NARRATIVE &
EXPERIENCE in
Multicultural
EDUCATION

Narrative and Experience in Multicultural Education *is dedicated to all the participants who have engaged in inquiry with us over the years—teachers, administrators, community workers, parents, and students—in Bay Street Community School and in other contexts. We are grateful to them for all we have learned about narrative inquiry, multicultural education, and life.*

Narrative & Experience in Multicultural Education

EDITED BY

JOANN PHILLION
Purdue University

MING FANG HE
Georgia Southern University

F. MICHAEL CONNELLY
*Ontario Institute for Studies in Education
of the University of Toronto*

SAGE Publications
Thousand Oaks ▪ London ▪ New Delhi

KH

For information:

Sage Publications, Inc.
2455 Teller Road
Thousand Oaks, California 91320
E-mail: order@sagepub.com

Sage Publications Ltd.
1 Oliver's Yard
55 City Road
London EC1Y 1SP
United Kingdom

Sage Publications India Pvt. Ltd.
B-42, Panchsheel Enclave
Post Box 4109
New Delhi 110 017   India

Printed in the United States of America

Library of Congress Cataloging-in-Publication Data

Narrative and experience in multicultural education / edited by JoAnn Phillion, Ming Fang He, F. Michael Connelly.
      p. cm.
Includes bibliographical references and index.
ISBN 1-4129-0582-6 (cloth) — ISBN 1-4129-0583-4 (pbk.)
1. Multicultural education—Cross-cultural studies. 2. Education—Social aspects—Cross-cultural studies. I. Phillion, JoAnn. II. He, Ming Fang. III. Connelly, F. Michael. l.
LC1099.N33 2005
370.117—dc22   2004025360

This book is printed on acid-free paper.

05   06   07   08   09   10   9   8   7   6   5   4   3   2   1

Acquisitions Editor:	Diane McDaniel
Editorial Assistant:	Marta Peimer
Production Editor:	Laureen A. Shea
Copy Editor:	Mary L. Tederstrom
Typesetter:	C&M Digitals (P) Ltd.
Proofreader:	Libby Larson
Indexer:	Pamela Van Huss
Cover Designer:	Janet Foulger

Contents

Preface

*N*arrative and Experience in Multicultural Education explores the untapped potential narrative and experiential approaches offer for understanding multicultural issues in education. The research featured in this book reflects an exciting new wave of social science thinking about human experience. The authors bring their personal experience to the inquiries, actively participate in the lives of the people with whom they work, care deeply about the concerns of their participants, and search for ways to act on these concerns. The studies focus on the lives of students, teachers, parents, and communities and bring forward experiences seldom discussed in the literature. The inquiries are far ranging in terms of content, ethnic groups studied, geographic locations, and other contexts.

As you read you will encounter work from different locations in the United States on African American concerns, Native American community and education issues, Latina/Latino parental concerns, multicultural teacher education issues, and more. You will also encounter work from various locations in Canada on teaching, inquiry, multicultural classrooms and schools, and links to a democratic vision, as well as work from Israel on teaching across great differences and historical divides. Several chapters deal with the methodology and background of this experiential research. Much of the work in this book reflects global considerations of increasing importance in multicultural education and teacher education. The special quality of this work that distinguishes it from other work in multicultural education is the emphasis on understanding experience and transforming this understanding into significant social and educational implications.

The work featured in *Narrative and Experience in Multicultural Education* is the culmination of more than ten years of inquiry by the editors. We have explored the potential of narrative inquiry and other approaches for understanding the meaning of human experience in the field of multicultural education and for understanding multicultural issues in society. Current multiculturalism research in education tends to stress theoretical approaches that yield generalizations. This effort has been important and has advanced the field; indeed it has made multicultural education a legitimate field of inquiry (see Banks & Banks, 2004). This book, however, has a different focus; it draws together new work that focuses explicitly on individual and group experience and explores the nuances of multicultural life. The origins of this approach primarily can be traced back to John Dewey's influential work, in particular to his theory of education and experience (1938). The significance of this new work is that it provides the nucleus of a complementary, new way of understanding the complexity of multicultural issues in education.

There are many texts that provide theoretical orientations to multiculturalism. New conceptual approaches in this book—reflexive, experiential, and practical—complement these texts with narrative accounts that offer specific research examples and a critique of the standard texts. This book provides research studies that offer new insights into particular multicultural topics, and the studies offer explicit methodological examples for researchers interested in each area. The exemplary work presented in this text has been provided by experienced qualitative researchers.

Instructors will find this book useful for studies of diversity because the research is conducted with different ethnic groups and takes place in diverse contexts, nationally and internationally. Students will find it useful, as it allows them to challenge their assumptions about multiculturalism and helps them link theory with practice and inquiry with life. It will also encourage readers to develop a critical, reflective view of how theory can be applied to particular contexts.

This book would not have been possible without the efforts of a great many people. We thank all the participants in our inquiries, the participants in the authors' inquiries in the book, and the authors themselves. Thanks to the support staff at the University of Toronto, Gary Pyper and Frances Tolnai, who helped organize the numerous manuscripts drafts we received throughout the two years of this project. We also gratefully acknowledge the suggestions provided by the reviewers of our prospectus and the draft of the book:

Jon G. Bradley, McGill University

Valerie-Lee Chapman, North Carolina State University

Cheryl J. Craig, University of Houston

Edmundo F. Litton, Loyola Marymount University

Joanna Mensinga, Central Queensland University

Francisco Rios, University of Wyoming

Frederick L. Yeo, Southeast Missouri State University

We hope this book provides you with fresh experiential ways of thinking about multicultural life and education.

The Editors:
JoAnn Phillion
Ming Fang He
F. Michael Connelly

References

Banks, J. A., & Banks, C. A. M. (Eds.). (2004). *Handbook of research on multicultural education* (2nd ed.). San Francisco: Jossey-Bass.

Dewey, J. (1938). *Experience and education.* New York: Collier Books.

1

The Potential of Narrative and Experiential Approaches in Multicultural Inquiries

JoAnn Phillion, Ming Fang He,
and F. Michael Connelly

In *Narrative and Experience in Multicultural Education* we explore the untapped potential that narrative and experiential approaches provide in understanding multicultural issues in education. We feature scholars whose work focuses on the lives of students, teachers, parents, and communities, while highlighting experiences seldom discussed in the literature. We believe that the experiential quality of this work is central to developing in-depth understanding of multicultural issues in education and in life.

As you read through this book, you will see that the authors bring personal experience to bear on their inquiries. You will see inquiry embedded in life and life embedded in constant change in relation to social, cultural, and political contexts. You will also be exposed to the ideas of self, others, and inquiry inter-related in complex and dialogical relationships over time and place. These scholars have developed their research questions, perspectives, and inquiry methods by drawing on what they care about passionately in life. Building upon their passion, these scholars engage themselves and others in a deeply reflective practice that has the possibility to transform everyday experience into insights with cultural, social, and educational significance. As demonstrated in each chapter, these scholars are not detached observers of, but active participants in, the lives of the people with whom they work. As they become immersed in the lives of their participants, they come to care deeply about their concerns and continuously search for effective ways to act on those concerns.

The authors in this book are diverse; the inquiries they engage in are far ranging in terms of content, ethnic group studied, and geographic location. We, of course, could not feature the entire spectrum of the authors' work, and there were many multicultural education issues that we were unable to cover, such as special needs, sexual orientation, gender, and the experiences of other ethnic groups. We believe that the significance of bringing this particular work forward is that it provides a new way of understanding the nuances of multicultural life and the complexity of multicultural issues in education. The special quality of the work featured in this book that distinguishes it from other work in multicultural education is its emphasis on understanding experience and transforming this understanding into significant social and educational implications.

Reading With an Experiential Eye and an Imaginative Eye

The chapters in *Narrative and Experience in Multicultural Education* are concrete, detailed, and filled with specifics of multicultural life and multicultural education. The inquiries in the book open the door to other inquiries and suggest new methodological approaches to multicultural research that have potential to enrich and broaden the understanding of experience in multicultural societies. We hope that readers will vicariously experience the complex multicultural life portrayed by the authors and will recognize the global multicultural issues toward which these chapters turn our minds.

We invite readers to read the chapters with an experiential eye—seeing, hearing, and feeling the nuances of multicultural life and illuminating the details of experience brought forward in each of the studies. We encourage readers to vicariously travel with each author into the research site, imagining themselves in that setting and experiencing the lives of the participants. Through reading with an experiential eye, readers will not only see, hear, and feel the multicultural lives of those under study but also, in some small way, carry on the inquiries alongside the authors.

We also encourage readers to read with an imaginative eye, exploring broad multicultural themes that drive each author's work. The imaginative eye inspires readers to see "unexplored possibilities," to nurture "reflectiveness and expressiveness" (Greene, 2001) and to search for the meaning of experience. We want readers to understand the experiences of authors and participants, not in a predictable, fragmented, categorized sense, but in relation to their own experience and in relation to the historical, geographical, sociopolitical, cultural, and other contexts of the inquiries. We also encourage readers to challenge themselves to look beyond stereotypes, the familiar, and what they take for granted in order to recognize the complexity of multicultural lives.

Reading with an experiential eye and an imaginative eye enables readers to deeply delve into the inquiries, to experience the passion and commitment of authors and participants, to puzzle over situations, to think about the meaning of the inquiries in relation to broader multicultural issues, and to envision possibilities for change in their own lives and the lives of those with whom they work. This method of reading a text can also be a method of reading the world. In addition, this method is a starting point for understanding narrative and experiential approaches to multicultural issues in education.

Structure of the Book and Outline of Chapters

Narrative and Experience in Multicultural Education is divided into six units. Three units address multicultural concerns of major North American ethnic groups—African Americans, Latinos/Latinas and Native Americans. One of the units focuses on international multicultural teacher education issues, and one unit is focused explicitly on narrative methodology in multicultural education research. The final unit addresses multiculturalism in democratic and community life. Chapters 2 through 10 and 12 through 14 contain an autobiographical introduction in which the authors connect the work presented in the chapter to their personal narrative histories. Each of these chapters concludes with further readings that were instrumental in the development of the authors' inquiry lines. Also at the end of each chapter, readers will find Reflective Questions that provide a starting point for discussion of the ideas in the chapter.

UNIT ONE: PERSONAL NARRATIVE, COMMUNITY NARRATIVE, AND THE AFRICAN AMERICAN EXPERIENCE

In Chapter 2, "Examining School-Community Connections Through Stories," Saundra Murray Nettles examines the emergence of a narrative that celebrates school and student strengths from a contrasting narrative, which characterized the school as deficient and harmful. She explores this school's narrative and the ways it changes using personal stories of two African American women—the principal and the author—and other information from the school community. The inquiry shows how interactions between the school community's narrative and the personal narrative of individuals contribute to the shaping and reshaping of a school's image. Nettles suggests that school-community connections in her research site contributed to a change in the context from one that was inconsistently supportive of student achievement to one that was consistently supportive.

In Chapter 3, "Black Women Writing Autobiography: Autobiography in Multicultural Education," Meta Y. Harris examines Black women writing autobiography and how teachers and students can employ autobiographical writing to develop better interactions between teachers and students and between diverse students in multicultural education. Harris found that writing autobiography provides the opportunity not only to explore history from a personal perspective, relative to the political happenings of the times, local events, Black community events, academic experiences, and other occurrences that impact life, but also to revisit those times from a "removed" perspective. Harris also found that writing autobiography opens avenues for individuals to examine how personal and educational experience impacts who they are and how they perceive, react to, and interact with others in multicultural societies.

UNIT TWO: LATINA/LATINO COMMUNITIES, FAMILIES, AND CHILDREN

In Chapter 4, "Being Educated in the Absence of Multiculturalism," Alma Rubal-Lopez and Angela Anselmo examine the experiences of two Latina Nuyorican sisters who were educated in the South Bronx (New York) during the 1950s and 1960s. Their narratives are used to recount their educational experiences in an oftentimes hostile and lonely environment. The authors compare what that experience was like and how it would be different today, and they address the role of multicultural education as a key factor in making that experience different.

In Chapter 5, "Between the Telling and the Told: Latina Mothers Negotiating Education in New Borderlands," Sofia A. Villenas discusses how Latina immigrant mothers face challenges in raising and schooling their bicultural children as they forge new communities in the United States. This chapter focuses on a conversation among Latina mothers, highlighting the spaces between the *telling* (the performances of dignity and strategic assertions of difference in the event of storytelling) and the *told* (the narrated events or descriptions supporting Latino family values and traditions). The women shared their struggles with assimilation, English language hegemony, bilingualism and biculturalism, the perils and necessity of doubling as working mothers in an unsupportive environment, and gendered ideologies about women's place in the home. These struggles reflected a process of teaching, learning, and negotiating life in new borderlands.

UNIT THREE: SOCIAL JUSTICE, EQUALITY, AND THE EDUCATION OF NATIVE AMERICANS

In Chapter 6, "White Teachers, Native Students: Rethinking Culture-Based Education," Mary Hermes discusses two White science teachers at tribal schools in the Upper Midwest of the United States. These teachers were identified by community members and school administrators as "successful" teachers. This chapter describes the experiences of these teachers as they wrestle with the daily effects of generations of oppression and poverty, as well as the beliefs and attitudes that help these teachers be effective allies and instructors for Native American students. Their experiences reveal the struggle with the contradictions of oppression, broaden the discussion of Native American culture-based education, and raise questions for the general applicability of cultural discontinuity as an explanation for Native American school failure.

In Chapter 7, "Journey Toward Social Justice: Curriculum Change and Educational Equity in a Navajo Community," Donna Deyhle provides a detailed narrative account of twenty years of participation in a school district with a large Navajo population. She documents the practical and policy struggles over the years to institute forms of schooling congenial to the Navajo community, and she describes the shifting imbalances between policy intentions and actual practices. In addition, she discusses how her role as researcher blends into that of community advocate and activist.

UNIT FOUR: MULTICULTURAL TEACHER EDUCATION IN INTERNATIONAL CONTEXTS

In Chapter 8, "Teachers as Transformative Healers: Struggles With the Complexities of the Democratic Sphere," Lourdes Diaz Soto presents narrative accounts of how teachers weave the post–September 11 World Trade Center tragedy into classroom curriculum to create transformative and healing spaces. These accounts demonstrate how issues of power became overwhelming and reveal that teachers' experience of this tragedy had emotional, intellectual, physical, and spiritual qualities. Soto depicts the complexities of the tragedy through teachers' working with young children as they struggled with the curriculum. This transformative process provided a space that enabled the researcher and the teachers to explore an education that moved beyond their current practice to one that was critically bilingual and multicultural.

In Chapter 9, "How Is Education Possible When There's a Body in the Middle of the Room?," Freema Elbaz-Luwisch explores the possibility of multicultural and diverse education in Israel. Elbaz-Luwisch tells the story of her attempt to figure out what might be learned from the situation of Jewish Israelis and Arab/Palestinian Israelis living with violence, with threats to personal safety, and with death part of everyday life. She draws on experiences of dialogue between Jewish and Arab/Palestinian Israelis in preservice and inservice settings at the University of Haifa to suggest that attention to feelings—to the expression of fear, vulnerability, and anger—and to the body, which carries these feelings and experiences, is needed in order to make such dialogue possible.

In Chapter 10, "Multicultural Perspectives in Teacher Development," Grace Feuerverger focuses on her experience of teaching a multicultural teacher education class. Feuerverger and her students inquired into the meaning of self in a multicultural context that invited collective stories of dislocation, survival, and triumph over adversity. She confronted her own multiple cultural identities, her sense of being on the margins, and her psychological "orphanhood" as a child of Holocaust survivors. She created a classroom as a site of cultural encounters and networks of personal and professional negotiations and as a means to explore issues of diversity and difference. Through an exploration of the relationship between personal and professional lives, Feuerverger creates a nuanced pedagogical discourse of intercultural understanding and harmony that stands as a moral and ethical challenge in the study of multicultural education.

UNIT FIVE: NARRATIVE INQUIRY IN MULTICULTURAL EDUCATION

In Chapter 11, "The World in My Text: A Quest for Pluralism," Carola Conle examines the idea of cultural pluralism as expressed in ten years of her academic writing. Searching for tensions, subtexts, and implicit agendas, Conle recognizes underlying issues important in cultural pluralism: reflection within encounters of difference, recognition, public spaces for social self-reflection, and discursive practices conducive to inquiry. She explores the conditions within which human beings safeguard their identity. Her narrative inquiry has developed in a congenial space where different experiences were heard and valued. Conle discusses how inquiry flourishes in pluralistic societies.

In Chapter 12, "The Art of Narrative Inquiry: Embracing Emotion and Seeing Transformation," Chris Liska Carger explores the experiences of a Mexican American immigrant family. Using narrative inquiry, she studied a Latino high school dropout and his family's struggles to become American citizens. She discusses narrative inquiry and the potential of this method to help teachers and researchers to understand diverse students' backgrounds and the implications of their experiences for education. Carger concludes that, for her, research is more than an academic exercise; rather, it is a form of social action.

UNIT SIX: DEMOCRACY, SCHOOL LIFE, AND COMMUNITY IN MULTICULTURAL SOCIETIES

In Chapter 13, "Narrative Inquiry Into Multicultural Life in an Inner-City Community School," F. Michael Connelly, JoAnn Phillion, and Ming Fang He explore the connection between multicultural education and narrative inquiry in Canadian social life. They trace twenty years of narrative inquiry in a Canadian inner-city school and argue that an understanding of multicultural life as a democratic life process is central to an understanding of the social purposes of multiculturalism. They believe that multicultural education and narrative inquiry have the potential for profoundly productive links in the pursuit of democratic life.

In Chapter 14, "Creating Communities of Cultural Imagination: Negotiating a Curriculum of Diversity," Janice Huber, M. Shaun Murphy, and D. Jean Clandinin inquire into the making of a diverse curriculum by attending to children's stories, teachers' stories, and stories of school. They focus on a particular curriculum space, peace candle gatherings, as the site for attending to the stories. The stories were collected in two classroom settings in Western Canada, an inner-city Grade 3–4 and a rural Grade 1. The authors examine the shaping influence of cultural stories and stories of school on curriculum.

In Chapter 15, "Narrative and Experiential Approaches to Multiculturalism in Education: Democracy and Education," Ming Fang He, JoAnn Phillion, and F. Michael Connelly borrow Dewey's key concepts—democracy and education—to conclude the book. They point out that a democratic vision, one of justice and equality for all, permeates the book. They believe that this vision, with equality and justice not only as catchwords but as genuine possibilities, is a vision of multicultural democratic life. They also discuss potentials and concerns of narrative and experiential approaches to the study of multicultural issues in education.

Multiculturalism Across Disciplines and in Education

As you go through each chapter with an experiential eye and an imaginative eye, we would like you to travel with us to explore some background that we think is relevant to a narrative, experiential approach to multiculturalism. Multiculturalism has become the key educational issue of our epoch. It permeates the discourse of many disciplines and has transformed thinking in many fields (Kalantzis & Cope, 1992). In the field of political science, multiculturalism in Europe, Canada, and the United States is increasingly linked to controversial discussions of democracy in global contexts (e.g., Dyer, 1996). Multiculturalism is of major concern in philosophical debates about cultivating human potential in a global context (e.g., Nussbaum, 1997), expanding notions of community to create spaces for genuine encounters among different people to reach common goals (e.g., Greene, 1993), and understanding the complex, changing nature of contemporary cultural and individual identity (e.g., Taylor, 1994). In women's studies, scholars are using multiculturalism as a lens to understand and critique gender and class issues and to expand women's epistemologies (e.g., Goldberger, Tarule, Clinchy & Belenky, 1996). According to Sue, Ivey, and Pederson (1996), the impact of multiculturalism in psychology is so strong that it has changed the entire discipline, and they describe this approach as the "fourth wave," after psychoanalytic, behaviorist, and humanist approaches.

No discipline is more profoundly affected by multiculturalism than education. Multiculturalism permeates all levels of education, from universities to public schools. In higher education, prominent universities have created centers, such as Princeton University's Center for Human Values, founded in 1991, to support teaching, research, and public discussion of fundamental questions related to diversity that span academic disciplines (Gutmann, 1994). Many universities have established cross-disciplinary courses on multiculturalism that fulfill undergraduate degree requirements (Nussbaum, 1997). Universities throughout the United States are engaged in preparing teachers and university professors to be multicultural educators.

In public school education, the interest in multicultural education relates to school practice (e.g., Banks & Banks, 1989; Cummins, 1989; Gay, 2000; Howard, 1999; Ladson-Billings, 1994; Nieto, 2000) and to scholarship and research (Banks & Banks, 2004). In elementary and secondary schooling, there is a rethinking at the policy level taking place in response to changes in societies, in particular in response to changing student demographics, especially in urban areas (Dentler & Hafner, 1997). There is also progressively more awareness of multicultural issues in areas not traditionally thought of as "needing" multicultural education, especially in rural areas (Yeo, 1999) and in predominantly White areas (Glazer, 1997).

Influential professional bodies, such as the American Association of Colleges for Teacher Education, the Association for Supervision and Curriculum Development, and the National Education Association, published policy statements on multicultural education as early as the 1970s (Gay, 1995). The National Council for the Accreditation of Teacher Education mandates that issues of diversity be integrated in teacher education in order for institutions to be accredited (NCATE, 2001). Educational bodies such as the American Educational Research Association have made issues of diversity of paramount importance (AERA, 1997).

One of the major shifts in multicultural education is the increasing recognition that multiculturalism has become a global issue rather than solely a North American issue (e.g., Grant & Lei, 2001; Moodley, 1992). Another shift is a move beyond Black and White issues to the inclusion of a diversity of ethnic and cultural groups (e.g., Seller & Weis, 1997; Wu, 2002). There is also a shift from demographic and population studies, combined with prescriptive action to be taken by policymakers and local educators, to studies such as those featured in this book—in-depth studies of the quality of multicultural life in communities, schools, and families (see also Soto, 1997; Valdés, 1996; Vasquez, Pease-Alvarez, & Shannon, 1994).

A Turn to Narrative and Experience

As you continue to explore background relevant to narrative and experiential approaches to multiculturalism, we encourage you to look deeply into the methodological approaches used in the inquiries in this book. Parallel with the increasing interest in multiculturalism, there has been a movement toward developing methods appropriate for the understanding of multicultural phenomena previously only explored from a Western scientific perspective. This perspective has limited understanding of multicultural issues (Sue, 1999). There is, however, a new wave of thinking in the field of educational research that challenges the Western scientific perspective. It has been called the "sixth moment" (Denzin, 1997), a time of questioning whose knowledge should be considered valid and a time when research participants have their own ideas about how their experiences should be interpreted, theorized, and represented. Many researchers have searched for ways to respond to the sixth moment. There are some researchers who have developed approaches to multicultural-ism in education that focus on in-depth understanding of diverse experiences of individuals, families, and communities. Much of that work has been done by women, many are ethnographers, some are narrative inquirers, many are from the same ethnic background as the people with whom they work, many are fluent in the languages of the communities in which they live and study, and many advocate on behalf of students, parents, and communities (e.g., Carger, 1996; Feuerverger, 2001; Soto, 1997; Valdés, 1996). Another major response to the sixth moment is a turn toward narrative, which Denzin and Lincoln (2003) call the "seventh moment." In addition, the use of narrative is in response to recognition of the complexity of human experience in increasingly diversified societies. In a broad sense, this book reflects the seventh moment in that it focuses on the study of experience in multiculturalism in education.

We call this study of experience *narrative inquiry* (Clandinin & Connelly, 2000), the specific focus on multicultural experience *narrative multiculturalism* (Phillion, 2002d), and the specific focus on cross-cultural experience *cross-cultural narrative inquiry* (He, 2003). Connelly and Clandinin (1988, 1990; Clandinin & Connelly, 1994, 2000) were among the first to bring an experien-tial focus to educational research. People from different educational fields are beginning to incorporate experiential aspects into inquiries regarding multicul-tural issues in education: for instance, Bell (1997), Carger (1996), and Valdés (1996) in language and culture issues; Ayers (2001), Foster (1997), and Sleeter (2001) in teacher narrative; Feuerverger (2001) and Soto (1997) in family and community narrative; Elbaz-Luwisch (1997), Hollingsworth (1994), and Phillion (1999, 2002a, 2002b, 2002c, 2002d) in multicultural teaching and learning; Conle (2000) and He (1999, 2002a, 2002b, 2002c, 2003, in press) in cross-cultural issues; and hooks (1991, 2000) in race, gender, and class issues.

One aspect of these inquiries is the idea of understanding experience in its own terms rather than categorizing experience according to predetermined structures and theories (Phillion, 1999). Many of these inquiries are "peopled" with characters rather than filled with categories and labels. Another aspect of these inquiries is the inquirer's recognition of sociopolitical and cultural contexts in shaping experience. The inherent potential of these inquiries lies in the possibility of effecting social change beginning with the individual and expanding into the greater community.

As narrative inquirers with strong interests in the lives of people living in diverse contexts, we feel that this kind of in-depth exploration that focuses on an understanding of experience, rather than on elaborating predetermined categories derived from theory, holds promise for ways to think about long-standing multicultural issues in global contexts. The chapters in this book contribute in this way to the history of work in multicultural education by examining issues through a more personal lens: the authors are committed to the participants in their inquiry and to the hope that the research will better participants' lives. The work illuminates and addresses structural inequalities in ways that bring life to issues that make them impossible to ignore. Researchers engaged in this work often take an active political stance, and many of the projects are directly aimed at making social and educational change. Although many of the authors would not describe themselves as being in multicultural education, we nevertheless find that these chapters illuminate multicultural issues. These are exciting chapters that tell us what it is like to do research at the "seventh moment" and give us a strong sense of what a turn to narrative and experience means in the study of multiculturalism in education.

Work featured in *Narrative and Experience in Multicultural Education*, embedded in lives and communities on the one hand and powerful ideas of being human on the other hand, is at the heart of narrative and experiential approaches to multiculturalism. As you go through the chapters with an experiential eye and an imaginative eye, we hope you will discover the particular qualities of these inquiries and the potential of narrative and experiential approaches to develop in-depth, nuanced understandings of multicultural issues in education. We also hope that this understanding will be transformed into hope and the possibility for better, more equitable lives in multicultural societies.

Recommended Readings

We would like to introduce readers who are not familiar with it to the theory of experience literature, in particular Dewey's work in *Education and Experience*

(1938), and to Schwab's theory of the practical (Westbury & Wilkof, 1978). The work of Dewey and Schwab draws attention to the experiential aspect of multicultural issues and to the potential of understanding experience to affect social and educational change.

Readers can also delve into related work in anthropology, such as Bateson (1994), Behar (1996), and Geertz (1995). This type of work enables readers to see culture as changing, fluid, and dynamic and multicultural inquiry as personal and embedded in history and place.

Exploring writing in philosophy on narrative imagination (Greene, 1995; Nussbaum, 1997) and notions of identity in pluralistic societies (Taylor, 1989) will help readers develop the ability to empathize with others, to perceive themselves not only as members of local communities but also as members of a world community, and to create possibilities for better lives in multicultural societies. These qualities are central to an understanding of narrative and experiential approaches to multiculturalism in education.

Readers might also benefit from exploring life-based literary narratives that focus on language, culture, and identity issues in real-life contexts. In particular, work such as Chamoiseau (1994) and Hoffman (1989) helps develop an in-depth understanding of lived experience from the perspective of participants. We believe that life-based literary narratives bring experiential qualities to multicultural theories and foster the development of narrative imagination—the ability to reflect on experience, question assumptions, and actively empathize with others (Phillion & He, 2005).

References

American Educational Research Association. (1997). *Report from the task force on the role and future of minorities*. Washington, DC: Author.

Ayers, W. C. (2001). *To teach: The journey of a teacher*. New York: Teachers College Press.

Banks, J. A., & Banks, C. A. M. (Eds.). (1989). *Multicultural education: Issues and perspectives*. Needham Heights, MA: Simon & Schuster.

Banks, J. A., & Banks, C. A. M. (Eds.). (2004). *Handbook of research on multicultural education* (2nd ed.). San Francisco: Jossey-Bass.

Bateson, M. C. (1994). *Peripheral visions: Learning along the way*. New York: HarperCollins.

Behar, R. (1996). *The vulnerable observer: Anthropology that breaks your heart*. Boston: Beacon Press.

Bell, J. S. (1997). *Literacy, culture, and identity*. New York: Peter Lang.

Carger, C. (1996). *Of borders and dreams: Mexican-American experience of urban education*. New York: Teachers College Press.

Chamoiseau, P. (1994). *School days*. Lincoln: University of Nebraska Press.

Clandinin, D. J., & Connelly, F. M. (1994). Personal experience methods. In N. K. Denin and Y. S. Lincoln (Eds.), *Handbook of qualitative research* (pp. 413–427). Thousand Oaks, CA: Sage.

Clandinin, D. J., & Connelly, F. M. (2000). *Narrative inquiry: Experience and story in qualitative research.* San Francisco: Jossey-Bass.

Conle, C. (2000). Thesis as narrative: What is the inquiry in narrative inquiry? *Curriculum Inquiry, 30*(2), 189–213.

Connelly, F. M., & Clandinin, D. J. (1988). *Teachers as curriculum planners: Narratives of experience.* New York: Teachers College Press.

Connelly, F. M., & Clandinin, D. J. (1990). Stories of experience and narrative inquiry. *Educational Researcher, 19*(5), 2–14.

Cummins, J. (1989). *Empowering minority students.* Sacramento: California Association for Bilingual Education.

Dentler, R. A., & Hafner, A. L. (1997). *Hosting newcomers: Structuring educational opportunities for immigrant children.* New York: Teachers College Press.

Denzin, N. K. (1997). *Interpretive ethnography: Ethnographic practices for the 21st century.* Thousand Oaks, CA: Sage.

Denzin, N., & Lincoln, Y. (2003). *The landscape of qualitative research: Theories and issues* (2nd ed.). Thousand Oaks, CA: Sage.

Dewey, J. (1938). *Experience and education.* New York: Collier Books.

Dyer, G. (1996). *Millennium.* Toronto: Canadian Broadcasting Corporation.

Elbaz-Luwisch, F. (1997). Narrative research: Political issues and implications. *Teaching and Teacher Education, 13*(1), 75–83.

Feuerverger, G. (2001). *Oasis of dreams: Teaching and learning peace in a Jewish-Palestinian village in Israel.* New York: RoutledgeFalmer.

Foster, M. (1997). *Black teachers on teaching.* New York: New Press.

Gay, G. (1995). Bridging multicultural theory and practice. *Multicultural Education, 3*(1), 4–9.

Gay, G. (2000). *Culturally responsive teaching: Theory, research, and practice.* New York: Teachers College Press.

Geertz, C. (1995). *After the fact: Two countries, four decades, one anthropologist.* Cambridge, MA: Harvard University Press.

Glazer, N. (1997). *We are all multiculturalists now.* Cambridge, MA: Harvard University Press.

Goldberger, N., Tarule, J., Clinchy, B., & Belenky, M. (1996). *Knowledge, difference and power.* New York: Basic Books.

Grant, C., & Lei, J. L. (Eds.). (2001). *Global constructions of multicultural education: Theories and realities.* Mahwah, NJ: Lawrence Erlbaum.

Greene, M. (1993). The passions of pluralism: Multiculturalism and the expanding community. *Educational Researcher, 22*(1), 13–18.

Greene, M. (1995). *Releasing the imagination: Essays on education, the arts, and social change.* San Francisco: Jossey-Bass.

Greene, M. (2001). *Variations on a blue guitar: The Lincoln Center Institute lectures on aesthetic education.* New York: Teachers College Press.

Gutmann, A. (Ed.). (1994). *Multiculturalism: Examining the politics of recognition.* Princeton, NJ: Princeton University Press.

He, M. F. (1999). A life-long inquiry forever flowing between China and Canada: Crafting a composite auto/biographic narrative method to represent three Chinese women teachers' cultural experiences (Featured article). *Journal of Critical Inquiry Into Curriculum & Instruction, 1*(2), 5–29.

He, M. F. (2002a). A narrative inquiry of cross-cultural lives: Lives in Canada. *Journal of Curriculum Studies, 34*(3), 323–342.

He, M. F. (2002b). A narrative inquiry of cross-cultural lives: Lives in China. *Journal of Curriculum Studies, 34*(3), 301–321.

He, M. F. (2002c). A narrative inquiry of cross-cultural lives: Lives in North American Academe. *Journal of Curriculum Studies, 34*(5), 513–533.

He, M. F. (2003). *A river forever flowing: Cross-cultural lives and identities in the multicultural landscape.* Greenwich, CT: Information Age.

He, M. F. (in press). In-between China and North America. In T. R. Berry & N. D. Mizelle (Eds.), *From oppression to grace: Women of color and their dilemmas within the academy.* Sterling, VA: Stylus.

Hoffman, E. (1989). *Lost in translation: A life in a new language.* New York: Penguin Books.

Hollingsworth, S. (1994). Teacher research and urban literacy education: Lessons and conversations in a feminist key. New York: Teachers College Press.

hooks, b. (1991). Narratives of struggle. In P. Mariani (Ed.), *Critical fictions: The politics of imaginative writing* (pp. 53–61). Seattle, WA: Bay.

hooks, b. (2000). *Where we stand: Class matters.* New York: Routledge.

Howard, G. R. (1999). *We can't teach what we don't know: White teachers, multiracial schools.* New York: Teachers College Press.

Kalantzis, M., & Cope, W. (1992, November 4). Multiculturalism may prove to be the key issue of our epoch. *The Chronicle of Higher Education,* pp. B3, B5.

Ladson-Billings, G. (1994). *The dream keepers: Successful teachers of African American children.* San Francisco: Jossey-Bass.

Moodley, K. A. (Ed.). (1992). *Beyond multicultural education: International perspectives.* Calgary, Alberta: Detselig Enterprises.

National Council for the Accreditation of Teacher Education. (2001). *Professional standards for the accreditation of schools, colleges, and departments of education.* Washington, DC: Author.

Nieto, S. (2000). *Affirming diversity: The sociopolitical context of multicultural education* (2nd ed.). New York: Longman.

Nussbaum, M. (1997). *Cultivating humanity: A classical defense of reform in liberal education.* Cambridge, MA: Harvard University Press.

Phillion, J. (1999). Narrative and formalistic approaches to the study of multiculturalism. *Curriculum Inquiry, 29*(1), 129–141.

Phillion, J. (2002a). Becoming a narrative inquirer in a multicultural landscape. *Journal of Curriculum Studies, 34*(5), 535–556.

Phillion, J. (2002b). Classroom stories of multicultural teaching and learning. *Journal of Curriculum Studies, 34*(3), 281–300.

Phillion, J. (2002c). *Narrative inquiry in a multicultural landscape: Multicultural teaching and learning.* Westport, CT: Ablex.

Phillion, J. (2002d). Narrative multiculturalism. *Journal of Curriculum Studies, 34*(3), 265–279.

Phillion, J., & He, M. F. (2005). Narrative inquiry and ELT research. In J. Cummins & C. Davison (Eds.), *The international handbook of English language teaching* (Vol. 2). Norwell, MA: Springer (formerly Kluwer Academic Publishers).

Seller, M., & Weis, L. (1997). *Beyond Black and White: New faces and voices in U.S. schools.* Albany: SUNY Press.

Sleeter, C. E. (2001). Epistemological diversity in research on preservice teacher preparation for historically underserved children. In W. G. Secada (Ed.), *Review of research in education* (Vol. 25, pp. 209–250). Washington, DC: American Educational Research Association.

Soto, L. D. (1997). *Language, culture, and power: Bilingual families and the struggle for quality education.* Albany: SUNY Press.

Sue, S. (1999). Science, ethnicity, and bias. *American Psychologist, 54*(12), 1070–1077.

Sue, D. W., Ivey, A. E., & Pederson, P. B. (1996). *A theory of multicultural counseling and therapy.* Pacific Grove, CA: Brooks/Cole.

Taylor, C. (1989). *Sources of the self: The making of the modern identity.* Cambridge, MA: Harvard University Press.

Taylor, C. (1994). The politics of recognition. In A. Gutmann (Ed.), *Multiculturalism: Examining the politics of recognition* (pp. 25–73). Princeton, NJ: Princeton University Press.

Valdés, G. (1996). *Con respeto: Bridging the distances between culturally diverse families and schools.* New York: Teachers College Press.

Vasquez, O. A., Pease-Alvarez, L., & Shannon, S. M. (1994). *Pushing boundaries: Language and culture in a Mexicano community.* New York: Press Syndicate of the University of Cambridge.

Westbury, I., & Wilkof, N. J. (Eds.). (1978). *Science, curriculum, and liberal education: Selected essays: Joseph J. Schwab.* Chicago: University of Chicago Press.

Wu, F. H. (2002). *Yellow: Race in America beyond Black and White.* New York: Basic Books.

Yeo, F. (1999). The barriers of diversity: Multicultural education and rural schools. *Multicultural Education, 7*(1), 1–7.

Unit One

Personal Narrative, Community Narrative, and the African American Experience

2

Examining School-Community Connections Through Stories

Saundra Murray Nettles

Autobiographical Introduction

My story almost ended nearly a decade ago. On January 19, 1995, doctors removed an orange-sized brain tumor that had grown up with me, undetected until days before the operation. While the tumor was scrambling my central nervous system, I had been learning about young people's psychosocial resilience, often defined as the ability to bounce back after adversity. Suddenly, at forty-eight, and in the middle of my career as an educational researcher with appointments at the University of Maryland and Johns Hopkins University, I began to look for others who had written about similar experiences of brain disease and a return to wholeness. But I could find only two books that told survivors' tales in their own words. Nothing existed about the experience of a middle-aged African American woman who relied on the creation of intellectual products for her livelihood.

I majored in philosophy at Howard University and later received a Ph.D. in psychology. I was thoroughly trained in experimental social psychology, but I found the methods alien to my humanistic sensibilities. I was intrigued with the achievement motivation of women and African American boys and men; my first job as a joint-appointed assistant professor of African American studies and of psychology seemed ideal. But I have a strong activist bent and segued into several years as an applied social scientist. I learned case study methods, as these were most applicable to the phenomena I studied in the "real world" of social service agencies and schools. In my spare time, I took creative writing classes and began two (still unfinished) novels. When I began my recovery from brain surgery in 1995, the creative and the human studies lines converged. I started writing a narrative of my illness and recovery, *Crazy Visitation*.

Although I have published articles based on secondary analyses, literature reviews, experimental studies, and case studies, in *Crazy Visitation* I found my form and my voice. While writing it, I discovered that, as a psychologist, I was not alone. While I had been trying to "do science," psychologists had discovered narrative as a root metaphor for emerging paradigms that sought to understand the individual in context. In educational research, narrative inquiry was taking form.

As a child of nine, I published one issue of a neighborhood newspaper. I wrote all the stories I had heard about our neighbors, typed them on a stencil, made copies using my father's mimeograph machine, and went door-to-door selling them for ten cents from a rusty red wagon. In high school, I wrote a column on my high school's activities for the Black newspaper *The Atlanta Daily World*. In college, I heard Charles Lloyd play "Forest Flower" and went to the dorm to write my first poem. In my fantasies as a young woman, I sat in a room filled with books, writing stories about people working and loving, seeing and changing, discovering and dancing. With my newly found narrative ways of knowing, the woman I am now meets the young woman I envisioned.

School Stories, Community Stories

The school building was in disrepair and its grounds unkempt when Frances Robinson began her duties as principal at the start of the school year in 1995. Just the semester before, *The Washington Post* had reported that Stanton Elementary School was one of eleven District of Columbia schools that had failed to pass fire code inspections. Ms. Robinson believed that the state of the building, built in the 1930s, was in part responsible for the flight of parents and students into other, more desirable places. "Based on what I had been looking at," she had written, "I could not blame them for their flight" (Robinson, 2000, p. 35).

As Ms. Robinson was assuming the duties of principal at Stanton, my colleagues and I at the Johns Hopkins/Howard University Center for Research on the Education of Students Placed At Risk (CRESPAR) set out to measure indicators of resilience and risk and to identity patterns that characterized children who did well, even thrived despite the presence of stressful life events and perceived violence. It was my responsibility to collect data at Stanton, one of three schools in the original study. The Stanton study soon expanded into a multifaceted effort in which I collected data as planned and also collaborated with Ms. Robinson and the Stanton faculty to apply principles derived from resilience research within the framework of the school's reform efforts. These efforts included districtwide instructional programs as well as enrichment activities that the school was conducting with "partners in education," including parents, churches, law firms, volunteers in government agencies, and community-based organizations.

Once the formal student data collection had ended in 1998, I remained as a partner in different roles: as judge for the science fair, as workshop designer and presenter, and "sounding board" for the principal. I also continued to collect information about the school, which led to an important discovery: the public image of the school was changing; it seemed to have more positive than negative elements. Concurrently, I continued to further my own understanding of resilience as it is expressed in narratives at the individual and contextual levels. In my own story of risk and recovery from a brain tumor (Nettles, 2001), I found that my experiences and the act of telling about them led to a new narrative whose theme was empowerment:

> As a black woman, I was all too familiar with the survival narrative; for many of us, it is the only story we know—how to get from day to day. But in reentering the world . . . I went beyond loss and survival to a new narrative. It is built on the two fundamental human tendencies that psychologists and others have identified. One is agency, expressed in strivings for power and independence. . . . The other motivational theme is connection, the strivings for love and intimacy. (pp. 148–149)

I began to ask of the Stanton data if it was possible that Stanton had recast an existing narrative. If so, how? The importance of this question was heightened when I read of community psychologist Julian Rappaport's (2000) work with a school in a Midwestern community, where he tried a variety of school-community programs. He wrote:

> Programs is not the answer. What is needed is a new setting narrative that speaks of the talents, skills, and abilities of the students, their families and neighbors. Frankly, such a culture change is working against entrenched narratives that are believed by both the oppressors and oppressed. (p. 21)

The purpose of this chapter is to uncover Stanton's narrative and how it changed, using as a lens the personal stories of two African American women— one the principal, and the other the author of this chapter. The overall narrative contributes to the literature of school-community connections by using narrative to explore the mutual influence of personal and school stories. My specific focus is school relations with agencies, churches, and other volunteers in the school.

I position the research within three converging lines of research. Two of them—on educational resilience and on school-community connections— have deepened our understanding that interrelated contexts can contribute to academic and psychosocial competence in children and youths (Christenson & Sheridan, 2001; Connell, Spencer, & Aber, 1994; Nettles & Pleck, 1994).

Resilience, typically defined as the individual's successful response to risk (Rutter, 1987), is increasingly described as a property of systems—school, home, community, health care—in reciprocal interaction with the child's personal characteristics (Pianta & Walsh, 1998). Research on empowerment (Perkins & Zimmerman, 1995), a third line of research, has identified characteristics of settings that contribute to and sustain characteristics (perceived competence and control, problem-solving ability, and empowering behaviors, such as participation in extra-curricular activities) associated with individual resilience (Werner, 1990). Researchers have used narratives to understand interactions between social contexts and individuals (Salzer, 1998) and to explore the role of narratives as resources for transformation at the personal level (Franz & Stewart, 1994) and in environments such as schools (Rappaport, 1995, 2000).

METHOD

Primary data sources included narratives that Ms. Robinson and I wrote. In the book *Is Urban Education Too Hard for God?* (Robinson, 2000), Ms. Robinson presented a plan for improving education based on her experiences in Stanton Elementary. Sources for my perspectives include a memoir, *Crazy Visitation: A Chronicle of Illness and Recovery* (Nettles, 2001), reflective notes, and papers presented at conferences. Ms. Robinson and I wrote our narratives independently. We had mentioned to each other that we were attempting to tell our stories, but we did not discuss content. We exchanged our books in Spring 2002 at Ms. Robinson's retirement party. The narratives were augmented with observations at school events, interviews with Ms. Robinson, and documents, including school improvement plans, agendas and minutes of meetings, materials from professional development workshops, and newspaper and online articles about the school. I drew on findings from data collected from students in Grades 2 through 6, using the following instruments: the Self-Description Questionnaire (Marsh, 1990), the Social Support Appraisal Scale–Revised (Dubow & Ullman, 1989), and the Motivations for Reading Questionnaire (Wigfield, Guthrie, & McGough, 1996).

The initial analysis was based on procedures for qualitative data analysis described by Miles and Huberman (1994). In the first stages of analysis, narratives, interviews, field notes, and documents were assigned descriptive and interpretive codes. I developed time-ordered matrices and prepared the first draft, a narrative of events. I integrated into the draft events, interpretations, and insights and findings from the three research areas noted earlier. The findings are reported as a narrative organized in sections using images from dance, also a form of expressive movement, as a way to convey the dynamic interaction between and flow through different stories.

THE SETTING

I had visited schools like Stanton many times in my career. Some were in Anacostia, the same Washington, D.C., neighborhood in which Stanton was located. Anacostia is a sprawling urban area east of the river of the same name. As a child, I had attended a school with a similar structure—brick, multistoried, with high ceilings—and academic program as Stanton's, located in one of Atlanta's most poverty-stricken neighborhoods. Students were performing at the low end of the scale. Fights, some in which I was a participant, broke out in the halls, the bathrooms, and the busy street in front of the school. Apart from my experience, I carried images of urban schools gleaned from films about the "hood," research reports, newspaper articles, and popular books about the lives of inner-city children. Rappaport (2000) calls these societal images and the stories they convey *dominant cultural narratives*. Like stereotypes, these narratives are persistent, difficult to change. They are often at odds with the realities of individual schools, in Rappaport's words, the *community* or *setting narratives*. Equally as important, community narratives are shared among members of the community and serve as the context for *personal stories*.

> True enough, we each negotiate the river of time with individual strokes we have learned to apply from our own particular canoe, fortified with our own supplies, but the currents that propel us are cultural and setting narratives. Communities tell stories. Settings tell stories. Visual symbols index stories.
>
> People change stories even as they act within them. Even as individuals are shaped by the community narratives they are given, those very narratives can be reshaped by the people who receive them. (p. 7)

When I first arrived at the school in March 1996, I found a nearly perfect fit between the setting and stereotype. True, AmeriCorps volunteers had painted the cavernous hallways, and the custodial staff was keeping a constant vigil to stem the flow of water from leaking toilets and sinks. Volunteers had been recruited to paint the auditorium. Amid repairs and refurbishing, Ms. Robinson had begun to assemble resources for upgrading academic achievement.

The school had had an erratic academic history since the predominantly all-White neighborhood changed after the schools integrated in the 1960s: the White population in Anacostia went from 82 percent in the 1950s to 14 percent in the 1970s. An article in the December 10, 1985, edition of *The Washington Post* describes the school's mostly poor and working-class students as scoring "at or better than the national average on standardized tests for several years" (p. C1), despite the lack of up-to-date textbooks and a deteriorating physical plant environment. When Ms. Robinson arrived, Stanton's academic program was, like the building, in a state of decline. At the start of the 1996–97 school year, the district would designate Stanton as a targeted assistance school (i.e., one requiring program improvement to increase student achievement). The enrollment of slightly more than 500 students was virtually all African American. Approximately 98 percent of the students were eligible for the free or reduced lunch program, and the median household income in the area from which the school drew its students was $12,000, an amount less than the U.S. federal poverty guideline of $15,150 for a family of four in 1995 (Stanton Elementary School, 1996).

The social conditions in the neighborhood surrounding the school were causes of concern. According to the 1990 Census of Population and Housing, in the school's zip code, of individuals eighteen years and older, 35 percent had not graduated from high school; the unemployment rate, at 10 percent, was twice as high as the national average; and 31 percent of families with children younger than eighteen lived below the poverty line. Violent crimes and drug use plagued the neighborhood. Indeed, we CRESPAR researchers had chosen the school because of its profile, its setting narrative.

MOVING INTO THE SETTING

I arrived at Stanton on the last Wednesday in March 1996. I was there to arrange a longitudinal study to understand how children's educational resilience (i.e., school-related performance and psychosocial adjustment) is influenced by neighborhood violence and life stress (called "vulnerability factors") and a protective factor—social support from family, peers, and teachers—hypothesized to ameliorate the effects of violence and stress. The plan was to conduct an initial survey of the third and fourth grade students, using standard instruments to measure the varied signs of individual resilience, as well as the children's perceptions of stressors. Another assessment would be conducted the following year. Previous research had produced mixed results regarding the role of particular protective and vulnerability factors (Luthar, Cicchetti, & Becker, 2000), and I hoped our findings would illuminate the discrepancies.

Ms. Robinson warmed to the idea. She explained that her first priority was to improve students' reading and math skills, that emphasis was consistent with assessment of resilience: children who function competently in the face of adversity can read and solve problems. She asked me to speak to parents and teachers, to gauge their interest in and willingness to approve the project, and further explained that a high proportion of the students had been exposed to drugs before they were born. She believed that poverty and household composition—many of the students were from single-parent homes—were also impediments. "What can you do to help the teachers deal with the conditions of the children's lives?" she asked.

I listened as Ms. Robinson spoke about things she was doing and wanted to do in the school. These items blended past and present. Some, such as refurbishing of the physical plant and installation of computers, were in progress; others, such as an all-male second-grade classroom, run military style, were barely outlines. In fact, we were meeting in a room filled with used computers, lined up neatly, unplugged, and ready to set up on the floor. I sensed that she would get to all the items on the list. Maybe it was her tone—authoritative but optimistic.

I still wondered what she thought she could do in this place. On the day of our meeting, another negative event occurred. As *The Washington Post* reported: "2nd-grader stabs 5 others with found medical tools" in a field next to the school. Ms. Robinson was appalled:

> During my first year as principal, my school made the news negatively—a principal's nightmare. A student had found lancets [small needles] on the community field on his way to school and used these needles to scratch a few classmates. The media blew the situation out of proportion and indicated that the possibility existed that the scratched students might be suffering from AIDS. I had no idea how anything positive could come out of that situation. Yet, the next day television crews came to the school to hear what I had to say. They went out of their way (most unusual for the media) to show what the little lancets resembled. However, columnist Courtland Milloy at *The Washington Post,* wrote an excellent article about Stanton, focusing on its programs and students, and focused on a first grade boy who was anchoring our school radio program. (Robinson, 2000, pp. 38–39)

I interpret this account as one example of how Ms. Robinson interrupted the public setting narrative, reframing it to highlight the school's assets.

Despite this glimmer of good news, the intellectual and physical deterioration of Stanton, if not intractable, seemed arrested, waiting, if history had its way, for the next decline.

In April, I presented the research plans to parents at their regular PTA meeting and to teachers at a faculty meeting. The parents were amenable. They seemed far more concerned about school environment, safety, and security than a research plan. Community volunteers had been recruited and would paint and clean the school in May. Representatives from the metropolitan police department were present at the meeting to answer questions about the lancet incident; parents and faculty enlisted their support in cleaning up the playing field and patrolling the area more frequently than before.

The teachers were more resistant to the research:

> One teacher put it bluntly: "We don't need another researcher coming in, getting publications at our expense, and moving on. We need help for these students."
> It was clear to me that I would not be doing an "objective" study, one in which I could maintain my distance. (Nettles, 2001, p. 133)

I countered their arguments with my history of work in the southeast Washington, D.C., community, one area of the city that had high crime and poverty rates. I had worked in a large antipoverty agency whose headquarters were located in Anacostia. I knew the community and many of the activists who were attempting to improve conditions there. I stressed my intention to examine student strengths instead of deficit. At the end of the meeting, the teachers offered their support. One aspect of the school story, teachers' beliefs about outsider intervention, had prompted me to reveal aspects of my own life. In turn, the teachers had created an opening for a cooperative relationship that offered possibilities for a different way of viewing students.

During April, May, and June, Ms. Robinson and I met to plan and discuss what I could do on my budget: provide information to teachers for their own use and development; conduct consultation on parent outreach, and perform a survey of Grades 2 through 6, using the complete battery of instruments. We planned the first staff development retreat for August and discussed ideas she had for the school. I became, in the process of consultation, a "partner-in-education."

BECOMING PARTNERS

Although Stanton did not yet have a robust home-school partnership, the school was building on an existing base that included two churches, a community-based service agency, and volunteer groups. A long-standing partner was Project 2000, Inc., a program launched by Dr. Spencer Holland and used to mentor Stanton students through high school (Holland, 1996).

The school's vision statement, set forth in the annual Title 1 improvement plan for 1996–97, highlighted the role of partners:

> The vision of the Edwin L. Stanton Elementary School is that it will serve as a beacon to this diversely talented school community, representing the highest standards of academic achievement and social deportment. Stanton will continue to forge partnerships that promote learning environments where the achievement of World Class Standards will become a reality. The school envisions confident students who will exit this learning community with outcome-based experiences, ethical standards, intellectual curiosity, and perseverance; prepared to perform competitively in a technological, global society. (p. 1)

Shadowing this hopeful vision was a complex reality. Already the needs statement referred to the "resilient urban child who is impacted by influences outside of the school which are brought into the school." A resilience narrative was becoming a part of the school's vision. But the document drew a dismal picture of one group of students: "Too many are substance abuse infected and affected children. . . . Teachers observe their uncontrollable behavior, hyperactivity, and learning disabilities. While they feel somewhat unprepared to meet their needs, they are making every effort to do so" (pp. 7–8).

Against that backdrop, late in August 1996, the faculty and Ms. Robinson came to Howard University's School of Law campus for the staff development retreat. The one-day retreat was more like a seminar among colleagues than a formal workshop. There were no handouts; neither was there an evaluation. We covered topics suggested by the faculty and Ms. Robinson and talked about student motivation, discipline, substance abuse, and neighborhood violence in the language of risk, resilience, and protection. In one of the three sessions, for example, we used Benard's (1991) threefold categorization of protective factors (high expectations, opportunities for participation, and caring and support) to brainstorm concrete examples in the Stanton school and neighborhood and in children's families. Throughout the workshop teachers expressed the need for Stanton's students to have opportunities beyond their neighborhood. One teacher's comment was representative: "Our students must not be locked into Southeast as their world. They must recognize their heritage and stand tall. Our world is made up of a very diverse population. They must give respect and demand respect" (Field notes, August 28, 1996).

One discovery we made in the session was that the school had indeed created opportunities for students to explore the world beyond their neighborhood, but only a handful of students in each grade had participated. A goal was established to involve as many students as possible in classroom activities, extracurricular clubs, and special events.

After the retreat the school year started, and my research assistants began the surveys in all grades but kindergarten and first. Throughout the school year, Ms. Robinson and I met often. In her office, with its high ceilings and African artifacts, we reviewed the programs that the school had attempted in recent years. The school, like other schools I had studied in my work, had many remnants of programs, components remaining from reforms never fully implemented or tried for a year or two with special funding that had ended. Also, the school had programs in the vestigial stages. Examining the remnants, Ms. Robinson identified her most urgent need: a child development specialist who could work with troubled children and their parents. Together, we searched for and found a recent doctoral graduate, who was hired part-time. We talked about ways to fill gaps in other programs, identifying contributions that community partners could make. Ms. Robinson asked me to search the literature for school programs for use with students who came from families in which drug use was prevalent. The resulting books and articles were the nucleus of a small collection of resources, housed in the library, for teachers to use.

The literature defines the partnership model as one based on mutuality of interests among social entities whose responsibility is to promote student learning. Swap (1993), who introduced the partnership as a "new vision" for schools, cited two-way communication and collaborative problem solving as foci that distinguish the partnership model from other forms such as the school-to-home transmission model. Looking back, I see that my relationship with Ms. Robinson was characterized by features the literature recommends in school-community partners. Our personal stories revealed some clues as to why this was so.

SUPPORTING ROLES

We had not traded resumes, but we soon learned though casual conversation that we shared a common background: Ms. Robinson and I both were graduates of historically Black public schools, colleges, and universities. Ms. Robinson was a graduate of the Calvin Scott Brown High School in Winton, North Carolina, the first Black high school in that state; I attended schools in Atlanta, one of which was Booker T. Washington High School, the alma mater of Martin Luther King, Jr. She received her B.A. at North Carolina Central University in Durham, North Carolina; I had received mine at Howard University in Washington, D.C. We both held graduate degrees from Howard. At those institutions, racially diverse faculty had been our instructors; some had been critics of the prevailing social order. We were both beneficiaries of a proud heritage: we walked on campuses with formally designated historical sites, we heard the history of African Americans from professors who had written original texts on the topic; we studied and participated in classes and clubs in which most others looked like us. Although I had a summer appointment with the Johns Hopkins portion of CRESPAR to do the research at Stanton, Ms. Robinson rarely mentioned my ties to that elite, predominantly White university. Indeed, in all of Stanton's literature, my name was paired with Howard University's role in CRESPAR. I sensed that she wanted the Stanton faculty, parents, and community partners to know not only that I was one of the community but also that she was proud her alma mater was engaged in the work of a national research center.

Perhaps because we shared similar educational backgrounds with a deeply ingrained sense of our shared heritage, in our personal stories we referred to professional forefathers and foremothers who, African Americans themselves, articulated a commitment of service to African Americans and other children of color. As an educational psychologist, I looked to Black women in the history of my discipline as role models of the scholar-activist.

> "Who must do the hard things?" Carolyn R. Payton posed this question in the title of the address she presented upon receiving the Distinguished Professional Contributions award from the American Psychological Association in 1983. . . . The pioneering black women of psychology were members of a small, elite group trained in the methods of experimental and developmental science, but they were also part of a tradition that emphasized the necessity of black women's activism. (Nettles, 1999, pp. 1, 7)

Ms. Robinson considered her work to be a Christian ministry, one reminiscent of the role of Calvin Brown, the founder of the high school from which she graduated. Respecting the separation of church and state, however, she did not use the language in her daily work, but in her memoir she wrote:

> If Dr. Brown, who was born in an era of slavery, was able to establish the first black high school in North Carolina before he was thirty years of age, what cannot we, who are educators born long after the Emancipation Proclamation was signed, accomplish in getting boys and girls of color to read, write, think, and speak literately? It must be noted also that such an endeavor necessitated funds that Dr. Brown did not personally possess. However, God placed men and women along the way to provide the financial backing for the first black school in North Carolina. (Robinson, 2000, pp. 17–18)

Ms. Robinson further believed that spirit-inspired

> principals, teachers, educational aides, partners-in-education, maintenance, office, and cafeteria workers can work in any situation and go anywhere when they know that where God sends them, He equips them to have never-ending victories .... With an unfaltering faith, educators can challenge children to conceive and dream the impossible. (Robinson, 2000, p. 33)

She wrote, "God promised me that Stanton would be turned around and be recognized across the country" (Robinson, 2000, p. 35).

I interpret Ms. Robinson's confidence in her own success and that of others as one key to the loyalty and generosity of community partners. Throughout the year, I had observed community partners—themselves a diverse group in terms of race/ethnicity and employment—in essential roles. "Book Buddies" from the Pentagon read to first graders. A community-based program provided mentoring for 35 girls in the fifth and sixth grades. A church partner arranged for General Colin Powell to speak at a school assembly. A coalition of African American professionals organized ninety volunteers to wire every classroom and office for the Internet. At a year-end awards ceremony, the PTA president, the assistant principal, and Ms. Robinson recognized eighteen community partners. Virtually all the students had received direct benefits from them.

CHOREOGRAPHY

Despite the efforts of the school faculty, the parents, and the community partners, the results of the spring tests were mixed. For example, in reading, a substantial majority of first graders (80 percent) scored at the basic level and above on the Stanford 9, but 58 percent of second graders scored below basic. In mathematics, 80 percent of third graders were at the basic level and above, however, fifth graders were almost evenly split, with 54 percent below basic and 46 percent at basic or above. The 1997–98 update to the school's improvement plan (Stanton Elementary School, 1997) placed literacy as the first priority, with the goal of ensuring that every child would be reading on grade level by the end of the school year. Improvement in mathematics was a close second. The plan to reach these goals included participation in a national trial of a reading program for first graders, contracting with a private provider of reading instruction for third graders, and tutoring—provided by community partners— for children in other grades. Other partners were continuing activities from the prior year and planning new initiatives.

Ms. Robinson believed that local planning was essential. In a chapter in her narrative, she described her ideas about the need for planning:

> We must know what is needed to make children learn, how to get them to learn, and what the end results will be. We do not need to be surprised at the end of the journey. In most cases, a sure and solid plan has yet to come into effect. In the absence of such a plan, we grab "get smart quick" and band-aid measures. We become susceptible to every dogma, paradigm shift, and research theory that comes along. We try everything and succeed with few things because there is no thought-out plan of action that is decent and in good order. (2000, p. 54)

Critiquing the susceptibility of educators to use external conceptions, Ms. Robinson insisted that teachers in the building take responsibility for plans and outcomes. In a monthly staff bulletin (December 1997), for example, she wrote:

> It is important that you keep lesson plans in your classroom. A class with no plans will go nowhere. Our students want to learn and are eager to be stretched many times much further than where we are willing to stretch them. If they and parents believe they are beyond the level of work in the classroom, do not hesitate to make parents partners in letting the child go even further. (2000, p. 3)

Over the summer, we reviewed the roster of partners and talked about various ways to include them in the overall instructional program. Like Ms. Robinson, I believed that sound plans were a vital part of action. In my work at Johns Hopkins University, I had used a method of action research, Program Development and Evaluation (PDE), to work with teachers and community agencies in projects as diverse as the Police Athletic League and Pittsburgh's Prospect Multicultural Center. The method called for extensive collaborative planning and implementation and was based in part on social psychologist Kurt Lewin's work.

But there was a difference in our rationales for using plans. I had accepted a framework and then worked within its boundaries. I had stood behind the power of external authority. Perhaps that accounted in part for why, in nearly twenty years of working with schools, I had lost some of my early enthusiasm. In my field notes, I'd commented:

> Where is the urgency I felt to use social science research to improve academic achievement of kids in urban areas? I used to feel a zeal, an urgency, a drive, a conviction. . . . Nothing has seemed to make a difference. Black kids, other kids of color are still often on the bottom. (Field notes, July 23, 1997)

Ms. Robinson and I talked about my discouragement, and she urged me to be optimistic, and she assured me that I could make a difference by providing information that gave the school staff a more complete picture of students' attitudinal strengths and dispositions.

As my collaboration with Ms. Robinson deepened, I realized that the school's actions to increase resilience would have to become part of the story. The student data would not be understandable without the emerging setting narrative. Parts of the student story—albeit told in group averages and standard deviations—and the school narrative were in dynamic interaction. But I had trouble starting on the expected technical report for Johns Hopkins University. The school was not relying on a "magic bullet," but carefully choreographing the old and new efforts of the entire school toward a vision that highlighted student achievement and confidence. In this day of "brand name" programs developed by leading researchers and administrators, this no-frills approach of using available resources would, we thought, probably be of little interest. But, for the record, Ms. Robinson and I decided to coauthor a technical report that told the Stanton story.

PRACTICING THE STEPS

The 1997–98 academic year began far from the city, at a rustic conference center in the hills and pastures of Northern Virginia. A community partner had underwritten the retreat for faculty and parents on the school staff. A consultant was present to facilitate the latest actions needed to implement a system-wide instructional initiative, and I was invited to present the results of the student surveys. The agenda was designed to prepare the faculty for the fall administration of the Stanford 9 and to inspire confidence and positive attitudes. A cookout and hayride punctuated the otherwise serious discussions and presentations.

I distributed a handout that summarized how Stanton students rated themselves. Overall, the students perceived themselves as capable and proud of who they were. Children thought they got along well with parents, liked them, and experienced parental acceptance and approval. On the dimensions of self-concept, ability, enjoyment, and interest, reading and math ranked high, and the number one motivation for reading among the students was the importance of reading. The students felt that they could rely on the teachers, their peers, and most of all, their parents, for support. These results, comparable to those of normative samples, suggested that the children in the study could draw on several kinds of resources to help them overcome adversity. I offered no explanations for why these results came about, but I suggested that the school and home environments seemed to be supportive of the strengths the children had.

The school year followed a predictable schedule: districtwide testing on the Stanford 9 in the fall and spring, daily instructional activities, school assemblies, field trips, a Parent Academy, and the creation of extra-curricular activities. Ms. Robinson made opportunities to communicate the school's vision. She stressed the need for writing and other forms of literacy:

> Standards must be set and assessed. I am not happy viewing sloppy writing that does not represent the best that children can do. Students should also read books outside of their class work. They should check books out of the library, be given book reports to do, and receive written or verbal feedback. (Stanton Elementary School, 1997, p. 3)

She and the teachers encouraged students to express themselves:

> The recognition of the school is increasing the self-esteem and importance of parents, students, and the staff of the school. . . . Four students entered the United Black Fund's annual citywide essay contest, "I Love Life and I Want to Live" in song, essay, and poster. Two students won first place in the essay contests. Another student won second place for the poster entry, and one teacher's entire third grade class won third place in the original song composition. (Robinson, 2000, pp. 42–43)

At the Partnership Summit in March 1998, an event celebrating the efforts of community partners, she said, "Children should be able to read, write, speak, think, and feel good about themselves." The partners had contributed to achieving the vision by providing regular tutoring and mentoring, implementing a Rites of Passage program, donating computers, providing training in peer conflict resolution, and donating resources.

During the summer of 1998, Ms. Robinson and I completed our technical report *Exploring the Dynamics of Resilience in an Elementary School* (Nettles & Robinson, 1999). It describes how the school was using two principles underlying resilience to improve the school: increasing available resources and mobilizing protective processes of high expectations, opportunities to participate, and caring and support. It reported significant gains schoolwide in reading and mathematics. We concluded:

> Resilience is emerging as an organizing principle that gives Stanton a means of integrating school improvement, regular and enhanced curricular offerings, and

processes that emphasize caring, high expectations, and opportunity. . . . We do not view this as another program to improve test scores and grades, although the results thus far are promising. Rather, we see this as a way of giving meaning to the phrase, "building on children's strengths." (p. 18)

The report describes a school in the midst of a changing narrative, and that change was positive and palpable. In May 1998, I had brought eighteen print journalists to the school. They interviewed teachers and students and listened as Ms. Robinson talked about the students, the parents, the teachers, and the community partners. Although I failed to grasp the significance of the comment at the time, I recall that one of the journalists turned to me and whispered, "I don't see any difference between this school and a school in the suburbs."

Summary and Discussion

Through personal stories of two participants who contributed to school change, in this chapter I examined the emergence of a narrative celebrating school and student strengths from one that characterized the school as deficient and harmful. The inquiry shows how interactions between the setting narrative and the personal stories of individuals contribute to the shaping and reshaping of a school's image. Further, the inquiry suggests that school-community connections contributed to a change in the context from one inconsistently supportive of student achievement to one with the characteristics of empowering community settings. This discussion focuses on three processes that encompassed interactions between setting narratives and personal stories: (1) creating and arranging, (2) practicing cultural sensitivity, and (3) uncovering parts in the whole.

CREATING AND ARRANGING

Choreographers, like school principals, have a vision, and they plan the steps that will realize their vision. In her role as principal of Stanton, Ms. Robinson linked the widely held goal of academic achievement for inner-city children with a parallel, divinely inspired vision of recognition of the school's accomplishments. Although she promoted classroom-level planning processes, she continually reviewed and revised schoolwide plans. She came from similar circumstances as her students; like them, she had attended a virtually all-Black school with Black teachers and leadership. She had achieved success in academic settings: she was an excellent role model. She had the skills to support and encourage others, as her interactions with community partners and with me indicated.

This picture is consistent with research identifying empowering community settings with leadership that is inspirational, shared, talented, and committed (Maton & Salem, 1995). Ms. Robinson also exemplifies characteristics of psychological empowerment. I interpret her critique of easy acceptance of externally generated theory and research as one piece of evidence of her critical awareness (Perkins & Zimmerman, 1995). Perhaps most empowering of all is the fact that she wrote her own story.

PRACTICING CULTURAL SENSITIVITY

With community partners-in-education, Ms. Robinson and the faculty created a setting that students viewed as supportive and that provided students with opportunities to participate in valued roles and activities. Again, this is consistent with research on the characteristics of empowering community settings (Maton & Salem, 1995).

In many respects, however, the Stanton setting resembles an intervention based on culturally sensitive theories and research. Tucker and Herman (2002) proposed self-empowerment theory (SET), which posits that academic success and behavior problems in African American children are influenced by self-motivation to achieve, perceived self-control, and other factors consistent with self-regulation and autonomy. Two things are unique: the premise that African American students are especially in need of empowerment to offset the persistent social injustices they face and the necessity of community mobilization, especially based in the African American community. Whereas some of Stanton's community partners came from outside the community, many were African Americans, some based in the neighborhood. They provided the kinds of assistance and modeling recommended by the Partnership Education Program (PEP, the intervention based on self-empowerment theory), such as pairing positive feelings about self with learning, management of negative emotions (as in conflict resolution training), and individualized academic tutoring.

UNCOVERING PARTS IN THE WHOLE

In this dance of narratives, I have uncovered parts in the whole: Ms. Robinson as principal, writer, and choreographer; the students' survey voices in concert; and I as researcher and narrator. The backdrop included teachers and community partners. One of the limitations of this inquiry is that it captures only selected parts. Many others can be uncovered: for example, parents and district administrators remain to be seen and heard. The spontaneous tales of students were absent.

In dance as in stories, people move onstage and then off. Sometimes they are dominant in the setting—as soloists or partners, and at others times they perform as a corps. The backdrop of the action—the props, the scenery, the lighting—is kaleidoscopic. With one twist, one motion, the pattern changes.

Thus, this story continues: Project 2000, a community partner, and Stanton students discussed strides made in academic achievement of Black boys on the November 16, 1999, broadcast of *Nightline*; *TIME for Teachers* (2000) published a feature on Stanton's efforts to foster resilience in its students, and the report that Ms. Robinson and I wrote was published in a guidebook on resilience for educators (Nettles & Robinson, 1999). Ms. Robinson has retired but still volunteers in the community. I have moved to another part of the country, but I follow Stanton's progress via the Internet. As of this writing, the school seems to be making steady strides in realizing its vision. If, as Rappaport (1995) notes, empowering resources include the ability to create one's narrative and to influence the collective narrative of one's community, then Stanton is telling its own story, moving to its own beat.

Recommended Readings

I mastered scientific discourse early in my career because that form allowed me simultaneously to hide behind authority and to become one in my own right. I started to find my own voice and to value stories of everyday experience in reading *Writing Down the Bones* (Goldberg, 1986); I return to that book whenever I start a new writing project. Nancy Sommers, in "Between the Drafts" (1992), reminds me, in her words: "My life is full of uncertainty; negotiating that uncertainty day to day gives me authority" (p. 29). Reynold Price's memoir, *A Whole New Life* (2003), taught me how to write from and about experience, and the essay, "Guidelines for Quality in Autobiographical Forms of Self-Study Research" (Bullough & Pinnegar, 2001), is a gem that supports my desire for good writing. I discovered *Common Ground: Personal Writing and Public Discourse* (Collette & Johnson, 1997) in a used bookstore near the University of Virginia. It is an indispensable guide to writing narratives of events (stories) and of ideas.

Reflective Questions

1. How will the foregoing narrative inform your decisions about your own work?

2. In collaborative research, trust between the research partners is very important. Describe the ways in which Nettles and Robinson developed a relationship of trust.

3. Empowerment can occur at individual, organizational, and societal levels. How did the narrative depict these levels and their mutual influences?

References

Benard, B. (1991). *Fostering resiliency in kids: Protective factors in the family, school, and community.* Portland, OR: Western Center for Drug-Free Schools and Communities.

Bullough, R. V., & Pinnegar, S. (2001). Guidelines for quality in autobiographical forms of self-study research. *Educational Researcher, 30,* 13–21.

Christenson, S. L., & Sheridan, S. M. (2001). *Schools and families: Creating essential connections for learning.* New York: Guilford Press.

Collette, C., & Johnson, R. (1997). *Common ground: Personal writing and public discourse.* Boston: Addison-Wesley.

Connell, J. P., Spencer, M. B., & Aber, J. L. (1994). Educational risk and resilience in African-American youth: Context, self, action, and outcomes in school. *Child Development, 65,* 494–506.

Dubow, E. F., & Ullman, D. G. (1989). Assessing social support in elementary school children: The survey of children's social support. *Journal of Child Clinical Psychology, 18,* 52–64.

Franz, C. E., & Stewart, A. J. (Eds.). (1994). *Women creating lives: Identities, resilience, and resistance.* Boulder, CO: Westview.

Goldberg, N. (1986). *Writing down the bones: Freeing the writer within.* Boston: Shambhala Publications.

Holland, S. H. (1996). Project 2000: An educational mentoring and academic support model for inner-city African American boys. *Journal of Negro Education, 65,* 315–321.

Luthar, S. S., Cicchetti, D., & Becker, B. (2000). The construct of resilience: A critical evaluation and guidelines for future work. *Child Development, 71,* 543–562.

Marsh, H. W. (1990) *Self description questionnaire–I: SDQ manual.* Campbelltown, Australia: University of Western Sydney, Macarthur.

Maton, K. I., & Salem, D. A. (1995). Organizational characteristics of empowering community settings: A multiple case study approach. *American Journal of Community Psychology, 23,* 631–656.

Miles, M. B., & Huberman, A. M. (1994). *Qualitative data analysis.* Thousand Oaks, CA: Sage.

Nettles, S. M. (1999, June). *Black women of psychology.* Paper presented at the National Conference on Black Women in the Academy II: Service and Leadership, Washington, DC.

Nettles, S. M. (2001). *Crazy visitation: A chronicle of illness and recovery.* Athens: University of Georgia Press.

Nettles, S. M., & Pleck, J. H. (1994). Risk, resilience, and development: The multiple ecologies of black adolescents in the United States. In R. J. Haggerty, L. Sherrod, N. Garmezy, & M. Ruttter. (Eds.), *Stress, risk, and resilience in children and adolescents: Processes, mechanisms, and intervention* (pp. 147–149). New York: Cambridge University Press.

Nettles, S. M., & Robinson, F. P. (1999). Exploring the dynamics of resilience in an elementary school. In B. Cesarone (Ed.), *Resilience guide: A collection of resources on resilience in children and families.* Champaign: University of Illinois, Early

Childhood and Parenting Collaborative. Retrieved March 15, 2004, from http://ceep.crc.uiuc.edu

Perkins, D., & Zimmerman, M. A. (1995). Empowerment theory, research, and application. *American Journal of Community Psychology, 23*, 569–599.

Pianta, R. C., & Walsh, D. J. (1998). Applying the construct of resilience in schools: Cautions from a developmental systems perspective. *School Psychology Review, 27*, 407–417.

Price, R. (2003). *A whole new life: An illness and a healing.* New York: Simon & Schuster.

Rappaport, J. (1995). Empowerment meets narrative: Listening to stories and creating settings. *American Journal of Community Psychology, 23*, 795–807.

Rappaport, J. (2000). Community narratives: Tales of terror and joy. *American Journal of Community Psychology, 28*, 1–24.

Robinson, F. P. (2000). *Is urban education too hard for God?* Fort Washington, MD: Silesia Companies.

Rutter, M. (1987). Psychosocial resilience and protective mechanisms. *American Journal of Orthopsychiatry, 57*, 316–331.

Salzer, M. S. (1998). Narrative approach to assessing interactions between society, community, and person. *Journal of Community Psychology, 26*, 569–580.

Sommers, N. (1992). Between the drafts. *College Composition and Communication, 43*, 23–31.

Stanton Elementary School. (1996). *Title 1 local school improvement plan, 1996–97.* Washington, DC: Author.

Stanton Elementary School. (1997). *Local school integrated improvement plan, update 1997–98.* Washington, DC: Author.

Swap, S. M. (1993). *Developing household partnerships: From concepts to practice.* New York: Teachers College Press.

TIME for teachers. (2000). Fostering resilience: What works. Retrieved March 16, 2004, from www.timeforkids.com/TFK/tgpdf/special/0005chevy.pdf

Tucker, C. M., & Herman, K. C. (2002). Using culturally sensitive theories and research to meet the academic needs of low-income African American children. *American Psychologist, 57*, 762–773.

Werner, E. E. (1990). Protective factors and individual resilience. In S. Meisels & J. Shonkoff (Eds.), *Handbook of early childhood intervention.* New York: Cambridge University Press.

Wigfield, A., Guthrie, J., & McGough, K. (1996). *A questionnaire measure of reading motivations* (Instructional Resource No. 22). Athens, GA: National Reading Research Center.

3

Black Women Writing Autobiography

Autobiography in Multicultural Education

Meta Y. Harris

Autobiographical Introduction

As a young Black woman coming of age and living in the Deep South during the civil rights movement, I had a deep concern for how Black people were perceived and judged, especially by people who knew nothing about us. My experiences during that time period fostered my fascination with writing autobiography. Historically, Black Americans have commonly employed the genre of autobiography to tell their stories (Harris, 2003). It was originally a means of appealing to White society for acceptance as human beings.

I find that writing autobiography gives me the opportunity not only to explore my history from a personal perspective, relative to the political happenings of the times, local happenings, Black community events, academic experiences, and other occurrences that somehow impinge on my life, but also to revisit those times from a "removed" perspective. I am able to visit my life as an "other." I also examine my autobiographical writings in light of the many ways I identify myself. The impact of these facts also affects how I respond to my life events today, not only in my personal interactions but also in my interactions as an educator, with my colleagues, and with my students. Certainly each teacher's identity and understanding thereof also impact his or her interactions with his or her colleagues and their students, depending on the backgrounds and the identities of those colleagues and students.

Autobiography can also be a means to share one's history and culture with others. The production of autobiography opens avenues for individuals to examine how the things their parents taught them, their formal education, and cultural and life experiences all impact who they are and how they perceive, react to, and interact with others. The sharing of insights gained from writing autobiography allows others to have a better understanding of the writer. Autobiography is therefore a valuable tool in multicultural education, where students and teachers both desire to learn about each other.

This chapter specifically examines Black women writing autobiography and how the use of autobiography writing by teachers as well as students can be employed in multicultural education to develop better interactions between the teachers and students and between diverse students in the classroom. Although this chapter is primarily based on research related to the autobiographical writings of Black women, this research is transferable and useful in the application of autobiographical writing in multicultural education and in other multicultural settings.

Why Use Autobiography in Multicultural Education?

When I enter a new class of students, I always begin by introducing myself and asking them to tell the class and me about themselves. My effort in this exercise is to get the students to think about their classmates and to consider and realize that there are different cultural perspectives. As time passes in the conduct of the class, I provide the opportunity for the students to share more and more of themselves and their experiences that are relevant to how they perceive the concepts we are studying. I find this to be effective in getting the students to open up to each other and to me in the classroom, and I have discovered that it fosters more camaraderie among the students.

Autobiography by Black people in America, as indicated previously, originally took the form of slave narratives, produced to show White people that slaves were indeed human beings, with all the same human qualities attributed to White people. Slave narratives were written also to appeal to the mercy of their White readers. These narratives would eventually be useful beyond that, however, to help uncertain Black people, generations later, define their identities from the life stories of former slaves. The slave narratives would give twentieth century Black Americans brief encounters with their past in the words of their ancestors.

Despite the fact that most Black people during slave-era America could not read or write, or even had the time or freedom to think in terms of "self-identity," the importance of the slave narratives to the lives of twentieth and twenty-first century Black Americans cannot be overestimated. The descriptions of Black women were particularly negative in the early literature about Black people, often presenting them as fat and doting mammies or as seductive temptresses and Jezebels, seducing and conquering with sex (Christian, 1985; Fox-Genovese, 1988). Still other stereotypical images of Black women include the submissive, unattractive, cooking-and-cleaning Aunt Jemima and the manipulative, controlling "Superwoman" (Bracks, 1998). The only way these images can be changed is for Black women to do it themselves, by writing their own stories about their lives (Christian, 1985; Harris, 2003). This simple act of penning one's own stories is a way for Black women to create their own identities, rather than those formerly created and promoted by White authors, filmmakers, television producers, and other Whites with access to the media (Coltrane & Messineo, 2000; Gray, 1989).

It has become necessary, for many reasons, for Black women to dispose of these exaggerated, negative, and false images of themselves and to create their own self-images. One major reason is that the previous sources of these images were unreliable and based their constructions on stereotypical, prejudiced, and distorted representations and ideologies. This is particularly troublesome because, generally, society in America bases its interactions with, and opinions of, Black women and men on those false stereotypical images. The need to challenge and reinvent the images of Black people and other people of color, and particularly women of color, has led to the establishment of autobiography as an important primary way of creating new images and encountering old images in multicultural classrooms. The redefinition of the self through the writing of autobiography places power into the hands of the writer to define who she is and to share her self-identity with the readers. This is the initiation of the changing of global societal views of Black women.

The Autobiographical Process

Aside from the fact that previous sources were unreliable, another major reason for destroying these historically negative images is that they have resulted in Black women being neglected or treated as inferiors in American society. This has impacted how Black women perceive themselves, as well as how they interact with others. There is a need for Black women to write their lives, as much for the correcting of the history of their lives as for the personal benefits they gain from engaging in the process of developing autobiography. The autobiographical process permits the writer to think deeply about her life and to develop a positive self-identity. The creation of autobiography is, in these ways, a therapeutic process that is useful to all who write their lives.

When I first wrote my autobiography for sharing in a classroom setting, I was able to express my anger against the "boxes" to which I was confined by society, especially by people who knew nothing about me. It gave me an opportunity to vent my feelings. The descriptions and images that were identified with me simply because I am a Black woman impinged on my self-esteem, self-concept, and ultimately my self-identity. This came out in my autobiographical writings. It was depressing, and it impacted all aspects of my life, but, in my writing, I was able to let go of some of the animosity that was keeping me from moving away from the unwarranted depictions that held me in a place that did not reflect who I really am.

Very often when I read the autobiographical writings of other Black women I am enthralled by their stories. I realize, however, that audiences who know no better may think that the story of one Black woman is the story of all or most Black women, including my story. This disturbs me because the continuing implication is the old, worn-out cliché that "all Black people are alike." Although Black people are still judged as a group, we are not all the same, or even nearly so, and I see that the sharing of my story will add to the literature on Black people, and especially to that of Black women.

One of the things I consider most important to do in my autobiography is to acknowledge my love and pride in Black people globally. However, I also find it necessary to inform readers that I am a Black American, not an African, and cannot claim any particular African heritage, as I have never traced my lineage. The act of tracing my ancestry beyond my great grandparents would be most difficult because of the rape of Black women by White men both during and after slavery, the absence of records documenting the family lineage of Black people in the South, and other circumstances that grossly impact the accuracy of such an effort. I also add in my writing that I know definitively that I am not *pure* anything and that my heritage is most certainly as mixed as it can possibly be, considering that I am definitely a descendent of slaves.

Until recently, self-ethnographic writing was considered suspect and largely ignored by the academic community because it was considered to be too personal and subjective to be of any real value in the world of scholarly research. Now, however, the self-ethnographic research tool is considered to be a primary resource for the scholarly investigation of peoples and cultures (Cobham & Collins, 1987; Stanley, 1993), which is why autobiography is an excellent tool for the study and discovery of other cultures.

Black women are beginning to experience the documentation of their lives as an important way to utilize their experiences and knowledge, for the expansion of their knowledge of self and others (Davies, 1999), as well as for sharing this self-discovery device with others. At the same time, the self-ethnographic process is a form of self-reflexivity that is at the core of methodological principles, "not in terms of self-absorption, but rather in order to use the interrelationships between researcher and other to inform and change social knowledge" (p. 3). This self-reflexivity is a turning back on oneself, a process of self-reference (Davies, 1999) in which the writer considers deeply the content of her writing with the intent of answering questions that she has about her own life story and of anticipating the questions that readers might have. The following brief excerpt from my autobiography illustrates this point:

Before I started school at six years old, I had experienced riding in the back of the city buses, and sitting in front with my aunt or my mother when they were taking the White children in their care some place. I realised that I was Black and lived in a society where the White majority hated me because of the colour of my skin, that my family was poor, and that I would have to work like mad to get myself out of poverty. I think that I must have started working hard from the day I realised these things, and I've been working hard ever since, to rise above the racism in America. This was not the way childhood should have been and it made for some pretty tough kids. Some of us would survive the marginalisation, while others would surely perish. Many of us have perished. (Harris, 2003, pp. 122–123)

Although autobiography as ethnographic research has been criticized as a self-indulgent and narcissistic literary genre (Davies, 1999) in which a linear and goal-oriented description of the individual achievements of a significant person, usually a White man, is given, the autobiographies of these men are usually widely accepted and highly respected documents. Yet the autobiographical writings of the nonfamous—women, and especially Black women—are usually criticized and afforded very little purposeful relevance (see Butterfield, 1974).[1] The writing of these autobiographies as self-ethnographic, cultural, and self-reflexive processes can offer the implementation of a new and different approach to both the interrogation of the personal experiences of Black women and the exchange of cultural knowledge in multicultural educational settings and in other settings.

The Parameters of Autobiography

Autobiography theorists and analysts have only recently begun to consider the importance of Black women's autobiographies in any scenario (Jelinek, 1980). Thus, the relevance of this genre in the multicultural educational setting is in dire need of significant scholarly research and further interrogation and examination. Aside from recognition of the importance of Black women's autobiographies, the past several years have seen considerable debate among theorists about the definition of autobiography. Stanley describes it as "ideological accounts of 'lives,' which in turn feed back into everyday understandings of how 'common lives' and 'extraordinary lives' can be recognised" (1992, p. 3). According to Stanley, the writer essentially tells the reader the story that she wants them to have and writes with that purpose, and not from the perspective of simply revealing her story to the world. Bearing this in mind, the autobiography writer may or may not decide to write a "true" story. That is, the writer may decide to present her story using fictional details and characters that for her may more fully convey the important themes of her life.

Autobiography is a genre of writing that is encompassed in the term *auto/biography*, which has over the past decade become representative of the many ways an individual can tell her life story (Stanley, 1992). Auto/biography includes fictional writing as well as "biography, autobiography, diaries, letters, social science productions, and uses of written lives or all forms of life writing and also the ontological and epistemological links between them" (p. 3). The practice of auto/biography involves the compilation of the history of a life, as perceived in memory and depicted by the person who lives or lived it (Harris, 2003).

Comprehensive auto/biography includes information from interviews with the writer (Smith, 1954), the words of acquaintances of the writer, any written documentation about the life of the writer, spoken communications, video and photographic data, fictive literary devices, and even other writing genres such as memoirs, diaries, journals, poetry, and novels based on the life of the person being documented (Stanley, 1992; Stein, 1933/1971, 1937/1985. See also Emecheta, 1972/1994, 1974; Jabavu, 1963). This opens incredible vistas for the creation of auto/biography and for increased accessibility to people wanting to create auto/biography. It also allows the opportunity for making life stories and life choices more understandable, both to those creating the auto/biography and to those reading and observing these auto/biographies. This interpretation of auto/biography is empowering to those who want to exercise the right to determine their self-identities and how their life stories will ultimately be told.

Initially, autobiographies such as the slave narratives were historical treatises that documented the lives of the people associated with the writer, as well as the life of the writer. Black writers of autobiography were especially rooted in this historical format and often left out any information that might be a clue to the reader about the writer's personal life. They wrote strictly about the general lifestyles of their time and place (Prince, 1831/1993, 1856/1990; Truth, 1850/1968) or about their professional accomplishments or their travels (Seacole, 1857/1988). More personal works came out of the religious testimonials of the times. Recently, Black women have started writing more personal autobiographies that pay attention to the personal details of their lives, such as how they handle different kinds of relationship situations, family issues, financial problems, and personal events that could affect their acceptance in their communities (Harris, 2003), their workplaces, and society in general.

Black women are expected to focus their autobiographical writing on political issues instead of personal lifestyle issues (Smith, 1984), which is sometimes problematic for them. Sometimes Black women want to tell their stories from personal perspectives. Although political issues are important, there is a great deal of knowledge to be garnered from the autobiographical writings that depict personal lifestyle issues as well. This is not saying that it is necessary to omit the political aspects of the writer's life, but rather it is necessary to iterate the importance of other aspects of life. The discussion of personal lifestyle issues can undoubtedly reveal how the writer copes with everyday hardships that rarely, if ever, come up when autobiography is written from a primarily political or historical perspective.

When writing my autobiography I found it difficult to write from a strictly personal perspective, because it was just as important for me to write about political issues that were happening at certain times in my life that also affected me personally. I could not have written my autobiography without writing about the civil rights movement or about moving from the segregated South to the home of my White foster parents in the northeast. I therefore intertwined the two perspectives to tell what I feel is a comprehensive story.

Although I have written quite openly about particular issues that I consider personal to me, I have been reluctant to write explicitly about my sex life and intimate relationships. Those experiences and relationships have deeply impacted the quality of my life and have made the difference in many of the decisions I have made in my life. My reluctance to make them a part of my auto-biographical record comes from the exposure that writing and publishing would give to these personal aspects of my life. It also comes from my attempts at exercising discretion and my desire to protect myself and others from unwelcome scrutiny by unknown readers who might not have my best interest in mind when scrutinizing me closely, from my own revelations.

In my close reading and analysis of the majority of the autobiographical writings in this research, I found that the authors often do not give their physical descriptions to the reader. Many Black women writers, including myself, give more details of surroundings when describing events than they give of self-descriptions. The reader will rarely find information in these autobiographies such as height, weight, face or body descriptions, or other indicators of appearance. Self-descriptions are strong indicators of the writer's self-esteem and self-identity and are important pieces of information for the reader in developing accurate perceptions of the autobiography writer. This is true for me as well. I do not describe my perceptions of my physical attributes or what I feel about how I look. I do, however, include photos of myself and of my family.

Many Black women writers of autobiography are now including more personal photographs in their books, in lieu of the previously absent, written descriptions of their physical appearances. The avoidance of physical descriptions also points to the deeply personal nature of autobiography. Most Black women autobiography writers are reluctant to reveal information that their families or communities might consider to be too personal and an invasion of the privacy of the writer or the privacy of others who might be mentioned in the autobiography. Ultimately, the inclusion of personal information in autobiography presents a more rounded and complete picture of who the person really is, even though it may leave the writer open to attack from the reader:

> Bracks suggests that when producing autobiography, the author must be open to the revelation of things that are usually kept secret, and that may even be so buried

that they are nearly completely forgotten. However, the choice to fully reveal themselves and admit their vulnerabilities to an openly hostile world requires lack of shame, as well as pride in who they are. (Harris, 2003, p. 56)

Some Black women theorists believe that the writing of autobiography is a way of creating self and community (Harris, 2003; Kolawole, 1997), as much as of sharing it. The creation of self and community are as much sociological explorations of the writer's environment as an examination of the individual's life. It is also accepted by feminist theorists that the social and individual are symbiotically linked (Davies, 1999; Stanley, 1993), therefore making the use of autobiography as ethnographic social research acceptable as a reflection of the communal values informing the writer's unconscious as expressed in the autobiographical writings (Harris, 2003). The Black woman who writes autobiography thus becomes a historian of her Black community.

Black Women Sharing Their Lives in Multicultural Settings

My autobiographical writing expresses my perception that certain things, both positive and negative, that happened in my Black community affected my self-identity as much as the positive and negative things that I encountered outside that community. Certainly, the fact that I am a child of the civil rights era significantly impacted my identity. My writing reflects those themes most important to me—equality for Black people and my self-identity, gender, personal challenges, and family issues. I think, write, and speak from the perspective of a Black woman living in a significantly racist society, where the majority of the people have some sort of bigotry toward Black women.

Sometimes, people who are familiar with me and who have read my autobiography will express to me that our memories of the same events are slightly or even grossly different. This is one of the reasons why autobiography is sometimes considered to be unreliable for research purposes. It is usually based entirely on memory, which is always subjective, and more often than not, on faulty memories. Autobiography is nonetheless a useful tool for learning the attitudes and beliefs of the writer and can provide a wealth of information about his or her culture and environment.

The sharing of autobiographical information with my students, and between the students, has positively affected the dynamics in my classrooms. When the students learn about their teacher, and about each other, and perceive that they can trust their environment, they become more open to participating in class and to sharing and learning. In a recent sociology class that I taught, there was a Gullah[2] student from South Carolina, who expressed to me that she was often not comfortable in her classes because she spoke in a different dialect from the other students, both Black and White. At the beginning of the class I had the students introduce themselves, as I always do, and because many of the students had been in my classes in the past, they were very open and spoke about their lives and goals quite easily. When the Gullah student heard the stories of the other students, she decided that she would be comfortable speaking in this environment and felt that she could tell her classmates about her discomfort in expressing herself in class. She was well received by the other students and became one of the most outspoken students in the class. This initial self-revealing act of sharing autobiographical information made a significant difference in how this young woman was able to become a viable part of the class and in how her peers were able to accept her and show her the respect she needed, so that she was able to freely and willingly participate in class discussions.

Readers' and listeners' reactions to personal autobiographies often prevent Black women from revealing important personal and cultural information. This almost always happens in the classroom as well. The concern with reader responses calls attention to the fact that the readers impact the interpretation of the autobiography, based on the readers' cultural backgrounds, personal idiosyncrasies, and other factors, such as geographic location. Therefore, it is important that the readers (or consumers) of the autobiographical products engage with the stories from culturally sensitive positions. This means that the reader has to be willing to hear what the writer is saying, without prejudging the writer's perspective.

The reader has the responsibility of giving the writer the opportunity to be heard, to be safe to write, and to speak freely. The reader should engage with the autobiography with an open mind rather than an overly critical attitude, paying attention to whether, and how, the writer moves from a childlike position to one of empowerment; this is a more appropriate critique of the life story than for the reader to engage with the work with the attitude that he or she is going to try to find holes in the story and to figure out whether or not the writer is being truthful. An effort to find the message in the text, not search for problems in it, will afford the reader a deeper understanding of the writer's world and of her real story.

The reader needs to keep in mind that the Black woman writing her life story is probably writing her autobiography in order to free herself from the stereotypical and derogatory images that have been inflicted on her historically (Bracks, 1998; Davies, 1994). The reader should also be mindful that the writer is sharing her intimate details, such as how she defines or identifies herself, the things that are important to her, and her beliefs and desires (Harris, 2003). The stories presented are in the words, voices, and artistic crafts of the women creating them and are their ways of obliterating the notions that previously hindered them, keeping them in the margins. These autobiographies challenge the readers to know the writers and to see how they live.

Carole Boyce Davies (1994) advises readers that

> Black women's writing . . . should be read as a series of boundary crossings and not as a fixed, geographical, ethnically or nationally bound category of writing. In cross-cultural, transnational, translocal, diasporic perspectives, this reworking of the grounds of "Black women's writing" redefines identity away from exclusion and marginality. (p. 4)

The readers' consideration of these factors is a way of constructively listening to what the writers are saying about the condition of their lives relative to their feelings of belonging or not and their prospects of dealing with and overcoming their feelings of alienation (Harris, 2003). These writings require a reading that incorporates the examination of the layers of meaning woven into the texts, which lose their meaning when read simplistically. The reader who wants to gain something from the reading of the Black woman's text must read it with an understanding of the struggle of the author and while making a linguistic interrogation beyond the language on the pages. Bracks (1998) suggests that the readers explore the writings, keeping in mind the "multidimensionality they express in language choice while being sensitive to the risks they [the writers] are taking making community knowledge available to an outside audience" (p. 21). Still, in any critical examination of the autobiographical writings of Black women, certain aspects of the writing must be highlighted and even deconstructed (Bracks, 1998). This examination should not be a hostile act, but one in which the reader engages with the text and accepts the possibility that the examination will yield useful information for better understanding the writer, her community of origin, and especially how she self-identifies. The same holds true when the writer of an autobiography shares his or her work with a group of people, such as in a multicultural education environment. This sharing can be between teachers of different cultures, between teachers and their students, or between students and their classmates.

In a recent class that I taught on Black women writers, I engaged my students by having them write about specific events in their lives that impacted them greatly as children. Although the students were all Black women, in the sharing of their writings we learned very important differences in lifestyles, backgrounds, experiences, and beliefs. The sharing of their stories allowed these students to see their classmates in a more personal light, which helped them to bond in the class and feel safe to share their lives with each other.

In another more multicultural and diverse class setting it was harder to establish a sense of togetherness among the students. The number of students was significantly higher as well, which is always a hindrance to the establishment of feelings of safety and camaraderie. However, when the students were requested to share personal experiences related to the social sciences concepts that they were learning, the students became eager to participate once the sharing started, and often the discussions had to be cut short so that the class could move on, because so many of the students wanted to share their life experiences. The discussions were even more involved and participatory when the students were sharing written autobiographical pieces on the topic of discussion.

As a writer of autobiography, I deliberately attempt to read my own writing in ways in which I think most readers will read my work. I try to be aware of the reader's impact on the text itself. I pay particular attention to the "hostile" reader. Although some of my writings are okay for me to read privately, the same text must be reconsidered and revised with the hostile reader in mind. I sometimes decide to change my text to prevent negative repercussions resulting from my revealing too much of my beliefs, my feelings about myself, and my feelings about others in my life. Ultimately, I often determine that the privacy rights of others in my life deserve the highest consideration. Even though I may alter the details of my text, I write to express what life has been like for me, as well as to release some of my anger and pain over perceived mistreatment and marginalization that I experience as a Black woman in the often hostile society in which I live.

Unfortunately, Black women writers of autobiography often fail to discuss feelings of anger and rage that may accompany their experiences of marginalization, harassment, and hostility associated with racial bigotry. Instead, the writer will usually focus on diplomacy, forgiveness, and humility. The writing of autobiography is a means of harnessing the negativity that these women encounter and survive. Audre Lorde writes,

> Women of Color in America have grown up within a symphony of anger, at being silenced, at being un-chosen, at knowing that when we survive, it is in spite of a world that takes for granted our lack of humanness, and which hates our very existence outside of its service. And I say symphony rather than cacophony because we have had to learn to orchestrate those furies so that they do not tear us apart. We have had to learn to move through them and use them for strength and force and insight within our daily lives. Those of us who did not learn this difficult lesson did not survive. And part of my anger is always libation for my fallen sisters. (Lorde, 1984, p. 129)

When students in the classroom write about anger in their lives, they tend to express their anger in frustrated or muted voices and seem okay with the fact that they are only beginning to be comfortable enough to write about their anger. The "muted voices" refers to the lack of development in their writings on the topic of anger. The students might express that they are mad or angry, without giving any details about the extent of their anger, how it is expressed, or how they deal with it.

The issue of validation of the autobiographical text is another common concern for Black women autobiography writers and may very well be a concern of students in writing their lives for the first time. Proving the truth of the autobiographical work can sometimes keep students from writing "true" documents and others from giving their full consideration to what the author is saying in her autobiography.

Some theorists say that all autobiography is fiction or that the retelling of past events inherently employs the use of fictive devices (e.g., Eakin, 1990; Stanley, 1993; Stein, 1937/1985). The fictive devices are many and virtually impossible to delimit and categorize because they are limited only by the mind of the imaginative writer. Students should be encouraged to make use of fictive devices to convey their stories. The autobiographical work should not only be a retelling of the facts as the author sees them but also be a way that the author conveys a sense of something that has deeply impacted her life and who she is and that she wants to share with others because of its great importance to her.

The use of autobiography in multicultural education is a concept that is rapidly taking hold in teacher education. It is one that should be actively promoted by educators for its value to multicultural education, as well as in helping teachers and students to identify where they can improve their interactions with people who are different from them. Autobiography is a way of introducing students to different cultures when the students are required to write about themselves and to share those writings with their teachers and classmates.

The art of writing is an important form of self-expression in modern culture. It can be extremely helpful in the formation of self-identity. However, the absence of good writing skills does not mean that those who lack them are lacking in the only acceptable form to express their self-identity. People who do not have good writing skills have other ways of developing and expressing their self-identities. The tradition of passing along history and life stories orally has been significant for centuries across many cultures, but the use of other artistic forms such as painting, drawing, sculpture, quilting, weaving, dance, music, and other activities are also effective ways of expressing self-identity.

The writing of autobiography for the purpose of sharing with others who are different and who want to learn about the writer is significant in the multicultural education setting because the writer is challenged to write about himself or herself as an individual and as part of the community. When writers are challenged to recognize their connection to their community, their birth families, and their separateness as individuals, they are apt to learn something about themselves and their communities. In this respect, I had to view myself beyond my identity as a Black person, or as a woman, and even as a member of my particular family and to see myself as who I am, separate and individual, a human being who happens to be a Black woman. The presentation of my knowledge of my "self" to others through the writing of autobiography is significant because it provides the readers or listeners with personal perceptions that determine my self-identity, which is necessarily reliant on my culture, environment, upbringing, and general background, as well as on my sex, sexual preference, and other factors that impact my life.

Conclusion

Unfortunately, the misperceptions and stereotypes about Black women not only are historical concepts but also still pose problems, as indicated earlier, with how Black women are perceived today. The current generations of youths are buying into stereotypes about young Black women that persist even when they are disproved and shown to be irrelevant. For instance, some young Black men will refuse to date young Black women with dark complexions because they claim that these young women have "attitudes" that make them undesirable. These young men thus choose to date only light-complexioned Black women or White women for their supposed better attitudes (Golden, 2004). The sad reality is that most of the dark-complexioned young women that these young men allude to are really in a defensive mode because they "have to work harder to be seen, heard, valued, accepted" (p. 59) than their lighter-complexioned counterparts. These Black women are often seen as unlovable and in many cases unsuitable for long-term relationships. They are considered to be the new "Sapphires,"[3] now called "Sheniquas" (p. 61). They are marginalized, "humourized," and considered "dark and ugly" rather than "dark and lovely" (p. 62).

The negative attributes with which these young Black women are labeled are perpetuated by youths who may have learned this attitude in their families, schools, or society in general. What are the personal experience stories of these women? How do they handle the challenges of being Black in societies that devalue them because of the color of their skin? These are the questions that can be answered by these young women and shared with their peers in their classes. How do other students relate to these young women, and what are their experiences in dealing with dark-skinned Black girls and women? When people are required to write about such issues from their own perspectives, they are challenged to confront their own prejudices. In the sharing of their ideas, feelings, and perceptions, they are displaying a willingness to be confronted about their attitudes as well as presenting the opportunity for others to challenge them to reform their misconceptions.

Educators must take responsibility for becoming actively involved in dispelling these negative images. Very often this will require that the educators start with themselves. One of the very viable and positive leads that educators can take in this effort is to encourage the writing and sharing of autobiographical writings by both faculty and students in the multicultural setting.

We can address specific themes for the focus of these writings, as well as allow the students to decide on the particular aspects of their lives that they want to address in their writings. We can direct how these writings will be shared within the classes and groups where they are discussed.

As indicated earlier, the educator must first address the topic from his or her own perspective. The discussion begins with each of us. This means that as educators we have to question ourselves about our own backgrounds and attitudes. We have to go through our own quest for the truth about ourselves as individuals. We have to be willing to get together and objectively discuss our attitudes about people who are different from us. We have to examine our own cultural experiences, how and what we were taught as children, and how our upbringings have made us who we are today. Furthermore, we have to determine whether our attitudes are being negatively imposed on the students and colleagues that we teach and encounter. The knowledge that this yields would set the stage to determine how we may need to make changes in our interactions to create more equity in our classrooms, better ways of interacting with students who are being negatively affected by our classroom behaviors, and better relations with and between our students and between our students and colleagues, thereby creating a more comfortable atmosphere.

We can initiate these discussions by creating an atmosphere of trust and safety in our classrooms. This is no small task. Most people are able to discern discriminatory attitudes and are more likely to be unresponsive when asked to reveal information about themselves and their communities in the face of them. In order to initiate such discussions in the classroom, students should not feel threatened, even if there is known discrimination in the attitudes of some of the class members.

The creation of a trusting environment might require that the teacher be willing to be the first to take the step of sharing a personal event that has affected who she or he is and discussing the impact of that event. The creation of a trusting environment that leads to understanding also requires that those in the position of authority—the teachers and professors—be receptive to all students, and not just the ones like themselves. When the educators in charge are able to display receptivity to all students in their classes, the classroom environment becomes open, and the atmosphere becomes one in which the students will feel safe to express themselves, without the fear that they will be disregarded because of their lives and their cultural heritage.

It all comes down to finding avenues to understand and accept people who are different from ourselves. Aside from helping race relations, autobiography can also help with gender relations, the relationships between persons with different sexual preferences, and even religious differences. Educators who are willing to challenge themselves by practicing autobiography as a way of tackling their own attitudes will find that they can become enlightened in their classrooms, and they will be able to encourage the same enlightenment among their students.

Recommended Readings

Black women writing autobiography and its use in multicultural education are concepts that continue to be explored by educators. The literature on the use of autobiography in multicultural education is extremely limited, but it is currently being more fully developed. I have relied heavily on Carole Boyce Davies's *Black Women, Writing and Identity—Migrations of the Subject* (1994) as a valuable analytical tool for examining the autobiographical works of Black women globally who live in societies where they find themselves marginalized.

I found that the autobiographical works of Buchi Emecheta (1974, 1994) provide useful illustrations of how the autobiographical writings of a Black woman can open the doors to greater understanding of her culture and how she is able to forge her self-identity, despite travails. It captures how Buchi coped with her marginalization both at home and in the geographical and cultural places that she migrated into. These works give the reader a glimpse into the bravery of the writer and the great skill that she must master in order to survive.

Marita Golden's work *Don't Play in the Sun* (2004) is another autobiographical work that permits the reader to enter the world and culture of the writer and expresses deep feelings about something rarely spoken of to those who are not part of the Black community. This work, at the same time, illustrates how autobiography is capable of unraveling the people of the culture, in the sense that it allows outsiders to get to know those people better.

The importance of Black women writing autobiography, and of it being useful in multicultural venues, cannot be overemphasized. Black women are recognizing their responsibility for telling their stories so that others can gain firsthand, invaluable information about the individuals as well as the communities from which they come.

Reflective Questions

1. What does a Black woman writing autobiography have to do with multicultural education?

2. What are the advantages to having the students write autobiography in the multicultural classroom?

3. How can school administrators incorporate the use of autobiography by teachers in multicultural classrooms and among their faculty to create more receptive multicultural environments in their school systems?

Notes

1. Butterfield even disputes the authenticity of the slave narratives as products of the slaves themselves, calling them "pseudo-narratives" and attributing them to White women (Butterfield, 1974, p. 201).

2. Gullah people are Black people who primarily reside on the barrier islands along the coasts of South Carolina and Georgia, whose ancestors retained much of their African culture, including a distinctive language dialect, until recent times.

3. "Sapphire" was the wife of Kingfish in the old *Amos and Andy* radio and television show; she was depicted as an argumentative, overbearing, and demanding Black woman who was always trying to control her husband.

References

Bracks, L. L. (1998). *Writings on Black women of the diaspora—History, language, and identity.* New York and London: Garland.

Butterfield, S. (1974). *Black autobiography in America.* Amherst: University of Massachusetts Press.

Christian, B. (1985). *Black feminist criticism—Perspectives on Black women writers.* New York: Pergamon.

Cobham, R., & Collins, M. (Eds.). (1987). *Watchers, seekers—Creative writing by Black women in Britain.* London: Women's Press.

Coltrane, S., & Messineo, M. (2000, March). The perpetuation of subtle prejudice: Race and gender imagery in 1990s television advertising. In *Sex Roles: A Journal of Research.* Retrieved March 2002 from www.findarticles.com

Davies, C. A. (1999). *Reflexive ethnography—A guide to researching selves and others.* London: Routledge.

Davies, C. B. (1994). *Black women, writing and identity—Migrations of the subject.* London and New York: Routledge.

Eakin, P. J. (1990). The vexingly unverifiable: Truth in autobiography. *Studies in the Literary Imagination, 23*(2), 129–144.

Emecheta, B. (1974). *Second-class citizen.* Oxford, UK: Heinemann Educational Publishers.

Emecheta, B. (1994). *In the ditch.* Oxford, UK: Allison and Busby Ltd. (Original work published 1972, Heinemann Educational Publishers)

Fox-Genovese, E. (1988). *Within the plantation household: Black and White women of the Old South.* Chapel Hill: University of North Carolina Press.

Golden, M. (2004). *Don't play in the sun.* New York: Doubleday.

Gray, H. (1989). Television, Black Americans, and the American dream. *Critical Studies in Mass Communication, 6*(4), 376–387.

Harris, M. Y. (2003). *Black women writing autobiography: Marginalisation, migration, and self-identity.* Unpublished doctoral dissertation, The University of Manchester, England.

Jabavu, N. (1963). *Ochre people: Scenes from a South African life.* London: Murray.

Jelinek, E. C. (Ed.). (1980). *Women's autobiography—Essays in criticism.* Bloomington: Indiana University Press.

Kolawole, M. E. M. (1997). *Womanism and African consciousness.* Trenton, NJ: Africa World Press.

Lorde, A. (1984). *Sister outsider—Essays and speeches.* Freedom, CA: Crossing Press.

Prince, M. (1993). *The history of Mary Prince: A West Indian slave, related by herself.* London: F. Westley and A. H. Daviseckley. (Original work published 1831, Ann Arbor: University of Michigan Press)

Prince, N. G. (1990). *Black woman's odyssey through Russia and Jamaica: The narrative of Nancy Prince.* New York: M. Weiner Publishers. (Original work published 1856)

Seacole, M. (1988). *Wonderful adventures of Mrs. Seacole in many lands.* New York and Oxford: Oxford University Press. (Original work published 1857)

Smith, M. F. (1954). *Baba of Karo: A woman of the Muslim Hausa.* New Haven, CT: Yale University Press.

Smith, V. (1984). Foreword. In A. Lee, *Sarah Phillips* (pp. ix–xxiv). Boston: Northeastern University Press.

Stanley, L. (1992). *The auto/biographical I: The theory and practice of feminist auto/biography.* Manchester, UK: Manchester University Press.

Stanley, L. (1993). On auto/biography in sociology. *Sociology, 27*(1), 41–52.

Stein, G. (1971). *The autobiography of Alice B. Toklas.* New York: Random House. (Original work published 1933)

Stein, G. (1985). *Everybody's autobiography.* New York: Random House. (Original work published 1937, London: Virago Press)

Truth, S. (1968). *Narrative of Sojourner Truth.* New York: Arno Press. (Original work published 1850, *New York Times*)

Unit Two

Latina/Latino Communities, Families, and Children

4

Being Educated in the Absence of Multiculturalism

Alma Rubal-Lopez and Angela Anselmo

Autobiographical Introduction

We have recently coauthored a book titled *On Becoming Nuyoricans,* which takes a very personal look at our experiences growing up in the South Bronx and describes how we negotiated an often hostile, racist, and confusing environment. Both of us are currently faculty members of the City University of New York, and we both have attained doctorates in bilingual developmental psychology (a doctorate in developmental psychology with an added concentration in bilingualism, sociolinguistics, and applied linguistics). Alma is a professor in the School of Education at Brooklyn College. She is also the program head of the Bilingual Teacher Program in Childhood Education and the undergraduate deputy chair. Alma's writings include research conducted in sociolinguistics, bilingual education, and multicultural education. Angie is the head of the SEEK program at Baruch College. She is also an interfaith minister and has authored work in the fields of pyscholinguistics and counseling.

The unlikelihood that two Puerto Rican females, from the same family living in the Patterson Projects in the South Bronx during the 1950s, would have taken such paths has led to a lifetime of people posing questions regarding why we chose to pursue our education and other questions regarding our educational experiences. Although the forces and developments that have led to our pursuing the paths that we have are central themes of our story, we also acknowledge how the lack of a multicultural approach in our education made our school experience an oftentimes hurtful and dreadful experience. Through our narratives we describe a time when homogeneity, a Euro-centered education, and an absence of any acknowledgment of any non-Western contribution to civilization was the norm. Because, quite often, we were one of a few or the only racial minorities in our class, we speak about the emotional and psychological ramifications of being educated in such an environment.

Introduction: First Generation Puerto Ricans in New York

We were part of the first generation of Puerto Ricans born and raised in New York during the 1950s and 1960s. Our generation paved the way for subsequent immigrant populations from the Caribbean, Latin America, and other non-European countries that settled in New York City. This generation of Puerto Ricans born in New York, also referred to as "Nuyoricans," was undoubtedly critical in helping to define issues of race, assimilation, and equity never before confronted by immigrants (African Americans notwithstanding) who were not White Europeans in a society that defined itself as a "melting pot."

As post–World War II children, we have witnessed major changes that have altered the very fabric of the United States. American society has changed in ways that we could never have imagined when we were children. One such transformation is the change of the U.S. population from one that was predominantly White European to one that is racially, linguistically, and ethnically diverse. This transformation in the demographics is the byproduct of changes in the immigration law, which now allows for larger numbers of immigrants from Asia, Latin America, and the Caribbean to enter the United States.

As children in the South Bronx we witnessed this change in the population firsthand; many of these new immigrants from the Dominican Republic and other Latin American nations became our neighbors when they settled in our already formed Black and Puerto Rican enclaves.

By examining excerpts taken from our soon-to-be-published book we describe our experiences during a time when homogeneity and the melting pot were the sacred cows, and then we look at how a different approach to our differences could have resulted in a better and kinder experience. We describe what it was like to be a member of a population of children who were ethnically, linguistically, and culturally diverse in a society that valued the opposite and in a political and social climate with little tolerance and acceptance for heterogeneity. We address issues of race, language, cultural values, and curriculum faced by us as children, and we examine how an acceptance and a respect for diversity and the institutionalization of a multicultural approach in education might have softened some of the blows that we endured.

One of the major forces impacting the lives of children during our early years was the introduction of television into the home. As illustrated in Steinberg and Kincheloe (1997), this transformed the very essence of family life. In general, the television programs aired during this period reflected an ideal American life. Although this captured the attention of the audience, the impact on children who did not fit within this framework was often detrimental. In describing the presence of television during this period, Alma explains,

> As children, television shows like *Father Knows Best, Donna Reed, Ozzie and Harriet,* and *Leave It to Beaver* made me wonder why we did not live in split-level homes with white picket fences. I remember looking out the window of my room and trying to find a star to wish on every night. My wish was to live in such a home. The mother who stayed home and the father who came home from work in a suit and said, "Hello dear. I'm home," was foreign to me. No one in my neighborhood went to work in a suit and no one returned home after a long day's work with the cheerfulness and energy depicted on any of those shows. A mother who never screamed or hit her children and who always looked good was not part of my life. A father who rarely shared any time with his family, a sick depressed mother who lived in the past with very little hope for the future, this is what showed when the curtain went up in my household. The tube depicted the Anderson family while I was stuck living in the Addams family.

These shows were dangerous to children of color because of the absence of any brown faces and the interpretations that could be made, especially by these children of color who were living in poverty. For the poor White child, the message was that maybe with hard work and discipline you can make it. After all, there are people like you who have made it. The poor White child might have an uncle or aunt that lives a different existence, but the chances of a poor Black or Hispanic child in the 1950s having a wealthy family member were slim. In fact, we who lived in the projects were the ones who were living well compared to our families and friends in tenements. For the poor White child, the hope is slim, but there might be a light at the end of the tunnel. However, for the Black or Hispanic child, the message is that there is no light at the end of the tunnel. In fact, there is probably no tunnel, either. There is only a long, long road that leads back to where you are, stuck in the ghetto and surrounded with poverty.

Furthermore, the isolation and segregation of public housing often resulted in false assumptions and dangerous interpretations made by children who looked at television without knowing anything outside of their immediate surroundings. If the only White people you "know" are those on television, then the assumption becomes that all White people are like those on the tube. Following, if the parents in these shows provided their families with the comfort that was seen on television, why can't you? And why is it that only White people are successful? These images quickly transform that father who was your knight in shining armor into Sancho Panza, the incompetent fool. The negative internalization of these images turns into a desire to be like those persons on the screen and to fantasize of a blonde, blue-eyed me, an impeccable home, parents who spoke proper English, and a mother and father who were not worn down by the everyday drudgery resulting from poverty and racism.

These thoughts occupied too much space in our young minds, and as a result, questions were formed, questions asking why life was the way it was, but the answers we received, when answers were given, were not adequate.

The messages encountered in the media were consistent with those encountered in school. For children, school is a source that informs them about their abilities, shows how other people see them, and ultimately contributes to molding their self-concept. For both of us, it was a source of achievement but also a source of unhappiness. Once we moved out of the projects and were forced to commute to a predominantly Irish and Italian neighborhood to attend school, our experiences negatively impacted how we saw ourselves. The insulation and racial and ethnic homogeneity of the projects had protected us to some extent from the reality of what it meant to be a Puerto Rican during this very intolerant period in American history. As our narratives in the following sections unfold, the relevance of our negative school experiences during the 1950s and 1960s illuminate multicultural educational issues still prevalent today.

Angie's Narrative on School

I would describe the period immediately following the move from the projects as the commencement of my ethnic wounding. It coincided with my entrance into the sixth grade. Feelings of shame about being Hispanic, poor, and different originated at this time. While living in the projects I did not feel different from anyone else. Although we were poor, we never felt poor, because everyone was in the same boat. The projects were the great equalizer.

The new school, St. Martin of Tours, was more modern and better equipped than my former school, St. Rita's, but its facilities could not help me cope with what I went through every day at that school. Having to spend Grades 6 through 8 commuting to a school that was in a predominately middle-class Irish and Italian neighborhood had a much more destructive impact on my self-esteem than did life in the projects.

I was the only Hispanic in my class. Thus, I became the "exception," or the Puerto Rican who was unlike the rest of the typical Hispanics. One of the nuns I was especially fond of suggested that I not refer to myself as Puerto Rican. It sounded better, more polite, to say that I was Spanish, especially because, as she told me, "I did not look or act like a Puerto Rican." No one could tell what I was, she reasoned, so why should I advertise it?

Prior to transferring to St. Martin's, I had never associated being Puerto Rican with anything negative. But the subtle message I got from that nun (who considered herself looking out for me) was that, because I was smart, was a high achiever, and had light skin, I did not represent my ethnic group. I was not like the rest of the Puerto Ricans, and I would be doing myself a great disservice by publicly identifying myself with them.

I soon learned that the parents of my new girlfriends were also more receptive to their daughters bringing home a Spanish girl rather than a Puerto Rican. Puerto Ricans ruined neighborhoods; they were loud, dirty, colored, dangerous, and usually carried knives and could not speak English. I remember going with a group of girlfriends to someone's home and not being allowed to enter with the rest of my schoolmates because the parents did not want Puerto Ricans in their home. I had to wait outside until they came out. I repressed this incident for many years. It came to light during an exercise, which was part of a cultural diversity training in which I took part decades later. I had shut down emotionally and went through similar childhood experiences like a sleepwalker. This was a way of not having to deal with the deep hurt and shame I felt. It never occurred to me to refuse to wait outside or to discuss it with someone or even to think that that treatment was unjust. I also do not remember inviting anyone from school to my home subsequent to the move from the projects. For one thing, they did not live near me and would have had to commute by bus. I also did not want anyone from school to see how I lived. Our apartment was shabby, cold, and rat invested.

I can trace the origin of a lifelong sense of inferiority and unworthiness to this time. I compared myself to these new classmates and always seemed to fall short. They lived in private homes that had front and back yards. My dad, unlike their fathers, was an atheist. He was not a member of the Holy Name Society like the fathers of my classmates, and my mother never went to church. During that time, she worked out of our home. The other mothers were housewives who cooked roast beef and potatoes. My mother cooked rice and beans with fried plantains. My father did not speak English properly, was rarely at home, and had views that were politically incorrect. His hero was Fidel Castro. I was taught in school that Castro was a dictator, a traitor, and above all else, a Communist. At home, Fidel was the great liberator who dared to fight American imperialism. Any discussion with Dad about Fidel turned into a major argument. I remember coming home from school one day and repeating to my father some minute piece of information I had learned, and he immediately went into a tirade about Yankee propaganda, the evils of capitalism, the inadequate American educational system, and the corruption of the church. Needless to say, my parents were not Ozzie and Harriet.

My only claim to fame was that I was a good student, and I received acknowledgment and recognition for this from teachers and fellow students. Academic achievement was what made me special, and because of this, doing well in school became very important to me; it was a way to receive acceptance into this new environment. The excitement of learning was there, but it took a backseat to the need to prove myself and to belong. Unfortunately, the more

I succeeded academically, the more I felt the pressure to continue to succeed. I became so identified with being a straight A student that I felt it was the only thing I had to offer. Without my grades I was nobody. Fear once again entered my life, the fear of academic failure and not living up to being the Puerto Rican who was an exception.

As I got older, enduring the surprised reactions people had when they learned that I was Puerto Rican was taking its toll on me emotionally. I was oddly conflicted. I understood that the intentions of some were actually meant to be positive; they felt that they were giving me a compliment by saying something like, "Don't worry, you are not seen like the rest of your people; no one would know to look at you. You can pass." These people had no idea that such sentiments exposed their prejudices. They were so sure they knew who the Puerto Ricans were and what they represented that they were convinced that I would be delighted to know that I was not being associated with the rest of them. They liked me well enough to allow me to enter their inner circles. After all, I was special, and this specialness of mine worked to mask who I actually was. In fact, I was liked not for who I was but in spite of who I was. As a result, my ability to fit in made me feel guilty about denying my identity. The price for belonging was a great one.

Alma's Narrative on School

School was just another source of anxiety. As one of four minorities in a predominantly White class of forty girls, I felt disengaged from school activities. The feeling of not belonging that would always be present throughout my life had risen to prominence while attending St. Martin of Tours School. For three years, Lillian, Alba, Esmeralda, and I, the only non-White students, were seated in the back of the room. In retrospect, we did what we were told and required little attention. None of us played any major role in the class activities. As I sat in the back, I viewed year in and year out those who were the teacher's pets, those who were disliked by her, and us, those who were nonexistent. My seat represented the marginal neighborhood, with Linda, the poor White trash of the class, seated directly in front of me. Ironically, the four of us were situated according to our skin gradation. The person with the lightest skin—me—sat closer to the front, and the one with the darkest skin sat in the very back of the room.

Oftentimes I wonder if Mrs. Terrilli or Ms. Canata consciously arranged our seats in this order or if our being ghettorically situated was just a coincidence. Whatever the case, our seating served to disengage us from the rest of the class. We were rarely called on and rarely volunteered for anything. Special events, such as school pageants and plays, came and went with us having very little interest or involvement. Although I would like to think that there was no malice intended in the way that we were treated, I know that teachers are not beyond making decisions based on certain attitudes and beliefs that they themselves have and are unaware exist. This may account for the fact that not one of the four of us during this time was ever selected to be a class monitor, chosen to execute a key role in a school play, or acknowledged for anything that we ever did well.

In the seventh and ninth grades we moved to Puerto Rico. After living there for one year we returned to New York. We both found that our high school experiences in New York centered around competition and a focus on individual achievement. The school environment encountered in Puerto Rico was one of cooperation and group orientation, whereas that of New York was of fierce competition and, in particular, unfair comparisons of Angie and me. Although we were born and reared in New York, we adapted better to the Puerto Rican approach. This is not surprising because the home environment and values of our home more closely resembled that of the Puerto Rican classroom.

Alma's Narrative on High School

My rebelliousness, as well as my worldliness, stood in the way of my ever coming close to Angie's saintliness, and quite frankly that was okay with me. I was more concerned about her obsessive studying than her praying, because I knew that I couldn't compete with her spirituality, and how could you measure a person's state of grace anyway? There were times when her compassion for people and her goodness did stand in the way of my being seen in a favorable light, but I could live with that.

However, those straight A's and her average, the highest in James Monroe High School for three years, were what I feared. The comparisons teachers would make between Angie and me were endless, and the damage was profound. Mrs. Laurie, my homeroom teacher in tenth grade, announced to the class while handing out report cards that I was not as smart as my older sister. Mr. Marcus, my math teacher, told my mother during open school day that I was not a serious student, despite my superior performance on the algebra and geometry regents. I remember taking the geometry regents and scoring a 95 percent, only to be told that it was unfortunate that I did not get 100 percent like Angie.

The comparisons went on and on. One teacher referred to me as Angie the entire semester that he had me in his honors Physics class, while others constantly expressed their disappointment that I was not the student she was. If Angie were just any honor student, the expectations of teachers would have been bearable, but she was not just any student. She was the highest performing student in a school that housed more than three thousand. This top ranking of hers turned my 90 grade point average (GPA) into something that was of little value. My efforts went unnoticed and were interpreted as not being good enough.

In retrospect, these unwarranted and unjustly deserved comparisons and judgments about my academic abilities were quite detrimental to how I saw myself and to how I approached competitive situations. I can honestly say that my reluctance to compete as well as the unrealistic and distorted perception of what is necessary to be considered worthy of acceptance, in some domains, have impacted choices I have made in my life.

As one of only a few minorities in the honor school at Monroe, I found refuge with Latino friends outside the honor school and two Jewish friends who were high-achieving students, but who were also outcasts in the honor school. The two non-Latino friends were also considered outsiders, because one was a gay male and the other a female whose mother had severe psychological problems.

Angie's Narrative on High School

From ninth grade to tenth grade I underwent a major period of transition. I went from a small, semirural parochial school to a large, urban public high school, James Monroe High School in the South Bronx. I was not placed in honor classes despite my excellent academic record. It was only when I completed my first semester at Monroe with a 95 GPA, and then insisted, that I was allowed to join the honor school. The honor school at Monroe was composed of approximately 250 students, or the top 10 percent of the school's population. There were few minorities in the honor school, which was mostly Jewish students and teachers; the student population of the entire institution was predominantly Black and Hispanic.

Students in the honor school were achievement oriented and focused on going to college. The cooperative spirit of Puerto Rico was replaced by fierce competition and single-mindedness. A few extra points earned by a classmate could change the test curve and negatively affect your final grade. Your performance could adversely affect someone else's success. Learning was no longer a win-win phenomenon, but by definition a win-lose experience; someone had to be on the bottom, and someone had to be on top. I worked hard to be on top and graduated salutatorian.

I had always aspired to go to college, but I had no practical information of what it would take to get there. It was a vague goal. I did not know how much money it would require or the kind of grades it would take. My parents were not college graduates, so I had no mentors to pave the way. I began to investigate and soon realized that most students in the honor school were going to one of the colleges of The City University of New York, which was free in those days. College was suddenly very doable, and I looked forward to continuing my education at City College. A visit with my high school guidance counselor changed my focus. He claimed that with my grades and class standing I could go to any college in the country. It was the mid-1960s and colleges were looking to integrate their campuses with talented minorities. I was a perfect candidate. He was very happy about the prospect of one of Monroe's students going to Harvard. Counselors who worked for Aspira of New York, the premier Puerto Rican educational and advocacy program at the time, were also delighted to have a young Puerto Rican girl with my educational background. I would be an excellent choice to open the path for other Puerto Ricans to break into Ivy League colleges. My father, who had never taken much interest in my education, was unexpectedly very excited about my going to Columbia University. He bragged to his friends that I was accepted to Columbia before I even applied. Once again, I felt an inordinate amount of pressure to excel for others—my father, my guidance counselor, my teachers, and my fellow Puerto Ricans. What would happen if I did not make these schools? I felt that I would disappoint everyone.

Speaking English, Being Puerto Rican

As members of a non-White, non-English-speaking ethnic group, language has always played a primordial role in defining who or what a Puerto Rican is. The decision of Nuyoricans to maintain our language, in the same way as our stance on race, which opposed our being dichotomized as Black or White, is still another example of how the Nuyorican has been able to adapt to living in two worlds. Our close ties to the island as well as our constricted living conditions in ethnic enclaves have all contributed to the maintenance of Spanish in New York.

The importance of knowing English was something that we realized at a very young age. The power of language and its role in determining one's status in American society were well understood by both our parents. Nonetheless, they had their perspectives about English and the role that it should play in the lives of their two girls. Our father, despite his wealth of knowledge of many subjects, always worked in low-paying jobs because of his lack of oral skills. His search for knowledge moved him to read the newspapers in English. However, his verbal skills were, and still are, very difficult to comprehend.

Our father, who was involved with the nationalist movement of Puerto Rico and was as anti-American as you could be without being a terrorist, refused to speak English in our home. He feared having children who did not speak Spanish. His stance on speaking Spanish at home was based on ideological reasons, while our mother's choice to speak English at home was based on social mobility and her need to protect us. Our mother was very aware of the codes of power that are played out in school and the disadvantages that a child has if she does not possess this code (Delpit, 1995).

My mother witnessed the very difficult time that Angie had when she first entered school. Angie followed my father's rule and spoke Spanish at home. When she went to school, she still spoke Spanish only, therefore my mother decided to speak to us in English at home. Our mother's proficiency in English was due to her high school education in Puerto Rico during a time when the island's language policy dictated the use of English at school. Needless to say, this choice was not available to many of my friends' parents who only spoke Spanish.

Our home's linguistic repertoire consisted of my parents speaking in two different languages when addressing us, the use of Spanish when speaking to one another, and our code switching when speaking to both of them. Both approaches have had their impact on our lives. The use of English at home did provide us with the linguistic code necessary for academic achievement. This was an advantage that many of our Spanish-dominant friends who had mono-lingual parents with less education did not have. Our English competency has allowed us to compete and succeed in academic and professional environments oftentimes restricted to those who have not been privy to this code. We have not suffered the shame and negative consequences of being labeled "limited-English-proficient," "uneducable," "stupid," or any of the many harmful and derogatory categories reserved for those who do not speak English. In fact, our success as students as well as professionals in the workplace has very often been interpreted as stemming from various sources while overlooking what may be the most important source, namely, our knowledge of the dominant language. We have at times been revered as persons who are the exception to the rule, when possibly language might be the underlying factor in our success.

In contrast, our command of Spanish has never reached nativelike competency. Although we can carry on conversations and function in any Spanish-speaking environment, English is the language that we feel most comfortable with when writing and performing any kind of academic work or official function. Our apparent dominance in English has led to our being criticized by those who perceive this as "trying to be Americana," and there are still others who feel the need to let us know when we are speaking Spanish that our pronunciation or usage is not that of a native speaker. Our mixture of Spanish and English, also referred to as Spanglish, is seen as an inferior code. The lack of nativelike Spanish competency has been a marker for our not being "true Puerto Ricans" and our subsequent exclusion from certain circles reserved for such individuals. The irony of this is that those engaged in the labeling have often been Puerto Ricans who are in pursuit of maintaining their language and culture, but who have often dealt with the Nuyorican in a prejudicial, exclusionary, and elitist manner, thus unwittingly becoming the oppressor. Our experiences were those of marginalized persons who were living in two worlds (Stonequist, 1961; Villanueva, 1993; Zentella, 1997).

To further complicate matters, native Puerto Ricans are constantly being criticized for how they speak Spanish. There are certain groups within the Spanish-speaking world that pride themselves on having the monopoly on speaking "correct Spanish." What these ignorant persons do not know is that we all speak a variety of one language or another, and it is not about one form being better or worse. It is about being understood. Teachers—in particular Spanish teachers, who have been taught by such linguistic elitists in college— continue to promulgate this lie about the inferiority of Puerto Rican Spanish. What they don't say is that La Academia Real has recognized Puerto Rican Spanish as one of the varieties of Spanish that they find acceptable.

The Misrepresentation of Puerto Ricans in American Curriculum

Exclusion of our native language was the most apparent missing element in school. However, it was not only the knowledge of ourselves that became lost when we entered school. What was taught in school, and more importantly what was chosen not to be taught, contributed to our not understanding vital issues about ourselves. One of the greatest challenges that the Puerto Rican population confronted in the 1950s and 1960s was one of ideology versus reality. The reformulation of the United States as a melting pot to one of a pluralistic society occurred during the past two decades. The period prior to this ideological transformation was a time of contradictions, confusion, and pain for Puerto Ricans who were segregated in tenements situated in ethnic enclaves in selected areas of New York City and who were employed in menial jobs with little room for social mobility. We were told that all immigrants who came to this nation were absorbed into the melting pot and thus were led to believe that our future would soon follow this same path. However, our reality did not reflect such an experience, leading to false assumptions about why we could not "make it," assumptions centered on notions of inability, laziness, refusal to conform, and many more explanations used to rationalize why our patterns of assimilation did not follow prior White European immigrations.

Schools did not provide clarity in understanding our situation. In the absence of such a precedent, schools remained true to a traditional Eurocentric view of knowledge that served to promote Western civilization and disregard the rest of the planet's population. What we learned is what fit into the paradigm that viewed Western civilization as superior to all other cultures. This experience is referred to by Lewis (1996) as the double-cross-reversal: the privilege of the dominant to talk at great length about that which is not and to stay silent about and ignore that which is. In this reversal, for socially subordinate groups, possibility is defined through denial, freedom is reinterpreted through constraint, violence is justified as protection, and in schools, contrary to the belief that it is a place where knowledge is shared, knowledge withheld articulates the curriculum. (p. 36)

Throughout our education, little was taught about Puerto Rico or its people. The one thing that we did learn was that Puerto Rico was given to the United States after the Spanish-American War. The island was also used as an example of a third world nation as well as an example of a poor country with uneducated people who were being saved from greater poverty by the United States. Furthermore, the United States opened its doors to us and provided us with the opportunity to improve our lives. Imagine, we had the opportunity to become civilized, and maybe if we played our cards right, we would move out of the ghetto.

What these teachers did not tell us was that after the Spanish-American War, Puerto Rico was given to the United States without the consent of its people. Puerto Rico went from having a fairly autonomous relationship with Spain to having one of colonial dependency with the United States. They also failed to inform us that American corporations had taken over Puerto Rican agriculture and transformed it from a self-sufficient multicrop economy into a mono-crop sugar economy that later resulted in adverse economic conditions that subsequently resulted in our migration to the United States.

Furthermore, many of our friends' fathers, including ours, had been drafted and had fought in World War II. In fact, the 65th infantry division was from Puerto Rico, a fact not known by me until I was an adolescent. Also, these very same soldiers who had been on the front did not have the right to vote in federal elections while in Puerto Rico, a right that many did not exercise until they came and settled in New York after having defended America.

More importantly, what they did not tell us was that our migration to New York City in the 1950s, during a period when industries were leaving the city for more profitable localities, would become for many Puerto Ricans a road to low-paying menial jobs for several generations to come. Our timing regarding our move to New York City was unfortunate. Here, we lived in segregated ghettos in a city that did not have the economic opportunities from which previous immigrants had profited. Our lack of economic prosperity and social mobility was thought to be due to our lack of desire to progress rather than as the byproduct of a postindustrial economy that did not meet the needs of a population that came to work in industries that were leaving New York.

As Pinar (1996) explains:

> We are what we know and also what we do not know. If what we know about ourselves—history, our culture, our national identity—is deformed by absences, denials and incompleteness, then our identity—both as individuals and as Americans—is fractured. (p. 23)

Such omissions regarding our place in history and our relationship to the United States are crucial. They transformed issues of colonialism, American economics, and military interests into personalized concerns of indebtedness for America's generosity without an understanding of why and how we ended up on the mainland. If curriculum is supposed to facilitate our understanding of the world (Grumet, 1996), then one can say that our curriculum provided us with an inaccurate purview.

What this does to a child's psyche is destructive. It tells you that you are poor and that this host nation is doing you a favor by allowing you to be here. This one-sided view results in blaming yourself and, in particular, your parents for your unfortunate place in American society. This facilitates the internalization of negative beliefs and stereotypes about one's culture and the inevitable acceptance of such beliefs by all, including yourself. You are like an uninvited guest at a formal dinner party that is reserved for those of a particular group, namely, White Europeans. You are hastily seated at the table but find yourself without eating utensils. This has a devastating effect on an immigrant child.

Could Multicultural Education Have Made a Difference?

Many of the Nuyoricans attending school during the 1950s and 1960s, like us, were educated to meet the demands of those decades, but found themselves in a pivotal period unprepared to meet the demands of the city's new economic order. They were the products of an education system that only knew how to function by proceeding forward regardless of the disparity in success and failures as measured by race, ethnicity, or socioeconomic group. This was a system that ignored the diversity of the population they were teaching. Only when these failures were of such magnitude that they could not be ignored did school officials begin to rethink their approach. Poor academic achievement was not confined to the African American, Puerto Rican, and poor White populations but also included a growing number of Dominicans, West Indians, Colombians, and many more who, because of the change in the immigration laws, began to grow in numbers. Thus, the population of persons of color who at one time were a relatively small group became the population of the Big Apple, and the need for major systemic changes became obvious. Not until this school-age population became significant in numbers and failure rates continued to rise were questions about how and why addressed. While the questions continue to be asked, solutions to such issues are fewer.

One possible remedy that emerged as a response to the challenge of educating a diverse population was that of a multicultural approach to education. This method addresses many of the concerns about how we were taught that surfaced while writing this chapter. While we both survived and succeeded as a consequence of our education, many whom we knew did not. We were the exception as reflected in the low high school completion rates and low representation of Hispanics in higher education. The dismal number of our generation who completed high school and the even smaller number who continued their education provide testimony to the idea that the ways children are taught must validate who they are in order to be effective. This is particularly true for children who come from homes in which the culture is greatly different from that of the classroom. In addition, children do not all learn in the same way.

One of the multicultural approaches to education as Nieto (2000) described is antiracist education. For Nieto, "Being antiracist and antidiscriminatory means paying attention to all areas in which some students are favored over others: the curriculum, choice of materials, sorting policies, and teachers' interactions and relationships with students and their families" (p. 306). Nieto proposes that multicultural education must be related to the core curriculum. It should permeate every aspect of school. This includes the school climate, physical environment, curriculum, and the relationships among teacher, students, and community. It must be included as a basic part of the curriculum rather than as a peripheral activity or interest. Not surprisingly, the canon must be transformed and expanded to include those cultures and people who have been traditionally excluded. The expansive nature of multicultural education makes it a process for all rather than something that is only for students of color, urban students, or the disadvantaged. Finally, multicultural education is a process that is ongoing and dynamic, with the purpose of putting our learning into action. In essence, education should be socially beneficial and meaningful. Schools should be a site of apprenticeship for democracy. If the aforementioned model of multicultural education had been the norm during our education, we would have had very different educational experiences. The expansion of the canon to include other cultures would in itself have made all of us better educated individuals. Yes, even Angie's White Irish Catholic friend's mother, who would not permit us into her home because we were Puerto Rican, might now have understood that our presence in New York was due to the same economic reasons as those of her family's. Maybe this knowledge would not have gotten us through the door, but hopefully her mother's prejudice would have been questioned rather than internalized by a child who did not know better.

KH

s israel
toric and ritual in colonial India (online)
Initials: sal Entry Date: Nov 4, 2005

ernment policy|zCalifornia
.es government policy california
ernment policy
ernment policy united states
electronic resource] : a perspective on
d by Richard J. Gilbert
nitials: sal Entry Date: Nov 4, 2005

rnment policy|zUnited States
es government policy united states
ernment policy california
tucky history
lectronic resource] : a perspective on
 by Richard J. Gilbert
nitials: sal Entry Date: Nov 4, 2005

In essence, the benefits of a multicultural curriculum are found not only in how it helps children of nonmainstream cultures but also in how it educates children of the majority culture. Everyone's ignorance of non-European cultures, histories, and religions when completing secondary school would have most likely been replaced by a better understanding and appreciation of Native American, African, Asian, and Latin American cultures. More important, the inclusion of where we came from, the contributions of our ancestors, and the forces that impacted our parents' migration to the United States would have given us a better perspective about who we were.

The impact of such knowledge on the lives of young children and adolescents must be underscored. Those feelings of anomie, incompetence, inferiority, and shame very often experienced by us, despite our outward attainment of success, would have been nonexistent and possibly replaced by feelings that would have facilitated success and social participation. Possibly, our choices would have been different, or at least clarity about our paths would have emerged earlier. Even more so, the emotional, psychological, and spiritual price paid by us for success would have been less. For children who did not succeed and paid a greater price by living in poverty for the rest of their lives, having a string of dead-end jobs that reminded them daily of the need for an education without any hope of one, such an approach to education as proposed by Nieto (2000) would have certainly impacted their lives.

Furthermore, for those in high school who were tracked in general education, then after graduation found themselves in a rice field in Southeast Asia fighting a war in a place that they could not even locate on a map, a connection with their lives and what was taught could have possibly made a difference between reading about a war and actually fighting one. They might have possibly joined the ranks of the privileged that went on to college and avoided being drafted. For those who did not speak the English language and who found themselves in classes of mentally challenged children, when just a short time before in Puerto Rico they were on the honor roll, multicultural education would have recognized that uniqueness and used their mother tongue in making the transition from Spanish to English. Their years wasted in classes for mentally challenged children, the negative labeling, a lifetime of self-doubt, and the insecurities and feelings of not being good enough that accompany such experiences might have been prevented. More important, the inadequate education resulting from years of little content learning received at the hands of teachers who wished to help without knowing how to could have been avoided. Even more dismal is the fact that some of these children became adults without being proficient in any language.

Although multicultural education is not a panacea for all that ails the education system, it is broad and inclusive enough to address much of what is not working. We commend schools that have acknowledged the value of a multicultural education. They have provided hope to our young and thus strengthened the future of all.

Recommended Readings

There are many books and articles related to multiculturalism and the education of minority children (see other chapters in the book). For those who want to read more on our particular topic, three books are most closely related to our experience of growing up as Puerto Ricans in New York, which in essence is about living in two different worlds. I selected those books that related directly to teaching and multiculturalism. The three readings are autobiographical: *Halfway to Dick and Jane* (Agueros, 1991), *Bootstraps from an American Academic of Color* (Villanueva, 1993), and *Growing Up Bilingual: Puerto Rican Children in New York* (Zentella, 1997).

Reflective Questions

1. How are the experiences of Nuyoricans different or the same from those of current immigrant groups in the United States?

2. How did the Puerto Rican immigration pave the way for other non-White groups?

3. How would the migrant experience of the Puerto Rican differ today as opposed to that in the 1950s regarding issues of race, class, language, and gender?

References

Agueros, J. (1991). Halfway to Dick and Jane. In C. J. Verburg (Ed.), *Ourselves among others: Cross-cultural readings for writers* (pp. 95–112). Boston: St. Martin's.

Delpit, L. (1995). *Other people's children: Cultural conflict in the classroom.* New York: New Press.

Grumet, M. (1996). The curriculum: What are the basics and are we teaching them? In J. Kincheloe & S. Steinberg (Eds.), *Thirteen questions: Reframing education's conversation* (Part 1, pp. 15–23). New York: Peter Lang.

Lewis, M. (1996). Power and education: Who decides the forms schools have taken, and who should decide. In J. Kincheloe & S. Steinberg (Eds.), *Thirteen questions: Reframing education's conversation* (Part 1, pp. 33–43) New York: Peter Lang.

Nieto, S. (2000). *Affirming diversity: The sociopolitical context of multicultural education.* New York: Longman.

Pinar, W. F. (1996). The curriculum: What are the basics and are we teaching them? In J. Kincheloe & S. Steinberg (Eds.), *Thirteen questions: Reframing education's conversation* (Part 2, pp. 22–30). New York: Peter Lang.

Steinberg, S., & Kincheloe, J. (1997). *Kinderculture.* Boulder, CO: Westview Press.

Stonequist, E. V. (1961). *The marginal man: A study in personality and culture conflict.* New York: Russell & Russell.

Villanueva, V. (1993). *Bootstraps from an American academic of color.* Urbana, IL: National Council of Teachers of English.

Zentella, A. (1997). *Growing up bilingual: Puerto Rican children in New York.* Malden, MA: Blackwell.

5

Between the Telling and the Told

Latina Mothers Negotiating Education in New Borderlands

Sofia A. Villenas

Autobiographical Introduction

While this chapter tells the story of a group of Latina mothers who were trying to make sense of how to raise children in a new community in the United States, it is also my own story as a daughter of Latino immigrant parents from Ecuador—a story of trying to broker between cultures, between my mother's voice and powerful institutions such as schools and hospitals and between self and collective identity formation within Los Angeles-based multicultural wars. My experiences growing up as a daughter of immigrants are in many ways similar to the experiences of other second-generation or U.S.-born children. For example, like so many language minority children, I served as a language broker or translator for my parents, particularly for my mother. I remember translating at hospitals, banks, grocery stores, and over the phone with real estate agents, telephone companies, police, and classroom teachers. I also grew up watching television in both English and Spanish; I watched *Laverne and Shirley* and *Little House on the Prairie,* but also *El Noticiero* 34 (News on Channel 34) and memorable *telenovelas* (Spanish-speaking soap operas). I went to theaters in the suburbs of Los Angeles to see *Rocky, Jaws, Grease,* and other Hollywood hits of the 1970s. But my parents also took us to *El Floral* drive-in theater in East Los Angeles to see Mexican comedian icon Mario Moreno Cantinflas, among other favorites. The Spanish-language television station offered Latino-focused news, which made me aware of Latin America as a vast part of the northern hemisphere. I also remember vividly the fear I felt at the nightly news of immigration raids in the Los Angeles *fabricas,* or sweatshops such as the ones in which my father worked. I feared that one day he would not come home because, even though he had legal residency, he might be picked up and sent back to Ecuador with no questions asked. I often wondered, do other kids know these things, share these fears, and understand what it is like living in these linguistic/cultural borderlands? But I also knew the answer. Schools and teachers pretended that this life did not exist—at least it wasn't in the textbooks, the songs we sang, the histories we studied, the families we learned about. And I certainly was not given the tools to comprehend cultural differences and coercive relations of power in our society. Without the language to articulate these life experiences, I became ashamed of speaking Spanish. I was tired of translating. It was not until college that many of us Latinos/as with the same experiences came together in Chicano and ethnic studies courses to learn how to question and articulate our bicultural realities and our histories. We felt rage at the silence we experienced in our schooling, but we also felt passion for working in our communities. We became teachers, public health workers, and *politicos*. I worked with Latino adults, mostly women, teaching English as a second language (ESL). Later I became a Spanish bilingual elementary school teacher and also taught the children of Latino immigrant parents. In both these settings, I listened to mothers' stories of dealing with hospitals, schools, and other institutions. I listened to their frustrations in trying to understand their children's lives and classroom experiences. I translated mail and explained school, all the time remembering and reliving my mother's and my own experiences. I knew well the huge gap that existed and continues to exist between Latina mothers' lives, their children's bicultural experiences, and the school environment. I have carried this sensibility to the research, writing, and teaching I do about Latino families, including the research with Latina mothers in North Carolina.

Context

In 1993 I arrived in North Carolina, bringing with me my mother's pedagogies— certainly a lifetime of teaching and learning in my family—as well as my bicultural experiences and my own middle-class, "professionally-informed" notions of mothering to conduct research about Latino family education in Hope City. Hope City[1] is a rural town in a central county with one of the fastest-growing populations of Latino families in the state, mostly recruited to work in the poultry industry. When I arrived in Hope City in 1993, there was barely a hint of a Latino community, but the population started to increase rapidly thereafter. By 1997, Latinos/as made up approximately 37 percent of the total population. In this rapidly changing landscape, I was interested in documenting how mothers forged community and family in a place with no previous Latino settlement. Would they face the same issues as Latina mothers in heavily Latino-populated Los Angeles, and to what intensity? How would they be positioned within differing racial/cultural dynamics (different from the U.S. Southwest), and in turn how would they position themselves vis-à-vis schools and health/social services? In this different borderlands context, was there hope for a different set of cross-cultural relations and a bridging between mothers' lives, their children's emerging biculturalism, and the public schools?

I spent two years in Hope City interviewing Latino parents, conducting oral life histories with Latina mothers, and working with Latinas[2] in ESL adult classes, parenting classes, and health classes. In conducting this study as ethnography, I was a participant observer in different home and institutional settings. I attended and taught ESL classes, served as bus driver for mothers attending parenting and health classes, attended family and town celebrations, and participated in school and social services meetings. In addition, I also conducted archival research using town documents and newspapers. I view this study as a small piece of history, as a snapshot of a historical moment of change in one community, particularly through the lens of the "new" arrivals.

In Latina mothers' life history narratives and conversations, they addressed the question of what it meant to raise children in the United States. Although at first, in hearing what was said or *told*, I listened to descriptions of their superior traditional family education with words of confidence, self-assuredness, and pride in their family values. But it wasn't until I carefully considered my feelings about the event of conversation itself, the *telling*, or how things were said—the various positionings they took vis-à-vis each other and imagined audiences of English-speaking *americanos*—that a fleeting picture emerged of the very processes of negotiating the challenges of raising bicultural children in these new borderlands of the rural Southeast. It was precisely in the spaces between the telling and the told where the terms of a viable family education were always in the process of being worked on and worked out. I have addressed some of the larger questions noted earlier elsewhere (see Villenas, 2001, 2002); however, in this chapter I examine the job of negotiating the ambiguities and "exigencies of living in the borderlands" (González, 2001)—borderlands that are between nations, between beliefs about "proper" parenting, gender roles, community rights, and citizenship in terms of who does and does not belong. In analyzing one conversation that took place among a group of Latina mothers one Sunday afternoon, I consider a particular moment in time as a creative and contested *performative* space where personal histories, local contexts, and larger power relations marked by race, class, gender, language, and citizenship status came together in negotiating the challenges of raising "successful" children and in constructing identities of dignity as capable mothers. Hence, this chapter also highlights the value of the struggle to recuperate the situational and bodily experiences of ethnography—to recuperate the saying from the said, as cultural anthropologist Conquergood (1991) writes, and to "shift the emphasis from space and time, from sight and vision, to sound and voice, from text to performance, from authority to vulnerability" (p. 183).

Between the Telling and the Told: A Borderlands Analysis

Inspired by folklorist Victor Turner's work on social drama and cultural performance, Conquergood (1991) explains how performance-sensitive ethnography "privileges particular, participatory, dynamic, intimate, and precarious, embodied experience grounded in historical process, contingency, and ideology" (p. 187). This sensibility to the body, kinetics, and emotion within particular historical contexts can also be elaborated from a borderlands perspective. "The border" and "Borderlands" refer to a shared historical and collective naming of the cultural and bodily experiences born of the physical border between the United States and Mexico/Latin America. As Chicana feminist Gloria Anzaldúa (1987) so aptly describes it, "The U.S.-Mexico border *es una herida abierta* [an open wound] where the Third World grates against the first and bleeds. And before a scab forms it hemorrhages again, the lifeblood of two worlds merging to form a third country—a border culture" (p. 3). In this way, the Borderlands refers to a brutal yet dynamic place of not only stark inequalities but also cultural survival and invention. For example, linguistic anthropologist Norma González (2001) discusses borderlands in terms of multiple and overlapping linguistic worlds that are used by the mothers in her study to invent, improvise, tinker with, and reproduce new social lives and ways of mothering that do not simply reproduce "tradition" in the Borderlands of Tucson, Arizona. In this way, borderlands are also the overlapping experiences between traditions, cultural sensibilities, ethnicities, gender roles, spiritualities, sexualities, and generations, as Anzaldúa has so often emphasized (see Keating, 2000). Thus, living in the physical and metaphysical B/borderlands has meant experiencing fragmentation and the dislocation of self under a history of colonization and domination responsible for continuing inequalities and discrimination in employment, housing, and schooling in the U.S. Southwest (see San Miguel Jr. & Valencia, 1998, for a history of Mexican American education). But it has also meant developing modes of survival to maintain integrity and dignity in living with the ambiguity that comes with straddling multiple realities. This ambiguity and straddling of multiple realities is often unseen and unheard; but they are in the body and emotions, in the said and in the unsaid—indeed in the interstitial spaces between the telling and the told. Thus, bringing together the idea of performance-sensitive ethnography with a borderlands sensibility allows for an embodied and engaged understanding of what is at stake in Latina mothers' conversations about themselves as mothers raising children in the rural American South.

Certainly, performance-sensitive ethnography and narrative analysis have been approached and developed from many different disciplines, including folklore, communications, social theory, feminism, cultural studies, theater, rhetoric, psychology, and counseling to name a few. While it is not my intention to do a detailed narrative and performance analysis of the Latina mothers' conversation in this chapter, I do want to briefly focus on two pieces of work that are personally relevant for me in articulating performance and borderland sensibilities in a close examination of narrative and discourse.

Communications scholar Soyini Madison (1998) provides an example of storytelling as an empowering act, particularly as it is "read" and coperformed through the lens of Black feminist and intellectual thought—just as I also am indexing a Latina *mujer-* or womanist-oriented borderlands perspective. Madison elaborates on the distinction between the telling and the told (from Bauman, 1986) in the oral life history narrative of Mrs. Kapper, an elderly African American woman. Mrs. Kapper tells about her life as an exploited field-worker who at one point talked back to the landowner. As Madison explains it, Mrs. Kapper was forthright and bold in confronting the landowner in the told or narrated event. In the telling, however, she spoke in a cautious, barely audible whisper as if the landowner had transcended time and space to hear her as she spoke miles away in a little room at the senior citizen center. Madison explains how "the years of resentment and fear embodied in her voice were present at this performative moment" (p. 330). But this performative tension between Mrs. Kapper's telling and her told story is important, as Madison continues, because it suggests a "broader performance tradition in African American culture, a tradition in which the contradictions and tensions in performance were a matter of survival: the tradition of the 'mask' or presentation of self constructed for white people" (p. 330). And yet, as Mrs. Kapper continued her story, it was through its performance, or the telling, that she experienced personal transformation. Although one may feel powerless and stripped of one's will and dignity in the event, it is in the retelling of the event that one can claim dignity and satisfaction. Mrs. Kapper reclaimed her dignity in also describing and euphorically performing her "real occupation" as someone who could nurture and raise farm animals. As Madison explains it, for Mrs. Kapper, who labored for others, work served as a site of repression devoid of creativity and pride. But it was in the telling and recasting of her work with pride that she was in control and independent because she owned the site of her labor and thus had ownership of herself.

Madison's experience with Mrs. Kapper and her attention to the performative aspect of storytelling resonates powerfully with my own experiences in

North Carolina. Indeed, what struck me most about the oral life histories and conversations with Latina mothers was not so much the content, but the performance of their words (both passionate and matter-of-fact) in reclaiming dignity in a context where they were often cast in negative ways by majority culture (see Villenas, 2001). I felt the urgency in their voices to speak beyond me as they recast their traditional family education and their gendered identities (or what it means to be a Mexican or Salvadorian woman) as superior to U.S.-based cultural practices. And yet at the same time, they were also struggling with continuity and change in terms of how to go about raising children and supporting their schooling. And of course, I was a coperformer in the storytelling, positioned at times as a bicultural "daughter" who had much to learn but also as a cultural broker who could offer information about "how things worked" in the United States. Thus, our performances were about "disambiguating" (González, 2001) the often conflicting borderlands between traditions, cultures, and generations. But what are some important aspects to attend to in terms of how to imagine and be attuned to these negotiations of the borderlands in the spaces between the telling and the told?

The work of linguistic anthropologist Stanton Wortham (2001) provides some very useful conceptual and analytic tools for examining discourse and narrative. Although it is beyond the scope of this chapter to provide the kind of detailed and rigorous analysis described in his work, I would like to call attention to some important conceptual tools that loosely guide my interpretations in this chapter. First, Wortham situates his social/cultural perspective of discourse and narrative as one that is opposed to approaches that rely solely on the cognitive content of talk. Instead, he emphasizes that power lies in the *interactional* event of storytelling where relationships are established and where narrator and audience are positioned in particular ways (e.g., as teacher and student, religious figure and potential convert, as "we" or me/you, as good taxpayer and welfare recipient, etc.). Drawing from Jakobson (1957/1971), Wortham distinguishes between the event of storytelling (referred to as the storytelling event) and the narrated event. Whereas most analyses may stop at the content or narrated event, Wortham argues for the fruitfulness of considering the performance of the storytelling event, how people are positioning themselves, and who is being addressed even if that audience is not in the room. Transformative power in autobiographical narrative, for example, is possible because it helps narrators "express and manage multiple, partly contradictory selves and experiences" (p. 7) in the event of storytelling vis-à-vis an audience and to possibly construct identities of agency and self-worth as Mrs. Kapper did in her life history narrative. But how does this happen?

Wortham develops his understanding of the storytelling event and the narrated event with powerful conceptual tools from the work of literary scholar and philosopher Bakhtin. From Bakhtin, we can understand language as dialogical in nature because humans are always responding to each others' words. In this way, words in any utterance have already been spoken by others and so people are taking positions with respect to past utterances. Wortham (2001) explains,

> Bakhtin claims that any utterance must take some position with respect to past words. . . . As Bakhtin sometimes puts it, all words "echo" with the "voices" of others, and, as interpreters, we try to understand the speaker's position with respect to the others who characteristically speak this way. . . . The speaker enters into dialogue with those past speakers, such that part of the current speaker's meaning and part of what he accomplishes interactionally through speech involves his relationship to prior speaker's positions. (pp. 21–22)

Drawing from Wortham's ideas, when I say I felt Latina mothers often talking "beyond" me, particularly in the event of oral life history narrative and in public settings including in-group conversations, I intuitively knew they were addressing past "words" about them as new arrivals in Hope City. While in the real-world undocumented immigrants' voices are denied a dialogue, in the performative event of storytelling they can "talk back" or enter into a dialogue with those past speakers who hold anti-immigrant and negative views about Latino families. Often and in many different contexts, the story-telling events in Hope City involved Latina mothers (and other Latino adults) addressing rhetoric about "illegal aliens"—a use of language that signals something less than human—and positioning themselves in relation to those *americanos* who produce these utterances. In doing so, Latinas also called into dialogue and positioned themselves vis-à-vis social groups within their own cultural milieu, for instance, "echoing" people who spoke like them with dignity as *personas bien educadas* (well-educated in the moral and holistic sense), as "good" and virtuous women, and as competent mothers. Of course, the meanings attached to definitions of *mujer* (woman) and motherhood were contested, but Latinas' positionings in relation to these various meanings were strategic depending on the storytelling event and the different "we" or "them" created and positioned with or against. These strategic positionings were part of the process of negotiating the ambiguities, uncertainties, and challenges of raising bicultural children in the midst of conflictive voices across cultural milieus and in the context of race relations in Hope City. Wortham (2001) thus provides effective analytic tools for highlighting the borderlands spaces of meaning-making between the telling and the told. As we shall see, these are the spaces where Latinas expressed and managed multiple and contradictory experiences in forging identities as competent mothers and dignified human beings.

The Story: A Conversation One Sunday Afternoon

A small group of *mujeres* (women)—Alba, Lydia, Marisela, Rocio, and I—gathered at the Hope City Memorial Library in North Carolina to discuss the transcripts of their life history interviews. As part of a project for the Southern Oral History program at the University of North Carolina in Chapel Hill, we were charged with producing a booklet based on the oral life histories about education from the Hope City Latino community. The following conversation took place that day:

Sofia: *¿Pues, hmm, que piensan que es importante de sus entrevistas para incluir en este librito?* (Well, hmm, what do you think is important from your interviews to include in this booklet?)

Alba: *Pues todo es importante.* (Well *everything* is important.)

Rocio: *Acerca de nuestros paises . . .* (About our countries . . .)

Alba: *Hablar de lo que se vivió antes, la vida en méxico, una vida muy activa porque trabajábamos y aquí la vida es muy monótona. Podemos hablar de las diferencias.* (Talk about how we lived before, life in Mexico, a very active life because we worked and here life is too monotonous. We could talk about the differences.)

Rocio: *Tambien deberíamos incluir como sufrimos en llegar acá.* (Also we should include how we suffered coming here.)

Sofia: *¿Y acerca de vivir en los Estados Unidos?* (How about living in the United States?)

Rocio: *La mujer americana no es hogareña.* (The American woman is not of the home space.)

Lydia: *En méxico, se pasa más tiempo con los niños. . . . El cambio es más difícil cuando los niños crecen y se acostumbran a la vida de acá.* (In Mexico, you spent more time with the children. . . . The change is more difficult when the children grow up and they get used to life here.)

Alba: *Quisiéramos que viviéran como uno se crió.* (We wish they could live the same way one grew up.)

Marisela: *Es difícil el cambio, el horario, la comida. El cambio más grande que van a sufrir es en la escuela, con el idioma. Aunque se crien en nuestro ambiente, van a absorbar las costumbre de aquí [de este país]. Van a sufrir, humillados.* (It's difficult the change, the schedule, the food. The biggest change they suffer through is at school, with the language. Even though they grow up in this environment, they absorb the customs from here [this country]. They will suffer, humiliated.)

Rocio: *Y el problema para nosotros es que no nos van a entender [riéndose].* (And the problem for us is that they won't understand us [laughs].)

Alba: *Pero entonces los niños van a dominar el idioma porque son pequeños.* (But then the children will master the language because they're little.)

Marisela: *Y otra diferencia es que aquí una trabaja y se descuidan las madres.* (And another difference is that here one works and the mothers neglect their responsibilities.)

Rocio: *Por amor, no porque muchas madres se descuidan.* (It's for love, not because a lot of mothers just neglect their children.)

Alba: *No es para descuidar a los niños, es mas bien para darles todo.* (It's not to neglect the children but rather to give them everything.)

Lydia: *Pero el tiempo que se les da, se da bien [riéndose suavemente].* (But the time that you give them, you make it good [laughs softly].)

Marisela: *Allá [en nuestros paises] se tiene a las tias y la familia. Los padres deben explicarles, inculcarles la razon osea la necesidad porque tienen que trabajar los padres.* (There [in our countries] you have the aunts and the family. The parents should tell them and explain to the children, inculcate the reason, the necessity of why the parents have to work.)

In our dialogue that Sunday afternoon, there was pride and self-assuredness, as well as ambivalence and insecurities about raising children and keeping their families "culturally" and emotionally intact while forging life in an unfamiliar context. The women, who were recent arrivals from Mexico and Central America, were gathered to talk about what to say publicly about their lives and how to portray themselves, their struggles, and their concerns to an English-speaking audience that had not the slightest knowledge of who they were. Certainly, on this occasion the women dialogued as competent and knowledgeable mothers with shared assumptions about their abilities to pass on values and a good family education to their children. At the same time, they also shared concerns about what it might mean to raise children in a town where they were economically, politically, and culturally marginalized (see Villenas, 2001). For example, Marisela's words, *"van a sufrir, humillados"* (they will suffer, humiliated), echoed some of these concerns about the effects of discrimination on children. And yet, there were other positionings that were taking place in this conversation related to "cultural" authority (the authority to speak on behalf of community) and to gender ideologies. For instance, Marisela's performance stands out as the "teacher" or authority advising the other mothers, even naming "the problem" of working mothers who might neglect their child-rearing responsibilities. But Marisela, whose children were living in Guatemala, was here under political asylum. How might the other women have viewed her child-rearing responsibilities and how was she positioning herself in this context? Moreover, as an unattached mother in Hope City, she also had to negotiate the gender rules of *honor y vergüenza* (honor and virtue; Villenas & Moreno, 2001) vis-à-vis the other married women, who were often critical of unattached mothers. These diverse positionings were thus not only in relation to a remote audience of English-speaking Hope City residents (and myself as representative link to this community) but also in relation to each other as women, mothers, and community members. We can consider these positionings, on a Sunday afternoon in Hope City, as a multilayered performance in history—that is, performances taking place in the context of structures (i.e., the racialized and gendered dimensions of economic restructuring and simultaneous migration), in the social world of discourses about gender and race (i.e., Latino patriarchy, beliefs about the "third world" and "legitimate" family lives), and finally in the context of personal lives of past and present.

It is important to begin by considering whom we were speaking to and how we were performing in interaction with each other while imagining and evoking a social world of people, discourses, and ideologies. Recalling Wortham (2001), in order to understand the power of narrative in transforming the self, one needs to ask about the particular positions that a speaker takes with respect to an audience and where the speaker places herself interactionally. In this case, it is important to consider how all of us women in the room were taking up certain positions as speakers with respect to different audiences—English-speaking Hope City residents, social service providers, academics, *los americanos* in general, other members of the Latino community, and a community of Latina mothers, including those in the room. While we all consistently positioned ourselves interactionally as "good mothers," our diverse performances highlighted our "theories of the flesh" (Moraga & Anzaldúa, 1983) carved from our complex, paradoxical, and ambiguous understandings of ourselves in relation to our social worlds.

What did our performances look like in relation to majority culture and to a situation of cultural and social marginalization in Hope City? The purpose of our meeting, to decide what to include in a public document about Latino education, and my own words that begin the discussion certainly signaled an outside audience of *los americanos,* as well as a context of "difference," alienation, and belonging/not belonging. From my own self-positioning as a

Chicana academic, daughter, and mother, I was responding to what literary scholar Leticia Garza-Falcón (1998) refers to as the "rhetoric of dominance"— that is, the invalidation and stereotyping of the people of Greater Mexico in the service of a dominative academic canon. In other words, I was responding to the silencing of Latinos' histories and bicultural lives in the public arena and school curriculum. Like Chicano historians and literary scholars, I too wanted to counter the rhetoric of dominance in Hope City, one that referred to Latinos and Latino family life as a "problem" by also "uncovering" voices unheard. Indeed, my own standpoint and actions as someone having experienced a rhetoric of dominance are powerfully evident in the artifacts I left behind in Hope City, including my talks at community gatherings, my voice in the town newspaper, and my addresses to town agency professionals. My own performance over the period of time I spent in Hope City is certainly not without its problems, to say the least, and illuminates missed encounters, understandings, and perspectives. Entrenched in Los Angeles identity politics, I am like Latino artists in the United States who, as Mexicano/Chicano artist Guillermo Gómez-Peña (1998) explains, work in the "flammable context of the multicultural wars and identity politics" (p. 135), defining ourselves as a culture of resistance. In defining ourselves as such, we sometimes miss differing perspectives about race, relationships, and alliance building. For example, as anthropologist Roger Rouse (1995) explains about the Latino migrant families he worked with, reciprocity and pragmatic affiliations, not identity politics, was primary in viewing the possibilities for building relationships across racial/ethnic groups. Nevertheless, my resistance to a rhetoric of dominance in terms of my personal history and my struggles as an educator and professional against negative notions of Latino families continually framed my performances in Hope City, as I positioned myself in relation to *los americanos,* even when they were not present, as on this Sunday afternoon.

Yet, from different backgrounds, Alba, Lydia, Rocio, and Marisela were also responding to a rhetoric of dominance. They were positioning themselves in interaction with discourses that questioned their right to live, work, and raise children in the United States, as well as responding to their cultural subordination and relegation to an inferior social/cultural status as "illegal aliens." In the conversation, the women stressed valuing the whole of their lives, emphasizing their cultural integrity and histories. In response to my question of what would be important to include in a booklet, Alba exclaimed, "*Pues, todo es importante*" (Well, *everything* is important), including as Rocio added, information about their countries of origin. As Alba elaborated, "*Hablar de lo que se vivió antes, la vida en méxico, una vida muy activa . . .*" (Talk about how we lived before, life in Mexico, a very active life . . .), I felt the women's urgency in presenting themselves as people with full and rich lives, lives full of meaning, activity, and knowledge. This urgency and response to dominance was true in so many different contexts. For example, in an interview for a newspaper story about our upcoming community meeting on Latino family education, Marisela very powerfully explained in Spanish, "The purpose of our meeting is to let people know that we have a rich education. Language and regulations hold us back. In some ways, things are worse here than in Guatemala [her home country]. Language prevents us from being ourselves" (October 19, 1995). Marisela's words for the newspaper story echoed similar positionings. With nods of agreement, the women were concerned with how the context of being undocumented in the United States changed how they were allowed to "be" in a new borderlands—or as Marisela suggested to the newspaper reporter, how language and cultural intolerance (not simply difference) rendered them different people. Rocio's suggestion that they should also talk about how they suffered in coming to this country highlighted how experiences of suffering and triumph were critical to portraying their humanity and in reframing the border-crossing experience not as an illegal act but as an act of courage. Stories of suffering in border crossing, poverty, and civil war were certainly central in the life history narratives of most of the women, particularly as stories exemplifying the value and valor of their humanity in response to a rhetoric of dominance in the United States.

In similar ways, the "rhetoric of dominance" (Garza-Falcón, 1998) was also explicitly challenged in the performative life history narratives of many of the women I interviewed. These women constructed their identities as "educated," intelligent, and resourceful mothers despite poverty and illiteracy in their home countries and racism in the United States. They performed their "special" and "better" education by actually teaching me through *consejos* (narrative advice) and stories. They positioned themselves interactionally in relation to me (an immediate audience) and to *los americanos* (a remote audience) as better educated—that is, highly educated in morals, values, respect, and the ethics of hard work. For example, Marisela continually emphasized learning the value of hard work from her mother. Lydia emphasized learning how to "*llevar el hogar,*" or how to keep house in terms of not only the physical work but also the emotional work, and to keep moral religiosity as good, kind, and noble family and community members. Lydia, Alba, and Rocio also emphasized the teachings of women's morality, how to keep clean, and how to serve in one's role as a single woman or as a married woman. Indeed, all the mothers (including me) at one point or another performed conversations and stories in relation to an audience of Hope City residents, social service professionals, or a generic group of *americanos.* Undoubtedly, these positionings in the *event* of storytelling (the telling) informed the narrated events in the stories (the told) concerning Latino working-class parenting and the embracing of dignity and a moral education.

Moreover, in positioning ourselves in relation to a "rhetoric of dominance" (Garza-Falcón, 1998), we also asserted difference. This strategic assertion of difference on my part came from my own experiences of cultural silencing in schools and of Los Angeles multicultural politics. In addition, as an ethnographic researcher, I was also wrapped up with the exigencies of an anthropological tradition, which despite much deconstruction, still depends on cultural boundaries and cultural "others" for its survival.[3] The women, too, strategically created boundaries at times to assert the value of their own education and child-rearing practices. Although Rocio's earlier comment that "*la mujer americana no es hogareña*" (the American woman is not of the home space) is certainly a stereotype, it is important to note how this critique served to position Rocio and her family education as "superior" vis-à-vis a supposedly "superior" American way of life. In her own oral life history, Rocio juxtaposed her perception of a licentious and morally lax U.S. society with the teaching of women's virtue and morality that are "*costumbres de nuestros países*" (traditions or customs from our home countries): "*Yo he visto que ya tienen novio se van se duermen con ellos y en méxico no es igual; es muy diferente la vida de allá. Alla es muy rara la mujer que fuma . . . como mexicanos tenemos que enseñarles las costumbres de nuestro país, pues aquí hay gente muy viciosa.*" (I've seen how when they [women in the United States] have a boyfriend they go and they sleep with them and in Mexico it's not the same; life is very different over there. There a woman who smokes is very rare . . . as Mexicans we have to teach them the customs from our home country; well here there are people with too many vices.) Rocio articulated what I might believe to be double-standard ideals with regard to women's sexuality, as cultural values of a better and superior Mexican family education. However, Rocio's strategic assertion of difference certainly made sense in the context of Latina mothers' negative framing in Hope City—evident in automatic assumptions about their need for parenting classes—and in the context of them as vulnerable "noncitizens" in this country. Drawing from and privileging a particular cultural frame of reference in which virtue and honor for women resided in their role as homemaker, Rocio positioned herself in a superior way vis-à-vis *las mujeres americanas* (U.S. women) as representative of *americanos* who echo voices of domination and discrimination.

Other positionings of difference stressed positive family lives and childhoods in the context of healthy environments and lifestyles in the women's home countries. Lydia's comment, "*En méxico, se pasa más tiempo con los niños*" (In Mexico, you spend more time with the children), and Alba's nostalgic remark, "*Quisiéramos que viviéran como uno se crió*" (We wish they could live the same way one grew up), pointed to a valuing of their "better" way of life and a real apprehension of the environment in which they found themselves in the United States. For example, in her life history narrative, Alba emphasized the monotony of life in Hope City, where she found herself and her children "*encerrados*" (locked up inside) all the time because of real and perceived dangers. In contrast, life in Mexico was about being outside surrounded by familiar people and feeling safe. Alba explained these sentiments in her life history interview:

> Allá [en méxico] la vida es muy diferente. En el pueblo todo el día pues se está uno pues afuera y los quehaceres adentro son pocos . . . se van corriendo los niños bien contentos todos a la escuela y aquí también no les gusta porque se van en autobús . . . y ya que llegan también corriendo de la escuela y todos a jugar con los demás niños pues afuera también.
>
> Over there [in Mexico] life is very different. In our town we spend all day well outside and our chores inside are few . . . the children go running, everyone happy to school and also here they don't like it because they have to take the school bus . . . and [in Mexico] when they get home also running all the way from school, everyone gets together to play with the rest of the children well also outside.

Alba's and Lydia's desires for a continuation of their own way of life—one that allowed for more time with the children and provided community and collective support for child rearing—contrasted sharply with assumptions in Hope City implying that Latinas did not have a good cultural basis for mothering. "*Cómo uno se crió*" (the way one grew up) was about safe and community-oriented environments and about a *buena educación* (good education) in terms of morals, respect, and dutiful behavior. These were performances of cultural continuity, of a taken-for-granted education, and of apprehension for change.

But on this Sunday afternoon, it was precisely at this nexus of apprehension and the desire for continuity of traditions and Mexican or Guatemalan ways of life that the women began to position themselves in relation to each other as parents dealing with assimilation, English language hegemony, and the conflicts of doubling as working mothers in Hope City factories. The audience was not *los americanos* anymore, but rather each other and other Latina mothers of the community. As parents, they worried about their children growing up in this country, about what "*el cambio*" (the change) represented for them when the children assimilated to this environment, as well as the effects of *el cambio* on the children themselves in struggling to fit in the U.S. mainstream. These changes also included language and the possible loss of communication in the family if English were to replace Spanish. However, while Rocio emphasized with humor, "*Y el problema para nosotros es que no nos van a entender*" (And the problem for us is that they won't understand us), Alba highlighted the positive feelings that many of the mothers felt toward their children's language learning, including pride in learning English and in being bilingual. Although it was unclear to me which language Alba was referring to when she said, "*Pero entonces los niños van a dominar el idioma porque son pequeños*" (But then the children will master the language because they're little), her positioning was one of confidence and pride in her children's language learning abilities, including the acquisition of English. And yet, as noted earlier, these words came from someone who was very apprehensive of the "dangerous" environment and lifestyle of isolation in Hope City (and the United States in general) as a place to raise her children. These ambivalent, often contradictory feelings were certainly the everyday negotiations of a newly forming Latino community who would face and were facing a situation of "subtractive schooling" (Valenzuela, 1999) for their children—an education that takes away rather than builds from the families' linguistic and cultural resources.

Moreover, the women positioned themselves not only as parents or educators but also as women and mothers who were workers in the burgeoning restructured economy of Hope City, now dependent on cheap immigrant labor (Fink, 2003; Griffith, 1995; Murillo Jr., 2002). Marisela, who brought up the issue of working mothers neglecting their children, was herself mothering across borders (Hondagneu-Sotelo & Avila, 1997) and working to send money to support her children in Guatemala. As a political refugee, Marisela felt forced to leave her children behind in the care of her mother, grandmother, and sisters. As briefly mentioned earlier, Marisela had much to negotiate vis-à-vis her status as an unattached woman and one who was not directly caring for her children. In this light, Marisela's harsh critiques about *el ambiente* (the environment) of the United States and about how much children would suffer here also might have been about trying to make sense of her own mothering across borders, even while performing with competence, self-assuredness, and authority as someone who was *bien educada* (well-educated in the holistic and schooling sense) and intelligent. Time and again, I witnessed Marisela position herself not only as different from *los americanos* but also as different from other Latinas in Hope City because she was a *political* refugee and not an economic refugee. Both of these critiques and assertions of difference, however, were embedded in response to U.S. cultural and economic dominance as well as to Latino patriarchy and gender ideologies. Marisela often explained that as a political refugee she *had* to leave her country, something she would otherwise not do for anything in the world because being in her country even while poor was better than mothering in what she believed to be a licentious and morally corrupt environment in the United States. At the same time, in the face of gendered ideologies about honor and virtue and women's place alongside their children, these performances positioned Marisela as a "better" mother. In contrast to other Latina mothers who were "willingly" raising their children in the United States because they were here for economic reasons, Marisela's children, as she often emphasized, were receiving a "superior" Guatemalan home education in the care of her mother and sisters. It seemed to me that, for Marisela, the spaces between the telling—how she positioned herself in this and other storytelling events as "different" from other Latina and U.S. mothers—and the told— the superior Guatemalan education versus inferior U.S. environment for child rearing—were the paradoxes and contradictions of maneuvering between

U.S. cultural hegemony, Latino patriarchy, and governmental abuse in her own country and now as an "invisible" transnational worker in the United States.

But Rocio, Alba, and Lydia would not let Marisela get away with her indirect criticism of their situation as working mothers in the United States. Rocio insisted that it was "*por amor, no porque muchas madres se descuidan*" (for love, not because a lot of mothers just neglect their children), whereas Alba, who was not working outside the home at the time, added that to work is "*para darles todo*" (to give them everything). Marisela again pointed to the differing context of mothering in the United States, where extended family is absent. Marisela acquiesced that adjustment and change to these new circumstances required, however, that parents make explicit or *inculcar* (inculcate) the reasons necessitating mothers' work outside the home. Thus, unlike Marisela, who faced the challenge of mothering across borders, these women were faced with the challenges of mothering in an unfamiliar environment and in the absence of kin and community support networks. For Rocio, Lydia, and even Alba, the spaces between the telling and the told—about negotiating the difficult tasks (and gendered ideologies) of mothering and working to cosupport households—were spaces of improvisation requiring resilience and the forging of new narratives about themselves as women, mothers, and educators of their children. For, indeed, the paradoxes of honoring and legitimizing their work *outside* the home ran alongside gender ideologies about women's place *in* the home, particularly as claiming the space of *el hogar* (the home) and criticizing U.S. women for not being of the home, positioned Latinas as good, if not "better," mothers. As I have written elsewhere (Villenas, 2001), the women's resilience in Hope City in the face of their deficit framing required a discursive commitment to *el hogar*—a cultural difference between Latinas and "*la mujer americana*" vehemently emphasized, albeit stereotypically, by Rocio and other Latinas. In these ways, all the women positioned themselves in relation to each other as parents, working mothers, and women within patriarchy, with a mixture of confidence and vulnerability, humor and seriousness, all the while laying open the very paradoxes and contradictions of mothering from the margins and across borders.

Conclusion: Toward Borderlands Pedagogies

In this chapter, I have discussed how a group of women at a moment in time positioned themselves in relation to different audiences, particularly in referencing *los americanos* and each other as parents, mothers, and "women." At this moment in time, the "rhetoric of dominance" (Garza-Falcón, 1998) was challenged as the women positioned themselves in interaction with racialized discourses that questioned the very legitimacy of their lives in the United States.

The event of storytelling—that is, the performances of dignity and the strategic assertions of difference—ran alongside the narrated events or descriptions of the challenges they faced in supporting a Latino family education of traditional morals, values, and customs. At the same time, in positioning themselves in relation to each other as parents, working mothers, and gendered beings, the spaces between the telling and the told began to unfold as ambiguous sites of contestation and negotiation. Women and mothers talking about their struggles with assimilation, English language hegemony, bilingualism and biculturalism, the perils and necessity of doubling as working mothers in an unsupportive environment, and gendered ideologies about women's place in *el hogar* (including their strategic claims to this space) was a process of teaching, learning, and negotiating life in new borderlands. And, certainly, my own positionings and performances as a Chicana coming from "a flammable context of multicultural wars and identity politics" (Gómez-Peña, 1998) and as a second-generation Diaspora Latina daughter and mother influenced and added to the context and content of these borderlands pedagogies. While being somewhat excluded from the conversation when the women addressed each other as their audience, I positioned myself and was positioned in that moment as the second-generation "daughter" who had much to learn from their experiences. This was often the way I performed and was positioned in the company of my mother and aunts even as a grown married woman with children. There were certainly uncross-able boundaries between myself, a U.S.-born, middle-class, English-speaking "professional," and the group of Latina mothers in Hope City, as we became aware of our different class and social locations. But as a U.S.-born "daughter" who didn't quite get things right, including the Spanish language and culturally appropriate social etiquette, I still felt as though there was familiarity and hope in their advice-giving performances.[4] For better or worse, I might have served as a reminder of what their own bicultural children might be like growing up in Hope City and the responses required on their part.

In short, our performances and positioning were but a glimpse of the "interstitial spaces" (Pérez, 1999), or gaps between the telling and the told, where the terms of a viable family education and identities of dignity were always in the process of being "worked out" in a borderlands context. Although these spaces were shaped by difficult political and economic circumstances like those of the border region between Mexico and the United States, it still remains that these were also borderlands spaces of improvisation and creative imaginings. For example, in terms of cross-cultural relationships, Latina mothers both retreated into strict categories of us/them as a mode of self-preservation, as in the conversation described in this chapter, and recast categories and refashioned identities as they accommodated and related with *mucho cariño* (much caring) to those *americanos* (both African American and White) who reciprocated genuine respect. As I've emphasized throughout, this borderlands sensibility was also required in terms of continuing a process of teaching and learning between adults and between adults and children in order to refashion a viable family education in a new place (see also Vasquez, Pease-Alvarez, & Shannon, 1994). Following Elbaz-Luwisch's (this volume) vision of a space where learning might take place, I would argue that more educators in the schools of Hope City and in the social services need to recognize the borderlands spaces they embody and the dialogic relationships they already inhabit with respect to the "other." In Hope City, as in other borderlands around the world, the processes of negotiating dignified identities, family education, and public schooling are wrought with injustices and pain; but there are always possibilities, some which cannot wait any longer to be realized.

Recommended Reading

This chapter highlights and raises a number of issues with respect to Latino education, including the context of Latino migration, work, and education in places with little previous Latino presence; Latina mothers' cultural and linguistic experiences in negotiating continuity and change in the experience of raising their children; Latino children's and their parents' experiences in the schools; and finally the processes of Latino immigrant parents' empowerment and advocacy on behalf of their children's schooling. *Education in the New Latino Diaspora* (2002), edited by Stanton Wortham, Enrique Murillo Jr., & Edmund Hamann, is a collection of writings detailing issues and experiences of newly forming Latino communities in Maine, Georgia, Kansas, Colorado, and North Carolina. In general, these chapters compare and contrast the host community's (especially school's) responses to Latinos as well as the Latino communities' views. Norma González's (2001) *I Am My Language: Discourses of Women and Children in the Borderlands,* on the other hand, focuses on the women of a long-established Mexican community in Tucson, Arizona, and details the intimate processes of language learning and teaching in families representing different generations (from first to third or fourth generation in Tucson). To get a sense of bilingual children's experiences in mainstream classrooms and schools, Guadalupe Valdés's (2001) *Learning and Not Learning English: Latino Students in American Schools* is an excellent study of how middle-school children actually fare in English-dominant classrooms. Although the instructional situation is bleak, Valdés gives recommendations for improving the educational opportunities for Latino English-language learners. So what roles do Latino parents play as advocates for their children's schooling, and how can they transform home-school relationships? Concha Delgado-Gaitan's *The Power of Community: Mobilizing for Family and Schooling* (2001) is an ethnographic study of a 15-year-old organization started by Latino parents seeking to help each other understand, work with, and change schools to meet the needs of their children. Like the Latina mothers in Hope City, we hear the voices of these parents express their pride, hopes, fears, and frustrations in carving a future for their children. Finally, for an overview of Latino education in general with historical and contemporary accounts to issues of Latino parental involvement, testing, bilingual education, and policy, Richard Valencia's second edition of *Chicano School Failure and Success* (2002) is an excellent resource.

Reflective Questions

1. Tell about an experience you have had with a storytelling event in which, thinking back, you were really attuned to what was happening in both the telling and the told. What positionings were taking place, and what was being negotiated? Did these feel like borderlands spaces of some sort?

2. This chapter argues for a performance- and borderlands-sensitive analysis of narrative and discourse. Were some issues illuminated or highlighted that might not have been with a content analysis? What role does my (the researcher's) personal history and interpretation of personal experiences play in this analysis, and what are other possibilities for interpreting the conversation among this group of Latina mothers?

3. What are some of the issues and challenges facing Latina mothers with regard to education (family and schooling) and specifically in the context of building new Latino communities in places with no previous Latino immigration and settlement?

Notes

1. Hope City is a pseudonym for a small town-like city in central North Carolina. According to the 1990 census, the town's population was close to 5,000.

2. I use the term "Latina" to refer to women of Latin American heritage. In Hope City, I met Latinas from many different parts of Latin America, including urban and rural Mexico, Guatemala, El Salvador, Honduras, and Colombia. I also use both Chicana and Latina to refer to myself, the first when indexing a political orientation—specifically to the identity politics born of *el movimiento,* the Mexican American civil rights movement—and the latter to identify a pan-ethnicity across generations and Latin American nationalities.

3. Cultural anthropologists are undoubtedly posing very serious questions about political engagement, continued colonialism, and issues around space, territory, and globalization.

4. I am inspired here by Edén Torres's (2003) conversation about the differences, tensions, and hope in the relationships between Chicanas and Mexican women nationals.

References

Anzaldúa, G. (1987). *Borderlands/La frontera*. San Francisco: Aunt Lute Books.

Bauman, R. (1986). *Story, performance, and event*. London: Cambridge University Press.

Conquergood, D. (1991). Rethinking ethnography: Towards a critical cultural politics. *Communication Monographs, 58*, 179–194.

Delgado-Gaitan, C. (2001). *The power of community: Mobilizing for family and schooling*. Lanham, MD: Rowman & Littlefield.

Fink, L. (2003). *The Maya of Morgantown: Work and community in the nuevo new South*. Chapel Hill: University of North Carolina Press.

Garza-Falcón, L. M. (1998). *Gente decente: A borderlands response to the rhetoric of dominance*. Austin: University of Texas Press.

Gómez-Peña, G. (1998). 1995–Terreno peligro/Danger Zone: Cultural relations between Chicanos and Mexicans at the end of the century (C. Ross, Trans.). In F. Bonilla, E. Meléndez, R. Morales, & M. A. Torres (Eds.), *Borderless borders: U.S. Latinos, Latin Americans, and the paradox of interdependence* (pp. 131–137). Philadelphia: Temple University Press.

González, N. (2001). *I am my language: Discourses of women and children in the borderlands*. Tucson: University of Arizona Press.

Griffith, D. (1995). *Hay trabajo*: Poultry processing, rural industrialization and the Latinization of low-wage labor. In D. D. Stull, M. J. Broadway, & D. Griffith (Eds.), *Any way you cut it: Meat-processing and small-town America* (pp. 129–151). Lawrence: University of Kansas Press.

Hondagneu-Sotelo, P., & Avila, E. (1997). "I'm here but I'm there": The meaning of Latina transnational motherhood. *Gender & Society, 11*, 548–571.

Jakobson, R. (1971). Shifters, verbal categories, and the Russian verb. In R. Jakobson, *Selected Writings* (Vol. 2, pp. 130–147). The Hague, Netherlands: Mouton. (Original work published in 1957)

Keating, A. (2000). *Gloria E. Anzaldúa: Interviews/Entrevistas*. New York: Routledge.

Madison, S. D. (1998). That was my occupation: Oral narrative, performance, and Black feminist thought. In D. Pollack (Ed.), *Exceptional spaces: Essays in performance and history* (pp. 319–342). Chapel Hill: University of North Carolina Press.

Moraga, C., & Anzaldúa, G. (1983). *This bridge called my back: Writings by radical women of color*. New York: Kitchen Table–Women of Color Press.

Murillo, E. G., Jr. (2002). How does it feel to be a problem? Disciplining the transnational subject in the American South. In S. Wortham, E. Murillo Jr., & E. Hamann (Eds.), *Education in the new Latino diaspora: Policy and the politics of identity* (pp. 215–240). Westport, CT: Ablex.

Pérez, E. (1999). *The decolonial imaginary: Writing Chicanas into history*. Bloomington and Indianapolis: Indiana University Press.

Rouse, R. (1995). Questions of identity: Personhood and collectivity in transnational migration to the United States. *Critique of Anthropology, 15*(4), 351–380.

San Miguel, G., Jr., & Valencia, R. R. (1998). From the treaty of Guadalupe Hidalgo to *Hopwood*: The educational plight and struggle of Mexican Americans in the Southwest. *Harvard Educational Review, 68*, 353–412.

Torres, E. (2003). *Chicana without apology: The new Chicana cultural studies*. New York: Routledge.

Valdés, G. (2001). *Learning and not learning English: Latino students in American schools.* New York: Teachers College Press.

Valencia, R. (Ed.). (2002). *Chicano school failure and success: Past, present, and future.* New York: Routledge/Falmer.

Valenzuela, A. (1999). *Subtractive schooling: U.S.-Mexican youth and the politics of caring.* Albany: SUNY Press.

Vasquez, O., Pease-Alvarez, L., & Shannon, S. (1994). *Pushing boundaries: Language and culture in a Mexicano community.* London: Cambridge University Press.

Villenas, S. (2001). Latina mothers and small-town racism: Creating narratives of dignity and moral education in North Carolina. *Anthropology & Education Quarterly, 32*(1), 3–28.

Villenas, S. (2002). Reinventing educación in new Latino communities: Pedagogies of change and continuity in North Carolina. In S. Wortham, E. Murillo Jr., & E. Hamann (Eds.), *Education in the new Latino diaspora: Policy and the politics of identity* (pp. 17–35). Westport, CT: Ablex.

Villenas, S., & Moreno, M. (2001). To *valerse por si misma* between race, capitalism, and patriarchy: Latina mother-daughter pedagogies in North Carolina. *International Journal of Qualitative Studies in Education, 14*(5), 671–687.

Wortham, S. (2001). *Narratives in action: A strategy for research and analysis.* New York: Teachers College Press.

Wortham, S., Murillo, E., Jr., & Hamann, E. (Eds.). (2002). *Education in the new Latino diaspora: Policy and the politics of identity.* Westport, CT: Ablex.

Unit Three

Social Justice, Equality, and the Education of Native Americans

6

White Teachers, Native Students

Rethinking Culture-Based Education

Mary Hermes

Autobiographical Introduction

Troubled by the consistent failure of schools to educate Native Americans and driven by questions of identity and culture, I have been drawn to the culture-based education movement. For the past twelve years I have been working in tribal schools, tribal colleges, and American Indian education programs within public schools. Often I hear people refer to culture-based education as the answer to a multitude of problems. This is a reasonable response, considering the damage inflicted by the boarding school era (1880–1924). In this era of self-determination in American Indian education, many people are turning to schools to help regain what has been lost. Many Native people, including those adopted like myself, are hoping to re-create culture and language for our children. "Culture-based education" sounds like a strategy that will heal our wounds. In my work, I critically examine what is meant by "culture-based education" in the hope of making it stronger.

My research has focused on asking community members, especially Elders, what they want from education, and then matching that with what I observe in schools. In the area on which my work focuses, Northern Minnesota and Wisconsin, very little research on tribal schooling has been done. I live near a reservation and am a part of their community, although I am not an enrolled tribal member. I want my children to know their Ojibwe culture and language as well as to be able to attend the college of their choice. I examine, teach, read, write, listen, and talk—hoping that asking the right questions will make the solutions (or at least the next direction) clear.

Beyond the professional expectations for research, as a community member I feel an ethical obligation to respond to community needs. Service is a natural outcome of research. Going back and forth between research and teaching (in the tribal community) is a given for me. For five years I was a staff member and teacher at a tribal school with a culture-based mission. I flourished at that school. I loved teaching Native children about things that I wanted to learn about—traditions, language, stories. I especially enjoyed tagging along with the culture staff on outings. We gathered rice, made maple syrup, went hunting and fishing, and tanned deer hides. Constant teasing and a feeling of familial closeness were woven into everything we did. These were times enjoyed by all. These were cultural experiences that would not likely happen in public schools. We hoped that somehow the bonding, the positive self-esteem, and the love of learning would transfer into a love of math and reading.

In my research I found that the distance between "culture" and "academics" was sometimes too wide for students to grasp. Although students had good relationships with teachers and learned some culture-based skills, they did not necessarily translate this into success in other academic subject areas. In fact, some students perceived an identity choice between academic and culture-based success: "be White" or "be Native." Being successful in subjects such as math and reading was understood as assimilating or "being White." Excelling in cultural activities was understood as "being Native." Although this choice is more subtle than the choice between attending a tribal or a public school, for example, it still represents a dilemma that need not exist. Culture-based tribal education has been *mostly* superimposed on standard public school education. We inhabit the systems we live in, and we have put culture-based education inside of a public school box. In doing this, we are not helping our students create an integrated identity as academically successful American Indian students.

Another area of concern identified in my research relates to socioeconomic oppression. Cultural curriculums do not always address the socioeconomic inequality and dysfunction that students experience outside of school. Sometimes the realities of this kind of oppression weigh so heavily on our students that schoolwork cannot be a priority. During hard times for these students, schooling must seem irrelevant. In this chapter, I highlight these concerns and wonder how the idea of culture-based education might be extended to consider the various life circumstances of students.

For the past four years I have been actively involved in the movement to make schools more academically challenging while at the same time approaching the teaching of culture in a different way. I have become part of a movement to start an Ojibwe language immersion school. It seems to me that teaching culture in English is one thing, teaching school through the Ojibwe language is another. Learning cultural traditions is important; regenerating culture through language is empowering.

Preface

Henry,[1] a superintendent of an Ojibwe tribal school, and Agnes, a teacher at another tribal school, talk about their own children. They believe that no matter what kind of or what quality education their children receive, they will go to college and be successful. Assured of their future, Henry says,

> See these kids? (He points to a portrait of his two handsome blonde, blue-eyed boys on the wall directly above his desk.) *No one can mess them up* [italics added]. There is nothing that can happen in school that will jeopardize their success.

I am dumbfounded. I think about these unsolicited personal references all year; they stand in stark contrast to the daily worry I feel about my two middle-class Native American children going to school in a town bordering the reservation. What a luxury it must be to feel assured that your children will be successful, regardless of their experience in elementary school.

The Culture-Based Movement

Culture-based curriculum has become complicated and contested terrain for Native Americans as postcolonial debates about identity and authenticity collide with archaic and racist colonial systems for schooling and tribal enrollment. In many ways, the mission of Native American culture-based schools has been diluted by the inability to create systemic change. The teaching of Native culture in tribal schools is often merely an addition to the existing state-sanctioned curriculum. Adding "culture" to a preexisting system of schooling sometimes results in the teaching of culture as content, sometimes in essentialized ways (Hermes, 2001). For example, teaching beadwork or Native dance without a deeper cultural context can intersect with mainstream stereotypes and students' notions of equating a Native identity with these traditions. The teaching of a Native culture-based curriculum must go much farther in order to create systemic change. Changes are needed in the organization of the school day, language of instruction, content, pedagogy, and approach in order to reflect the epistemology of the indigenous people (Hermes, 1995).

The culture-based movement in Indian education was a response to the boarding-school era and the tremendous loss of culture and language that subsequent generations of Native people suffered. In many ways, the idea of culture-based education opened the door for understanding and defining a different approach to schooling for Native Americans. However, culture-based curriculum has become the catchphrase for success in Native education. Often "culture" in education is expected to remedy complex and deep-seated social problems. And yet, the development of a nation-specific culture-based curriculum (e.g., Ojibwe culture-based math curriculum) has not been a funding priority for research and development. For example, very few if any books, textbooks, or other curriculum resources have been published in the Ojibwe language. Further, many of the indigenous knowledge bases and languages have been fragmented through colonialism, making curriculum production even more difficult. Individual tribal members who are certified teachers often do not have language fluency or extensive cultural knowledge. On the other hand, many elders with culture and language knowledge have suffered abuse in boarding schools and are not eager to go back into any school. Because of their experience in schools, they were not likely to become teachers. Consequently, the majority of certified teachers in tribal schools in the Upper Midwest are non-Native.

Within this context, I asked the following question: (1) How do White (or non-Native) teachers become successful teachers at Native culture-based schools? (2) How do they fit in with the school's mission of teaching in a culture-based way? I wanted to understand their interpretation of the meaning of a culture-based curriculum and how they understand their own positionality. These are middle-class White teachers of generally poor brown students. Their students are from the reservation and the inner city; the teachers are from the suburbs and border towns, and yet there is trust. "Mr. Joe! Mr. Joe! Look at this homework. . . ." "Agnes, want to see a picture of my baby?" I hear their students trusting them, and I know I am in the right classrooms. The students volunteer stories of their lives; they privilege these White folks in ways that are rare. I am quite happy to hear the teacher's struggles, to ask how they've lasted five, six, seventeen years at the tribal school. The teachers wonder aloud about other jobs that pay more and cost less. I am content looking from the inside at the outsider.

The teachers in this study interpret the culture-based mission of their schools as going beyond what is being taught in culture classes. They talk about high rates of absenteeism. They talk about poverty and the socioeconomic status of families. In their minds, their students' performance in school is affected most vividly by the family circumstances of poverty. They understand the socioeconomic oppression of Native Americans as deeply intertwined with culture. Their responsiveness to students' needs is shaped by this knowledge as much as by awareness of the cultural differences.

In the following sections, I consider some of the theories that have informed Native American education within the broader context of minority school failure. I am interested in how dominant and narrow the culture-based approach can be. Next, I briefly describe the methods used in this research and then present data that describe how these teachers strive to understand and fit into their Native culture-based schools. I offer an analysis of data that underscores the teachers' attempts to weave an understanding of socioeconomic oppression into the schools' mission of culture. My research suggests that theory needs to be updated to reflect these current understandings in practice. I end my discussion by challenging the dominant position that sees culture in a narrow sense within Native American education and by attempting to broaden this notion.

Theoretical Framework

This research is situated within the larger literature and debate concerning minority cultures and educational failure. Because this debate has been extensively detailed elsewhere (Foley, 1991; Trueba, 1991), I only briefly refer to it here. Theoretical underpinnings for work on minority cultures and educational failure stem from at least two main areas of educational research. First, sociolinguistic (and microethnographic) research suggests that a lack of cross-cultural communication, or "cultural discontinuity," can result in minority student failure (Dumont, 1972; Erickson & Mohatt, 1982; Greenbaum & Greenbaum, 1983; Phillips, 1983). Second, work by critical theorists suggests that larger societal variables such as power structures, institutional racism, and opportunity structures also play an important role in minority student failure (Deyhle, 1995; Lipka, 1994; McCarty, 1989; Ogbu, 1978).

The first strand of research, cultural discontinuity, or the "communication process" explanation (Erickson, 1987), has been interpreted by some practitioners to mean that continuity between home and school would promote success (Au & Jordan, 1981). This approach, the cultural-based approach, has also had much popular appeal with Native American communities. The thrust of the Native American civil rights and self-determination movements in schools has been to reclaim Native cultures and languages and to rebuild self-esteem (Lomawaima, 1995). The primary vehicles to meet this aim have been culture-based schooling and culture-based curriculum. The culture-based movement has grown in the past thirty years to include Native American culture and language in public and tribal schools. The culture-based movement in Native American education has contributed to improve the identity, self-esteem, and attitude toward schools of many Native Americans (Deyhle & Swisher, 1997).

The debate between macro and micro explanations of failure has been revisited by many scholars (e.g., Erickson, 1987; Foley, 1991; St. Germaine, 1995). Is there something about a clash of cultures within the classrooms that causes Native students to fail? Or is the low socioeconomic status of many Native Americans the most significant factor in school failure? Although it is beyond the scope of this chapter to resolve this debate, I see the need to be aware of both micro and macro forces at work within the school. I am concerned with developing a theoretical approach that is not prone to reinscribing cultural barriers, as some interpretations of cultural discontinuity and learning-styles theory do (Henze & Vanett, 1993). My approach does not assume that there are already fixed and tangible boundaries between cultures to be studied, but rather that there are ongoing relationships that are always affected by the larger systems and structures of which they are a part (Levinson & Holland, 1996). In exploring the ways that Native students and White teachers work successfully in the classroom, I hope to gain insights into what else is going on besides "culture difference." In what ways do successful White teachers approach the teaching of Native students? How does the teacher's awareness of structural inequalities affect teaching? In my research, I explore the relationships between students and teachers, especially the beliefs of the teachers that support their particular practices.

Methods

The methods for this study were ethnographic or, stated broadly, interpretive (Erickson, 1986) and were generally influenced by narrative inquiry (Connelly & Clandinin, 1990). These methods have been adapted to a Native epistemology (Crazybull, 1997; Hermes, 1998). Care was taken to follow Ojibwe cultural protocols and research priorities. For example, consistent with Ojibwe oral traditions, narrative methods in data collection and interpretation were utilized (Peacock & Miller Cleary, 1997). Data were gathered in a two-state area of the Lake Superior band of Ojibwe over a two-year period (from September 1999–August 2001). Four tribal schools were included as a representative sample of Ojibwe tribal schools in Minnesota and Wisconsin. In this chapter, two teachers at two tribal schools are discussed in-depth. These two particular teachers were chosen because they are both high school level science teachers.

Community members and/or administrators were briefed on the research project and asked to nominate "successful" teachers. I did not ask for White teachers or for science teachers. These teachers were recognized as excellent science teachers, and in both cases, the teachers were recommended by an administrator and a respected community member. Also in both cases, the community member was a culture teacher at the school and a parent of children attending the school. For the nominators, I defined the criteria for "successful" as a teacher who taught for academic success, critical consciousness, and/or cultural competence (Ladson-Billings, 1995). The nominators qualified their choices as teachers who met at least two and, in some cases, three of the criteria.

Teachers were observed on a series of six to eight teaching occasions throughout the school year; in-depth field notes were taken. A series of three in-depth interviews were conducted with each teacher. The first interviews were broad and explained the purpose of the study. Participants were asked open-ended questions about their position at the school, their classes, and their feelings about teaching Native students. The second interviews focused more on the teaching of Ojibwe culture and the teacher's own cultural identity. The third interviews were generally reflections on the first two, with participants often rethinking what they had said and revising statements. After reading transcripts of their interviews, the teachers were given the opportunity to make corrections or clarifications. On several occasions, I also informally interviewed individuals and small groups of students. Data were collected over the aforementioned two-year period, transcribed, and then coded. After identifying and hand-coding themes, I interpreted the themes, and now, influenced by these themes as a frame of reference, I retell the teachers' narratives.

Results

POVERTY: IT'S EASIER TO TALK ABOUT CULTURE

When asked whether cultural differences between home and school were a contributing factor to student failure, most teachers thought the impact of poverty was a much more prohibitive factor to school success than culture. At Big Lake School, introducing my project to an administrator, I told him I was interested in how culture affects schooling. His response was "Well, that depends on which culture you are talking about, the traditional Ojibwe culture, or the culture of poverty. The culture our kids grow up in is not traditional Native American culture. It's a low social-economic poverty culture."

This comment was common for nearly the entire first year of interviews. When asked about culture, participants raised the issue of poverty. The words of Agnes (a teacher at Native Peoples School) directly echoed the administrator: "More than being Native American they are inner city/poverty influenced."

As teachers and administrators were anxious to talk about poverty, I wondered how I could have overlooked it. In fact, how could the whole of Native American education ignore it? Workshops and inservices on culture in the curriculum are abundant. American Indian education programs in the public schools often specialize in adding culture, developing culture-based material, and making things that reflect Native culture and values. But what about the fact that we are the poorest, least-educated, and least-employed minority in America? Surely this is connected to Native success and culture in school. I feel as if I have stumbled upon to a topic that is painfully obvious. The teachers hold open their hearts and point to it; they know it well. They make a plea to understand it, but academics, intent on culture and identity, seem embarrassed even to name it.

TEACHERS TALK ABOUT CULTURE AS POVERTY

Agnes has been a teacher at the Native Peoples School for three years. The school was born in the 1970s. A survival school located in the inner city, its mission is to build healthy self-esteem through educating Native students about their identity and heritage. It is called a "survival school" for the survival and revitalization of Native culture. The students come from many indigenous nations, predominantly Ojibwe and Lakota. Many of the cultural teachings at the school are drawn from these two tribes. Ojibwe language is offered and, at the time of the study, the lead culture teacher was an Ojibwe woman highly respected for her cultural knowledge and involvement in traditional ceremonies.

Joe is a fourth-year science teacher at Ojibwe Tribal School. Located on a small Ojibwe reservation in the north, the school is a couple of hours away from a major metropolitan area. Joe's school was also founded in the 1970s and has a similar philosophy of teaching in a culture-based way. Many traditional subsistence activities are carried out at the school on a regular basis; for example, ricing (the practice of gathering wild rice), hunting, and sugar bush (gathering maple sap for syrup) are taught in a hands-on technique at the school every season. Ojibwe language is offered throughout the K–12 level, but as a second language. Like other courses, it is scheduled a few times a week for an hour or so. Important times at the school are marked by feasts. Community members and elders can be seen frequenting the school for these events.

Agnes and Joe teach at tribal schools where cultural traditions are taught. To them, poverty and socioeconomic oppression are larger day-to-day factors in students' ability to concentrate and succeed in school than are the differences between Native American and White cultures. In May 2000, Agnes told me,

> I say this was profound [the idea of poverty along with culture] because I could see where today's questions [to the students] about "culture" seemed a bit abstract. I could sense there were so many pressing things, things they had no way to talk about. How abstract must the "baby in utero" sound when their basic needs are not met. Culture must sound nearly like a luxury—although all of them recognize it is important. In fact, they hold onto it like a mantra. Culture. They could not tell me what it was or where they learned it, or even why it was important to them, but they surely held fast to the belief that it is.

Both Agnes and Joe struggle with low attendance, lack of school readiness, and poor attention from students. They attribute these issues largely to poverty and factors beyond the students' control. They struggle not to blame the students or their families because they see it as part of the history of oppression of Native peoples in the United States. Their beliefs are contradicted by the larger school systems and cultures that do hold individual students accountable. These teachers have adjusted and do not hold students to the same behavioral expectations that they would in another setting. They put students' needs first. They try not to lower academic expectations but instead to adjust behavioral (nonacademic) expectations. Agnes said,

> We were talking about it before—about how they have to survive every day. They have to find food, because they're children of poverty, so they have to find a home and food, and I mean things so surprising to me, not having dealt with people from poverty. But to see when they open up their purse, they just don't have a wallet and a comb in there, they have a toothbrush in there, because they don't know where they're going to spend the night and they want to have a toothbrush with them. I mean that breaks my heart. So seeing them having to contend with helping to raise their brothers and sisters because they have an unhealthy home, or being homeless themselves, or I mean that stuff, that's really hard to deal with . . . some of our expectations are just too high. You can't expect them to have a pencil because they don't have a home. You can't expect them to have a notebook or to remember to bring it because they haven't eaten a meal in twenty-four hours.

At the reservation school, Joe often talks about the secondary effects of socioeconomic oppression—drinking, drug abuse, fighting, and stealing. He sees these behaviors as coming directly from dysfunctional families and poverty and as being in conflict with traditional Native values. Joe cites poor attendance and inability to concentrate as the main reasons for failure in his classes. He adjusts his teaching, remains flexible, and spends much of his time helping individual students catch up. He has invented several systems of files and teaches students to be responsible for what they have missed. In the following example, he directly links home and poverty to problems he has communicating with students:

> It's like you get beat up, or my father's drunk, or you go without dinner or breakfast, and I'm sure that hurts. And they look at me, and you know, I have everything. And I really wasn't prepared for that. It's a culture of poverty. The poverty, or whatever you want to call it, it's difficult for me, but I'm getting better at it. When I see the student comes in and one day she's just the best student you could ever hope for. And the next day she's swearing at me and everything I say is wrong and whatever. And I'm starting to get upset, and I see that she has a bruise on her eye. No wonder she's upset—someone hit her. Something happened that's really tough. And those are the kinds of things that I guess really keep me coming back because that's something I think I can help students with.

Acknowledgments of the effects of socioeconomic oppression greatly influence teachers' decisions in responding to students, especially in terms of behavioral expectations. When they plan for and consider being responsive to students, the overriding consideration is the day-to-day struggles of their students. This means considering factors other than just Native American culture in a narrow sense. It means considering the historical circumstances that have resulted in low socioeconomic status and a myriad of related issues.

NATIVE AND MAINSTREAM CULTURE AND CHANGE

Given this broad and critical understanding of the oppression of Native people in America, the teachers constantly question what they have come to think of as the norm for classroom expectations, Native culture, and their own Whiteness. Their understanding of culture—one that is underscored by recognition of change as a constant—is a second unifying theme in these interviews.

The understanding that Joe and Agnes have of Native culture is continually evolving. They both have a complex understanding of culture as something immanently important, always changing, and difficult to pinpoint. Further, they realize that their understanding of Native culture has been informed by both experience and stereotypes. As noted earlier, they have had to adjust their idea of "culturally responsive teaching" to include socioeconomic circumstances. In other ways, they struggled to hold a notion of culture as something alive and changing. The teachers described culture as "everything and nothing." They puzzled over the definition of culture in several interviews. Most often they referred to examples from their tribal school teaching or from their own backgrounds to illustrate their definitions. Their difficulty in describing culture confirms the idea that they see it as complex and not easily defined. In terms of teaching at an Ojibwe culture-based school, Joe attempted to describe culture this way:

> And that's just it, again—what is culture? If I teach a student how to do sugarbush— I learned one way. I learned that you go out to the farm and there are a lot of old Germans sitting around drinking a lot of beer. And there's a huge tractor and you drive around the woods, and it's like a farm and you eat—so that was sugarbush. Basically you end up with pretty close to the same product, but obviously the process is quite a bit different. The only way I can learn about the actual culture (Ojibwe) is to go out and do sugarbush with people that live in the area. I'm sure there's a lot of different ways, you know, one Native American will do it a lot different than the next. And of course I can read about Nanabooshu[2] and the story of the lazy people drinking the sap right out of the tree, that's cultural too. There are many Native Americans today that have huge operations for syrup, which is a lot different than using a sumac with a file and birch bark.

I interpret Joe's beliefs about culture this way: there is no one right way; culture is a process even within the same group of people, and there is variation across time and place. He does not expect one way to define tradition or hold one way as more authentic than another. He does, however, make a distinction between "traditional Ojibwe" and "mainstream" culture.

> But then how is culture played out in everyday life? How they live at home, to me, is just much more mainstream culture than what they have at school. That I see is the same as a lot of whites, especially the pop or the recreational culture. They are huge football fans—they all love the Minnesota Vikings, and they all hate the Packers. They love rap music. They wear color in their hair. I mean they keep up with what's going

on—which is mainstream culture. It is very important to them. In my opinion, it's
more important for them to keep up with that than the traditional [Ojibwe culture].

Joe raises the issue that mainstream culture complicates a clear dichotomy
between home (as traditional) and school (as mainstream culture), which was
assumed in early research in Native education (Mohatt & Erickson, 1981;
Phillips, 1983). Both Joe and Agnes thought that most of their students learned
more traditional Ojibwe culture, or at least cultural activities, from the school.
Some parents work forty or more hours and do not get the time off needed to
participate in seasonal activities, which are labor intensive. On the other hand,
some employers, like the school or the tribe, will grant time off for "ricing," for
example. In many instances, *because of economic change,* it has become the job
of the school to teach Ojibwe hunting and gathering skills.

BEING WHITE IN A NATIVE SCHOOL: NOT THE EXPERT

If teaching traditional cultural activities is partially the job of the school,
then what is the responsibility of the White teachers? In responding to students'
immediate needs, Joe and Agnes read this mission broadly. However, they both
toe the margins when asked specifically about teaching culture. Joe described
his position this way: "Probably the best way I can teach the culture is to have
some respected community member come in and do it. That's the way." Joe
holds the belief that he is not an expert on teaching Ojibwe culture. He sees
himself as an outsider and an ally, someone who can best support cultural
learning. He feels it is not his place to directly teach cultural skills, but does his
best to enhance and support that learning in his science classroom. Agnes, the
teacher at Native Peoples School, has a similar perspective on her position:

> Culturally based curriculum ideally would be given in the Native language of that
> culture, whatever that would be, and the curriculum would relate to that culture.
> Because, to me, it would be cool if it could be an immersion-type program. But
> unfortunately what happens in schools, especially at the middle school and high
> school levels, is you don't find people competent in a specialized area that are also
> strong in that culture. So I've been put in the position of not being Indian, not
> being a Native person, and trying to incorporate some of the culture of which
> I know just a very limited amount into my science classroom, and that's really
> difficult. It's really a difficult thing to try to do—just because I'm not. I mean, I
> shouldn't be doing this really, I shouldn't. Really, it should be a Native person, an
> American Indian person out there teaching physics. Because they would know,
> they would know off the top of their heads how to relate whatever particular topic
> they're speaking on to the culture. And I don't. I have to stretch.

Although I do not agree that persons of Native heritage would necessarily
know "off the top of their heads" how to connect physics and Native culture,

I think Agnes's admission that she is not the expert leads her to think of herself as an ally and not the sole source of information for her students. This position opens a space for discussion, direction, and self-reflection that is not always found in the more familiar stance of teacher as expert (Britzman, 1991). In an important way, it is this appropriate discomfort with and critical reflection upon their own whiteness that positions these teachers as allies and underpins their success.

Both teachers talk directly about their whiteness. Their teaching approach is informed by an awareness of being part of the dominant culture. They have both been called "whitey" and don't particularly like it, but they understand that they are outsiders in a community that has been colonized by European Americans. They don't expect every Native teen they meet to be at peace with that. As Agnes said,

> You know, it's really hard on the students to come from culture class, where they've learned this horrific history of their people done to them by White people, and then come up and respect me when I stand up and try to teach them physics. That's a hard transition to go through.

More important than knowledge of Native culture is the awareness of how the history between Native Americans and European Americans affects the position of White teachers in Native schools. These teachers do not expect to be experts at teaching culture; they see their role as allies. They are there to teach science and to support culture. Their thinking about what it means to support culture is always changing, and in this area they see themselves as learners. Although they are teachers, they do not assume that they are experts in every area, especially when it comes to Native culture.

HOW DO TEACHERS COPE WITH ALL THIS UNCOMFORTABLE INFORMATION?

Some people living and/or working in Native communities self-medicate. Some find extended families or other sources of support; others turn to traditional Native culture and spirituality. Work in communities that have endured generations of trauma is difficult. Peacock and Miller Cleary (1998) have written extensively about teaching in Native communities that have survived the devastating impact of oppression. I talked to Agnes about how she dealt with this situation:

> Oh well, I cried every day on the way home from work. I mean, thank God I have like a 20- to 30-minute commute, because by the time I got home I was in some kind of frame of mind to deal with my family. But it's just heartbreaking. And then somehow I guess you just kind of get a little perspective of, I don't know . . . you

can't let it keep affecting you that way because it's just too exhausting. So somehow you kind of put it aside.

Throughout this research, the teachers told me that they enjoyed talking to me. These interviews created an opportunity for support and critical reflection. As a Native person and a teacher who is not a community member, I had both insider and outsider status. I was an insider in that I have also had the experience of teaching and living in Native communities; I could deeply empathize with their struggles. On the other hand, I was neither a community member nor a tribal member in the communities they were teaching in, and so I was an outsider. I had neither family connections nor influence over their jobs.

Each teacher did find a person in his or her community in whom they could confide. Each teacher created a friendship with a Native person who was a teacher at one time. That person was not a direct authority and thus could be an internal support and critic. That friend was the person who referred me to them for this study.

Teachers are busy, but these teachers saw it as part of their responsibility to take the time and initiative to create a friendship with community members. They would often turn to such friends for advice or to brainstorm ideas for lessons. If they had a conflict with a Native person, they could first ask their friend for advice on how to proceed. I believe that in doing this they displayed a sense of respect for the boundaries of local community and culture that in part comes from an awareness of their positions. Similar to their stance on not being the expert at teaching Native culture, they accepted their own outsider status when dealing with personal issues as well. Figuring out their place in the community, what is a stereotype and what is real, requires a kind of community learning that is not found during the typical school day.

Although they were both exposed to stereotypes, Agnes and Joe have worked to see Native people as they see culture—complex, changing, and full of individual variation. Both teachers were openly reflective about what they have learned and what they have had to unlearn as teachers at their respective schools. Joe, for example, grew up in a border town to the Menominee reservation in Wisconsin. He said he could have ended up either way, as an ally or as a racist. He was fortunate to witness someone close to him working with Native youth in spite of the current stereotypes. He grew up in Shawano during the time the Menominee reservation had been terminated by the government. The community members, supported by AIM,[3] had taken over a building in order to fight termination. Joe remembers,

Well, I just heard stories about how they [the Menominee] went and had gotten horses and stuff, and were eating the horses in there because there was no other way to get food.[4] And I can't remember exact stories, but I just remember that there were some pretty bad things going on there. I had dreams that Indians were taking over our community—that's how bad it was. I can remember having these dreams where I was hiding and Indians were coming. I'm sure it was from that experience on the reservation. You couldn't drive through the reservation because you heard stories of someone shooting at cars. You would pull over and people were actually killed, so you're never supposed to drive through there. On the other hand, it was my father who was the high school football coach, wrestling coach, and worked on the track. So a lot of the Native American students he knew very well, and I got to know them. I would just hang out with my father at wrestling or whatever, so I knew all these people and they certainly weren't the ones you heard about. I mean, they sure weren't the ones you were afraid of. So, luckily, I had that background. I think that helped a lot.

Joe and Agnes understand Native culture as changing, fluid, complicated, and having survived colonialism. One of their responses is to position themselves as teachers who are not cultural experts, but rather who are supporters of culture. They are constantly working out ways within their particular contexts to do this. They resist the position of teacher as an isolated expert.

Rethinking Culture-Based Education

Two important and related ideas emerge from my interpretation of this data. First, the idea of discontinuity between home and school cultures is not understood as the primary cause of educational failure as expressed by these teachers, and cultural difference alone does not inform their ideas about their students. This finding directly challenges the idea that cultural discontinuity alone can account for Native student failure. The teachers in this research bring the idea of low socioeconomic status to the forefront as they discuss how they go about meeting student needs. Second, my understanding of their narratives identifies them as allies with, not instructors of, the Native identity of their students. In the position as teacher/ally they are simultaneously in the center (as teachers) and on the margins (as White community members). They are able to inhabit this delicate position because they are aware of their own identities in relation to the context of Native American oppression. Advocating the idea of culture-based curriculum, this finding suggests that non-Native teachers acting as allies can have a supporting role to play in the development of a positive Native student identity. I believe this research provides insights into what Erickson (1987) calls

> culturally responsive pedagogy . . . one kind of special effort by the school that can reduce miscommunication by teacher and students, foster trust, and prevent the genesis of conflict that moves rapidly beyond intercultural misunderstanding to bitter struggles of negative identity exchange between some students and their teachers. (p. 355)

These interviews detail the "special effort" made by White teachers in Native schools. More than just responsive to cultural differences, they are aware of the history in which these differences are rooted. They are aware that "difference" is only defined in terms of relationship meaning; they are aware of the relationship between European and Native American. There is a place for non-Native teachers within Native culture-based schools—as allies. This kind of movement requires reflection on the part of the teachers and a willingness to look at more than superficial cultural traits. As whiteness is so often invisible to White teachers (Landsman, 2001), this type of reflection may be especially challenging. Both Agnes and Joe have found space for reflection with the careful construction of friendships within the tribal communities in which they teach. The teachers' own identities and positions as "not the expert" serves them particularly well within this context.

The implication for the teaching of preservice teachers is clear: teaching about Native cultures in a narrow sense is not in and of itself enough. For the teachers in this research, more powerful than their knowledge of cultural difference was their knowledge of the big picture—the context of socioeconomic and cultural oppression of Native Americans. Looking at the bigger picture may help teachers not to place blame on students for their failure to come to class prepared. For example, a teacher's awareness of outside pressures on students helps in not placing blame on the families. The teachers in this research repeatedly responded to such circumstances by adjusting their expectations. Furthermore, the decisions of Agnes and Joe not to position themselves as experts in terms of teaching culture were also informed by their awareness of the history of Native and White relations.

Peacock and Miller Cleary (1998) emphasize the need for a critical consciousness among teachers of Native students. In this research, the successful teachers (Agnes and Joe) were cognizant of oppression, cultural change, and their own cultural identity. Specifically for Native peoples, the socioeconomic change that has accompanied colonization has had a great effect on intergenerational cultural transmission. Policies of assimilation, termination, and removal, for example, have had a direct effect on the severe language and cultural losses that are now an everyday part of life for many Native students. Peacock and Miller Cleary point to understanding the complicated effects of oppression and internalized oppression as an essential part of good teaching for Native students:

> The effects of European colonization on the indigenous people of America and the accompanying devastation of many American Indian tribes that resulted have adversely affected the harmony and balance of generations of individuals and tribes. To make conscious decisions in solving problems, teachers and schools need to understand the roots of overt, covert, and institutional racism and historic oppression. (p. 61)

In terms of theory, our understanding of failure in Native American education should be expanded to include both the contribution of critical theorists that states structural inequality affects school performance and the suggestion by sociolinguists that inclusion of culture and cultural patterns of communication could help improve performance. The study described in this chapter dramatically points out that the notion of differences between cultures alone is an inadequate explanation for failure. Building on the work of other scholars who are trying to bridge the macro-micro debate (Ladson-Billings, 1995), effective theory in Native American education needs to include the understanding of oppression as both cultural and economic. As attested to by the teachers in this study, often our students are not afforded the luxury of such artificial categories. The understanding and the critical consciousness of teachers must not be solely preoccupied with one culture or class to the exclusion of the other.

Expanding Culture-Based Curriculum Theory and Practice

Rigidly defining cultures and carving cultural boundaries in stone have proved less than accurate in the modern world, to say the least. Yet, if culture resists essentialism, how can it become the content subject within a school? How can culture-based curriculum alone account for the devastating and traumatic socioeconomic change of the past 500 years?

The culture-based curriculum movement in Indian country is faced with these questions today. Some scholars and activists are looking toward language as a deeper signifier of culture, one that is a conduit, not an essence (Hermes, 2001). One tribal school in this area has completely redefined the idea of culture-based curriculum and will only teach the Ojibwe language, believing that transmitting culture will follow from teaching the language in a more natural way (Hermes, 2001). Other communities are working more closely with the elders and the language to understand indigenous epistemologies as embedded in the language (Lipka, 1991; Watahomigie & McCarty, 1994) and are building connections to the mainstream curriculum from that vantage point. Perhaps for indigenous people, making a cultural curriculum is more about bringing people together than it is about extracting knowledge from books (Archibald, 1990; Sheridan, 1991). How do we teach Native culture in schools? Will teaching Native culture remedy the many wounds of oppression? It is fitting that there is not one uniform response to such enormously important questions.

In challenging the theory of cultural discontinuity, I do not believe we should abandon the culture-based curriculum movement. The evidence that showed us the patterns of communication were different for Odawa children and teachers than for their mainstream counterparts fueled a popular movement to bring culture into Native American and public schools and propelled us to reexamine assumptions about teaching. Teaching Native culture in schools has brought community members into schools, created an interest in the creation of culturally based curriculum materials, and had positive effects on self-esteem (Demmert, 1994; Dick, Estell, & McCarty, 1994).

More than a narrow definition of culture must be incorporated into both the theory and the practice of Native education. Ideas of culture alone can intersect with popular and prevalent stereotypes and acts of appropriation. "Culture" brought into schools alone to remedy the complex elements of failure is often essentialized (Levinson & Holland, 1996). Culture and the history of Native American oppression together create the opportunity for critical awareness that is needed by teachers.

The teachers discussed in this research were successful because they were aware of the history, culture, and current circumstances of their students. Most important, they were aware of and comfortable with their own identity as White teachers. As outsiders and allies, they were able to find their place within the community. Beyond teaching cultural skills, they were able to support the identity and culture of their students by being aware of the complex interplay of class, culture, and identity. In articulating continuities and discontinuities, we point to layers of intersecting oppressions; in telling stories of teachers who struggle, we are moving beyond explanations for failure and moving toward an understanding of how some teachers thrive despite the odds.

Afterword

The stories of these teachers, and my analysis, make me think about identity politics as well as culture-based curriculum. By identity politics, I mean the nasty idea that some identities are more valuable than others (as if an identity is a permanent, unchanging thing). It is an internalized belief that some groups of people are better than others (e.g., Native teachers are better than White teachers in Native schools). This generalization (a variation on internalized racism) is lodged deep within my unconsciousness. It is surely how I have been most hurt by racism. I see the world in racialized terms. Sometimes this is useful, sometimes it is not useful. When a judgment is attached, it is no longer a useful analysis, but rather an artifact of racism. This way of judging—call it identity politics—seems to wrap around my consciousness in layers. Try as I might to peel the layers off, it continually resurfaces (wretched dandelions!).

I see these teachers pouring their hearts and minds into this work, and I am humbled. I say "hurray!" and remember that individuals can collectively produce social change. In fact, it must be this way. What this research has done for me is to make me notice and deeply appreciate the work of these teachers—and the hundreds (maybe thousands?) of other White teachers working across boundaries who are quietly changing the world. Next time I walk into a Native school, I won't be so quick to think, "What is *she* doing here?" Maybe instead I will think, "I wonder if that is a Joe or an Agnes?"—working late hours, worrying about students, and doing her best to understand her own place in the struggle. (There, one less dandelion to pull.)

The teachers written about here are—like the concept of culture invoked in this chapter—complex, constantly changing products of their own culture. This means they are not without internal contradictions. Their identities are not one unified and fixed object. It would be wrong to represent them as one-dimensional. These teachers offer us excellent models of teachers/allies and outsiders who act in support of Native cultures. They will also be the first to admit that they continually struggle with their own internalized stereotypes about both race and class. I do not mean to paint a picture of perfect teachers for all to aspire to. I mean to inspire all of us who struggle. For this time, I shine the light on their best words and work, and I write this afterword to acknowledge that working across differences is always a work in progress. After all, dandelions also have flowers.

Recommended Readings

This chapter brings together a number of issues relating to teaching, learning, and working across differences. The idea of culture-based education is not specific to Native Americans; other peoples in and outside the United States are challenging the forces of cultural colonization through schooling. For theoretical work on the idea of culture-based education, I recommend "But That's Just Good Teaching! The Case for Culturally Relevant Pedagogy," by Gloria Ladson-Billings (1995). In this easy-to-read chapter, Ladson-Billings outlines three criteria for "successful" culture-based education used in this study.

For students wanting to know more about Ojibwe culture, I recommend Peacock and Wisuri (2002) *Ojibwe: Waasa Inaabidaa* (We look in all directions). This book contains accurate, up-to-date accounts of Ojibwe life. It is written for a general audience in a narrative style.

To learn more about American Indian education, and the research that has been done on schooling, there are two main texts. The recent collection edited by Karen Swisher and John Tippeconnic (1999), *Next Steps: Research and Practice to Advance Indian Education,* is a vibrant collection of articles from many disciplinary perspectives on the current problems and proposed solutions in Indian education. Most of these articles touch on culture-based education in American Indian communities. Last, *Collected Wisdom: American Indian Education,* by Tom Peacock and

Linda Miller Cleary (1998), gives a bird's-eye view of American Indian education as told by teachers of American Indian students across the United States. This broad view of American Indian education is an excellent complement to this chapter, which focuses narrowly on one people and one place. The words of the teachers in this book echo the concern for understanding a multitude of socioeconomic problems that are voiced by the two teachers in this chapter.

Reflective Questions

1. How will you balance challenging or motivating students in school with the knowledge that they may be struggling outside of school? How will you find the balance between being demanding and yet understanding of personal circumstances?
2. All students struggle with identity. What will you do in your classroom to support student identities, while not privileging any one identity? Will you intervene if you see students setting up an identity pecking order?
3. Consider the way the teachers in this chapter used theory and story. How are both of these analytical tools useful and practical?

Notes

1. All personal names are pseudonyms.
2. "Nanabooshu" is the traditional trickster who appears throughout Ojibwe country and is held as sacred within the oral tradition. My understanding of the Ojibwe oral tradition is that stories involving this character should not be written down, nor should they be told outside of winter time.
3. AIM is the acronym for the American Indian Movement.
4. This is a reference to the time on the Menominee reservation when AIM members occupied a church abbey in protest of the federal government terminating the tribal status of the Menominee nation.

References

Archibald, J. (1990). Coyote's story about orality and literacy. *Canadian Journal of Indian Education, 17*(2), 66–81.

Au, K., & Jordan, C. (1981). Teaching and reading to Hawaiian children: Finding a culturally appropriate solution. In H. Trueba, G. P. Guthrei, & K. H. Au (Eds.), *Culture in the bi-lingual classroom* (pp. 139–152). Rowley, MA: Newbury House.

Britzman, D. (1991). *Practice makes practice: A critical study of learning to teach.* Albany: SUNY Press.

Connelly, M., & Clandinin, J. (1990). Stories of experience and narrative inquiry. *Educational Researcher, 19*(5), 2–14.

Crazybull, C. (1997). A Native conversation about research and scholarship. *Tribal College Journal, 9*, 17–23.

Demmert, W. (1994). *Blueprints for Indian education: Languages and cultures* (ERIC Document Reproduction Service No. RR93002012). Charleston, WV: Appalachia Educational Laboratory.

Deyhle, D. (1995). Navajo youth and Anglo racism: Cultural integrity and resistance. *Harvard Educational Review, 65*(3), 403–444.

Deyhle, D., & Swisher, K. (1997). Research in American Indian and Alaska Native education: From assimilation to self-determination. In M. W. Apple (Ed.), *Review of research in education* (pp. 113–194). Washington, DC: American Educational Research Association.

Dick, G. S., Estell, D., & McCarty, T. L. (1994). Saad Naakih Bee'enootiji Na'alkaa: Restructuring the teaching of language and literacy in a Navajo community school. *Journal of American Indian Education, 33*(3), 31–46.

Dumont, R. (1972). Learning English and how to be silent: Studies in Sioux and Cherokee classrooms. In C. Cazden, V. John, & D. Hymes (Eds.), *Functions of language in the classroom* (pp. 344–369). New York: Teachers College Press.

Erickson, F. (1986). Qualitative methods on research on teaching. In M. Wittrock (Ed.), *Handbook of research on teaching* (pp. 119–161). New York: Macmillan.

Erickson, F. (1987). Transformation and school success: The politics and culture of educational achievement. *Anthropology and Education Quarterly, 18*, 335–356.

Erickson, F., & Mohatt, G. (1982). Cultural organization of structures in two classrooms of Indian students. In G. Spindler (Ed.), *Doing the ethnography of schooling* (pp. 132–174). New York: Holt, Rinehart & Winston.

Foley, D. (1991). Reconsidering anthropological explanations of ethnic school failure. *Anthropology and Education Quarterly, 22*, 60–85.

Greenbaum, P., & Greenbaum, S. (1983). Cultural differences, nonverbal regulation and classroom interaction: Sociolinguistic interference in American Indian education. *Peabody Journal of Education, 61*, 16–33.

Henze, R., & Vanett, L. (1993). To walk in two worlds—or more? Challenging a common metaphor of Native education. *Anthropology and Education Quarterly, 24*, 116–134.

Hermes, M. (1995). *Making culture, making curriculum: Teaching through meanings and identities at an American Indian tribal school.* Unpublished doctoral dissertation, University of Wisconsin, Madison.

Hermes, M. (1998). Research methods as a situated response: Towards a First Nations' methodology. *International Journal of Qualitative Studies in Education, 11*(1), 155–168.

Hermes, M. (2001, April). *"Ma'iingan* is just a mis-spelling of the word *wolf"*: Inserting Ojibwe culture into tribal schools. Paper presented at AERA 2000, Seattle, WA.

Ladson-Billings, G. (1995). But that's just good teaching! The case for culturally relevant pedagogy. *Theory Into Practice: Culturally Relevant Teaching, 34*(3), 159–165.

Landsman, J. (2001). *A white teacher talks about race.* Lanham, MD: Scarecrow Press.

Levinson, B., & Holland, D. (1996). The cultural production of the educated person: An introduction. In B. Levinson, D. Foley, & D. Holland (Eds.), *The cultural production of the educated person: Critical ethnographies of schooling and local practice* (pp. 1–54). Albany: SUNY Press.

Lipka, J. (1991). Toward a culturally based pedagogy: A case study of one Yup'ik Eskimo teacher. *Anthropology and Education Quarterly, 22,* 203–223.

Lipka, J. (1994). Language, power, and pedagogy: Whose school is it? *Peabody Journal of Education, 69,* 71–93.

Lomawaima, K. (1995). Educating Native Americans. In J. Banks & C. McGee Banks (Eds.), *Handbook of research on multicultural education* (pp. 331–342). New York: Macmillan.

McCarty, T. (1989). School as community: The Rough Rock demonstration. *Harvard Educational Review, 59,* 484–503.

Mohatt, G., & Erickson, F. (1981). Cultural differences in teaching styles in an Odawa school: A sociolinguistic approach. In H. Trueba, G. Guthrie, & K. Au (Eds.), *Culture and the bilingual classroom* (pp. 105–119). Rowley, MA: Newbury House.

Ogbu, J. (1978). *Minority education and caste: The American system in cross-cultural perspective.* New York: Academic Press.

Peacock, T., & Miller Cleary, L. (1997, fall). Disseminating American Indian educational research through stories: A case against academic discourse. *Journal of American Indian Education,* 7–15.

Peacock, T., & Miller Cleary, L. (1998). *Collected wisdom.* Boston: Allyn & Bacon.

Peacock, T., & Wisuri, M. (2002). *Ojibwe: Waasa inaabidaa (We look in all directions).* Afton, MN: Afton Historical Society Press.

Phillips, S. (1983). Participant structures and communicative competence: Warm Springs children in community and classrooms. In C. Cazden, V. John, & D. Hymes (Eds.), *Functions of language in the classroom* (pp. 370–394). New York: Teachers College Press.

Sheridan, J. (1991). The silence before drowning in alphabet soup. *Canadian Journal of Native Education, 18*(1), 23–33.

St. Germaine, R. (1995). Drop-out rates among American Indian and Alaska Native students: Beyond cultural discontinuity (ERIC Document Reproduction Service No. RR 93002012). Charleston, WV: Appalachia Educational Laboratory.

Swisher, K., & Tippeconnic, J. (Eds.). (1999). *Next steps: Research and practice to advance Indian education.* Charleston, WV: Appalachia Educational Laboratory.

Trueba, H. (1991). Comments on Foley's "Reconsidering anthropological explanations." *Anthropology and Education Quarterly, 22*(1), 87–94.

Watahomigie, J., & McCarty, T. L. (1994). Bilingual/bicultural education at Peach Springs: A Hualapai way of schooling. *Peabody Journal of Education, 69,* 26–42.

7

Journey Toward Social Justice

Curriculum Change and Educational Equity in a Navajo Community

Donna Deyhle

Autobiographical Introduction

I grew up in a military family. My father, originally from Ohio, was a pilot in the air force, and my mother left her home in rural Alabama for the first time to travel the world with my dad, my brother, and me. I often say, as a military dependent, I lived here, there, everywhere, and nowhere for long. Over the course of my years in school I lived in New York, Alaska, Colorado, Texas, New Mexico, England, France, and Germany. These travels opened windows to diverse lifestyles, cultures, and landscapes, resulting in experiences that have had a profound effect on my life and fueled my interest in anthropology and education.

I have focused my scholarly research on schooling as an institutional setting in which diverse cultures interact—and power relations are played out. As a high school teacher in Brazil, I worked with the Karaja Indians in Brazil in the development of a culturally specific curriculum and a native teaching

AUTHOR'S NOTE: Over the past twenty years my research has been supported by the University of Utah, the Spencer Foundation, and the Navajo Nation. I thank them for their support. I would also like to thank Audrey Thompson for her insightful and delightful comments on this chapter. And, finally, I would like to thank all the gracious Navajo people who have supported my work and spent endless hours contributing to my education.

training program for their community. In New York, I taught low-income students, who left school more frequently than they graduated, and adults that continued their education after high school. In New Mexico, I taught native student teachers from Acoma, San Felipe, Laguna Pueblos, and the Navajo Nation. And over the past twenty years, I have been working among a Navajo community in Utah with the schooling of their children.

In the fall of 1983 I traveled to this district in southern Utah to start a study of Navajo and Ute high school youth, their families, and the surrounding communities. As a newly hired Assistant Professor of Anthropology and Education and Multicultural Education at the University of Utah, my aim was to "discover" the causes of school conflicts that lead youth to leave school and use this information to enhance the training of teachers. Trained as an anthropologist, I was prepared to learn about cultural differences between American Indians and Whites and apply this knowledge in school reform efforts. These academic efforts became enfolded in the court case that is the focus of my chapter.

My early research was framed by a "cultural difference" perspective, which argued that much of the conflict and failure experienced by Navajo youth was due to cultural differences between the home and the school. This argument is evident in articles published on testing in *Curriculum Inquiry, The Journal of Educational Equity and Leadership,* and *The Peabody Journal of Education,* on culture and child development in *Theory into Practice,* on parent involvement in the *International Journal of Qualitative Research in Education,* break-dancers in the *Anthropology & Education Quarterly,* and dropouts in the *Journal of Navajo Education.*

My current research examines how power and racial relations contribute to the academic struggles of Navajo youth. Examples of this research appear on cultural integrity and racism in the *Harvard Educational Review,* on Navajo mothers and daughters in the *Anthropology & Education Quarterly,* on break dancing and heavy metal in *Youth & Society,* on cultural identity and dropouts in the *Journal of American Indian Education,* and in a review of the field of American Indian Education in the American Educational Research Association (AERA) *Review of Research in Education.* As I write these words I am continuing to work on a book about three Navajo women, whom I met in 1984, and their families' life experiences as daughters, mothers, and wives during the past two decades.

"Trust Us. We Are Now Sincere."

In May 1993, the newly appointed district director of bilingual education attended a parent meeting at an elementary school whose population was

100 percent Navajo. More than thirty Navajo parents and their children attended. The director, an experienced educator who did not speak Navajo, stood and spoke to the group. "We want to do what your kids need. So we are going to develop a bilingual program. So your kids can learn better in their classes. We think it will help." Parents expressed disbelief. "But you were supposed to be doing that when I was in school," one said. "And you still aren't. How do we know you will use Navajo to teach our kids?" Another agreed, "You were sup- posed to be doing that bilingual education because of the court case. But it still isn't going on." Visibly uncomfortable, the director nodded his head in agreement. "Yes. I know it wasn't done. But we are going to do it now. Trust us. We are now sincere." These Navajo parents had reasons to question the sincerity of the district efforts to educate their children. They had heard the same refrain of "trust us" almost twenty years before when *they* were students in this school.

In 1976, San Juan school district came to an out-of-court agreement in a case filed by Navajo parents. The district was required to build two high schools on the Navajo reservation and develop a bilingual and bicultural pro- gram for all grades. Within eight years the high schools were built. The bilin- gual and bicultural program sat unused, gathering dust in the district's materials center for fifteen years. In 1991, the district was found to be still out of compliance with federal English-as-a-Second-Language (ESL) requirements by the U.S. Department of Education's Office for Civil Rights.[1] After three years of unacceptable bilingual plans from the district, Attorney General Janet Reno authorized the Justice Department to intervene in this case as a party-plaintiff. The Navajo Nation also joined the lawsuit. Based on a preliminary investiga- tion, the Justice Department decided that the school district had discriminated against American Indian students, violating federal law and the Fourteenth Amendment, by failing to adopt and implement an alternative language pro- gram for limited-English-proficiency students. The district was accused of denying American Indian students the same educational opportunities and services provided to Anglo students, such as equal access to certain academic programs, as well as denying qualified American Indian persons employment opportunities equal to those provided to Anglos. This case represented only the second case regarding American Indians and education that the educational litigation department in the Justice Department had intervened in during the previous twenty-five years.

I present a narrative of this "battle" through the lens of this court case. Over the past twenty years, Navajo parents have continued to fight for educa- tional equity, and the White community and school district have consistently resisted a vision of local multiculturalism that would include Navajo language and culture. I start with a snapshot of the ethnohistorical and contemporary context of the Navajo and White communities.[2]

Whites and Navajos: Shared But Uncommon Landscapes

According to tradition, Navajos have lived in their current location since the 1500s. The Navajo Nation today covers more than 16 million acres in four different states. Although Navajos today might not match the textbook image of "traditional Navajos," there are hundreds of ways of "being Navajo": they remain a culturally and socially distinct group of people, and the persistence of their culture creates distinctions between Navajos and their White neighbors. Unlike Navajos from other parts of the reservation, who were removed to a prison camp by Kit Carson in 1868 during the "Long Walk," the Navajos here have never left their homeland. The White population in this country arrived in the 1880s as pioneers from the Church of Jesus Christ of Latter-day Saints (LDS), or as they are commonly called, Mormons. Sent by Brigham Young, the 236 settlers were to start a colonizing mission among Navajo and Ute people and to increase the land base and religious influence of the LDS church throughout the region.[3]

Over the past 125 years, the White population, predominantly LDS, has expanded and prospered. The Navajo and Ute populations have also expanded, today making up 52 percent of the county's almost 13,000 population, but they remain poor, with marginal public voices compared to the White population. Today, nearly 90 percent of those in the county on public assistance are either Navajos or Utes. The unemployment rate of Navajos and Utes is almost 40 percent, compared to 5.8 percent for the entire state population. The percentage of residents below the poverty level in the state of Utah is 11.4 percent; this rises to 36.4 percent in San Juan County.[4] Only 1 percent of homes in Utah lack indoor plumbing; this rises to 28.8 percent in San Juan County and 54.8 percent in the Navajo Nation.[5] In Utah, 85 percent of adults have a high school diploma; this drops to 60 percent in the county, and 36 percent in the Navajo Nation.[6] Statewide 65 percent of adults have post–high school education, whereas only 37 percent of adults in the county and 21 percent of adults in the Navajo Nation have post–high school education.[7] These disparities paint a stark picture of inequality between Navajos and Whites in the economic, social, educational, and political spheres in the county.

This county is one where families stay together. In the United States nearly 10 percent of residents live alone; this figure drops to 4.2 percent in San Juan County.[8] White, predominately LDS families are enveloped in community activities surrounding their church. Navajo families, living mostly on the Utah strip of the Navajo Nation, also surround themselves with family and kin. Navajo traditional religious practices, the Native American Church, and activities in various denominational churches also envelop Navajo families' lives.

I was not surprised that so little connection exists between Navajo and White communities, for only frail surface threads bind the two together: those touched as people pass through public institutions such as schools, banks, businesses, and restaurants. A deeper fabric of the community is composed of one's social connections with family and kin. Most Navajos and Whites do not socialize as friends; as a consequence, the shared practices and beliefs for each group remain fundamentally different. Cultural differences, miscommunication, and racist treatment all combined to make Navajo parents and students feel profoundly alienated from schools. But these people have not been passive in their response to their situation, as the lawsuit illustrates.

The 1974 Lawsuit: Navajo Parents Versus the Board of Education

On behalf of forty-eight individual Navajos, Jimmy Sinajini filed a lawsuit against San Juan School District in the United States District Court in 1974. In terms of geographic area, San Juan is the largest school district in the United States; the district occupies 7,884 square miles. The southern one-third of the district is part of the Navajo Nation. According to the 1970 census, the county had a population of 9,600. Approximately one-half of the population was Navajo, and almost all of the Navajos in the county resided on the reservation. In spite of the larger Navajo population in the southern portion of the district, the only two high schools in the district were located in the northern portion of the district. Although several other issues were involved in the complaint (including the district's failure to provide a legally sufficient bilingual program for Navajos), the most important issue in the case revolved around the long distances Navajo children had to travel to attend high school. The two longest bus routes were instructive. In one, Navajo students were bussed up to 166 miles round-trip each day. In the other, Navajo students were bussed for up to 112 miles round-trip each day. The 220 Navajo high school students who were bussed by the district rode on the bus an average of 86 miles each day of the school year. The average Navajo student traveled four times as far to school as did the average non-Indian student. Each year, on average, Navajo students traveled more than 15,000 miles, spending the equivalent of 120 school days physically sitting on a bus just to attend school. For the students at the end of the longest bus routes, the figures rose to 30,000 miles each year and 240 school days on a bus. These miles for the most part were on rutted, eroded, unpaved roads that frequently washed out during rains. The complaint in this lawsuit was based on the premise that the failure to construct high schools in the Navajo portion of the district denied Navajo children an equal educational opportunity and constituted illegal racial discrimination.

Attached to the out-of-court settlement requiring the district to build two high schools on the Navajo reservation was a bilingual-bicultural and cultural awareness program. By 1978, the district agreed to have a bilingual-bicultural program, utilizing both Navajo and English, operating in Grades K–6 in elementary schools Navajo students attended. A cultural awareness plan was to be developed and used for all students, White and Navajo, in the district. In theory, this was to be a research-based two-way bilingual plan. But in practice it became a transitional Navajo-to-English program. On paper the language and cultural programs were excellent. In practice they were nonexistent.

"Are You Friend or Foe?"
The Bilingual-Bicultural Program

In October 1984 I had been living for several months in the district, starting an ethnographic study of Navajo youth and schooling. After interviewing the superintendent, I was told, "Go talk to the director of the Curriculum Materials Center. He can tell you about our bilingual program." Arriving at his office I was invited in and asked, "Are you friend or foe?" He laughed at my stunned silence and continued, "I always ask, because it's not popular here. I am only one of two in the district that is supportive of the bilingual program. None of the principals are in support of bilingual education. One elementary school has one, but it is just total immersion in English. Navajo will be used as a last resort, but it is not stressed or taught." He reached behind his desk and pulled a packet off the bookcase and handed it to me. "Here is a copy of the plan we developed after the court case. Look at it carefully. It says that we will provide cultural awareness for all students, that means the Whites too. But that never happened. Their parents would never let it happen." He sighed and shook his head as he continued, "People here don't understand bilingual programs. They think, 'I can learn a foreign language. If the Navajos can't learn English they must be dumb.' They don't understand that when we teach a foreign language in school we provide instruction about the language in English, but they don't seem to make the transfer to the Navajo situation here."

Copies of the court-approved bilingual plan were printed in his office and sent to all of the teachers. "There was money for bilingual then, but because we have a decentralized district, principals can do what they want, and the money was used for other purposes they felt was important. And when we had cutbacks, the Navajo aides were the first to go. We lost all but at the lower primary K–3." He took me on a tour of the curriculum center, specifically focusing on the Navajo materials he and his staff had developed. "We have nine films, like 'Coyote and Rabbit,' 'Coyote and Skunk,' 'Coyote Learns Subtraction.' The young kids love them. But the teachers don't use them much. And here is our section on guides, manuals, and textbooks. We developed fifteen on cultural awareness for our teachers. And over here we have thirty-five Navajo experience booklets with cassettes in English and Navajo. We have over fifty other filmstrips and instructional kits and packets in both Navajo and English. But our teachers don't use them." When we returned to his office he showed me a set of order forms. "Look. We have larger orders for our materials from New Mexico, Arizona, even Colorado. Schools with Navajo students love our materials. But our teachers here don't use them. They think it is not worth the effort. And that the kids need to be learning English. Isn't that ironic? This stuff is supposed to help them learn English." I left his office with a copy of the bilingual program. I was excited about the materials. I was depressed to hear they were not used in the district.

Over the next several years I asked the teachers in the district, who were overwhelmingly White, about the bilingual plan they were required to use. Responses ranged from surprise to disbelief. None of the teachers remembered seeing the district's bilingual plan. Over the next ten years of my fieldwork I saw no uniform bilingual-bicultural program in existence in the district. On an individual basis, some teachers did attempt to integrate Navajo words and cultural information in their elementary classrooms. In some classes, an alphabet lining a classroom wall used Navajo words for the letters. Navajo clan names were printed neatly on the side of a chalkboard in several classrooms. Occasionally, Navajo elders would visit classrooms. On a school level, yearly "cultural days" included Navajo songs and dances, Navajo food, and speeches from Navajo educators and politicians. In the high schools, the inclusion of Navajo culture and language were rare. Walking through the halls and classrooms at night gave no clues that in the morning the schools would be filled with young Navajo students.

On the district level, little was done to implement the bilingual-bicultural program. In 1984, the superintendent explained that although he was concerned about equal educational opportunities for Navajo students, "there is no real bilingual program in place now. The use of a model that uses native language first is not enforced here in the district. We had problems with this program. There were not enough Navajo-speaking teachers, and later cutbacks led to reducing Navajo teacher aides. We have new efforts to get at the heart of the curriculum to develop a literary model." Expressing concerns that the district was not addressing bilingual needs, he asserted that the principals were not in favor of bilingual education and that it was out of his control. "We have a decentralized district here, principals have total control over their schools. It's like ten districts." He explained that the lawsuit was the reason for the existence of a formalized bilingual plan—a direction he seemed to question. "The main question is not answered. It's 'What affects the Navajo student to become involved in the English curriculum?' There is not interest in their involvement with Navajo language. We need to bring kids up to grade level to avoid any future court cases, then we will have done our job," he explained. He left the superintendent position the following year.

Renewed Resistance: Navajo Parents Reopen the Court Case

In 1990, Navajo parents, frustrated with the high dropout rate and low achievement rate of their children, and claiming the district was not in compliance with the consent decree, filed to reopen the 1974 court case. They firmly believed the district "had not done their job." At the same time the Director of the Utah Division of Indian Affairs (UDIA) and the U.S. Office for Civil Rights of the U.S. Department of Education (OCR) were informed of the lack of a bilingual-bicultural program in the district.

Within a year, the OCR conducted a compliance review of the educational program and services provided by the district for limited-English-proficiency (LEP) students. OCR found that the district did not have effective procedures in place to identify and assess LEP students and that the district was not implementing an effective program for LEP students to ensure each had an opportunity to learn English and to participate effectively in the district's educational program. OCR concluded that the district was in violation of Title VI of the Civil Rights Act of 1964 and its implementing regulations with regard to the issue of providing LEP students with meaningful access to the district's educational program.

At the same time the district submitted the plan to OCR, it was distributed to all principals. In that document was a list of the barriers to Navajo students' academic success.[9] All reasons for school failure pointed in the direction of the Navajo community. It was perceived that Navajo youth lacked self-esteem and came from inadequate homes with families that lacked parenting skills. They were viewed as having limited cultural enrichment opportunities and limited basic vocabulary and language development. Fetal alcohol syndrome, poor attitude and motivation, and poor attendance were central barriers. Only two out of fifteen barriers pointed in the direction of the school system—"questionable teacher support" and "curriculum not relevant." The blame had shifted from lack of school language programs to meet the instructional needs of the Navajo students to the students themselves and their families.

The OCR again rejected the district's plan and turned the case over to the U.S. Justice Department. After an investigation, the U.S. Justice Department and the Navajo Nation entered into the Sinajini lawsuit as party plaintiffs against the San Juan school district. In 1993, I filed an affidavit for the plaintiffs based on my ten years of research. In the following section, the academic record of Navajo youth, from the beginning of the court case in 1974 to the early 1990s, almost twenty-five years, was detailed in this affidavit. My data clearly showed that "the district had not done their job."

Navajo Student Achievement and School Leavers: A Job Undone

In 1984, I began a dropout study of Navajo and Ute students from San Juan school district. The district provided me with full access to all relevant records. I tracked six cohorts of students from two high schools from the ninth grade to their graduation or leaving school. Ten years of school records, a database of 1,489 youth, 168 questionnaires of dropouts, observations in more than 300 high school classes, more than 100 formal interviews, and 200 informal interviews with school administrators, teachers, parents, and students created a complex database to assess Navajo and Ute school achievement.[10]

The figures from the U.S. Department of Education in 1986 showed an average attrition rate (data that show the proportion of a given entering high school class that does not graduate four years later) in the state of Utah for the class of 1984 to be 21 percent. The dropout rate of American Indian students was almost double the state average. The graduate rate of 59 percent is lowered to 49 percent when reporting only students who graduate on time in the traditional high school program. Almost half of the school leavers felt their teachers did not care about them or did not help them with schoolwork. Home difficulties were also mentioned by more than half of these youth. These numbers painted a dismal picture; at the same time, the combined figures glossed over patterns determined by examining the academic records of these youth year by year and school by school. Almost 20 percent of these youth were physically in school for twelve years and still did not graduate. Over half, 55 percent, of the youth that dropped out did so during the twelfth grade. Persistence on the part of the students was not the problem. The students from Whitehorse High School, with a 99 percent Navajo student population, were more successful at completing school than their peers at the racially mixed (50/50) San Juan High School. These statistics raise questions that challenge the assimilatory assumptions behind the belief that Navajo youth are hindered in school because of their Navajo language and culture. Quite the opposite— the Navajo youth who are living in their homes in the Navajo Nation, firmly rooted in their Navajo community, are more successful in completing school than their peers in town who have a more strained and distant connection to their language and cultural foundations. This was not the message the district wanted to see in my data. I gave my database to a principal who, in trying to refute the results of my study before he left the district, found a slightly higher dropout rate in his own study. Racial relations and conflicts, however, appeared strongly in both our findings. Navajo youth responded differently to the racial treatment they experienced. Many left school. Others faded into the background of their classroom. All, however, spoke of the burden of racial discrimination in their day-to-day lives in schools. This racially charged context was at the foundation of the lawsuit.

Surveillance by the U.S. Justice Department: The Curriculum Committee

In late August 1997, I drove to the district offices for the first meeting of the court-appointed curriculum committee. The previous April, the U.S. Justice Department, the Navajo Nation, Sinajini et al., and the San Juan School Board again came to a court-approved plan. In a unique agreement that combined three different lawsuits against the school district, four committees—bilingual education, curriculum, finance, and special education—were formed to develop new school district instructional plans. Each committee consists of three school-appointed and three Navajo Nation and Justice Department educational experts. One of the issues the district was accused of was denying American Indian students the same educational opportunities and services, such as equal access to certain academic programs, provided to Anglo students. My research had been used in the court case, and I was appointed by the Navajo Nation to serve on the curriculum committee.

As I drove the 350 miles to meet the other members of the committee, I thought of what little improvement in educational achievement had occurred since the case against the district was initiated in 1974. As measured on the California Test of Basic Skills (CTBS), Indian students at the eighth-grade level made little gain in a decade from 1977, when the average was a 5.0 grade-level equivalent, to 1987, when the average was 5.6. In 1990 and 1991, eleventh graders at Whitehorse High School scored in the 15th percentile in reading. With a change to the Stanford Achievement Test (SAT) in 1997, achievement scores were still dramatically low. In 1997, eleventh graders designated FEP (fully-English-proficient) averaged the 23rd percentile in reading, while their PEP (potentially-English-proficient) peers scored in the 9th percentile. From 1984 to 1990, Whitehorse High School graduated only 63 percent of its Indian students, and San Juan High School graduated less than half of its Indian students. In a 1992 "report card" sent to all post office box holders in the county, the district reported that the dropout rate for non-Anglo students was four times higher than for Anglo students. The district also reported that the dropout rate had increased from 1989 to 1991. The average Indian graduate was reading at only the seventh-grade level. Most of the dropouts were at least six grade levels behind the national average. From 1977 to the present, Navajo students show little real gains in academic abilities. In September 1997, the Utah Taxpayers Association rated the district as the worst in the state based on school testing results. The district got an F+ for its 1996 SAT scores, a C for its 1995–1996 test improvement, an F+ for its test scores with a poverty index, a D- for a 1996 final grade, and a cumulative grade covering the previous five years of a D+. Some school district personnel blame this dismal record on Indian students and their families. One White woman bitterly explained,

> It's so cultural! As soon as one of them bobs above the water a bit they pull him back down. It's innate! It's so destructive. They [Navajo families] pull everyone down if one tries to succeed. Some people give me that line, "They walk in beauty stuff"— it is certainly a good part of the traditional stories and culture—but this other is so negative. They are such a negative people. They make sure most don't succeed.

Navajo families blame low academic achievement in part on racism and inadequate schooling. A Navajo student's description of her experiences in high school illustrates what this felt like:

> The teachers really don't listen to the Indians much. Like an Indian would raise up their hands. These White teachers don't want to take the time to work with Indians. Then they just look at them and they ignore their hands and stuff like that. But when a White person, a White student raises up their hand, they'll go to them first. So, it's like Whites, they get first served and then the Indians last. . . . Probably because they want the Indians to be dumb. . . . They probably think that the Navajos don't know much. That they don't really care to go to school.

In many ways, these different perceptions and experiences were at the heart of the lawsuits against the district. These issues were on our minds during our first meeting.

The six of us chosen as the curriculum committee sat across from each other in a conference room in the district's main office. One retired superintendent, an assistant superintendent, and the district's assistant superintendent represented the school district; a thirty-year educational expert for the Justice Department, a bilingual expert from the Navajo Nation, and I represented the Navajo plaintiffs. The district assistant superintendent opened the meeting.

The 1997 agreement of parties listed the following outcomes as mandatory:

> The district agrees to continue to incorporate a Native American cultural awareness component into its curriculum and to formulate a more formal cultural awareness plan. The district shall make educational programs available so that all students are offered an equal educational opportunity and shall use its best efforts to provide equal access to educational services and courses that are substantially similar.

An examination of the district's four high schools' course offerings was the first action item of the meeting. The Justice Department expert provided handouts for the committee. "I took all of the courses in each school and compared the offerings. I was really shocked. I haven't seen anything so bad since the 60s in the South." Bodies stiffened across the table. The committee silently read the charts. Of the district's twenty-one offerings in social studies, only three were offered at Whitehorse High School—U.S. History, World Geography, and U.S. Economics. Of the thirty-two different kinds of English/Reading courses offered in the district, only the basic Language Arts 7, 8, 9, 10, and 11 appeared in the list of possible course choices for students at Whitehorse High School, along with eleven different sections of Basic Reading. Math 7 and 8 and General Math Review were offered in ten different classes, and only two classes were offered in any higher math course—a combined Algebra/Geometry class. These Navajo students did not have the opportunity given to students at the other district high schools to take Algebra I, Algebra II, Calculus, or Trigonometry. Earth Systems, Physics, and Chemistry were also missing from the schedule. Sixteen different teacher instructional hours were filled with special education courses. High-achieving students from this school could not gain admission to the University of Utah, even with a diploma, due to lack of math and science courses. When we had had time to peruse the handout, the educational expert spoke again, "Any high school that has to have eleven reading courses tells me the schools are simply not doing their job. I have never seen anything as bad as this." In a nervous and defensive stance, the assistant superintendent quickly asserted, "The district recognizes the problem. We are devoting our efforts this year at reading for all the Navajo schools."

Over the next year and a half the committee worked toward a districtwide curriculum plan. Although not seamless, both sides worked in the spirit of changing the educational experience of Indian youth in the district. In January 1999, the school district, the Navajo Nation, and U.S. Justice Department approved the curriculum and heritage language plans. Our committee was charged with overseeing the implementation of these plans for three years or until both sides agreed the district was in compliance with the court agreement. Our hope on both sides was to see academic improvement among the Navajo students.

Curriculum Committee
Evaluation Meeting, November 1999

My colleague and I left Bluff shortly after sunrise to drive through Monument Valley for the first formal evaluation of the school district's reform efforts. For forty-six miles the two-lane road undulated up and down and across the red sandstone landscape. The road seemed small and out of place as we drove between the monoliths scattered along the side of the road. We climbed up a small pass and descended into the shimmering red valley. The high school sat alone, surrounded by stunning mesas, monoliths, and buttresses. A lime-green playing field established an artificial boundary between the Navajo Nation and the school district.

We gathered in the faculty room just before first period for coffee, juice, and doughnuts. Most of us had been with the committee from the start. The directors of secondary education, elementary education, and special programs now represented the district. The tensions of earlier years were subdued, although we were cognizant that we represented different constituents. We were all educators committed to making a difference, and we knew each other.

We reviewed our evaluation sheets. "We have streamlined the observation forms. Teachers have been confused and want to know what we are looking for," explained the director of special programs. The principal, who had shared the forms with her teachers added, "My teachers have seen the form and agree, good teachers should be doing this." We focused on four areas. First, we wanted teachers to have daily, unit, and yearly lesson plans with assessable behavioral objectives of what was to be taught. Simply, we felt teachers should know what they were going to teach when they stood in front of a class. Second, we wanted teachers to be able to identify the students most in need, the limited English speakers, and show how the teachers were addressing their needs. Basically, the youth most at risk should not be ignored, even if they are sitting quietly in their seats. Third, we wanted teachers to have a plan that promoted cognitive and academic interaction, rather than simple nonverbal seatwork. And fourth, in Navajo classes, we wanted teachers to teach in the Navajo language, using English only in a limited way. In reviewing our "vision," everyone agreed that we were asking for what any outsider would consider "good instruction."

We divided up to observe specific classes. I went to Algebra I. When I entered the classroom, students were working alone at long rows of desks facing the front of the classroom. The teacher was working at his desk computer. Two problems were written on the board as examples of the steps the students were expected to follow to solve the problems. The topic for the day was rational numbers. I sat in the back of the classroom, apparently unseen by the teacher. After fifteen minutes, a student asked the teacher a question. The teacher moved to the board to work out the problem and quickly moved back to his desk. There was a general feel of a traditional math class—math problems on the board, students working individually and quietly on problems in their text. One Navajo boy worked with a White girl on several of the problems. The two Navajo girls in front of me filed their nails, talking and reading *Scholastic Magazine*. The teacher remained seated at his desk for the next twenty minutes.

Almost forty minutes into the class he noticed the Navajo girls' lack of attention to the math problems and an absence of calculators. Moving over to them he said, "Now you know you are supposed to have calculators. Move up front to share with the other students. Get your books together and move up to someone with a calculator." He returned to his desk. The girls stood up but did not move. Several minutes passed, and the bell rang. As I left the room he came over. "I didn't see you in here. I don't have my lesson plans. I left them at home. But I could go get them for you." I told him not to bother. "The next time I visit I will look at your lesson plans for the year." He didn't smile as he shook my hand.

Moving to an English Enrichment class, I was joined by two of the district administrators. On the shelves surrounding the room were stacks of student folders from the last several years. Student manuals and reading texts filled several bookcases. The writing on the front board read, "Things to do today— Review KWLS, Work on Bib/Note Cards, Record research reading in logs." All available wall space was filled with posters of American Indians, Navajo stories, and pictures of Monument Valley. Next to the door was a large poster of Navajo values, "The Beauty Way of Living and Learning." A smiling, confident face of a young Navajo woman claimed your attention. There were seven students in the room, three of whom were resting their heads on the large center table. They didn't bother to look up when we entered the room. Cheerfully, the teacher hurried over to explain the day's activities. She had been the ESL teacher since 1984. She fumbled in her blouse pocket to find a bathroom pass for a student. "They are working on their level. Each of them has a portfolio. They do research and things and then record their findings in their log. And then they take a test on the computers to see if they can move to the next level." She walked us over to the computers in the center of the next room. "Only eight of the twenty-two computers in this ESL lab are working. But we are working on this." Back in the class she moved from student to student, bent over them, and quietly asked if they needed assistance. Most shook their heads. Few were working on their assignment. If they remained quiet, she moved to the next student. I looked at their papers. I could not describe this as an enrichment class. Short worksheets did little to promote critical thinking or reflective thought: boring lessons, bored students. At the end of the evaluation, all of us agreed that this class, or type of class, was failing students; it was not the other way around. And we had begun with high hopes; we left this class feeling disturbed.

Right before lunch I decided to attend a Biology class. The lesson was on "living parameters," specifically the pH level of solutions. With a graphic organizer on the board the teacher explained H_2O, acids, and bases. Energetically but quietly, he moved throughout the class. In an evenly divided class, the Navajo and White students sat side by side in teacher-assigned seats. Students were attentive as he wove around the classroom. An observer could see youth reaching out to correct a chemical equation on their neighbor's lecture notes or hear soft verbal corrections to each other's notes. The air felt comfortable and pleasant. Prearranged partners for lab experiments ensured face-to-face inter-actions. During this day there was much laughter and task-engaged behavior. I walked through the classroom during the experiment asking about the class. One Navajo student explained, "It's a fine class. We get along. And he makes this biology real interesting. He teaches us." His White partner grabbed his pencil, "He gives me all the answers!" They both laughed. It was an excellent, well-prepared class that engaged both White and Indian students. I saw engagement in a science lesson that on the surface might be seen as "not con-nected to Navajo lives," but there was excellent instruction, nevertheless. I went to lunch with hope renewed.

The hope soon faded. It was a disappointing afternoon. After lunch, a district administrator and I attended an eighth-grade U.S. History class. When we entered, the teacher, who was an American Indian, was sitting on a stool in front of the classroom reading a newspaper. Half of the students had their heads down on their desks. The others were quietly reading. No lesson plans were in sight. Seeing us, he turned to the class, "Listen here, in the paper it says, 'Indians urged to support census.' This means you guys should all get counted." A few students moaned. "OK, let's start." He folded the paper and moved to the front chalkboard. He had written, "Veterans Day: What it's about. Remembrances and Respect." He asked the class, "What is November 11? At 11:00?" No one answered. He persisted, "What's this date?" Several of the students yelled out, "Cool!" or "Style!" The teacher sighed, looked at us, and then back to the class, "It's the V word. Veterans Day." Students again yelled out, "Vegetables," "Veterinarian," or "VD." Gentle laughter rolled through the room.

The teacher moved to the back of the room and read from a report stapled to the bulletin board. "This is about the Navajo code talkers. They are credited with winning the war. Because they used Navajo, and none of the Japanese could understand Navajo." This did not perk the students' interest. Half of the class still had their heads on their desks. Ten minutes had passed since the beginning of class. The teacher seemed nervous with our presence. "Ok, let's do this worksheet. Get into your groups." Students slowly turned their desks to form groups of three. The handout had one question, "Why do we have Veterans Day?" with three subsections, History, Clinton's Letter, and Demographics. The teacher said, "Now the seventh graders wrote almost a page on this assignment, so you should do more." One student responded, with a grin, "Ours is in invis-ible ink." Several students laughed, "Yeah," and "For us only." Ignoring this comment, the teacher said loudly, "And this is the day that you should all find a veteran and thank him. For saving our country." Students spent the next thirty minutes thumbing through their 1978 Merrill Publishing Company text,

American History, for answers to the question. The administrator and I almost fell asleep. When the bell rang, relief showed on the teacher's, as well as the students', faces. Along with the students, we quickly left the class.

I went out of the main building to temporary trailers, where I found the reading classes. "Reading Right" was a class required of all students. The bell had just rung, and students were slowly entering the room. Clusters of round tables and chairs filled the room. Nothing covered the light-green walls. A large plastic book-display case next to the front door stood empty. There were no chalkboards in the room. The teacher was finishing writing the assignment on the freestanding white board. It read, "Mural: Picture painted directly on a wall or ceiling. Intimacy. Silhouette. Curiosity. Spasmodically. Petrified." Students entered the classroom, put their books and notebooks on the tables, and went to pick up their reading folders. The teacher explained, "The folder tells them what level they are at. They go to the library and get a book at their level in the reading series. Then they come here and read it and take a test at that level on the computer." Everyone knew the routine. Young men with oversized blue jeans and unlaced athletic shoes moved to claim their folders with little interest. Three young women, in blue jeans, sweaters, and athletic jackets, sat comfortably on a couch. They were reading well-worn romance novels. Within the first ten minutes, half the class left to check out books at the library. Several failed to return. The others returned with less than half the period remaining. None seemed to acknowledge either the teacher or the assignment board. By the end of the period all the remaining students were reading. The class was quiet. The teacher remained at her desk, grading and recording student papers. There was a void of interaction either between students or with the teacher during the class. The students seemingly passed the time in silence, protectively disconnected from the school around them. I had no confidence that this was helping with their reading. Over the past fifteen years I had seen many reading classes similar to this one. I thought about the "flat line"—little visible improvement—of reading test scores over the past two decades, and I sighed as I left the classroom.

At the end of the day, the committee gathered to talk about our shared observations. In general, we were disappointed with the quality of the teaching we had observed. All the teachers had been told that we would be in the school that day, and still many did not have their required lesson plans. Most teachers' in-class instructional time accounted for only a few minutes during each fifty-minute period we observed. The vast majority of students' time in class was spent working individually on projects, worksheets, or chapter-end question assignments. Attempts at question-and-answer sessions were only marginally successful in most of the classrooms. An overall picture of what we had seen was of students sitting unengaged in the lessons—but engaged in something else—during lectures. For the most part, they were letting the day pass around them. Life with friends was good. What happened in most of their classes, however, was uninteresting and disconnected from their lives.

2002: Three Years Into the Monitoring of the School District

I was switched from the high school to the elementary school monitoring team for the April 2002 school visits. As a previous high school teacher before I became a university professor, the elementary school environment was not a familiar one. One of the district committee members and I joined the building's reading specialist to observe a first-grade English literacy class.

As I sank into a tiny wooden chair, a young Navajo girl with shining black braids bounced over to me, put her hands on my knee, and with a broad smile demanded, "Who are you?" To which I replied, "I'm a teacher from Salt Lake City." She responded, "We have lots of people visit us. You can stay here and watch us read." She turned and ran to join twenty classmates who had already taken their places in designated bright squares and circles on the floor rug. The entire group of children turned around and waved at us, giggling and holding onto their neighbors. The teacher smiled and explained, "They are real assertive. This is their classroom and they like to know who is coming to watch them." She turned back to the group and continued with the reading lesson. It was a wonderful lesson. The children's little bodies moved back and forth with excitement and interest as the story unfolded about a lost pig trying to find a home. "Wow! He needs a home!" exclaimed one boy. His neighbor agreed and said, "My grandfather has a bunch of sheep. I bet he would live with them." To which several of the children nodded in agreement as they thought of their own parents and grandparents with their livestock at their homes on the reservation. The teacher quickly picked up the student's references to their lives and took the opportunity to make this connection. "Yes, Navajos have many sheep and horses and cows. And I bet a pig could find a nice home there." Giggles rose as the teacher continued to turn the pages of the large, glossy book. The reading lesson continued for almost thirty minutes. The children were attentive, excited, and largely on task. All of the children read, and several were seen helping and correcting their reading partners. It was a remarkable lesson. All of us from the monitoring team were beaming when we left the room. The teacher was respectful of the children, and they of her. And they were reading at high levels. It was what we had been working for.

We left and moved to observe a combination third- and fourth-grade Navajo language lesson. The classroom was filled with examples of Navajo and English literacy. The walls were covered with bright posters showing Miss Navajo Nation, Monument Valley, Manhattan, flowers, animals, and smiling children of all colors and nationality. The fourth-grade Navajo teacher was a recent graduate from the University of Utah, with special certification in reading, but she was unsure of her Navajo language teaching skills so she had joined with a more experienced Navajo teacher. As in the first-grade classroom, students were verbal, eager, active learners. When observing other Navajo language classes, we most often saw "labeling" (naming the objects) and very little active verb-based interactions. The language was present in the classroom, but it was not used in conversations. This class was different. The two teachers passed out paper cups and half filled the cups with juice. In pairs, the students took turns pouring the juice for each other and explaining the action in Navajo. A soft murmuring of Navajo rose from each of the pairs. Very little English, except in an emergency, could be heard. "OK, I'll say this once in English for you," said a girl to her partner. "I am filling this in for you." And she repeated it in Navajo. With a nod of her head, her partner responded in Navajo. The Navajo language was being used, not just displayed.

During that day, we observed active learning and teaching throughout the school. This does not mean that we did not also see some off-task or bored students, as well as some "teaching moments lost." What was reassuring, however, was the acceptance of the Navajo-ness of the students as a resource rather than as a barrier to overcome. Navajo language was central to instruction. No one spoke of the limitation of the students. No one dismissed the importance of building on the cultural experience of Navajo students. High expectations were felt throughout the school. This was a huge change from my very first observations in this school almost twenty years ago.

During the previous three years, the monitoring team had seen many wonderful instructional lessons, but many depressing classrooms. Now we were seeing the promise of the new curriculum and the heritage language instructional models in classrooms across the district. Heritage language (Navajo and Ute) classes were available to all students, in all grades, and in all appropriate schools. Elementary schools required thirty minutes of literacy instruction in Navajo per day and fifteen minutes of a content area in Navajo per day. Secondary schools offered two levels of Navajo language classes. Navajo culture and government classes in Navajo were scheduled for EDNET broadcast the following year, sponsored by Utah Education Network. All English and Navajo teachers became ESL endorsed and certified. Navajo and Ute language teachers were hired at each school site. All the courses needed to get into postsecondary institutions in Utah were now available to Navajo students. Each elementary school provided staff development and "best practices" demonstrations, led by their principal, each month. Parent involvement activities had increased at all schools. And almost all teachers had lesson plans to guide and organize their instruction. This last change was not easy. The effective teachers, for the most part, were already using lesson plans. The teachers who needed them the most resisted the most. Our insistence gained us the not-so friendly label "Lesson Plan Police." Teachers, the monitoring team, and district administrators had struggled together to effect change at the classroom level. We were now looking to see if these changes had made a positive difference in the schooling experience of Navajo students.

October 2, 2002: A Step Backward? The End of the Monitoring

The message being left on the answering machine woke me up. It was my colleague on the consensus team urging me to call: "You won't believe what I got by mistake when I opened up my e-mails." He was right. Within two hours I was on a conference call with lawyers from the lawsuit, the U.S. Justice Department, the Navajo Nation, and our team. One careless press of the "forward" key from a paid consultant for the school district revealed a shocking picture of what the district was doing behind our backs. We learned of planned meetings with the new superintendent and state senators in Washington, D.C., the following week, strategies to stall our fall monitoring of the schools and classrooms, and a desire to stop our monitoring efforts—all apparent plans to ignore the agreement of parties that all had signed in 1997. We were deeply dismayed. Our team desperately brainstormed ways to salvage the somewhat collaborative relationship we had developed over the past five years. "I know we have support with many of the teachers and some of the principals. It's the administration," my colleague argued. The lawyers from the Navajo Nation argued the district was "trying to muzzle the Nation" by exclusion. We were seeing a shift to political intervention as a means to ignore the courts and our local agreements. If we were refused entry into the schools for the monitoring process, we would be pressured into one of two options: walk away and hope some of the educational progress we saw continued or go back to court to gain entry into the schools. Their lawyers had told them that if they returned to court they would win the case. Our lawyers disagreed. We ended the meeting continuing to fight.

November 2002 was the last monitoring visit by our team. We spent a tense week observing in classroom, seeing some excellent instruction and some teachers still struggling. At the end of that week, at the "debriefing meeting" usually reserved for our meeting with principals, we were told that the school district would no longer allow us into the schools for observations. An administrator moved to the board and wrote two dates: December 7, 1941, and August 8, 1945, and asked us what the dates represented. After silence he responded, "The beginning and end of World War II." He then wrote April 7, 1997, and today's date, November 8, 2002. "We have been at this longer than World War II. And now, on January 8, 2002, No Child Left Behind was enacted, and we will have to answer to that. Our new board members do not agree with the consensus plan. We have to more forward and get this lawsuit behind us to serve the needs of our students." We were then presented with the district's new direction. The letter sent to the U.S. Justice Department was shared with the team. In it we were accused of "burdensome program and process requirements" that were forced on the district by our "high pressure negotiation tactics" and "outlandish interpretations of broad legal requirements" in the original 1997 consensus agreement. Our twice-a-year monitoring visits were "highly intrusive" and resulted in "disruption to our staff and programs." In general, the district argued that the curriculum plan caused an "adverse effect on students." In addition, the district argued that they could not adequately teach the state core curriculum because of the "loss of class periods to obligatory Navajo language classes." At the elementary level, due to "inflexible Navajo language requirements," fine arts, physical education, health, science, and social studies programs had suffered. At the secondary level, the district argued that they had to "abandon or de-emphasize" the Sterling Scholar program, the science fair, and the Academic Decathlon because of the demands of the monitoring team. In addition, required curriculum and heritage language plans were responsible for causing the district to lose several faculty members and more than $200,000 of vocational funding and made it difficult to recruit teachers. The final assertion stated, "The Plan requirements and the monitoring activities are impeding our ability to respond to the No Child Left Behind legislation."

We received a new language development and curriculum plan—a plan we called the "nonconsensus plan." This plan moved Navajo language from a required curriculum offering at each southern school (majority of Navajo schools) to one that would be optional, dependent on an adequate number of students registering for the class. In a district that had a history of reducing Navajo teachers and Navajo language and culture classes, this was an ominous echo of the past. The put us back full circle, where Navajo language and culture was seen as a frill available to be deleted during times of budget tightening or when more time was needed for physical education, health, technology, and social studies classes or extra-curricular activities. During the 2002–2003 school year, the San Juan school district and the Navajo Nation tried to come to a consensus, once again, over the revision on the revision of the revisions of our original plan. As of this writing, lawyers from both sides are reviewing the document in preparation for a new agreement between parties. In the final plan, at the unwavering insistence of the Navajo Nation, the Navajo language is again a mandatory districtwide course offering.

Reflections on Social Justice–Driven School Change

In critical race theory,[11] storytelling is a research form that can be helpful to expose racism and, in the case of schooling, unequal educational opportunities.

I believe the narrative storytelling of this court case provides a different kind of picture of "multiculturalism." Not only one of learning about each others' cultural differences, in which mutual understanding and respect will result, but one that paints the complexity of power relations over the very ideal of "multiculturalism." Using a critical race perspective, Gloria Ladson-Billings captures the essence of this conflict: "Critical race theory sees the official school curriculum as a culturally specific artifact designed to maintain a White supremacist master script" (1998, p. 18). Individual teachers may like and respect their Navajo students and work hard to help them succeed. However, institutional structures are in place that track and limit students' opportunities regardless of a teacher's efforts. Reflecting the history and persistence of racism in U.S. schools, Nieto's words seem to echo the situation I described here.

As institutions, schools respond to and reflect the larger society. It is therefore not surprising that racism finds its way into schools in much the same way that it finds its way into other institutions, such as housing, employment, and the criminal justice system. Overt expressions of racism may be less common in schools today than in the past, but racism does not just exist when schools are legally segregated or when racial epithets are used. Racism is also manifested in rigid ability tracking, low expectations of students based on their identity, and inequitably funded schools (Nieto, 2004, p. 39).

The history in San Juan County of segregated schools and assimilatory educational goals for Navajo students is reflected in the current practices and thinking of White citizens of the county. Resistance to the use of school dollars for Navajo language and cultural instruction emerges in daily discourses. Local historian Robert McPherson clearly captures these feelings and what it means for the consensus plan in his 2001 book *Navajo Land, Navajo Culture: The Utah Experience in the Twentieth Century.* I quote at length, as he is an "insider" to these issues—having lived his entire life in the county and written dozens of scholarly studies on southern Utah.

> While this plan was implemented in various stages in 1998, there are some people who still voice complaints. They argue that the system hinders the acquisition of English-language skills for those who need the help the most; that the whole plan is politically and legally motivated and does not consider the welfare of the children; that the Navajo tribe, which has a voice in the adoption of the curriculum, is foisting family responsibility for teaching language and heritage onto the schools, where it does not belong; and that here are not enough staff to implement a true bilingual model. After listening to these arguments, a Navajo man serving on the school board countered: "I think we should withdraw every Navajo student from the San Juan School District. That's when you will be happy. Take care of it once and for all. Just sweep the floor and go home. You have no interest in educating Navajo students in San Juan School District."[12]

Over the course of almost twenty years, my role has shifted from ethnographer to Indian lover to lawsuit enemy to expert witness and now back to ethnographer. Ironically, in March 2002, I was asked by the district to "create an alliance with research academics" to help the district research "pockets of excellence." I was delighted and agreed, immediately starting to work on a research plan and team. After the district prematurely ended the monitoring team's efforts, they also reversed the offer. In February 2003, I received an e-mail from the administrator who I had worked with on the consensus team explaining that the "pockets of excellence" project has been placed "on hold" because of the new responsibilities placed on the district by the No Child Left Behind Act. The research was just too threatening for what it might expose. In a sincere way, I believe, he ended with, "We appreciate your concern for our students." I have to remind myself that the narrative I write here is not simply about the "good guys" and the "bad guys." It is a narrative that shows Whites advantageously orchestrating economic, political, and social control over this landscape. And it shows Navajos as resilient and persistently claiming this same landscape and wealth. It also shows Navajos as active agents contesting and demanding equity in and out of schools, rather than as merely victims.

In the district's September 23, 2002, letter to Assistant Attorney General Ralph Boyd, the district argued that the consensus team's curriculum and heritage language plans had nothing to do with improving student performance; quite to the contrary, our monitoring efforts had had "adverse effects" on students' achievements. Based on my experiences in this district over the past twenty years, I would argue otherwise. When the Navajo Nation insisted on the inclusion of Navajo language, they were arguing for a fundamental tenet of their continued sovereignty and identity as a people. This is no more than the White citizens already have in place, and this is key to Navajo youths' positive self-esteem, serious school effort, and school success.[13] The very fact of having Navajo culture and language required of the district is dramatic when viewed against the backdrop of the 100-year-old battle over equal educational opportunities. And there is an abundance of research that connects the power of social justice in a multicultural schooling context to positive schooling experiences and success. Of course, I would not argue that all positive change has been due to the intervention of this lawsuit. Much effort has been undertaken with state support for K–6 reading, for example. But I do think the existence of this consensus team's efforts have forced outside public attention to the neglect of Navajo language opportunities; to the restrictive, vocationalized curriculum provided to Navajo students; and to many teachers' indifference, racism, incompetence, and lower expectations. It is my hope that these changes have opened up the space for the possibility of change, but for such change to be productive, White faculty and administrators will have to move beyond comfortable folk explanations for Navajo school failure and study their own complicity in problematic pedagogies.

Recommended Readings

When introducing multicultural research to students, I think it is critical to provide a historical framework for students to understand issues of racism, power, and contested space and place within the United States' diverse population. An excellent book that I use in my undergraduate and graduate courses is Ronald Takaki's (1993) *A Different Mirror: A History of Multicultural America*. Sonia Nieto's (2004) text *Affirming Diversity: The Sociopolitical Context of Multicultural Education* also seeks to provide readers with examples of institutional racism (traced historically) and its connection to student achievement in today's school. Specifically focused on American Indians and Alaskan Natives are the following excellent books: K. Tsianina Lomawaima (1999), *They Called It Prairie Light: The Story of Chilocco Indian School*; Jerry Lipka, Gerald V. Mohatt, and the Ciulistet Group (1998), *Transforming the Culture of Schools: Yup'ik Eskimo Examples*; and Teresa L. McCarty (2002), *A Place to Be Navajo: Rough Rock and the Struggle for Self-Determination in Indigenous Schooling*.

Reflective Questions

1. Deyhle started this research as an outside ethnographer and then became a political actor in the lawsuit. What are the ethical issues surrounding this change of roles?

2. What might a more positive collaborative relationship between Navajo parents and their children and school officials and teachers look like?

3. How is the concept of "multiculturalism" challenged or problematized by the example of this court case?

Notes

1. The *Lau v. Nichols* court case decision required school districts to provide some kind of alternative educational program if students did not speak English, the language of instruction. One perspective of the ruling was that minority students are entitled under the Fourteenth Amendment to an educational experience tailored to their unique linguistic, cultural, and developmental needs. The specific language program was to be decided at the district level. Some districts moved to bilingual education, others to ESL, some programs were transitional, others dual-language maintenance. To neglect the language needs of students, however, amounted to denying them equal educational access to school instruction. In response to *Lau v. Nichols*, the Department of Education issued a decree for districts to follow. See U.S. Department of Education, Office of Civil Rights (1975). Also reprinted in *The Linguistic Reporter 18*, no. 2 (1975): 1.

2. In my past publications I used the term "Anglo," which more specifically referred to peoples of Northern European heritage to avoid the essentialization implied

by the term "Whites." Throughout this chapter, however, I will use the term "Whites" most often to describe the European American population in the county. I am fully aware of the essentialized nature of using this term to describe all "nonpeoples of color," but this is the term used by the groups I describe. First, historical documents, almost exclusively written by European Americans from this area, and contemporary interviews I conducted most frequently used the dichotomous terms "Indian" and "White." Second, almost all the Navajo and Ute people used these terms in daily life. I use "Anglo" here when this was the specific term used, such as in a legal court document.

3. The history of this region has been extensively researched, which has aided my understanding of the relationships between Navajos and Whites. See, for example, Cuch (2000), Lyman (1962), McPherson (1988, 1995, 2000), Perkins, Nielson, and Jones (1968).

4. U.S. Bureau of the Census (1995, p. 2). At the time of this writing the Census 2000 information is not available. Based on my observations during the 1990s, I would argue that little has changed other than the population size.

5. U.S. Bureau of the Census (1996, April 24, p. 2).

6. U.S. Bureau of the Census (1996, January 17, p. 2).

7. U.S. Bureau of the Census (1996, March 20, p. 2).

8. U.S. Bureau of the Census (1996, July 10, p. 2).

9. Memo document distributed during a district principals' meeting.

10. For more in-depth analysis of this data on Navajos and school failure see Deyhle (1992, 1995).

11. Critical race theory (CRT) has its historical genesis in the work by predesegregation African American legal scholars such as Charles Hamilton Houston and Thurgood Marshall. However, CRT was born in the writings by civil rights lawyer and academic Derrick Bell. Among others, legal scholars Lani Guinier, Kimberlé Crenshaw, and Richard Delgado have been extremely influential in the development of critical race theory. William Tate IV and Gloria Ladson-Billings have been key in bringing CRT to the field of education. See Ladson-Billings and Tate (1995) and Tate (1997).

12. McPherson (2001, p. 230). The Navajo man's quote comes from "Bilingual Proposal Gets Cold Reception from Educators and Parents," *Blue Mountain Panorama*, October 8, 1997, 2.

13. There is a significant body of research that argues that youth's native language and culture are assets to school success, not barriers. For a review of this research see Deyhle and Swisher (1997).

References

Cuch, F. S. (Ed.). (2000). *A history of Utah's American Indians*. Salt Lake City: Utah State Division of Indian Affairs, Utah State Division of History.

Deyhle, D. (1992, January). Constructing failure and maintaining cultural identity: Navajo and Ute school leavers. *Journal of American Indian Education, 31*, 24–47.

Deyhle, D. (1995). Navajo youth and Anglo racism: Cultural integrity and resistance. *Harvard Educational Review, 65*, 403–444.

Deyhle, D., & Swisher, K. (1997). Research in American Indian and Alaska Native education: From assimilation to self-determination. In Michael W. Apple (Ed.), *Review of Research in Education* (Vol. 22, pp. 113–194). Washington, DC: American Educational Research Association.

Ladson-Billings, G. (1998). Just what is critical race theory and what's it doing in a nice field like education? *International Journal of Qualitative Studies in Education*, *11*(1), 7–24.

Ladson-Billings, G., & Tate, W. F., IV. (1995). Toward a critical theory of education. *Teachers College Record, 97*, 47–68.

Lipka, J., Mohatt, G. V., & the Ciulistet Group. (1998). *Transforming the culture of schools: Yup'ik Eskimo examples.* Mahwah, NJ: Lawrence Erlbaum.

Lomawaima, K. T. (1999). *They called it Prairie Light: The story of Chilocco Indian School.* Lincoln and London: University of Nebraska Press.

Lyman, A. R. (1962). *Indians and outlaws: Settling of the San Juan frontier.* Salt Lake City, UT: Bookcraft.

McCarty, T. L. (2002). *A place to be Navajo: Routh Rock and the struggle for self-determination in indigenous schooling.* Mahwah, NJ: Lawrence Erlbaum.

McPherson, R. (1988). *The northern Navajo frontier, 1860–1900: Expansion through adversity.* Albuquerque: University of New Mexico Press.

McPherson, R. (1995). *A history of San Juan county. In the palm of time.* Salt Lake City: Utah State University.

McPherson, R. (2000). *The journey of Navajo Oshley: An autobiography and life history.* Salt Lake City and Logan: Utah State University Press.

McPherson, R. (2001). *Navajo land, Navajo culture: The Utah experience in the twentieth century.* Norman: University of Oklahoma Press.

Nieto, S. (2004). *Affirming diversity: The sociopolitical context of multicultural education* (4th ed.). Boston: Pearson.

Perkins, C. A., Nielson, M. G., & Jones, L. B. (Eds.). (1968). *Saga of San Juan.* San Juan County: Daughters of Utah Pioneers.

Takaki, R. (1993). *A different mirror: A history of multicultural America.* Boston: Little, Brown.

Tate, W., IV. (1997). Critical race theory and education: History, theory, and implications. In M. Apple (Ed.), *Review of Research in Education* (Vol. 22, pp. 195–247). Washington DC: American Educational Research Association.

U.S. Bureau of the Census. (1995, December 13). *The San Juan Record,* p. 2.

U.S. Bureau of the Census. (1996, January 17). *The San Juan Record,* p. 2.

U. S. Bureau of the Census. (1996, March 20). *The San Juan Record,* p. 2.

U.S. Bureau of the Census. (1996, April 24). *The San Juan Record,* p. 2.

U.S. Bureau of the Census. (1996, July 10). *The San Juan Record,* p. 2.

U.S. Department of Education, Office of Civil Rights. (1975). Task force findings specifying remedies available for eliminating past educational practices ruled unlawful under *Lau vs. Nichols. The Linguistic Reporter.* Washington, DC: Department of Health, Education, and Welfare.

Unit Four

Multicultural Teacher Education in International Contexts

8

Teachers as Transformative Healers

Struggles With the Complexities of the Democratic Sphere

Lourdes Diaz Soto

To transform the world is to humanize it.

—Freire, 1985

Autobiographical Introduction

My childhood memories are those of a return migrant from Puerto Rico and New York City. Like the families and children I have interviewed (Soto, 1997a, 1997b, 1999, 2001a, 2001b, 2002a, 2002b, in press), I am a displaced border crosser experiencing the complexities of hybridity, oppression, and newly found privilege in academia. The South Bronx elementary school I attended (PS #20) has been destroyed, as was 1024 Fox Street—the building where my family and I lived. There are small row houses standing in the places where I rode my scooter, where my friends and I jumped rope, and where the kind "trick-or-treat lady" was mugged by the boys from Simpson Street.

AUTHOR'S NOTE: A note of appreciation is extended to the teachers I worked with in New York City during 2001 and 2002. My gratitude is extended especially to Tracy Schneider, Juliana Lasta, Grace Morris, and Kate Martin for their friendship and assistance in gathering children's depictions. I would also like to thank Lottie Almonte, Antoinette Cloete, Tatyana Klein, Monisha Bajaj, and all of the "the Freirians" for their support, wisdom, and courage.

As a Puerto Rican woman/mother/grandmother/privileged faculty living in the mainland/metropolis I continue to reflect on the complexities of multiple postmodern concerns. *Somos los de aqui y los de alla.* (We are from here and from there.) We are Puerto Rican American citizens with ties to the mainland and to the island. A long-standing concern for many of us has been the sterilization of one-third of Puerto Rican women in a federal government program that constitutes the highest rate of genocidal sterilization in the world (*La Operacion*, 1982). The most recent concern leading to multiple protests has been the continued bombing of the Puerto Rican island of Vieques. Following the September 11, 2001, tragedy, Puerto Ricans have felt compelled to dress in patriotic garb, but I have not seen patriotism extended to allow the U.S. Navy to practice bombing on Martha's Vineyard.

My concern also centers on how monolingually, linguistically, ethnically, and culturally diverse children are mapping their lives in the contemporary private and in the postmodern public sphere. In the private sphere, there are complex daily challenges faced by children, families, schools, and communities. My many years of teaching out of my own being and learning from English-only speakers, international students, and U.S.-born ethnically diverse learners have helped me to gain insights and to move to a space that I sense is more critical, more insightful, and more loving. My goal has been to move beyond the pain and immerse myself as a cultural worker continually struggling as an ally of contemporary postmodern learners.

My focus has been the children—the children who attempt to make sense of "why do they hate us so much?" after the September 11, 2001, tragedy (Soto, in press): for example, the child in my daughter's Washington, D.C., day care center that volunteered, "Put on my Power Ranger outfit and save the day!" Children can energize adults in our society who make the decisions, who wield the power, who need to ponder carefully ways in which we might be able to "save the day."

Scholars like myself seeking additional wisdom want to explore *consejos* (advice) from diverse peoples. Maori researchers have shared these profound guidelines that I find very valuable: (1) *aroha ki te tangata* (a respect for people); 2) *Kanohi kitea* (present yourself to people face to face); (3) *titiro, whakarongo . . . korero* (look, listen . . . speak); (4) *kia tupato* (be cautious); (5) *Kaua e takahia te mana o te tangata* (do not trample over the mana of other people); and (6) *kaua e mahaki* (don't flaunt your knowledge) (Smith, 2000, p. 242).

Teachers as Transformative Healers

Teachers are envisioned by Giroux (1988) as "transformative intellectuals" capable of educating learners about the possibility of democracy and social justice. His view of democracy (1993) includes both the discourse and the practice that inform freedom, equality, and social justice. He states:

> At the same time the challenge of democracy resides in the necessary recognition that educators, parents and others will have to work hard to insure that future generations will view the idea and practice of multicultural and multiracial democracy as a goal worth believing in and struggling for. (p. 1)

In this chapter I maintain that New York City teachers moved *beyond transformative intellectuals to transformative healers* during the September 11 tragedy. Although it was not my intention, it may be that in some ways this chapter is reminiscent of the genre of Latin American *testimonio* because it includes a view of hegemonic discourses from subaltern voices expressing a therapeutic and public testimony (for a discussion of *testimonio,* see Brabeck, 2003).

This circular narrative weaves the post–September 11 tragedy as a backdrop to describe how a set of teachers moved beyond transformative intellectuals. We (the teachers and I) moved into a space that can only be described as transformative and healing. This space integrates the complexities of the self—including the intellectual, the emotional, the physical (the body), and the spiritual nature of our own beings. This evolving liminal space of transformation and healing required that as we reached out to each other, to ourselves, and to others, in light of the catastrophic rupture, we experienced love and compassion.

Giroux's words relating the challenge to democracy certainly ring true at this post–September 11 juncture when the democratic principles of the United States of America are being contested. Among President Bush's initiatives, we are seeing military tribunals limiting the rights of defendants, the detention of an undetermined number of people, and the government listening to people's private conversations, thereby demonstrating that our democratic ideals are standing on fragile ground.

Our narratives describe the "ways people experience the world" (Connelly & Clandinin, 1990). Our perceptions and our lenses were embedded in the emotional, the intellectual, the physical, and the spiritual as issues of power overwhelmed us during the September 11 tragedy. Issues of power, not just as Foucault (1977) describes as a technique or action that individuals can engage in, but as Merleau-Ponty (2002) describes: how we can process prereflective and practical participation within the world. As you read this chapter, you will be introduced to the teachers who were forced to summon their courageous wisdom to deal with the tragedy as it impacted them, the children they were teaching, and both the local and the international community. I envision them as "transformative healers" because they not only critically analyzed the immediate and distant experience but also were totally engaged in how best to meet the needs of the New York City children they were meeting every day in their classrooms.

As a visiting professor at Teachers College, I observed how the September 11, 2001, tragedy had a profound impact on many lives. The tragedy took over our daily lives and our thinking about the needs of our learners and ourselves, because we know we can only teach out of ourselves. My students and I compiled three slices of data depicting the complexities of the tragedy including (a) a slide presentation focusing on the children in the United States and Afghanistan, interlaced with New York City (NYC) children's drawings; (b) teacher narratives depicting the daily lived realities working with young children at the time of the tragedy; and (c) how we struggled with the curriculum that semester. These elements helped us explore the need for an education that moves beyond our current practices to an education that is critically bilingual/multicultural and provides spaces for transformative healing.

Concern for the Children

The teachers shared their experiences as they worked with children in New York City who were attempting to understand the September 11 tragedies. Imagine being in a classroom with a room full of young children viewing the entire episode that the rest of us viewed on the television screen. Louise (pseudonym), a teacher and a mother, reflects on her thoughts at the time:

> My reaction to the entire September 11th tragedy was one of disbelief and horror. Sorrow and anger eventually set in, but it took me about a week to come out of denial. I believe this tragic event needs to be addressed by educators, parents, families, and government. Students of all ages need to be informed. The silence in the schools reminds me of the silence there once was about children doing drugs. It was no one's responsibility, especially in the schools. We should be "frightened" . . . if we become desensitized to human suffering and tragedy. We can reflect upon the people, things, issues, values, and so on that give us a sense of peace . . . [W]e will come closer to being able to live with one another in a peaceful, accepting manner. One of the ways we can begin to do this is by exposing children to differences in cultures, religions, customs, gender issues, and so on. This way they can grow up with a well-developed sense of critical evaluative knowledge and a widened periphery of our world and the issues therein.

The September 11, 2001, events left a legacy that continues to haunt many teachers, students, and families. This one day changed our lives: our daily realities and our thinking about how Americans are viewed in the global theater. No one could have predicted the magnitude of the event. Imagine the struggle for teachers such as Louise and her students when every minute of the assault was replayed daily by media coverage: funerals, people carrying pictures of their loved ones on their chests, smells, fears, sirens, tears, huge trailers and construction equipment, noisy trucks. Most schools asked children to draw pictures of the event and brought counselors and psychologists to spend time with the children. Teachers also described instances where they were advised not to discuss the event with their students, even though Martin Luther King Jr. had reminded us long ago that silence can serve as betrayal:

> We must speak with all the humility that is appropriate . . . we must speak. (2001–2002, p. 24)

One teacher, Mercedes, who felt that it was important to address the September 11 tragedies in the classroom, observed, "We need to stop treating the classroom as a separate entity. Everything that happens in the classroom should relate to the real world. If it doesn't then I will ask why bother teaching it?" Mercedes's perspective relays how the curriculum should reflect children's needs and their daily lived realities. Mercedes was reaching for the transformative space of healing. Britzman (2002), like Mercedes, has noted

> the disillusionment toward knowledge persists as one of this century's great epistemological themes and is acted albeit unconsciously, in the fields of curriculum. This illusion is supported by a series of defenses the fields of curriculum employs: the curriculum as technical, as government, as genealogy, as preparation, as something that is capable of speaking for itself. (p. 96)

Teacher Narratives: Struggling With the Curriculum

How to address the tragedy with learners and with the community became the subject of discussion in both schools and the academy. The tragedy facilitated reflection on multiple issues including but not limited to personal safety, sociohistorical dealings, nationalism, international relations, the curriculum, social justice, the economy, and peace.

Three teachers shared their thinking at the time about the tragedy and the inherent complexities in their daily lived realities and the curriculum inside and outside the classroom. The first voice (Sandra) describes perceptions, the second voice (Lisa) provides advice for classroom teachers, and the third voice (Jennifer) refers to "flag-toting Americans" at a time when the American flag became a prominently displayed symbol in stores and homes and on cars and clothing. These narratives taken together reflect the complexities faced by teachers and children. The struggles included elements of patriotism, social justice, equity, war, and peace. The teachers envisioned a curriculum that affords learners an opportunity to reflect and critically view the world. Their feelings ranged from outrage, anger, and fear to helplessness, mourning, and concern for others. In some ways these selected voices begin to theorize and envision possibilities for classrooms and for their own pedagogy. These teachers were embarking on the transformative healing process.

Sandra: I sit in my cushy papasan and wrapped in worn serapes, drinking the queen's tea. I peer at my piece of the sky . . . I am at home. I feel connected and I feel grateful. I hear talk in the distance regarding "the evil one." I hear talk in the distance of the barbarians . . . [I]t is us versus them, our liberty . . . they want to take away our freedom and we can't let them. My body shudders at this manipulation of words, spoken for the sake of maintaining hegemonic power structures at the expense of people like me who want to be proud of something less oppressive and dominating. My ancestors were American long before it was limited to the United States . . . and I'll be damned if I'll let someone else define my piece of the sky for me.

Lisa: Shall we talk about the 9/11 tragedy in our class? Yes. We should let our children know what happened in our country regardless of what age the children are. They will know the facts sooner or later. [We need to] pay close attention to the children's reactions, especially those who have lost families or friends on September 11. I can surely do my part for the children such as . . . create a secure and safe classroom atmosphere; return everything to routine as quickly as possible; read extra books for the children and help them deal with the events; encourage children to help each other. We are brothers and sisters in one nation . . . keep monitoring the situation. This is a time to bring us closer together. We share bitterness and happiness together.

Jennifer: My government tells me that those responsible belong to a non-secular group whose mission is to develop a supreme establishment whereby the members espouse the fundamentalist practice or die. . . . The trend for flag-toting Americans to spread their nationalism and rally sentiment for the "right" cause no longer appeals to my sense of solidarity. I find the majority of the nationalists act like supremacists. No wonder the rest of the world thinks we're an arrogant bunch bent on sticking our policies where it best fits the interest of our prosperity. I do too, and I live here. I would like peace but it's not possible at this time, and, realistically, peace for the world will never happen as long as human beings have the intellect to justify their actions.

The narratives of Sandra, Lisa, and Jennifer reflect the complexity of the struggles teachers faced post–September 11. As they critically reflected on the September 11 tragedy, they realized that their concerns about patriotism, social justice, equity, war, and peace not only impacted their lives and the lives of their students but also impacted the lives of people around the world. To embark on a process of healing, teachers had to develop their ability to transform their anger into possibilities for classrooms and for their own pedagogy. You can envision this process in the following teachers' narratives. Sacho reflected on how she and two of her roommates responded after the initial shock:

> I decided to donate my blood. I called the Red Cross. But the operator said, "There are too many people who want to donate the blood."
>
> Day after day, I walked around the town and tried to find something I can do for them. I donated daily stuffs. I attended church. I attended candle service. But I cannot be satisfied myself. I was talking about the issue with my roommates who are from Japan. One girl is majoring in philosophy, the other is an art major, and I am in TESOL [Teachers of English to Speakers of Other Languages]. All of us are depressed. We all thought, "A philosopher cannot do anything, an artist cannot do anything, an ESL [English as a Second Language] major cannot do anything." We walked around and called the Red Cross to volunteer. "We need someone who has a special skill [firefighter, police officer]." We could not find the meaning of what we were doing now and started doubting. A few weeks later . . . each of us found we might do something by using what we are doing in the future. The girl majoring in philosophy thought she could talk to many people asking them to think about what is a human life. The girl majoring in art realized art could save humans. Actually, many museums have exhibition for the New Yorkers to cure people's mind. And I as an ESL teacher realized what I can do is to keep telling my students about the disaster and teach them how precious human lives are and the importance of love and peace in the world. I think this is the mission for teachers.

Nadia, a fourth-grade teacher, reflected on the effects of terrorism on her students and her classroom:

> The fear of terrorism is currently more profound than ever. As an antiterrorist precaution, the United States' borders have become very stringent. Antiforeign sentiment is more evident . . . and innocent ethnic groups are being blamed and mistreated. How will these current trends . . . affect the daily lives of our bilingual/ bicultural students? Although the current problem is creating the most serious difficulties for people of Middle Eastern decent, the surge of racism is affecting all recent immigrants living in the United States. As a result of the attacks, statements such as "go home where you belong" are being heard along the streets from New York to Los Angeles. . . . It is unfortunate but the events of September 11 have now made our jobs as bilingual/bicultural educators even more difficult than they once were!

Jonathan reflected on multiculturalism and a national identity:

> The trend in social studies education towards multiculturalism has become too maligned by those who seek to simplify it as a vilification of White male dominance. There is nothing wrong with studying the history of the dominant culture, but to tout it as the only true history becomes problematic. . . . [It] is necessary to

ensure the formation of a national identity that truly reflects the makeup of its people. . . . The sought-after objectivity does not allow the students to develop their own ideas.

Gloria revealed her feelings about injustice:

Historically, in education, we have robbed our children of the truth. Growing up I believed that if we, as Latinos and other oppressed peoples, worked hard in school to become educated, nothing could stand in our way. Slowly I watched people who were important to me drop out of school. . . . [O]ur educational system is not set up for the success of people of color. This idea sickens me. . . . Our voices have been so silenced that many of us can no longer speak. . . . [W]e must have an educational system that does not oppress but provides knowledge and choices for our children. That is my vision.

Peter stated his goal as a teacher:

My goal is not to teach them to be unpatriotic or anti-USA but I want them to look at the world with a critical eye. I recently heard President Bush talking to students in a D.C. public school. He kept talking about how we weren't fighting the people of Afghanistan but we were fighting evil people. I really thought that was inappropriate. The Taliban has been responsible for some really awful things. People did some awful things on September 11. But for our president to call people evil is a judgment call that I'm not sure I think any human being should make about another. We've done a lot of things that are very subversive and could be considered evil. I do support our involvement in Afghanistan but I am bothered by anyone calling another person evil.

These narratives demonstrate how these teachers attempted to make sense of their world. Their daily lived realities became layered with political and emotional complexities and curricular possibilities. Teachers realized that critical reflection on their experience and the experiences of their students, coupled with a critical discussion with their students about the experience of the September 11 tragedy could become a transformative space for healing.

At the Academy: The Struggle for the Curriculum

At Teachers College (and other institutions of higher learning) we experienced multiple moving teach-ins where voices spoke about the September 11 tragedy and how it had affected their life and their memories. Some faculty felt that the tragedy did not relate to their courses, while many of us, including my students and me, felt that we could not ignore an event that was affecting local, national, and international policies and activities.

My students and I struggled with the curriculum in a seminar I was teaching titled "Language, Culture, and Power." Freire's (1970, 1985) notion of "reading the word and reading the world" had been uppermost in our minds. With the advent of the September 11 tragedy we decided to begin our discussions by conducting "informal" discourse analyses of the initial news coverage. We found the language of war prevalent with little discussion about peace. We knew our nation was headed for war.

My students and I reflected on the "language of war" that the media began to insert quickly after the September 11 tragedy. We also examined our own experiences and discussed the multiple lenses available to us as well as the complexities of the event. We relied on *hermeneutics* (the art of interpreting reality) and *bricolage* (a variety of disciplines and traditions). We explored multiple layers including the emotional, the corporate, the racial, the political, the sociocultural, the feminist, the realities of worker exploitation, the silencing of immigrants, and the spiritual intersections with issues of ethics, solidarity, and public responsibility.

We found that a critical bilingual/multicultural lens centering on the complexities of power afforded us the opportunity to examine how power regulates discourses and how the multiple realities of power construct our consciousness. The students in the seminar designed a postmodern multimedia minireader theater representing a slice of our discussion while portraying a critical analysis with a pedagogy of feminist hope and change. The students dramatized our therapeutic dialogue to members of the Teachers College community. Along with the dramatization, several students designed a timed PowerPoint slide presentation depicting the events on a large overhead screen that was presented at the same time as the mini-theater. We saw several audience participants weeping, and we knew that there was still need for additional dialogue and critical bilingual/bicultural pedagogy centering on the complexity of the issues the event provided. We were searching for a space of healing that we could pursue together.

We began to dream about possibilities. We envisioned a postmonolingual society and a critical bilingual/multicultural pedagogy where our mutual interests of world peace and understanding could be pursued. This type of inclusive curriculum would offer the opportunity to have an informed nation that can understand, critically analyze, and interpret the complexities of multiple issues. If all of our learners are seen as contributors of wisdom, language, and culture, then a learning community can be created where issues of social justice and equity can be discussed, solved, and healed. How much easier would it be if young children were socialized to understand and befriend culturally and linguistically diverse people? Perhaps we could avoid global conflicts if our children could envision peaceful resolutions.

The following series of vignettes capture the post–September 11 feelings. The initial vignette is excerpts from Brooklyn poet Suheir Hammad's first poem after September 11:[1]

> 1. there have been no words.
> i have not written one word
> no poetry in the ashes south of canal street.
> no prose in the refrigerated trucks driving debris and dna.
> not one word. . . .
>
> . . .smoke where once was flesh.
>
> fire in the city air and i feared for my sister's life. . .
>
> first, please god, let it be a mistake, the pilot's heart failed,
> the plane's engine died.
> then please god, let it be a nightmare, wake me now.
> please god, after the second plane, please, don't let it be anyone
> who looks like my brothers. . . .
>
> 3. the dead are called lost and their families hold up shaky
> printouts in front of us through screens smoked up.
> we are looking for iris, mother of three.
> please call with any information. we are searching for
> priti, last seen on the 103rd floor. she was talking to her husband
> on the phone and the line went. please help us find george,
> also known as adel . . .
> i am looking for peace. i am looking for mercy. . . .
> (Hammad, 2001–2002, p. 7)

I found these words inspiring, as I browsed in a New York City bookstore, the week of September 11, 2001:

> we must raise the international of hope.
> Hope above borders, languages, colors, cultures,
> sexes, strategies, and thoughts,
> of all those who prefer humanity alive.

CONSIDERING THAT WE ARE:

For the international order of hope, for a new and
just and dignified peace.

For new politics, for democracy, for political liberties.

For justice, for life, and dignified work.

For civil society, for full rights for women in every regard, for
respect for elders, youth, and children, for the defense and
protection of the environment.

For intelligence, for culture, for education, for truth.

For liberty, for tolerance, for inclusion, for remembrance.

For humanity. (Zapatistas, 1998, pp. 51–52)

The advent of the September 11 tragedy led us to realize that we needed to find a space of healing and empowering moments filled with hope, possibility, and love.

As our president announced that our nation was now at war, we continued to pursue and reach for a "space of healing." Our lived realities included horrific insights and sounds of daily funerals, police sirens, and family members carrying pictures of loved ones.

In this chapter I have shared a "testimony," demonstrating how teachers, students, and many others were inextricably linked as we experienced and continued to experience the September 11 tragedy. Several of the students I met during my appointment as visiting professor still maintain contact with me. One student and I have written a chapter together and presented it at the American Education Research Association. Another student calls every so often asking, "So . . . how are you?" while several continue to e-mail their progress. We learned multiple lessons about the complexities of the democratic sphere as well as the strength of the human spirit and the strength of transformative healing. We learned just how important it is for the curriculum to reflect the daily lived realities of learners, or as Mercedes pointed out, "Why bother teaching?"

When I reflect on our experience, I find myself admiring the "transformative healing" the teachers so willingly engaged in for the children's sake, for their sake, and for the sake of the community. Can you imagine how you might have reacted in similar circumstances? I keep relying on Freire's (1985) words that "to transform the world is to humanize it." The courage and wisdom we (teachers, children, and the community) shared in solidarity as an integral part of our collective memory was an act of love.

Recommended Readings

If you are interested in gaining more insight about the issues discussed in this chapter, you may want to experience the writings of bell hooks, Paulo Freire, F. Michael Connelly and D. Jean Clandinin, Joe Kincheloe, Peter McLaren, and Gloria Anzaldúa. You can choose among many of their writings to understand multicultural education, critical pedagogy, narrative inquiry and the importance of a "feminist lens." My personal favorites are the following: Anzaldúa's (1999) *Borderlands: La Frontera* highlights issues of "border crossing" in an interesting personal manner that includes poetry and a Latina feminist lens. Clandinin and Connelly's (2000) book *Narrative Inquiry: Experience and Story in Qualitative Research* has become standard reading for all my students. One of my students, Yu-chi Sun, recently won the outstanding dissertation award in Pennsylvania for her piece on Chinese immigrant daughters, and she was influenced by Connelly and Clandinin as well as Ming Fang He's (2003) inspiring publication *A River Forever Flowing: Cross-Cultural Lives and Identities in the Multicultural Landscape.*

My dear colleague and *hermano* Joe Kincheloe's (2001) *Getting Beyond the Facts* is extremely valuable to teachers interested in understanding educational social realities of the contemporary sphere. Kincheloe and Steinberg's (*hermana*) (1997) *Changing Multiculturalism* is a genius of a piece for gaining a critical lens in the field of multicultural education. Peter McLaren's (1997) *Revolutionary Multiculturalism* will also help you gain deeper insights into critical multiculturalism.

bell hooks's work also spans many contemporary issues. I recommend *Teaching to Transgress* (1994) for teachers who can envision themselves as "transformative intellectuals" and *Sisters of the Yam* (1993) for notions of healing and self-recovery. I humbly add my own work *Language, Culture and Power: Bilingual Families Struggle for Quality Education* (Soto, 1997b), depicting the daily educational realities of Steel Town. There are certainly many more salient readings, but at least this list will contribute to your journey.

Reflective Questions

1. Are there particular ethical and moral roles teachers have after a catastrophic rupture such as the events of September 11?

2. What does it take for a teacher to participate in "transformative healing"?

3. What is our role as teachers in the complexities of the democratic sphere?

Note

1. Poetry by Suheir Hummad is reprinted with permission.

References

Anzaldúa, G. (1999). *Borderlands: La frontera. The new Mestiza* (2nd ed.). San Francisco: Aunt Lute Books.

Brabeck, K. (2003). Testimonio: A strategy for collective resistance, cultural survival and building solidarity. *Feminism and Psychology, 13*(2), 252–258.

Britzman, D. (2002). The death of the curriculum. In W. E. Doll & N. Gough (Eds.), *Curriculum visions* (pp. 92–101). New York: Peter Lang.

Clandinin, D. J., & Connelly, F. M. (2000). *Narrative inquiry. Experience and story in qualitative research.* San Francisco: Jossey-Bass.

Connelly, F. M., & Clandinin, D. J. (1990). Stories of experience and narrative inquiry. *Educational Researcher, 19*(5), 2–14.

Foucault, M. (1977). *Power/Knowledge.* New York: Pantheon Books.

Freire, P. (1970). *Pedagogy of the oppressed.* New York: Seabury.

Freire, P. (1985). *The politics of education: Culture, power, and liberation.* South Hadley, MA: Bergin & Garvey.

Garcia, A. M. (Director/Producer). (1982). *La Operacion* [Videorecording]. New York: Latin American Film Project.

Giroux, H. (1988). *Teachers as intellectuals: Toward a critical pedagogy of learning.* South Hadley, MA: Bergin & Garvey.

Giroux, H. (1993). *Living dangerously: Multiculturalism and the politics of difference.* New York: Peter Lang.

Hammad, S. (2001–2002, Winter). First writing since September 11. *Rethinking Schools,* p. 7.

He, M. F. (2003). *A river forever flowing: Cross-cultural lives and identities in the multicultural landscape.* Greenwich, CT: Information Age Publishing.

hooks, b. (1993). *Sisters of the yam: Black women and self-recovery.* Boston: South End Press.

hooks, b. (1994*). Teaching to transgress.* New York: Routledge.

Kincheloe, J. (2001). *Getting beyond the facts.* New York: Peter Lang.

Kincheloe, J., & Steinberg, S. (1997). *Changing multiculturalism.* London: Open Press.

King, M. L., Jr. (2001–2002, Winter). When silence is betrayal. *Rethinking Schools,* p. 24.

McLaren, P. (1997). *Revolutionary multiculturalism: Pedagogies of dissent for the new millennium.* Boulder, CO: Westview Press.

Merleau-Ponty, M. (2002). In A. Edgar & P. Sedgwick (Eds.), *Cultural theory* (pp. 158–160). New York: Routledge.

Smith, L. T. T. R. (2000). Kaupapa Maori research. In M. Battiste (Ed.), *Reclaiming indigenous voice and vision* (pp. 224–247). Vancouver, Canada: University of British Columbia Press.

Soto, L. D. (1997a). Boricuas in America: The struggle for identity, language, and power. *The Review of Education/Pedagogy/Cultural Studies, 19*(4), 349–365.

Soto, L. D. (1997b). *Language, culture, and power: Bilingual families and the struggle for quality education.* Albany: SUNY Press.

Soto, L. D. (1999). Toward a critical postmodern narrative inquiry. *Contemporary Psychology Journal, 45*(1), 14–16.

Soto, L. D. (2001a). Childhood memories. *Anthropology and Education Quarterly, 32*(1), 1–9.

Soto, L. D. (2001b). The politics of civility: Struggles of a Latina in the Academy. *Taboo, 4*(2), 5–10.

Soto, L. D. (2002a, Fall). Latino children's perspectives of bilingualism: Altruistic possibilities. *Bilingual Research Journal, 26,* 723–733.

Soto, L. D. (Ed.). (2002b). *Making a difference in the lives of bilingual/bicultural children.* New York: Peter Lang.

Soto, L. D. (in press). Children make the best theorists. In L. D. Soto & Swadener (Eds.), *Power and voice in research with children.* New York: Peter Lang.

Zapatistas. (1998). *Zapatistas encuentro: Documents from the 1996 encounter for humanity against neoliberalism.* New York: Seven Stories Press.

9

How Is Education Possible When There's a Body in the Middle of the Room?

Freema Elbaz-Luwisch

Autobiographical Introduction

This chapter tells the story of my attempt to figure out what might be learned from the situation of living with violence, threats to personal safety, and death as part of the everyday. Born in Canada, I moved to Israel in 1983, and I've been involved since 1986 in teaching in a multicultural setting at the University of Haifa, where the student body includes recent immigrants to Israel, students from the Palestinian community within Israel, as well as students from veteran Jewish Israeli families of a range of ethnic backgrounds. In recent years, much of my teaching and research has focused on bringing about experiences of dialogue between Jewish and Arab/Palestinian Israelis in preservice and inservice settings. In doing this work I draw on my own family history as a daughter of parents who immigrated to Canada from Eastern Europe and who lost many family members in the Holocaust. Having been drawn to narrative as a research method, I began paying more attention to my own story, past and present, as well as to the stories of students. The focus on narratives told and written by students has led me to believe that it is of paramount importance to give place in the classroom to the expression of feelings, such as fear, vulnerability, and anger, and to the body, which carries these feelings and experiences. A pedagogy that integrates feelings and makes room for bodily experience is difficult to manage in a traditional university setting, yet this is what is called for in order to make dialogue across difference possible.

How Is Education Possible?

There's a body in the middle of the room. We ignore it. I, as the teacher, show students how to do this, and they follow my lead. Because my students are teachers and prospective teachers, trained by years in classrooms, they are already inclined to ignore the body. But the fact that I set an example is undoubtedly reassuring. Usually, of course, we ignore the body by ignoring it—we don't speak about it, we don't look directly at it, we change the subject quickly if there's a risk of noticing it. Sometimes, however, we have to ignore it by speaking about it— by saying the right things and then carrying on with our assigned topic.

In an intriguing philosophical reflection on education, Vanderstraeten and Biesta (2001) formulated a provocative question: "How is education possible?" Their question relates to the very possibility and significance of intersubjectivity in education. They respond to the question through two texts, in which they explore somewhat different lines of thought. Both take Dewey as a starting point, but Vanderstraeten goes on to reflect on social systems and on the results of empirical research, while Biesta explores the work of Arendt. They conclude, together, that what educates is the educational "situation," by which they refer to the in-between space that results from the difference between educator and student. Their two texts are intended to embody this insight: they insist that the two texts could not be combined, nor could a third, definitive text be written. It is not Dewey, or Arendt, who provides the answers, nor is there any other privileged conceptualization by the authors that might answer their question. The meaning resides in the space between, in the dynamic of the dialogue itself. But what kind of meaning can be forged when, in the space between, lies a body?

The question—how is education possible—comes from a paradoxical, postmodern space in which speech has become problematic and meaning has become problematic, thus conveying that meaning through speech—without which it is, indeed, hard to conceive of education–can no longer be taken for granted. This paradoxical space is a relatively familiar one in current academic discourse, but in everyday life most of us manage to conceive of the world as a relatively orderly place in which the possibility of communication is taken for granted. We do so despite the evidence of the evening news, despite the history of the last century in which so many millions were murdered, despite the mysterious logic of globalization that seems to pervade every corner of our lives, and despite the hallucinatory nature of popular culture. Such is the power of the need to make meaning, to construct a story that hangs together for our lives.

Since October 2000 my colleagues and I have been trying to conduct the business of education in an Israeli university, while around us much of reality has seemed to be crumbling into dust, violence has become taken for granted, and the possibility of dialogue with others cannot be assumed in advance. We ask the question "How is education possible?" and our actions tell us that education is still possible because we continue to do our work. My personal attempt to refocus the question began in late August 2001 when I attended a meeting at Givat Haviva, the Jewish-Arab institute of the Kibbutz movement. A group of Jewish and Arab/Palestinian Israelis[1] was invited to meet with Palestinians from East Jerusalem; the participants were people who had worked in various contexts to foster Israeli-Palestinian dialogue, and the meeting was convened to discuss ways of continuing. After the meeting, a press conference was scheduled—an opportunity to demonstrate publicly that Israeli-Palestinian cooperation still took place after a year of violent clashes and the suspension of the peace process, a chance to show that talking was still possible. In the middle of the meeting, one of the guests took a call on his cell phone and returned to the room to inform us that a prominent Palestinian had just been killed—assassinated, in the language of one side, "taken out" for the sake of preventing further violence, in the language of the other. After some comments on this event, the conversation continued, no less friendly than before. But when we moved to the room where the press conference was to be held, we found that everyone was there but the press. Most of the reporters had been sent to cover the assassination, and our message that dialogue was still possible would not be heard that day. The situation felt very familiar, and the theme was simple: every time we try to conduct a dialogue, we are stopped because there's a body in the middle of the room.

Multicultural Dialogue in Teacher Education

All this time, while my colleagues and I have been teaching prospective teachers, working with experienced teachers and other practitioners in the context of graduate study, attending meetings, planning programs, discussing faculty policy, advising students, and even moving to new offices, we've had one ear tuned to the news. We hear of the latest suicide bombing and reach for our cell phones to check on family members and friends. We hear of the latest military action and go to our computers to receive anguished messages from observers in Ramallah or Jenin. We sign petitions and send e-mails. In between, because we're at our computers anyway, we keep writing. We go to class, distribute bibliographies, lecture, and conduct discussions. Our students represent the diversity of Israeli society: Arab students make up 20 percent of the student body at the University of Haifa, paralleling their proportion in the population, while about a third of the Jewish students are of Sephardic origin (North Africa and Asia), and about 20 percent of those of Ashkenazi origin (Europe) are immigrants from the former Soviet Union. Until recently, our campus was a stage on which many of the relationships and conflicts of the larger society were played out in small, passionate but homely dramas

(Elbaz-Luwisch, 2001b; Hertz-Lazarowitz, 2003). Since October 2000, however, student demonstrations on campus have been closely monitored and have alternated with periods of restriction in which political demonstrations were banned. There has been an ongoing atmosphere of tension.

Many of the courses I teach for prospective teachers focus on multiculturalism, and as I have conceptualized these courses, dialogue among students from different backgrounds is always one of the main vehicles for learning about multiculturalism in education. Generating such dialogue has never been a straightforward matter, and I have puzzled over it repeatedly (Elbaz-Luwisch 2001a, 2001b). Since the breakdown of the Israeli-Palestinian peace process in the fall of 2000, however, the situation has become even more difficult. Many students would prefer the university classroom to be a protected space in which political events and circumstances are left outside the door and in which the focus is exclusively on some "neutral" course content. On one occasion, when an Arab student suggested we talk about "Israeli identity" (a topic that was quite relevant to the course content), he was greeted by groans from most of the Jewish students: "We talk about it all the time, we're sick of it." As violence has escalated, it often seems that students are unwilling even to sit in small groups to talk with members of the "other" side. In one course, students were asked to write stories of an encounter with an "Other"; I learned that the Other may be one's cooperating teacher, a friend who betrays one's trust, or a foreign worker. If Jews and Arabs are in fact Others to one another, apparently it's not safe to talk about it. But whether we talk about it or not, there's a body in the middle of the room.

Dialogue in Situations of Violence

Trying to understand how death, violence, and the threat of violence impact the lives of teachers and students in this context has become a preoccupation, if not an obsession; probably it's also a survival mechanism for me. I have spent months searching out texts, images, and resources that could help me create meaning in the present moment. My search has taken me backward to familiar texts and vaguely recalled imagery, sideways to literature in unfamiliar areas, and sometimes, one hopes, forward to new ideas. In the educational literature well-meaning statements abound: The world's children are our future, and war affects children in many complicated and tragic ways, says Byrnes (2001). After September 11, thoughtful articles began to appear with suggestions for how to conduct discussions in schools and university classrooms (Kardia, Bierwert, Cook, Miller, & Kaplan, 2002) and how to encourage respect for difference (Bruffee, 2002), but these, and the more familiar narrative treatments of diversity (e.g., Conle, 1996)—including my own earlier work (Elbaz-Luwisch, 2001a,

2001b)—seem far away from the situations I encounter now working with practicing and preservice teachers in Israel. In the refuge of the library, I found violence to be a hot topic, recurring in a range of journals dealing with culture, spirituality, media, anthropology, and religion; one day I left the library carrying a small book with a red and white cover, titled *High Explosives and Propellants* (Fordham, 1980). This is a time of clashing images and disharmonious sounds, of bad lighting, poor acoustics, and half-baked ideas.

I began my personal exploration with a return to *The Interpretation of Cultures* (Geertz, 1973), remembering an image that Geertz had presented from fieldwork in Indonesia of a child who died suddenly while living in the home of a relative. Political and religious conflict in circumstances of rapid change, instability, and jockeying for power among local leaders all contributed to an awkward and painful situation: the child could not be buried until agreement was reached about which rituals were appropriate for the family in question and who was authorized to conduct them. Finally, after hours of agonized waiting, the process of preparing the body was begun. By then so much time had gone by that the body was stiff and difficult to hold, and the family members were almost too distressed to perform the traditional task of holding and washing the body. The image is a stark one that underlines how disruptive cultural and political changes can appropriate even the deeply personal experience of losing a loved one.

Another image is provided by Rosaldo (1988), who describes what he learned from the acute grief over his wife's accidental death while conducting fieldwork in the Philippines. The phenomenon of headhunting had been difficult or even impossible to understand before he experienced his personal tragedy. Later, his own experience of grief provided an avenue of emotional connection that enabled him to make sense of the experiences of the Ilongot people who, as one of them explained it, cut off human heads because "rage, born of grief, impels him to kill his fellow human beings" (p. 178). What Rosaldo found in common with the experiences of the headhunter was not just the grief itself but the fact that this "rage born of devastating loss" is situated at rock bottom, not susceptible to further justification or accounting: "This anger at abandonment is irreducible in that nothing at a deeper level explains it" (p. 191).

What I begin to learn from these examples is that we may share some common emotions across cultures, yet these emotions may be situated in different ways, both within ourselves and within or outside of our explanatory frames of reference. In the Middle Eastern context, Palestinians often claim that suicide bombers are acting out of deep despair and hopelessness, but this explanation is one that most Jewish Israelis can hardly hear. They cannot see a connection between despair and the taking of innocent lives; in fact, they are often outraged at the idea that explanation is possible, just as headhunting as a response to grief initially made no sense to Rosaldo. He wonders at the fact that "most anthropologists write about death as if they were positioned as uninvolved spectators who have no lived experience that could provide knowledge about the cultural force of emotions" (1988, p. 193). His argument suggests that we will be unable to understand one another unless we draw on our own lived experience.

Lived experience, however, can be both a powerful tool of understanding and a trap. There is no simple, unmediated feeling (see Boler, 1999). For example, Ribbens (1998) comments,

> I have found . . . that my voice concerning my moral obligations towards my child subverts, or drowns out, my feeling voice as a basis for my mothering. Further, these moral voices may well monitor and reshape the feeling voices, so that I may only experience the correct feelings appropriate for a good mother.

Ribbens speaks primarily about the way that the personal expression of feeling is shaped by public discourse. In the local context, it is apparent that one may come to experience the correct feelings appropriate for a good Israeli or Palestinian.

The shaping of discourse is a material, commodified process as well as a social and intellectual one. In Israel, there has long been a tendency to focus on home and family in difficult times. This seems like a "natural" response: in times of war and threat to personal safety it is natural to remember who and what are really important; and besides, many people naturally prefer to stay home when restaurants and discotheques are prime candidates for bombings. However, how we live in our homes is never entirely a private matter. Focusing on the media, one notices that television programming is replete with cooking and home decorating programs from around the world, as well as local versions copied by Israeli channels. The messages conveyed by these programs seem to reach into unexpected places, leading me to wonder if it would it be appropriate to include in an academic paper the Naked Chef's recipe for a salad of grilled vegetables and couscous. In a time of economic recession and high unemployment, it is ironic that one of the dairy companies recently introduced a new line of yogurt, with a large number of new flavors that have not only names but personalities: Blushing Raspberry, Innocent Apple, Optimistic Berry, Shy Fig, and Peach in Love. An example at the other end of the economic spectrum is an advertisement for a new shopping plaza that features shops selling exclusive furniture and home design products. The full-page advertisement tells the reader that, in these times, all of us turn inward and focus on our homes. We're invited to come to the new center, which features the best security arrangements possible; apparently, buying a new sofa may take the edge off the latest report on the TV news.

> The interval between the ignition of the fusehead and the bursting of the detonator is known as the reaction time and the interval between the breaking of the fuse wire and the bursting of the detonator is known as the induction time. (Fordham, 1980, p. 113)

Despite these distractions regularly thrown my way from the popular culture, my attempt to learn something from the experience of violence is ongoing. Wilcox (2001) discusses the 1998 murder of Matthew Shepard in Laramie, Wyoming, arguing that this act can be considered a form of "symbolically disruptive violence," an act that threatens a particular group's symbolic world. She considers the various media and community responses to that murder as indications of attempts to reconstruct those shattered worlds. Many of the events of the past year and a half in the Middle East have carried symbolic meanings that seemed too heavy for the actual events themselves to bear—the death of a young Palestinian boy, Mohammed Al Dura, caught in crossfire while huddled against his father; the bombing that took place in a hotel where Israelis, many of them elderly, were gathering to celebrate the Passover seder. The main disruption caused by such events is of the fragile vision of two states living in peace; but the more problematic disruption in an educational context is of the very possibility for ordinary people on both sides to continue to see that those on the other side are, like themselves, ordinary people. It is this disruption that forces me to question whether education is possible, whether it is still possible to speak about dialogue across cultural differences.

Suicide bombings, combined with the characterization of the bomber as a "martyr" for the Palestinian cause, is undoubtedly the one phenomenon that makes dialogue most difficult for Jewish Israelis. This observation led me to readings on the theme of sacrifice. Driver (2000) defines human sacrifice as "any ritually justified taking of life" (p. 101). Driver is not talking about acts of terrorism or about struggles for independence, much less about the actions of duly constituted national military forces. He explores the ritualized violence of a variety of religious practices, ancient and current, and suggests also that "there is something ritualistic about the crimes of serial killers" (p. 111). To make sense of this, he draws on Artaud's definition of cruelty: "Cruelty signifies rigor, implacable intention and decision, irreversible and absolute determination" (p. 110). Not all the violence of the past year and a half in the Middle East has reflected these qualities, but some of it has. Seeking the roots—the motives and impulsions—for acts of violence, Driver suggests,

> Ritual arises when human beings set out not only to perform an act that is irreversible, as all acts are, but also to demonstrate this irreversibility . . . the demonstration of the power to act may very well be undertaken for one's own benefit—to lift confidence, perhaps, or to obtain the clarity and exhilaration that come from heightened attention to one's own behavior. (p. 111)

Engaging in acts of violence conveys power, awesome power that perhaps is easier to wield when it is ritualized, given transcendent meaning by myths, declarations of communal purpose, and calling. Driver's analysis suggests that there is also a liberative potential to ritual and that it does not have to be fulfilled through violence. Theorists such as Girard and Kristeva, however, argue that violence is the organizing principle, so to speak, of society—that collective identity is forged through violence. Anderson (2000) contrasts these two theorists, arguing that "in achieving collective identity by way of sacrifice patriarchal cultures have denied sexual difference and love in immolating the lives of others as the Other" (p. 217). Reading Kristeva for a way to subvert the violence of patriarchy, she suggests that, according to Kristeva, violence is sexually differentiated, repeating in a mimetic fashion the primordial rupture between the infant and the body of the mother. Anderson sees hope of reconfiguring "the nature of our desires, in recognizing violence as the *force* of love, in order that the other might be welcomed and not sacrificed for the same" (p. 226). I'm not sure I fully understand Anderson's argument, but it is by reading with my body rather than my intellect alone that I sense something important here. In a recent discussion among a group of Jewish and Arab teachers (in an inservice workshop on multiculturalism), one of the moments of understanding occurred when some of the women spoke about their fear, fear for the physical safety of their children and husbands. Speaking about their children created a sense of shared feeling among Jewish and Arab participants, which interrupted what had been a very heated argument moments before. But this sort of feeling can be and is manipulated to serve public ends. In "Stabat Mater," Kristeva (1992) underlines how maternal feeling has served the power of the patriarchy. One has only to recall images of wartime ceremonies honoring the mothers of fallen soldiers as they are presented with the military decorations earned by their sons. However, Anderson suggests that we might be able to draw on the same resources to imagine something different.

An Example From Teacher Education in the Israeli Context

Through my meetings with teachers and prospective teachers, I try hard to imagine something different. Paying attention to my own body is the beginning of this. One day I tripped on the stairs on my way to class. A sprained ankle slowed me down enough to become aware that I could hardly bear to go to class; I no longer had the energy to teach Jewish and Arab students who seemed so unwilling to talk to one another, even though I could well understand their reasons. Thinking about it so directly made it impossible to continue as I had before, and the only option I could imagine was to speak about it with the students, to open up the class to discussion about the situation if they so wished. I did so in two different groups, and the response both times was similar: first silence, then a hesitant response, and finally a heated discussion that greatly disturbed some students but was a relief to others. Informal conversations with students in the days that followed, as well as their written feedback at the end of the course, indicated that the discussion seemed to give rise to some interesting outcomes. The following describes some of the discussion in one of the two classes.

The first to take up the challenge was Alia,[2] who raised her hand and said that she had been very hurt by the fact that a Jewish student group had protested the activity of Arab students who collected financial and other contributions for residents of the Palestinian areas. She saw this act as purely humanitarian and could not understand the protest against it. This, of course, was a sufficiently provocative statement for the Jewish students to enter the discussion. Sitting next to Alia, Bella tried to explain her fear that money thus raised might be used for purposes that were not humanitarian, that is, to finance further terror activities. Carim told us that he has been involved in a Jewish-Arab group that went to Jenin to see what had happened there and that it had been shocking. He told us that terror acts inside Israel also shocked him and that he had visited Poland and toured a concentration camp and was horrified and saddened there. He said he had stood in silence a few weeks ago on Holocaust Memorial Day with other Arab students, but had been angered when he saw that some Arab students, who chose not to observe the two-minute silence, were met with the comment from a Jewish student that "they are nothing but lice and should be eliminated." Dana later commented that as a Jew she was saddened and upset that after the Holocaust, her country, which should have been a place of supreme tolerance and respect for the other, did not appear to be so.

As the discussion went on, there were some very strong expressions of anger: two or three Jewish students found that shouting was necessary to express what they were feeling. Elana told the Arab students that she expected them to be appreciative of the soldiers who were giving their lives to protect all the citizens of Israel, Arabs as well as Jews, from terror. Frank told us that he had been on reserve duty and had been shocked to see a young Palestinian using an elderly man as a shield. Frank's voice was so loud that a student from the class next door came to our room and stood in amazement for a few moments watching. After each outburst the discussion was relatively calm for a while, until the next. For the most part, the students did try to conduct an orderly discussion and to listen, although it is impossible to know if some people had not tuned out early on after an upsetting comment by the "other side."

Our class was held in a large classroom with long rows of desks fixed to the floor. There were about twenty-five students in the room. At the beginning I had suggested that students could sit around the perimeter of the room facing in so as to see one another. At one point Gila, who was sitting in the front row and facing me rather than the group, said quietly that she had lost a friend in the helicopter disaster of several years ago, that a student of hers had died in a recent terror attack, and that it was very hard for her to participate in the discussion at all. She got up and left the room. I asked people to be silent for a few moments simply to acknowledge what had been brought into the discussion. A few minutes later, Alia got up and also left the room. Later, she and Gila returned together, and Alia told us that they had spoken and had come to some understanding.

Toward the end of the class, Helena told us that as a Christian she had been opposed not only to violence but especially to suicide bombings and the idea that a suicide bomber could be a "martyr" for the Palestinian cause. But after recent events, she was beginning to understand the suicide bombers. Several other Arab students related to the desperation of the bombers. Their comments were received angrily by Jewish students, even though they had said they "understood" the bombers, not that they supported them. But their Jewish listeners accused them of "identifying" with them. Someone said, "If you can understand, that means you identify with them." Jenny, a Jewish student, originally from the former Soviet Union, said she had been raised to be loyal to her country no matter what and could not accept that the Arab citizens of Israel did not seem to feel such loyalty. Another Jewish student, Keren, said that she lives in a town where Jews and Arabs have long lived side by side, but that now she finds herself fearing and suspecting her Arab neighbors: recently an Arab from that town was found to have assisted a suicide bomber. At this point, one of the students pointed out that there was much generalizing in the discussion: everyone tended to speak of "us" and "them" or used the second-person plural to address the "other group" in class.

By the end of class, our discussion had been full of bodies: the victims of terror attacks, the bodies of the suicide bombers, the victims killed in the territories in recent weeks. There was also the tired body of at least one student, Lisa, who said she has eight hours of class in a row on Wednesdays, and the discussion had upset her so much that she did not know how she would get through the rest of the day. "This is not what the course is supposed to be about, and it's a waste of time," she argued, "because none of us [are] going to change our minds." I suggested that the usefulness of the discussion is not measured in whether or not people change their minds. "Is it therapy then?" she asked. I replied that I didn't know how to separate the emotional from the cognitive and that one of the useful things we might be learning is how to relate to difficult issues in the classroom, issues likely to come up in the schools where these students will be teaching in the future.

When class ended I thanked all the students, including those who had been silent; it was clear to me that all of them had contributed to making the discussion possible. A few people thanked me; many left with closed expressions I could not read. I left the classroom with mixed feelings. Reflecting on the class, I was glad I had seized the opportunity. I could point to several moments during which something worthwhile might have happened: a few students had had the opportunity to get something off their chests; there was an important moment of connection between Alia and Gila; and a few people reiterated the idea that talking together was the only option, thus reinforcing an idea and a hope that have become extremely difficult to sustain in recent days. Emotionally and physically, however, I felt drained, as if I had been crying. Looking back, I realized that while the number of Jewish and Arab students who participated actively in the discussion was about equal, the strong outbursts of anger all came from Jewish students, for whom, I realized, it was safer to express themselves. In two cases I supported those outbursts with my body, by going and standing behind the students and by signaling to other students who wanted to respond to wait until the outburst was over.

When we met again a week later, we briefly discussed the previous class. Several students stated their feeling that the shouting had been inappropriate and should have been "controlled" in some way by me as teacher. I'm not sure they accepted my explanation that there was shouting because there was so much strong feeling and that, without letting some of that feeling come to expression, there could not have been a discussion. However, the majority of students seemed to agree that it had been important and useful to talk, and the atmosphere in the class now seemed quite different. When we carried on with our scheduled program, working in small groups, there were a number of groups in which Jewish and Arab students worked together.

The Place of Bodily Experience in Dialogue Across Difference

Engaging in discussions of this kind, in which there is room for the expression of strong feeling, and in which all the different positions can speak out (including those that are far from the mainstream and even those that are not "socially acceptable," e.g., the terrorist), has been referred to as "sitting in the fire" (Mindell, 1995). The approach developed by Mindell stresses that it is important in any conflict to listen to all the voices and opinions. Further, the emphasis is on integrating and transforming violence and other negative forces. The discourse of Western culture has focused on seeking to eliminate violence, to resolve conflict, and to eradicate suffering rather than to search out deeper understandings of both the circumstances and their underlying meanings. But there are some attempts to think differently; for example, Wilkinson (2001) proposes "thinking with suffering." In some postmodern feminist work, there is a similar understanding of the need to process conflict, to "face up" to evil, to the imagery of violence, particularly with respect to the nuclear complex (e.g., Keller, 1990). I note the imagery of "sitting" used by Mindell and that of "facing up" by Keller. In situations of conflict, our bodies are mobilized by ancient programming to fight or flee. To ask of students and ourselves to remain calm, to listen attentively, to respond with empathy and understanding, in short to engage in a disembodied and disinterested dialogue when virtually everyone feels that his or her physical safety may be at stake and indeed, our very existence as a group seems threatened (whether it is or not), is not reasonable. We need to find ways of allowing bodies—live bodies—to enter that in-between space where education can take place. If we don't enter the space together, the media, politics, power, and fate will take up the space and fill it with lifeless bodies.

Since Johnson (1989) proposed that the knowledge of teachers is embodied, too little work has been done that directly pursues this idea. The body-mind split continues to hold sway on the thinking and living of educators. Yet when a Finnish colleague and I examined the stories of teachers from Finland and Israel, we found that even in two cultures with quite different patterns of physical expressiveness, teachers' accounts of their lives and work were full of bodies—theirs and their pupils' (Estola & Elbaz-Luwisch, 2003). In my classes I saw this knowledge of the body in the students' reaching out to one another, in their expression of a common fear for their own safety and that of their children. This implicit knowledge is waiting to be brought forward and used, and if we want to move into that space between, we will need it.

> Another person is something perceived, exposed to us, and circumscribed by our vision. His intentions are exposed by the way he stands and moves, by his body kinesics, and by his words. His actions and his body are also exposed to our operations; his space is in the common world. He is exposed to being violated, outraged, wounded by us. . . . And for us to defer to another, to subordinate our behavior to some extent to him, is to expose ourselves to him—expose ourselves to being violated, outraged, wounded by him. To approach another with respect is to expose our seriousness of purpose to the flash-fires of his laughter, to expose our cheerfulness to the darkness of his grief, to let him put his blessing on our discomfiture and suffering, to expose ourselves to the shock waves of his curses. It is through our wounds that we communicate. (Lingis, 2000, p. 179)

Lingis is a philosopher writing from an ecological perspective, and his words evoke the body as vulnerable, as living in a shared space with others, and as providing ground and possibility for communication. Horowitz (1992), a political philosopher with a different agenda, comes to a similar conclusion: he argues for a form of "groundless democracy" in which the lived experience of the body becomes a kind of touchstone: bodies constitute "a field of lived meanings that are not derived solely from linguistic forms" (p. 161), and as such they carry wisdom about their own felt needs. Listening to the body, according to Horowitz, we will discover the need for sharing, for reciprocal relations with others. In the experience of the body, "there is compassion, the listening and feeling together of self and other" (p. 163). I find these understandings of the body as a foundation, the organizing template for individual and shared experience, useful in orienting to a pedagogy that would pay attention to the body.

In trying to act on this sense of the importance of our implicit knowledge of the body, I have conducted two different activities, both in small groups, which seemed to mobilize bodily understandings. In the first activity, students were asked to present a program or curriculum that fostered multicultural understanding; it could be an existing program or one they developed. Their task was to prepare a poster and make a brief presentation about the program they chose. This is quite an ordinary sort of activity, but in the context of a diverse group it had some effects that were unexpected, and this despite the fact that most of the students worked with people from their own group or background. The students chose many different kinds of programs to present, but the common denominator was that all the programs were designed to foster understanding between diverse groups. There were a number of surprises both for me and for the students. First, we were surprised to discover the wide range of resources already available, as well as the creativity of some of the students in developing their own ideas. Second, we had the opportunity to *see* all of the students standing in front of the class talking about a program they found interesting. In a situation where both sides often find it easier and less painful to simply ignore the existence of the other, this is not trivial. For example, we saw a group of Arab students present a program designed to teach students about the history of Jerusalem as a city that is sacred to three religions. We also saw two Jewish students, future literature teachers, present a plan to teach Jewish pupils the history of the many Arab villages left behind in 1948, using a short story told from the perspective of an Arab child. We saw a group of Jewish and Arab students who had worked together to propose a unit on games and toys in different cultures. What we saw, in effect, was prospective teachers from all the different groups standing up and declaring themselves, in a variety of ways, as supporting coexistence and intercultural understanding, supporting it not just at the level of beliefs and opinions but at the level of physical action. For every program presented there may well have been students in the class who did not agree with the content as laid out in the given program (the program on the Arab villages prior to 1948 is an example that would draw fire if it were implemented in a Jewish school). After each presentation, there was a discussion and critique of the various programs, but the impact of this activity seemed to go beyond cognitive understandings, creating some common ground where all of us could stand together in support of our diversity.[3]

The second activity, which seemed to engage students emotionally and bodily as well as intellectually, is one in which each person is asked to write the life story of someone who has had an important influence on him or her. Students write about a parent or family member, a friend, or even a political or literary figure who has influenced them. They are asked to be descriptive and to include telling anecdotes that will enable the reader to get a good sense of who the person is and what his or her influence has been on the life of the writer. Some included photographs or illustrations of various kinds. Most of the students choose to write about people who really are or have been important in their lives, and to the extent that the writers are indeed fully engaged in the writing. The students are then organized by me into groups of about five to share their stories and to explore the various issues that arise from a meeting of their stories. Bodily understanding comes into this activity in a number of ways: in the life stories themselves, the body is evident in their physical descriptions of their subjects, in the accounts of caring they received from parents or grandparents, and in anecdotes about the actions, exploits, working lives, suffering, and living of the persons written about. In the group activity, the body is engaged as well. The students work in their groups for about half the semester, sitting together and getting to know one another. They have to find ways to get along because the group work constitutes half of their mark for the course, so they are also involved in practical considerations related to dividing up the task and getting it done. One of the subtasks requires each student to write an appreciation of one of the other stories in her group. Thus, one student, who was born in the Soviet Union, expressed his admiration for an Arab man who had ten children and had managed to help all of them attend university. A Jewish student was impressed by the story of the life of Jesus as told by a Christian student. And Suha, a Muslim woman, told her group that she took the same message from Dina's story of her mother who had immigrated to Israel from Argentina as she found in Abir's story of her father who had left his village in 1948 and spent several years in Lebanon before being able to return home. Both of them love their country and have a sense of belonging to something larger than themselves, Suha pointed out.

Another subtask is that of identifying stereotypes and ideas that people hold about other groups and cultures that are brought to the fore and questioned by students as they encountered the different life stories. Becoming aware of the stereotypes one harbors is difficult under any circumstances, and asking students to reveal these stereotypes to others in a group is perhaps intrusive as well. I debated this point with myself for a long time, feeling at an impasse. Eventually I decided to follow an instinct and to simply imagine that it was easy. On the list of guidelines for the group assignment, one item simply reads, "Make a list of the stereotypes that you discovered in working with the stories (at least 3)." The groups had no difficulty complying with this task. One student (mentioned earlier) noted his stereotype that large families were always economically and educationally disadvantaged. Another, after reading the life story of the Egyptian woman writer Nawal El Sadawi, indicated the stereotypical view of women's limited abilities prevalent in his background. Several had been led to question stereotypical views of religious people after reading one of the life stories. Perhaps the students did not have great revelations as a result of this activity, but only listed common stereotypes that were elicited by the stories; nonetheless, the activity probably had some usefulness in reminding them of the need to watch for stereotypical thinking and generalizations about various groups.

Finn (1992) discusses the possibility of "being-otherwise-than-being a man, a woman, a Christian, a Jew, a mother, daughter, father, son, etc." (p. 112). She imagines a space that is "between experience and expression, reality and representation, existence and essence: the concrete fertile pre-thematic and an-archic space *where we actually live.*" This space is the site where learning might take place, a space where it is possible to engage with

> judgement and critique, creativity and value, resistance and change. It is the ground of the critical intentions and originating experiences which enable us to call the political status quo into question . . . the only place from which the conventionality, the contingency ("the arbitrariness") of reality (of political positivities and identities) can be seen and challenged. (p. 113)

The good news for educators is that according to Finn this space does not have to be created; it is where we already live. And although the terms in which they describe it are different, it seems that this is close to the space that Vanderstraeten and Biesta (2001) also imagine. We recognize it in our experiences of excess, confusion, ambiguity, chaos, and chance—experiences that have been common fare in the last few years in the Middle East, but are also well known to many around the world, in developing countries, and in North America and the West in the aftermath of September 11, 2001. It is a space that disappears when we retreat into the categories that define who we are— Christian, Muslim, Jew—and forget that we are always "more and less than what we stand for in the polis and what stands for us" (Finn, 1992, p. 113). And yet, to say that we are more and less is clearly not to make facile declarations of common humanity, nor to stake the claims of a common and transcendent spirituality. We are more, and less, than these as well. Engaging with life stories that matter to them, and with curricular materials that speak of possibilities for making a difference, the students are perhaps better able to see one another as more, and less, than members of particular groups. The various activities in which I have engaged with them do seem to bring them into contact with the place where they already live, with their own life experience and resources, as well as their difficulties. Engaging with the students and with the real materials of their lives, in this way, makes education almost possible.

Recommended Readings

To gain a better understanding of the complicated reality that is discussed in this chapter, I suggest reading a number of different kinds of work. The particular situation of Jewish and Arab students on the campus of the University of Haifa was studied by Hertz-Lazarowitz (2003) in the framework of her courses in the faculty of education; her article discusses "Arab and Jewish Youth in Israel: Voicing National Injustice on Campus." A philosophical study that examines attitudes toward the past and practices of memory in Israel and Palestine is Gur-Zeev's (2001) article "The Production of the Self and the Destruction of the Other's Memory and Identity: Israeli/Palestinian Education on the Holocaust/Nakbah." Two studies that look at the immigrant experience in Israel are an anthropological study by Golden (2001) titled "Storytelling the Future: Israelis, Immigrants and the Imagining of Community" and Lieblich's (1993) study from a psychologically oriented narrative perspective, "Looking at Change: Natasha, 21, New Immigrant From Russia to Israel." An account that lies on the border between journalism and literature is Grossman's (1993) book *Sleeping on a Wire: Conversations With Palestinians in Israel,* which describes the situation of Palestinian citizens of Israel based on conversations with them. Finally, reading Grace Feuerverger's chapter in this book (Chapter 10) will add to the reader's understanding of the present chapter as well.

Reflective Questions

1. The metaphor of "the body in the middle of the room" used in this chapter grew out of a specific experience in the context of a situation of violent political conflict. But it is pertinent to many other situations that affect teachers and students today: many children carry on their bodies the scars of physical and emotional abuse, poverty, hunger, and drug abuse, for example. You are invited to consider what body or bodies may be found in the middle of your own classroom, now or in the future, and what impact that might have on teaching and learning.

2. Paying attention to physical experience in the present was helpful to me in the teacher-education class discussed in this chapter. Think about a significant classroom event for which you have retained a memory of the physical experience: try to recall it in detail, to feel what it was like, perhaps to describe it in writing. Ask yourself why this particular physical experience might have stayed in memory and what connection it might have to your life at present or to your teaching.

3. Have you experienced situations in which conflict was expressed openly in the classroom and addressed in a useful way, or has it more often been brushed aside or dealt with outside the classroom? What is your attitude to conflict in the classroom, and what theories or approaches are you familiar with that might be helpful in dealing with conflict?

Notes

1. Identity is a complicated matter for the Arab/Palestinian citizens of Israel, as reflected in the diverse ways they refer to themselves—they speak Arabic; are Palestinian in cultural, historical, and ethnic affiliation; Muslim, Christian, or Druze by religion; and Israeli citizens. Here, because I also refer to the Palestinians who are residents of the occupied territories, for the sake of clarity I refer to the Israeli Arab/Palestinian teachers and students with whom I work as Arabs. I'm aware that many would define themselves as Palestinians, some as Druze, and others in various combinations of all the above.

2. All names are pseudonyms; I used the letters of the alphabet in order to help keep a sense of the sequence of the discussion.

3. I carried out this activity three times, with more than 100 students, and I have to report that, in one case only, the presentation (about a bilingual Jewish-Arab school) gave rise to a heated argument, not because of its content but because the presenting students used the term "Nakbah" ("catastrophe" in Arabic, the term used for what happened to the Palestinian community in 1948), and in response to a question from a Jewish student translated this term as "Holocaust." Several Jewish students took exception to this, and in the ensuing fray insults were traded and the class was unable to proceed. Eventually there were apologies and the presentation was finished. This was the last class of the semester, and many students left deeply discouraged. However, the students who had been engaged in the argument—a Jewish man and two Palestinian women—stayed behind and talked for almost an hour and eventually shook hands and parted on good terms.

References

Anderson, P. (2000). Sacrificed lives: Mimetic desire, sexual difference and murder. *Cultural Value, 4*(2), 216–227.

Boler, M. (1999). *Feeling power: Emotions and education.* New York & London: Routledge.

Bruffee, K. (2002, January/February). Taking the common ground: Beyond cultural identity. *Change, 34*(1), 11–17.

Byrnes, D. (2001). War and conflict: Educators advocating for the protection of children. *Educational Foru, 65,* 227–232.

Conle, C. (1996). Resonance in preservice teacher inquiry. *American Educational Research Journal, 33*(2), 297–325.

Driver, T. (2000). The act itself: Tracing the roots of violence in ritual. *Soundings, 83*(1), 101–117.

Elbaz-Luwisch, F. (2001a). Personal story as passport: Storytelling in border pedagogy. *Teaching Education, 12*(1), 81–101.

Elbaz-Luwisch, F. (2001b). Understanding what goes on in the heart and in the mind: Learning about diversity and co-existence through storytelling. *Teaching and Teacher Education, 17,* 133–146.

Estola, E., & Elbaz-Luwisch, F. (2003). Teaching bodies at work. *Journal of Curriculum Studies, 35*(6), 1–23.

Finn, G. (1992). The politics of spirituality: The spirituality of politics. In P. Berry & A. Wernick (Eds.), *Shadow of spirit: Postmodernism and religion* (pp. 111–122). London & New York: Routledge.

Fordham, S. (1980). *High explosives and propellants* (2nd revised edition). Oxford, UK: Pergamon Press.

Geertz, C. (1973). *The interpretation of cultures.* New York: Basic Books.

Golden, D. (2001). Storytelling the future: Israelis, immigrants and the imagining of community. *Anthropological Quarterly, 75*(1), 7–35.

Grossman, D. (1993). *Sleeping on a wire: Conversations with Palestinians in Israel.* New York: Farrar, Straus and Giroux.

Gur-Zeev, I. (2001). The production of the self and the destruction of the other's memory and identity: Israeli/Palestinian education on the Holocaust/Nakbah. *Studies in Philosophy and Education, 20*(3), 255–266.

Hertz-Lazarowitz, R. (2003). Arab and Jewish youth in Israel: Voicing national injustice on campus [Special issue on Youth Perspectives on Injustice and Violence]. *Journal of Social Issues, 59*(1), 51–66.

Horowitz, G. (1992). Groundless democracy. In P. Berry & A. Wernick (Eds.), *Shadow of spirit: Postmodernism and religion* (pp. 156–163). London & New York: Routledge.

Johnson, M. (1989). Embodied knowledge. Personal Practical Knowledge Series. *Curriculum Inquiry, 19*(4), 361–377.

Kardia, D., Bierwert, C., Cook, C., Miller, A., & Kaplan, M. (2002, January/February). Discussing the unfathomable: Classroom-based responses to tragedy. *Change, 34*(1), 19–22.

Keller, C. (1990). Warriors, women and the nuclear complex: Toward a postnuclear postmodernity. In D. R. Griffin (Ed.), *Sacred connections: Postmodern spirituality, political economy, and art* (pp. 63–82). Albany: SUNY Press.

Kristeva, J. (1992). Stabat Mater. In T. Moi (Ed.), *The Kristeva Reader* (pp. 160–186). London: Blackwell.

Lieblich, A. (1993). Looking at change: Natasha, 21, New immigrant from Russia to Israel. In R. Josselson & A. Lieblich (Eds.), *The Narrative Study of Lives* (Vol. 1, pp. 92–129). Newbury Park, CA: Sage.

Lingis, A. (2000). Ecological emotions. In R. Frodeman (Ed.), *Earth matters: The Earth sciences, philosophy, and the claims of community* (pp. 175–187). Upper Saddle River, NJ: Prentice Hall.

Mindell, A. (1995). *Sitting in the fire: Large group transformation using conflict and diversity.* Portland, OR: Lao Tse Press.

Ribbens, J. (1998). Hearing my feeling voice? An autobiographical discussion of motherhood. In R. Edwards & J. Ribbens (Eds.), *Feminist dilemmas in qualitative research* (pp. 24–38). London: Sage Ltd.

Rosaldo, R. (1988). Grief and a headhunter's rage: On the cultural force of emotions. In E. Bruner (Ed.), *Text, play, and story: The construction and reconstruction of self and society* (pp. 178–195). Prospect Heights, IL: Waveland Press.

Vanderstraeten, R., & Biesta, G. (2001). How is education possible? Preliminary investigations for a theory of education. *Educational Philosophy and Theory, 33*(1), 7–21.

Wilcox, M. (2001). Murderers and martyrs: Violence, discourse, and the (re)construction of meaning. *Culture and Religion, 2*(2), 155–178.

Wilkinson, I. (2001). Thinking with suffering. *Cultural Values, 5*(4), 421–444.

10

Multicultural Perspectives in Teacher Development

Grace Feuerverger

Autobiographical Introduction

It has been twelve years since I began my faculty position in the Centre for Teacher Development at the Ontario Institute for Studies in Education/ University of Toronto (OISE/UT), and my teaching and research spaces have been filled with a myriad of issues focusing on language, culture, and identity in educational contexts. I acknowledge my own linguistic and cultural life history as a child of Polish and Jewish refugees of the Holocaust, growing up in the Montréal of the 1950s and 1960s. This legacy has provided a significant guiding motif in my professional life. Emotionally, I will forever be wounded in the face of the stark realities of my life history. I have always searched for a sense of personal belonging within the protective layers of my professional life—that is, in school when I was very young and in university when I was older. I found this healing connection when I encountered the embrace of other cultures and languages. Learning languages and writing about the cultures they represented became my foster home: a place where I could negotiate communities that were full of life and energy and continuity.

It was not an accident that I entered the teaching profession after I received a bachelor of arts degree with joint honors in French and Italian literature from McGill University, although I did not know that at the time. I had been involved in some master's courses in Italian literature at the University of California at Berkeley when I happened, quite serendipitously, upon a graduate seminar on the topic of bilingualism being offered at the school of education. This became a pivotal moment in my professional life. I understand now that the texture and meaning of my life began to take shape at that time. I think of the words of Mary Catherine Bateson (1989, p. 29), who said that "composing a life involves a continual re-imagining of the future and reinterpretation of the past to give meaning to the present." My specialization in the PDAD (Professional Diploma After Degree) program at the University of Alberta in Edmonton was in bilingual education. I subsequently taught for seven years as an extended French and French immersion elementary classroom teacher in a bilingual school in a small Franco-Albertan town called Vimy, forty miles north of Edmonton, and in public schools in Edmonton and in Toronto. Those seven years of classroom teaching are the foundation upon which my academic life now firmly stands, and the fruits of those years continually nourish me in all my graduate teaching and in all my research work.

My scholarly writing has always been directly informed by what happens in classrooms and in schools. For me education is about the search for freedom, or as bell hooks (1994) calls it, "the practice of freedom." It is about creating classrooms as sites of cultural encounters and networks of personal and professional negotiations. It is the kind of thoughtful and dynamic process embodied in Paulo Freire's (1970) revolutionary perspective of education as social liberation. Thich Nhat Hanh, the Vietnamese Buddhist monk, acknowledges the teacher as a healer and sees education as a holistic and spiritual practice.

Indeed, when I began my faculty position in the Joint Centre for Teacher Development, I hoped that I was ready to confront my multiple cultural identities, my sense of being on the margins, my psychological "orphanhood" as a child of Holocaust survivors. My desire was to resurrect the lost texts of my past within this new professional world.

The multilayered academic journey that has evolved since then has been both overwhelming and fascinating as it illuminates my interaction with students, colleagues, research participants, friends, relatives, my partner—and, in short, my whole life. My recent book, *Oasis of Dreams: Teaching and Learning Peace in a Jewish-Palestinian Village in Israel* (Routledge/Falmer), is a reflexive ethnography focusing on the two bilingual, bicultural educational institutions in this place of peaceful coexistence—an elementary school where Jewish and Arab children study together and the "School for Peace," which is a conflict-resolution outreach program for Israeli and Palestinian adolescents and their teachers. This book is based on a nine-year study that I carried out as researcher in this extraordinary cooperative village. It is about hope in the midst of deadly conflict, and it has forever changed my life, both professional and personal.

In this chapter, I explore the ways in which discussion formed the basis for creating a spirit of community within the classroom and a vehicle toward intercultural understanding through a strong interactive relationship between my graduate students and me. This chapter is dedicated to the tapestry of meaning that was woven together in my first graduate seminar, "Multicultural Perspectives in Teacher Development."

A Pathway to Narrative: My First
Graduate Course as a Pedagogical Adventure

As I write this piece, a flood of warm memories sweeps over the page from that springtime of my university career, and I feel privileged to have had those experiences to share and to cherish. The story I tell of my own beginning university faculty experience attempts to make sense of the cultural narratives that my graduate students and I created within a setting of pedagogical and collaborative caring (Noddings, 1991). What we searched for was a "communion" in Buber's (1958, 1965) terms—the dialogue between individuals that results in a sense of community and also in a deeper understanding of cross-cultural communication. It turned out in that first year that all the students were women. We gathered to share our professional stories of dislocation, survival, and triumph over adversity. This emergent spirit was very much in keeping with the planned objective of the course, which was to explore issues of diversity and difference within school contexts. Although we came from different places around the world, we had a similar, albeit implicit, agenda in mind—to discuss our research stories as they interacted with our investigations of multicultural classrooms. An experiential approach to the topic appeared to me to be the only methodology that could do it justice. I began to appreciate narrative as a process of making meaning of experience by telling stories of personal and social relevance through conversation and journal writing (Connelly & Clandinin, 1990, 2000) as I began to realize that "we gather other people's experiences because they allow us to become more experienced ourselves" (Van Manen, 1990). Sam Keen (1990) says that

> storytelling is a communal act; it requires community and it creates community. In the telling, there is a teller and a listener, and so it removes the isolation of the sufferer. In the telling, we remember our past, discover our present and envision our future. In the telling, we overcome loneliness. The sharing of our stories cures us. We exchange our unconscious myths, for the conscious autobiography. That is the task of a life.[1]

In order to make sense of the complex cultural worlds we inhabited, my graduate students and I focused on our autobiographical narratives within the context of our professional lives. We jumped out of our compartmentalized boxes to find ourselves in what Ruth Behar (1996) named "a borderland between passion and intellect, analysis and subjectivity, ethnography and autobiography, art and life" (p. 174). In an early journal entry, I acknowledged this strong autobiographical thread among us and concur with Robert Coles (1997) that "intense self-scrutiny is, one hopes, an aspect of all writing, all research," and furthermore "the search for objectivity is waylaid by a stubborn subjectivity" (p. 87). Craig Kridel (1998) underscores the "power of autobiography and biography—the construction of landscapes and the act of making history personal" (p. 122). This was a way to open a textual space for understanding and honoring the struggle of "otherness" without and within ourselves. In one of my first journal entries I wrote,

> I feel privileged to have been allowed into the lives and dreams and nightmares of my students. . . . I sense that we have something deep in common. We have been wounded, but we are survivors. We have come together to give each other support in the retelling and rebuilding of our life stories. We will nurture each other. I think that in a psychological sense we are cultural orphans, all of us. But we are orphans who are determined to succeed. We are the lucky ones. I sense anger in my students, but it is a righteous anger. It is a liberating anger. (September 30, 1991)

Teaching is a highly personal enterprise. William Ayers (1993) captures the essence of it when he writes "that teaching is primarily a matter of love" (p. 18). Any caring teacher understands instinctively that it certainly is not merely a question of mastering certain technical skills. It is relational and interactive. As in any profession where there develops over time an intimate relationship between practitioner and client, teaching is more an art than a science. There is a well-known adage that even the best curriculum materials will fail if the teacher's heart is not in it. As I look back at that first course and all the ones that followed, I am reminded of the eloquent words of Anne Michaels (1996), who says that "the best teacher lodges an intent not in the mind but in the heart" (p. 121). This notion is consistent with Freire's (1994) idea that pedagogy has "as much to do with the teachable heart as the teachable mind, and as much to do with efforts to change the world as it does with rethinking the categories that we use to analyze our current condition within history" (p. 64).

The study of teachers' narratives—that is, teachers' stories of their own experiences—is increasingly being seen as essential to the study of teachers' thinking, culture, and behavior (Goodson, 1991). Indeed, a growing number of scholars now recognize that because teachers are key players in education, their voices need to be heard; they have a right to speak for and about the teaching-learning experience. Furthermore, narrative research is becoming accepted as a means of understanding teachers' culture from within (see, e.g., Carter, 1993; Clandinin & Connelly, 2000; Cole & Knowles, 2000; Eisner, 1991; Goodson, 1991; Schön, 1991; Tabachnick & Zeichner, 1993). However, educational investigators have generally paid too little attention to teachers' voices, especially those on the margins of the system. Pinar (1998) suggests that identification with marginalized social groups is of utmost educational importance. Giroux (1994) claims that "multiculturalism has become a central discourse in the struggle over issues regarding national identity, the construction of historical memory, the purpose of schooling, and the meaning of democracy" (p. 325). Such theoretical notions informed the discussions about multicultural school-based research throughout the term of my first course and very much shaped the relationship that my graduate students and I developed week by week. The central question for my professional self will always be the one that I posed in my first graduate course and still do today: Why does one go into teaching in the first place?

Case study and narrative methodologies were examined to document the construction and reconstruction of the meaning of teaching and learning from a moral perspective for my students as teachers in their particular settings. Research was therefore seen as a social process but also reflexive as it is focused on the individual teacher/researcher. As participant-observers in their everyday classroom activities, my students explored the dynamics of power and identity and of cultural and linguistic difference and equality. We discussed various qualitative methods of research (Clandinin & Connelly, 1994; Eisner, 1991; Eisner & Peshkin, 1990; Glesne & Peshkin, 1992; Hopkins, 1987; Hornberger, 1990; Huberman & Miles, 1984; Schön, 1991; Yin, 1984; etc.) in order to focus on how the curriculum and pedagogical strategies in schools can be reconstituted in such a way that they can offer, as Torres-Guzman (1992) explains it, "cognitive empowerment," allowing students to become critical thinkers in dialogue with their teachers.

In this chapter I choose a narrative approach in order to give voice to the moral/educational initiatives that my students and I created in our respective classrooms. Thus, the research approach of this piece is naturalistic. Carol Witherell and Nel Noddings (1991, p. 239) state that we "as educators are inescapably involved in the formation of moral communities as well as the shaping of persons," and I highlight the phrase Maxine Greene adapted from Toni Morrison's novel *Beloved* to say that "moral education requires becoming friends of one another's minds, even, perhaps especially, when the 'other' is 'stranger'" (see in Witherell & Noddings, 1991, pp. 238–239). In this process, all of us were encouraged to reflect on our own personal philosophy on intergroup relations vis-à-vis the teaching and learning experience within a culture of diversity. The emphasis was on "thick" description, on process, and on the natural setting (i.e., the classroom, the home, or the village) as the source of data (see, e.g., Geertz, 1988, 1995; Janesick, 1991). I think Geertz (1995) captures the exploratory sense of it beautifully when he states that ethnographic research planning is "hardly . . . a straightforward matter . . . 'on s'engage, puis on voit,' plunge in and see what happens." (p. 117).

In the fall of 1991, I was hired as assistant professor by F. Michael Connelly, who was founder and head of the (then) Joint Centre for Teacher Development at OISE/UT. He opened the door to a new professional world and helped "give me permission" to embark on the journey of qualitative inquiry by telling me as he did in my first meeting with him that "*doing narrative is not a crime.*" I have taught "Multicultural Perspectives in Teacher Development: A Reflective Seminar" each year since that fall of 1991, and each time it has been a very special experience. That first course, however, will be etched in my memory forever. I created the syllabus for this course over the summer. I remember being surprised at how quickly it came together, as if all my undergraduate, graduate, and postdoctoral work, as well as all my elementary teaching years had been a dress rehearsal for this one shining moment. I floated into that first class in the late afternoon on a Tuesday in September 1991 on a cloud of euphoria. The sheer delight of walking back into a classroom as the teacher after a hiatus of a decade was magical. This time it was a classroom of graduate students, and it was exhilarating.

The Context of Toronto:
Inquiring Into Our Cultural Selves

Cultural pluralism is the very essence of Canadian education, and the official Multiculturalism Act was enacted in 1971. Over the past three decades, Canadian immigration levels have gone from approximately 85,000 to 220,000 annually. Statistics Canada indicates that the population of Canada is more than 30 million (Canada Census, 2001). Almost 20 percent of the population are foreign born, while more than 200 ethnic groups live in Canada. Toronto, Vancouver, and Montréal attracted almost three-fourths of the immigrants in 2000; 70 percent of them came to Toronto, Canada's largest urban center. In 2004, more than 40 percent of the students in Toronto's schools were foreign born; almost 60 percent speak a language other than English or French at home—and that does not include children born in Canada who are of English as a Second Language (ESL) background. If you add this group into the picture, almost 70 percent of Toronto's school population comes from an ESL background. It seems only reasonable to assume that within this context of diversity, the issues of multicultural education cannot be viewed as being peripheral to mainstream schooling.

Indeed, the United Nations has recently named Toronto the most ethnically diverse city in the world.[2] Furthermore, the Canadian societal fabric is built upon the notion of a multicultural mosaic where, at least officially, the maintenance of minority languages and cultures is encouraged (Cummins & Danesi, 1990). In the Canadian province of Ontario, the multicultural reality was addressed by establishing the Heritage Languages Program (HLP) in 1977 to provide classes in the languages and cultures of minority language children for the purpose of promoting a sense of self-esteem and a fuller understanding of respective cultural backgrounds (see Cummins & Danesi, 1990; Feuerverger, 1989). The intention was that such a program would offer the potential for a deeper sense of connection and community within the educational experience. However, issues of multiculturalism continue to be at the center of political controversy (see Berryman, 1988; Feuerverger, 1994). This is because the issue of cultural and linguistic diversity is layered, complex, and manifold in symbolic meanings within Canadian society. Multicultural and multilingual education, by its very nature, engenders emotionally intense discussions—situated as it is at cultural crossroads that have been so dramatically altered over the last few decades in all Canadian urban centers, and especially in Metropolitan Toronto. It was clear to me that a course focusing on these issues of diversity from the perspective of practicing teachers in classrooms was sorely needed in order to develop more effective directions for promoting cross-cultural cooperation and understanding at all levels of schooling. I decided to create it.

Because I was hired in the summer, the description of my course did not appear in the OISE bulletin. I remember wondering if anyone would show up. The course was intended to be a "hands-on" exploration of how teachers/educators can prepare themselves in a fundamental way to reflect on their underlying personal and professional attitudes toward the multicultural microsociety of their classrooms. We would focus on how teachers can begin to unearth the "unconscious myths" that motivate them in the planning of curricula and in their choice of interpersonal classroom strategies. We would consider how multicultural education provides pedagogical opportunities for students, teachers, and researchers within interactive spaces that engage issues of personal and cultural identities. The intent was to examine the epistemologically complex implications of understanding teacher development as autobiographical/biographical text (Connelly & Clandinin, 1988).

Toward a Collective Consciousness of an "Engaged" Pedagogy

In this section I examine how my graduate students and I acknowledged the "foreigner" whose language, culture, values, and traditions are different from the mainstream. The intent was to, as Maxine Greene (1988) put it, "communicate a sense of our lived worlds" (p. 388). We were, right from the beginning, involved in a transformative process toward a collective consciousness—a group of individuals with a commonality of purpose, that is, to create a more nuanced pedagogical discourse of intercultural understanding and harmony. Our inquiry led to exciting new insights into our personal and professional lives and to a more compassionate understanding of the teaching-learning experience within diversity and to moral and ethical dilemmas in education. Within this discourse lies Nel Noddings's (1984, 1991) notion that a good education must be based on caring relationships in terms of "how to meet the other morally," thus opening a space for contemplation. We focused on the necessity that students and teachers find common ground in the midst of seemingly insurmountable differences. We stressed, as Henry Giroux (1991, 1994) does, the development of pedagogical contexts that "promote compassion and tolerance rather than envy, hatred and bigotry, and that provide opportunities for students to be border crossers" (p. 508). Teachers need to be border crossers too. They need to create a bridge filled with communication, with real *dialogue*. Indeed, Buber's (1958, 1965) theoretical focus on the centrality of dialogical meeting—that is, on an understanding of the self as both personal and social in an ongoing process of construction and reconstruction through encounters with other selves—informs the discussion that follows. Moreover, according to Bourdieu (1996),

> to write an educational program is a philosophical act in favor of reason. Forms of collaboration across boundaries have an urgency in this time of restoration.... We must defend open-minded and democratic educational endeavors in a time when dark forces in society are trying to eradicate reason.[3]

The interpretive approach that I use in this piece is in congruence with many postmodern theorists interested in issues of intersubjectivity and reflexivity in research activities. I focus on the cultural narratives of my graduate students and their professional longings—and how their lived experiences were revealed in their fundamental values, their beliefs, their perceptions of education, and, in fact, in the worldview that they carried (consciously and unconsciously) with them into our classes every week. bell hooks (1994) discusses the need for rethinking ways of using life history to focus on issues of identity and to challenge the notion of identity as static. Thus, the centrality of emotion in this pedagogical journey suggested that issues of identity cannot be explained solely through an intellectual and cognitive process, but rather through a different focus on affect, interaction, and interpretation. In other words, the lived experience needs to be seen as an interpretive rather than a causal story. In terms of the "biographies of vulnerability" that permeated the discourse of my graduate course, I as instructor/researcher was mindful of Olesen's (1992, p. 218) claim that "body and self are intertwined." We need to attend to cognition and emotion, using both phenomenal and interactive approaches. Indeed, I observed how emotionally powerful these weekly university encounters were both for myself as instructor and for my students in our struggle to reenvision and reshape an understanding of multicultural education.

For my graduate students, one theme question would be "In what ways has our personal story influenced our research interests, and how do both of these interact with what we are discovering through observation and conversation in the classroom setting?" Another would be "How is our research story evolving through this process?" These issues are in keeping with bell hooks's (1994) notion that "progressive, holistic education, 'engaged pedagogy' . . . emphasizes well-being . . . and therefore a process of self-actualization" (p. 15). Through journaling, my students and I became more familiar with our unique personal perceptions of our place in society and in what ways we may contribute to teacher development. Discussing our subjective perceptions of ethnic identity involved a great deal of personal reflection, which struck at the core of how we defined ourselves in the world. We discovered that our language and ethnicity were connected to our sense of purpose and self-worth in society. We examined our individual, familial, and cultural differences to find that within these differences we had much in common. We had all come into the course balancing at least two cultural identities and languages. From the start I wondered, as others may have, how our juggling acts informed our personal practical knowledge (Connelly & Clandinin, 1988) in our multiple roles (as women, teachers, researchers, daughters, wives, mothers). I encouraged my students to construct new meaning for their texts while searching for professional identity. We all became fellow travelers in our educational landscapes, and the journal writing became a shared enterprise. We heard the voices of the "other" within our lived experiences, and, as a result of this influence, our own stories became reconstructed and retold from a fresh perspective. It seemed as if a story of collective professional identity evolved as we shared our individual narratives.

The Voices Emerge: Narrative and the Formation of Personal and Ethnic Identity

The narratives generated by the students and by myself explore our life histories of living within and between various cultural worlds, struggling to find voice, meaning, and balance. We became involved in a "reflection-in-action" (Schön, 1987) on our own philosophy of teaching and learning and on the search for our personal and collective Canadian identity. Our individual voices began to emerge within a developing dialectical relationship between personal and professional reflections, between theory and practice as a means of understanding the "self" in relation to the "other." It was in these painful and hopeful pedagogical musings that we felt summoned to, in Maxine Greene's (1988) words, "the tasks of knowledge and action."

I recall an incident in class wherein some of my highly gregarious students (socialized in Western society, which places a premium on "talk") tended to dominate the conversation. I was mindful of the quieter students from Eastern cultures who continued to be dominated by their Western sisters, and my impulse was to step in tactfully. But I waited, hoping that things would work themselves out. Later, I received an e-mail message from one of the "silent" students, who complained that a few of her Western peers were "hogging" discussions in class and that she was becoming increasingly frustrated. I knew then that I had to intervene. Yet my desire was to avoid offending sensitive egos, including my own, because as a beginning university teacher I wished very deeply for a warm rapport with others also journeying toward self-knowledge. But, in spite of my own inner tensions, I did raise the issue of conversational inequalities, and it opened a space for dialogue about the desire to be in the "limelight" and its effects on classroom interaction. One of the students saw for the first time that she was still trying to get the attention of her parents at the kitchen table. Her epiphany came when she realized that she was reenacting her "family scene" in her role as teacher, who kept a tight lid on the responses of the pupils in her classroom. Another was just so overwhelmed with the changes taking place in her personal life that she simply had become too immersed in her own story to listen to the others. Yet another was grateful that, in spite of her father's lack of higher education, he had placed such an emphasis on learning and had inadvertently showed her the way to a teaching career; thus, she hung onto this professional identity with perhaps too much intensity. The discussion allowed us all to become more sensitive to the complexity of the "other" in the classroom and to continue on our reflective pedagogical journey.

The discourse of caring and intercultural understanding was exemplified in a growing trust in me as facilitator and was reciprocated in my own actions and journal writing sentiments. As one of my journal entries expresses,

> We are all very compatible. Problems arise and we look for solutions. All issues can be raised because everything is negotiable. What I feel most proud of is the sense of honesty and openness that my students and I share in class. We trust each other. We feel safe in the telling of our stories. And we are striving to find meaning in our stories. Our stories intersect to become new stories with new life and direction. We are in search of our personal identity. (October 20, 1991)

In the spirit of Witherell and Noddings (1991), we enacted a pedagogical "search for enlightenment, responsible choice, perspective or means to solve a problem [considered] mutual and marked by appropriate signs of reciprocity" (p. 7). As I experienced these dynamics in class, I was reminded of Belenky, Clinchy, Goldberger, and Tarule's (1986) notion of "real talk," wherein careful listening, emergent ideas, and mutually shared understandings shape pedagogic encounters. I have recently returned to Belenky et al.'s text only to ponder the possibility that the "real talk" in our course discussions released an energy within us. This energy was described by one student, who wrote in her journal,

[She had] half forgotten what kind of magic really good classes can do to you. They give you confidence in yourself, inspiration, and most of all, energy. One person's story triggers so many other new stories which have been forgotten. No, actually, not forgotten, but waiting to be brought to light, to be "reconstructed." (September 25, 1991)

A major theme that emerged from this graduate seminar awakened us to the power of the "family" narrative, which creates "unconscious myths" that drive our professional actions and choices in educational careers. Many of us explored what Belenky et al. (1986) name the "epistemological atmospheres of our families" by discussing the kind of discourse used within our families that either nurtured or constrained us as women (p. 157). In reflecting on my beginning university teaching narrative, I am more convinced than ever that the ethnolinguistic group from which we originate colors the lenses through which we look at the world and influences all our interactions, including teaching. Narratively speaking, "culturally and socially embedded metaphors have a powerful shaping influence on the way in which teachers come to know teaching" (Connelly & Clandinin, 1988, p. 9). Our stories concur with the research of Feuerstein (1979), which suggests that intellectual development plays an important role in clarifying emotional turmoil. As one of my graduate students put it, this process of intellectual development began for her as a child and has extended into her adulthood through journaling activities:

I have been a "loner" during many periods in my life. It might explain why I often feel that I do not belong, even when I am at the hub of activity. I remember escaping, as a child, into the world of books. They were all the companions I needed. . . . And so I went seeking an identity in the magic world of words. . . . Only recently have I begun keeping a journal—more for academic purposes than any personal quest, though the two are intimately intertwined at this stage. (October 27, 1991)

Images of a Multicultural Home

In the reading of assigned texts from the scholarly literature on multicultural issues in education, my students and I built bridges to one another, which initiated a process that challenged others to expand their listening space. I had in mind the intent that my graduate students should become participant-observers as teachers/researchers in elementary or high school classrooms where cultural and linguistic diversity constituted the teaching-learning experience. I gave the students the freedom to interpret "classroom" for themselves. Several students, who were on leaves of absence from their boards, expressed interest in inquiring retrospectively into their teaching experiences. These particular students inadvertently expanded the planning of my own curricula by exploring their underlying personal attitudes toward their multicultural classroom experiences. They brought to the course a window of opportunity through which the rest of us more closely examined how our past teaching-learning experiences shaped our present inquiries in classrooms.

In the same way, my graduate students also shared stories of the teaching-learning experience within a multicultural/multilingual context. Here is an example of a Chinese graduate student's journal writing, illustrating her participation-observation as a researcher in an ESL classroom with newly arrived children:

> [The teacher] takes advantage of every opportunity to impart a feel of the language to her students. I watched her speaking English in a very playful and lively way even though most of the students may not yet be able to understand all the words. . . . Her sensitivity to the ESL students' cultural backgrounds is so clear. Their first language and culture are respected. While introducing the mainstream Canadian culture, she makes sure that learners get a chance to share their own culture with the others and that their identity is not denied. . . . They are encouraged to read in their own language while learning English and to share their readings. This is a very important way for the students to retain their own identity, which is crucial to their self-concept. Consequently, kids also get to know about different cultures, and a multicultural awareness is cultivated. When the Chinese girl finished telling a story from her culture, I heard an Iranian boy saying that he wished that he could read Chinese. As a result, students learn to admire and respect those who come from other backgrounds and languages, rather than to be prejudiced against them. I believe that this is such an important part of multicultural teaching. (October 15, 1991)

A Japanese student, teaching an after-school heritage language class and reflecting on it in her journal writing, wrote metaphorically about her own teaching self:

> I like using metaphors when I describe my teaching, and in this case a metaphor of baking comes to my mind. Being a teacher is like baking a cake. You mix eggs, sugar, and flour. What comes out is not like any of the ingredients; yet the quality of the cake depends on the quality of the ingredients. If you use stale eggs, the cake will smell stale too. Teaching is the same: what I do outside of my classroom is not directly related to the activities that I employ in my teaching. However, one can tell from my teacher-self, I believe, the quality of my other "selves." What I bring into the classroom is what I am interested in now, who I am as a whole person. (November 12, 1991)

Her later journal writing not only reflected a transformation in her metaphor of "baker" to "shopkeeper" to "shop owner" but also reflected my own theme of the course involving the cultural orphan trying to heal herself by becoming whole:

> Over the past few months, the metaphor of shopkeeping has become more and more fitting to describe my teaching. I, as a novice shop owner, started off with high ambitions, stocking up all sorts of goods that I thought customers would like. Then realizing that the shop was not selling as well as she had predicted, the owner realized that not everyone has the same taste as she does, that she had to cater more to her customers' different tastes. She started to have more variety, even things she never liked herself. She became more sensitive to the "customers' needs." She started to buy goods that sold well in a larger quantity and diminished the amount of goods that were unpopular. (December 1, 1991)

As a means of improving writing skills in her classroom, this graduate student decided to have her pupils write journals as she herself was doing in our course. The results were far more powerful than she had anticipated:

> I never expected that writing would become a tool for communication between my students and me. But some students started to tell their life stories, and I felt morally obliged to do the same. . . . I learnt to respond to my students in narrative [as we were doing in the graduate seminar]; I tell my stories to them to illustrate my point. It involves a certain risk. By doing this, I am revealing my private self to them. I become more vulnerable. What if my students show what I write to their parents, other teachers, even other students? . . . My students are taking the same risk. They have enough trust in me to know that I would not do such a thing. Then I must have the same degree of trust in them too. You cannot expect someone to tell their lived experience when you are not prepared to commit yourself.
>
> This all amounts to respecting different voices. I have a voice both as a teacher and as someone with a dual cultural and linguistic heritage. Each of my students has a voice too, each of them just as important as any other, including mine. And what a diversity there is among them. When I realized this, I stopped developing a curriculum that was coherent only in my eyes. . . . My students made me realize that they are their own people and that they have their own agenda. . . . My teaching is the same. I no longer expect every student to learn every single thing that I teach in class; however, I do hope that I have something to offer every one of them, that they learn at least one or more things in my course, in the real sense of the word. (December 1, 1991)

This student of mine had decided to apply what was happening in our graduate seminar to her heritage language teaching, and it had worked! Our graduate seminar itself became a multicultural home wherein "different voices" were respected and the "whole person" was treated as a significant phenomenon of schooling. This is one example of a phenomenon of schooling that F. Michael Connelly and D. Jean Clandinin might consider to be a personally and socially meaningful experience. A view of the whole person emerged from the course as students reflected on and wrote about their participant-observation experiences. Perhaps not surprisingly, then, reflections on childhood dominated as a theme in the journals, and certain "narrative threads," involving tensions and the necessity of resolving tensions, emerged. The first example identifies an Anglo-Canadian graduate student's personal childhood struggle between "selves" and a new awareness of "torn identities" of the children that inhabit the classrooms of multicultural Toronto:

> I look back on my childhood. There seems to be two dominant themes that run the course of my life . . . narrative threads: intellectual independence fostered by my father, and "fitting the mould" advocated by my mother—be it the patriarchal one set up by my father, or later the one defined by my husband. . . . The "dream world" portrayed by my father was far more eloquent than the realities laid down by my mother. Which did I choose? Is it possible that the strife I live as adult stems from the child, from a time in which conflicting messages were impinged on my being at a young and supple age? Is it conflict born of the struggle between the "self" I am expected to be and the "other" I want to be? So many children in classrooms in Toronto live this kind of torn identity because of their immigrant status. I now am more aware of their cultural conflicts because of the discussions in this course. (November 9, 1991)

A number of other graduate students told me directly that they would never have been able to delve so deeply into the labyrinth of their multiple identities had I not opened up my own narrative to them. This South Asian student shows that struggle is part of the healing process; she believes that writing can help heal repressed wounds by articulating latent pain.

> One MUST write to discharge the tensions. In seclusion. To channel the excess and diffuse energy. To question beliefs and opinions by learning and refining the art of writing the silent selves. That is strength and growth. . . . To lay bare the pain is part of the process of healing. . . . "We can't imagine what we can face, and we can't face what we can't imagine." It takes courage to imagine! It takes courage to explore, to dig out, and to express the repressions of oppression. To recover our own experiences, knowledge, and possibilities. (October 19, 1991)

A Chinese student who shared her journal writing with the rest of us during the term sensitized us to her experiences in the Chinese Cultural Revolution. Although she was one of the quiet ones in the class, her action of journal sharing became a catalyst for a deeper level of reflective sharing. She helped us open up different parts of ourselves as we lived out the mythology of "cultural orphan" collectively. She had a wonderful, deep laugh that was contagious. She explained that laughter became her survival mechanism during her hard times in the Cultural Revolution. She had had a choice between tears or laughter, and she had chosen laughter, the life force. When I looked at her I saw a lovely flower shining with hope. One of her metaphors for the power of teaching was indeed the fragrance of the osmanthus blossoms. I do not believe that I have ever seen or smelled this flower, but she described it as "white at the beginning, golden in full blossom, tiny but sweet. The fragrance stays long and spreads a distance" (October 1991). When I would look at this student, I could see the osmanthus. "I am lucky to remain positive and optimistic toward life after experiencing so much suppression and severe disruption as I had," she wrote. She also told us how she was given a great gift by her father: Taoism.

In the Taoist perspective, the world, that web of time and change, is a network of vortices like a moving and dangerous torrent of water; the ideal Taoist is a person who has learned to use all her senses and faculties to improvise the shapes of the currents in the world, so as to harmonize herself with them completely. Meanwhile, the person remains an individual, a unique individual, who owns her ever-increasing senses, faculties, and ways of improvisation.

Therefore, this student's laughter was to express "a sadness so deep." She laughed because it was the only way she could express herself. It was an act of defiance, of dignity, and of identity. At the end of term she wore her "own costume" to the holiday party. This action eased the tension of herself as stranger who, although feeling "culturally different here," found the strength to share herself with us. In her words,

> Open is the word to describe the class. We are all open to ourselves as well as to others. Both the teacher, Grace, and the students presented their true cultural and personal voices. We could be who we really were. Thus a caring relationship, caring for both others and different parts of ourselves, was created, where every person was co-operating, supportive, learning, and teaching. (December 3, 1991)

A Visit From an Author

A Canadian graduate student from the Maritimes who grew up in a homogeneous society read from her journal one evening in class,

> This is a whole new exploration for me as a teacher. In so many cases these newly arrived students are trying really hard to fit into Canadian society as quickly as possible but it's so tough—trying to be what their parents want them to be culturally. The kids feel like it's holding onto the past, and they want to get to the future! How do you bridge the two worlds? (November 10, 1991)

The theme of "bridging" that our journal writing created was brought to a new level by an author's visit. Ibolya (Ibi) Grossman, in her autobiography *An Ordinary Woman in Extraordinary Times* (1990), which she wrote at the age of seventy-four, enchanted us with her maternal quality, while contributing to and participating in the dynamic of the class during her visit. In her moving account as a Hungarian-Jewish Holocaust survivor, Ibi faced persecution, loss, and exile. She was branded "stranger" within her homeland, as was the student in our seminar who endured the Chinese Cultural Revolution. Similarly, the foreign students in the class, by virtue of their status, amounted to strangers to

Canada. They expressed feeling "different" and "out of step" in the Ontario school system, as did even those of us who were Canadians, but from outside of Ontario.

Perhaps more meaningfully, the personal sense of stranger status resonated for us as women who walk the tightrope of multiple cultural lives (Gilligan, 1982). In the "Stranger's Story" (1991), which we read in our class, Shabatay recognizes the quality of what it means to live on the edge and of what the stranger, by her very presence, requires of those with whom she comes into contact: an openness toward difference that helps constitute caring relationships between teachers and students. Furthermore, I came to understand from interviewing participants in a multicultural literacy project in an inner-city school (which began in that first year of my faculty position) that the image of "stranger" is central to many immigrants' experiences (see Feuerverger, 1994). As participant-observer in this school, I came to recognize that knowing the existence of the "foreigner," as Julia Kristeva (1991) puts it, is a central aspect of language awareness that I believe can be defined as sensitivity to and a conscious understanding of the myriad languages and cultures in our world, as well as their role for humanity. This study has helped me to understand more fully the dialectical relationship between language and thought in practical educational settings (see, e.g., Bakhtin, 1981; Dewey, 1938; Vygotsky, 1962). As discussed earlier, I have been involved in multilingual education both personally and professionally as far back as I remember, and I believe that the bilingual (multilingual) classroom must be a space where dialogue is seen as a necessary way to relate authentically to one another through collaboration, reflection, and expression (see, e.g., Ada, 1988; Banks, 1989; Cazden, 1989; Corson, 1993, 1999; Cummins, 1989, 1994; Delgado-Gaitan, 1997; Fine, 1993; May, 1994; Nieto, 1992; Wong-Fillmore, 1991; and so many more).

This experience of the immigrant as stranger brought my graduate students together in the same way that immigrants find one another in a new land. They began to create a vibrant sense of community out of loss and tension. This reminds me of the words of William Pinar (1998): "Living on the margins may be dangerous but at least you can breathe there." In my own journal writing on my multicultural literacy project, I wrote that

> I could immediately identify with the anxiety in the eyes of many of the participants as they brought back sharp memories of my own parents' post–World War II struggle four decades ago, as refugees and immigrants trying to pick up the pieces of their broken lives in a new land that offered the hope of personal freedom and economic potential. (October 30, 1991)

In another piece wherein I share more of my early tensions as a child of immigrant parents, I explain how I transcend cultural and linguistic barriers through my classroom teaching and my school-based research work:

I, in my role as teacher/educator and researcher, am also retelling and reliving my personal story through this multicultural literacy project. Perhaps this project resonates with me because I sense their confusion and loneliness. Their childhood stories are in many ways my childhood story. I too would return home from school to parents who felt totally powerless in their new society and who were intimidated by my teachers and the educational system in general. I never shared any of my schoolbooks or lessons with them. Many times I would have to translate what the teacher would have to say about me to them on parents' night. How small and weak my parents would seem in this circumstance. How they were diminished in my young eyes. On some level I must have sensed the injustice of the situation. (November 12, 1991)

My own theme of literacy imbalance within my immigrant family's experiences (which I have also documented as a more general phenomenon of the immigrant experience: see Feuerverger, 1991, 1994) deeply affected one of my graduate students who came from Portugal. She shared her story of tension in her family vis-à-vis literacy and higher education:

I early perceived cultural differences between my parents. My father subscribed to all the papers and was the local news reporter. His barbershop was like a cultural center; my mother was not part of any discussion. He did not value her opinions and sometimes I heard him calling her "ignorant." It was my father who taught me how to read, and I remember him always with a paper or book in his hands. I did not forget two of his favorites—Victor Hugo's *Les Misérables* and Dostoevsky's *Crime and Punishment.* There were several volumes, and I remember trying hard to read them and finding them very boring. My mother threw the books away when he died. She did not value books. . . . At that time I could not understand why she did that. Now I realize that these books for her might have been obstacles, barriers, walls erected between the two of them. Was she also afraid of losing me when I went to the big city to study? Was that why she was never a great supporter of me pursuing an education? (November 30, 1991)

Mothering in the World of Teaching

Perhaps the previously described situation suggests one possible dimension of a mother-daughter relationship involving connection through separation, uncertainty, and loss. The theme of motherhood was in part enacted in our discourse of caring that reflected the "politics of talk" (Belenky et al., 1986) within families. Some of my students displayed a great ambivalence toward their mothers, and they sought to know more about their mothers' lives. Some felt it was too late to restructure their mother-daughter relationship but were optimistic that they would do their best to be more fully "present" for their own children and for their students. It is clear that we had only touched the surface of the complicated mother-daughter story as it relates to the teaching story, but we at least had the courage to begin the process. In the following excerpts from two different graduate students' journals, the theme of mother-daughter relationships is apparent. In the first example, a Jewish-Canadian student explores the traditional messages her mother communicated and the tension she, as the daughter, clearly felt:

> So here I am growing up with a vision of personal freedom [gathered from my father's wonderful stories] conquering new horizons as my imagination roams asunder. . . . My mother did not endorse such an outlook on life. As far as she was concerned, a young girl's life led to family, children, community service—the traditional role of women in archaic, patriarchal societies. The message was loud and clear in the example set at home, as well as the preaching that went along with it. . . . I'm not quite sure I know what I am doing. I don't seem to be able to separate my mother's stories from myself. As a matter of fact, the only way I seem to be able to relate to her, now that she is dead, is through images and stories revolving around the mother-daughter relationship, which I immediately turn on its head looking at my own daughters, asking myself what is the message they received over the years and how has this affected my professional life? (November 2, 1991)

In the second example, my Chinese graduate student wished to become like her mother, the "well-accomplished person" and professor. But the point remains that this student, too, is trying to understand how her own professional story fits with that of her mother's:

> My mother does not fit the "good" mother model. She used to teach at university before [she] retired. . . . I liked to go to her apartment at university where there was always messiness. . . . My mother is direct, open, and has a bad temper. . . . She smokes, plays cards by herself every day, and reads novels every day. It is fun to watch her read—laughing and crying with the authors but never bothering to remember the names of the authors or the titles of the books. But I bet she has read all the novels available in the Chinese language (classical, modern, and those translated from other languages). She did not mother my brother and me in the way a traditional Chinese mother should have done. . . . She practices Tai Chi every day and loves gardening. She is a well-accomplished person instead of a traditional mother model. I am proud of her because she is not a "good" mother in the usual terms. Because of my mother's mothering, I can see myself on the way to becoming as well accomplished as she is, in my own way in my career. I don't have to be a "perfect" woman or a "superwoman." (November 6, 1991)

The theme of motherhood within the context of education, was, in part, enacted in our seminar through our encounter with our author visitor. One South Asian student in the class compared our visitor Ibi directly with her own mother and then reflected on my "mothering" in class:

> Ibi was such an addition to the class. I was overwhelmed by her honesty and her motherliness. It made me think of my own mother and how distant she was, really.

I could never go to her for any good advice; she was always so critical of me. Ibi made me feel how much I have missed and it saddens me. Her devotion to her son in the midst of all her suffering is so inspiring. She lost her husband in the war but kept on being the best mother she could be. How young she was and how strong! I will never forget her cracked voice when she spoke of losing this man who was her husband for such a short time. The tears were hot and stabbing my eyes. I looked around. We shared this tragic moment together. At the next class, we all began to talk about our mothers and mothering in general. It happened so spontaneously. I heard M. mention that Grace was motherly in her teaching role. The more I think about it the more I agree. She lets us "be"; she lets us grow. She cares about us personally and professionally. She is nurturing. (October 30, 1991)

Ibi's hug, a maternal embrace, comforted one student whose tears of suffering flowed in connection with her life story. Drained by yet another "stranger's" story, we all were left feeling shipwrecked but alive and one step closer to the wholeness of being that was at the core of our journey. Our personal memories brought us closer to "solidarity with one another" (Delpit, 1992). The next journal excerpt is an example of a first introduction to "otherness." There is a sense in the following piece that the Roma/Gypsy women embody a different way of life that also entails magic and enchantment and "wistful dreams." How powerful to identify with another culture and language and, in the process, to transcend the difficulties of one's own personal background:

In my little Portuguese village, the Gypsies always came in late spring when the bright yellow blooms of acacias contrasted with the blue skies. . . . Was my fascination an unconscious recognition of the difference between their lives and the way my parents were bringing me up? Was I already longing for the independence I now value so much? Most of the time the Gypsy children did not pay much attention to me, but once in a while I played with some of the girls. We did not exchange many words. This upset me because I loved the music of their language. I wished I could speak like them. I did not understand everything they said, but I understood there was another linguistic code, another way of communicating. Was this my first encounter with a foreign language? Gypsy women were beautiful, I loved their long skirts, and I could not help following them when they went into the village. The owners of the stores feared them because they said the women were capable of stealing things right in front of their eyes. Sometimes the women convinced some adults to have their palms read, and I was intrigued by their knowledge. They had come from other places, they must have learned these things somewhere else. When the villagers said the gypsies were witches I did not believe them. They cooked, and took care of the children—I could watch them from the bridge. They were like everybody else—just different because they traveled. The whole summer was enchanted. Groups of gypsies came and went, they never stayed long. I used to watch them disappear down the road, and I had wistful dreams of being stolen by them. (November 1, 1991)

Like Pinar (1988), curriculum for all of us became a search for self-knowledge that actively pursues a construction of self-identification with marginalized social groups. I searched for ways within my teaching to create a sense of a collective cultural home that would thrive in a university setting, shaping personal and professional destiny. Perhaps I was working toward becoming not only a caring professor but also as Belenky et al. (1986) would describe it, as a "midwife-teacher" whose participation in narrative inquiry lends support to the evolving multicultural consciousness of others. In the spirit of making a home of the classroom, I held the last class in my house. Everyone prepared a recipe representing their own culture, thus contributing to a multicultural feast. The warmth of our words filled us all with emotion that had developed in the sharing of our narratives throughout the term. I wrote a journal entry that evening, and it stands as a tribute to this educational experience:

> Throughout the term, we peeled off the layers of our (cultural) past, week by week, until what we stared at was the potential of our future. A glimpse of paradise; a broken promise made years ago. Within the landscape of our cultural diversity we shared a common goal. We were in the process of discovering our stories. They had been lost in the maelstrom of political, social, psychological violence. Our voices had been silenced in the storm but we survived, shipwrecked but alive. And suddenly we found each other in this course. No wonder the sparks began to fly. We began to write our journals and we shared the grief and pain and anger and joy. This is what education is all about: this gem of community and learning. (December 1991)

Recommended Readings

I highly recommend Bill Ayers's (1993) book *To Teach: The Journey of a Teacher*. He captures the essence of the journey when he writes "that teaching is primarily a matter of love." My book *Oasis of Dreams: Teaching and Learning Peace in a Jewish-Palestinian Village in Israel* (2001b) is based on a nine-year research study that I carried out in an extraordinary village, and it is about hope in the midst of deadly conflict. I explore the woundings and sense of victimhood that both peoples—Israeli Jews and Palestinians—feel in their very different ways. I focused on the two bilingual, bicultural educational institutions in this place of peaceful coexistence—an elementary school where Jewish and Arab children study together and the "School for Peace," which is a conflict resolution outreach program for Israeli and Palestinian adolescents and their teachers. The research journey that took place in this village quite literally changed my life, and I wrote it as a "thank you" to these courageous people. The methodology that Clifford Geertz (1995) offers in *After the Fact: Two Countries, Four Decades, One Anthropologist* has informed postmodern ethnographers who, in spite of having their qualms about the "authorial voice," make themselves more visible and sometimes even central to their research enterprise as a means of better understanding and interpreting their findings. Ruth Behar's (1996) book *The Vulnerable Observer: Anthropology That Breaks Your Heart* allows me to teach and write more "vulnerably" in terms of "the need to be able to draw deeper connections between one's personal experiences and the subject under study" (p. 13). Reading her book was a transformative experience for me.

Reflective Questions

1. Discuss this quote from the chapter in terms of your own understanding of multicultural education and narrative: "What we searched for was a 'communion' in Buber's (1958, 1965) terms—the dialogue between individuals that results in a sense of community and also in a deeper understanding of cross-cultural communication."

2. Carol Witherell and Nel Noddings (1991) state that we "as educators are inescapably involved in the formation of moral communities as well as the shaping of persons," and I highlight the phrase Maxine Greene adapted from Toni Morrison's novel *Beloved* to say that "moral education requires becoming friends of one another's minds, even, perhaps especially, when the 'other' is 'stranger'" (see in Witherell & Noddings, 1991, pp. 238–239). For example, it has been stated that moral education is the only kind of education. How do you respond to these reflections within the perspective of these quotes?

3. After having read this chapter, how do you regard the notion of "multicultural education"?

Notes

1. In a PBS television interview with Bill Moyers.
2. This statement was made by a UN official in the context of a discussion about international issues at a conference on democracy in multicultural societies (personal communication with the author, June 1993).
3. Quote from a lecture given at the University of California, Berkeley, April 6, 1996.

References

Ada, A. F. (1988). The Pajaro Valley experience: Working with Spanish-speaking parents to develop children's reading and writing skills in the home through the use of children's literature. In T. Skutnabb-Kangas & J. Cummins (Eds.), *Minority education: From shame to struggle* (pp. 223–238). Avon, England: Multilingual Matters.

Ayers, W. (1993). *To teach: The journey of a teacher.* New York: Teachers College Press.

Bakhtin, M. (1981). *The dialogic imagination.* Austin: University of Texas Press.

Banks, J. (1989 [April]). *Teacher education and ethnic minorities: Conceptualizing the problem.* Paper presented at the annual conference of the American Educational Research Association, San Francisco.

Bateson, M. C. (1989).*Composing a life.* New York: Atlantic Monthly Press.

Behar, R. (1996). *The vulnerable observer: Anthropology that breaks your heart.* Boston: Beacon Press.

Belenky, M. F., Clinchy, B. M., Goldberger, N. R., & Tarule, J. M. (1986). *Women's ways of knowing: The development of self, voice, and mind.* New York: Basic Books.

Berryman, J. (1988). Ontario's heritage languages program: Advantages and disadvantages of three models of organization. *Multiculturalism/Multiculturalisme, 11*(3), 18–21.

Bourdieu, P. (1996, April 6). *Democracy, society and education.* Lecture given at the University of California at Berkeley, Wheeler Auditorium.

Buber, M. (1958). *I and thou.* New York: C. Scribner's Sons.

Buber, M. (1965). *The knowledge of man.* New York: Harper & Row.

Canada Census: Statistics Canada (2001). Ottawa: Queen's Printer.

Carter, K. (1993). The place of story in the study of teaching and teacher education. *Educational Researcher, 22*(1), 5–12.

Cazden, C. (1989). Richmond road: A multilingual/multicultural primary school in Auckland, New Zealand. *Language and Education, 3,* 143–166.

Clandinin, D. J., & Connelly, F. M. (1994). Personal experience methods. In N. K. Denzen & Y. S. Lincoln (Eds.), *Handbook of qualitative research* (pp. 413–427). Thousand Oaks, CA: Sage.

Clandinin, D. J., & Connelly, F. M. (1995). *Teacher's professional knowledge landscapes.* New York: Teachers College Press.

Clandinin, D. J., & Connelly, F. M. (2000). *Narrative inquiry: Experience and story in qualitative research.* San Francisco: Jossey-Bass.

Cole, A., & Knowles, G. (2000). *Researching teaching: Exploring teacher development through reflexive inquiry.* Boston: Allyn & Bacon.

Coles, R. (1997). *Doing documentary work.* Oxford, UK: Oxford University Press.

Connelly, F. M., & Clandinin, D. J. (1988). *Teachers as curriculum planners: Narratives of experience.* New York: Teachers College Press.

Connelly, F. M., & Clandinin, D. J. (1990). Stories of experience and narrative inquiry. *Educational Researcher, 19*(5), 2–14.

Corson, D. (1993). *Language, minority education and gender: Linking social justice and power.* Toronto, Canada: OISE Press.

Corson, D. (1999). *Language policy in schools: A resource for teachers and administrators.* Mahwah, NJ: Lawrence Erlbaum.

Cummins, J. (1989). *Empowering minority students.* Sacramento: California Association for Bilingual Education.

Cummins, J. (1994). From coercive to collaborative relations of power in the teaching of literacy. In B. M. Ferdman, R. M. Weber, & A. G. Ramirez (Eds.), *Literacy across languages and cultures* (pp. 295–331). Albany: SUNY Press.

Cummins, J., & Danesi, M. (1990). *Heritage languages: The development and denial of Canada's linguistic resources.* Toronto: Our Schools/Ourselves Educational Foundation: Garamond Press.

Delgado-Gaitan, C. (1997). Dismantling borders. In A. Neumann & P. Peterson (Eds.), *Learning from our lives: Women, research and autobiography in education* (pp. 37–51). New York: Teachers College Press.

Delpit, L. (1992). The politics of teaching literate discourse. *Theory Into Practice, 31,* 285–295.

Dewey, J. (1938). *Experience and education.* New York: Collier Books.

Eisner, E. (1991). *The enlightened eye: Qualitative inquiry and the enhancement of educational practice.* New York: Maxwell Macmillan.

Eisner, E. W., & Peshkin, A. (Eds.). (1990). *Qualitative inquiry in education: The continuing debate.* New York: Teachers College Press.

Feuerstein, R., Rand, Y., & Hoffman, M. (1979). *The dynamic assessment of the retarded performer: The learning potential assessment device, theory, instruments and techniques.* Baltimore, MD: University Park Press.

Feuerverger, G. (1989). Ethnolinguistic vitality of Italo-Canadian students in integrated and non-integrated heritage language programs in Toronto. *The Canadian Modern Language Review, 46,* 50–72.

Feuerverger, G. (1991, Spring). University students' perceptions of heritage language learning and ethnic identity maintenance in multicultural Toronto [Special Issue on Heritage Languages in Canada]. *Canadian Modern Language Review, 47*(4), 660–677.

Feuerverger, G. (1994). A multicultural literacy intervention for minority language students. *Language and Education, 8*(3), 123–146.

Fine, M. (1993). You can't just say that the only ones who can speak are those who agree with your position: Political discourse in the classroom. *Harvard Educational Review, 63,* 412–433.

Freire, P. (1970). *Pedagogy of the oppressed.* New York: Seabury Press.

Freire, P. (1994). *Pedagogy of hope: Reliving pedagogy of the oppressed.* New York: Continuum.

Geertz, C. (1988). *Works and lives: The anthropologist as author.* Stanford, CA: Stanford University Press.

Geertz, C. (1995). *After the fact: Two countries, four decades, one anthropologist.* Cambridge, MA: Harvard University Press.

Gilligan, C. (1982). *In a different voice.* Cambridge, MA: Harvard University Press.

Giroux, H. A. (1991). Democracy and the discourse of cultural difference: Towards a politics of border pedagogy. *British Journal of Sociology of Education, 12*(4), 501–519.

Giroux, H. A. (1994). Insurgent multiculturalism and the promise of pedagogy. In D. T. Goldberg (Ed.), *Multiculturalism: A critical reader* (pp. 325–343). Cambridge, MA: Blackwell.

Glesne, C., & Peshkin, A. (1992). *Becoming qualitative researchers: An introduction.* New York: Longman.

Greene, M. (1988). *The dialectic of freedom.* New York: Teachers College Press.

Goodson, I. (Ed.). (1991). *Teachers' lives and educational research. Biography, identity and schooling: Episodes in educational research.* London: Routledge/Falmer.

Grossman, I. (1990). *An ordinary woman in extraordinary times.* Toronto: Multicultural History Society.

hooks, b. (1994). *Teaching to transgress: Education as the practice to freedom.* New York: Routledge.

Hopkins, D. (1987). Enhancing validity in action research. Research Paper #16. London: British Library.

Hornberger, N. (1990). Creating successful contexts for bilingual literacy. *Teachers College Record, 92*(2), 212–229.

Huberman, A. M., & Miles, M. B. (1984). *Innovation up close.* New York: Plenum.

Janesick, V. J. (1991). Ethnographic inquiry: Understanding culture and experience. In E. Short (Ed.), *Forms of curriculum inquiry* (pp. 101–119). Albany: SUNY Press.

Keen, S. (1990). Interview with Bill Moyers. PBS TV Series.

Kridel, C. (Ed.). (1998). *Writing educational biography: Explorations in qualitative research.* New York: Garland.

Kristeva, J. (1991). *Strangers to ourselves* (Trans. Leon S. Roudiez). New York: Columbia University Press.

May, S. (1994). School-based language policy reform: A New Zealand example. In A. Blackledge (Ed.), *Teaching bilingual children* (pp. 19–41). London: Trentham Press.

Michaels, A. (1996). *Fugitive pieces.* Toronto: McLelland and Stewart.

Nieto, S. (1992). *Affirming diversity: The sociopolitical context of multicultural education.* White Plains, NY: Longman.

Noddings, N. (1984). *Caring: A feminine approach to ethics and moral education.* Berkeley: University of California Press.

Noddings, N. (1991). Stories in dialogue: Caring and interpersonal reasoning. In C. Witherell & N. Noddings (Eds.), *Stories lives tell: Narrative and dialogue in education* (pp. 157–170). New York: Teachers College Press.

Olesen, V. (1992). Extraordinary events and mundane ailments: The contextual dialectics of the embodied self. In C. Ellis & F. Flaherty (Eds.), *Investigating subjectivity: Research on lived experience* (pp. 211–229). Newbury Park, CA: Sage.

Pinar, W. F. (1988). Autobiography and the architecture of self. *Journal of Curriculum Theorizing, 8*(1), 7–35.

Pinar, W. F. (1998). *Curriculum: Toward new identities.* New York: Garland.

Schön, D. (1987). *Educating the reflective practitioner.* San Francisco: Jossey-Bass.

Schön, D. (Ed.). (1991). *The reflective turn: Case studies in and on educational practice.* New York: Teachers College Press.

Shabatay, V. (1991). The stranger's story: Who calls and who answers? In C. Witherell & N. Noddings (Eds.), *Stories lives tell: Narrative and dialogue in education.* New York: Teachers College Press.

Tabachnick, B. R., & Zeichner, K. M. (1993). Preparing teachers for cultural diversity. In P. Gilroy & M. Smith (Eds.), *International analyses of teacher education* (JET Papers One; pp. 113–124). London: Carfax.

Torres-Guzman, M. (1992). Stories of hope in the midst of despair: Culturally responsive education for Latino students in an alternative high school in New York City. In M. Saravia-Shore & S. F. Arvizu (Eds.), *Cross-cultural literacy: Ethnographies of communication in multiethnic classrooms* (pp. 477–490). New York: Garland.

Van Manen, M. (1990). *Researching lived experience: Human science for an action sensitive pedagogy.* London and Canada: University of Western Ontario Press.

Vygotsky, L. S. (1962). *Thought and language* (Trans. A. Kozulin). Cambridge, MA: MIT Press.

Witherell, C., & Noddings, N. (Eds.). (1991). *Stories lives tell: Narrative and dialogue in education.* New York: Teachers College Press.

Wong-Fillmore, L. (1991). Language and cultural issues in the early education of language minority children. In S. L. Kagan (Ed.), *The care and education of America's young children: Obstacles and opportunities* (pp. 64–79). Chicago: University of Chicago Press.

Yin, R. K. (1984). *Case study research.* London: Sage Ltd.

Unit Five

*Narrative Inquiry in
Multicultural Education*

11

The World in My Text

A Quest for Pluralism

Carola Conle

Confronting the world from moment to moment is also confronting the self.

—Gergen & Gergen, 2000

M any educational researchers now accept the above as a condition of their work. Can we turn this "truism" around and say that confronting the self over a period of time is also confronting a world? My intent in this chapter is to confront ten years of my academic writing in order to examine the world of which that writing has been a part. Why? I sense an unstated hypothesis and an implicit agenda hidden among the rather far-flung topics of my work. This hypothesis and agenda are likely connected to the world confronted by me at the time of writing. Laurel Richardson wrote her book *Fields of Play: Constructing an Academic Life* (1997) in an attempt to contextualize ten years of sociological work (Richardson, 2000) and found that self and contexts were very much interdependent. Becoming clearer about what may only be indirectly expressed at the time may bring greater clarity about important issues, then and now.

More than a half-century ago, philosophers began to draw attention to the inseparability of subject and object in human endeavors, including the endeavors of research and the writing that aims to tell about research. What made subjects and objects stand together in this way is the inevitable presence of interpretation. I am always an interpreter because I cannot rid myself of my personal history, nor can I step out of the world in which I live when I confront whatever objects I chose to explore. Interpretations permeate perception, inquiry, and representation. Gathering some of my interpretations, putting them side by side and seeing where there are connections, where the rubbing points are, the incongruities and the questions, I confront myself and, I hope, simultaneously shed some light on the world the interpretations are struggling to characterize.

In our current era, this is not a straightforward task, because in a multicultural world filled with multiple interpretations for seemingly similar phenomena, knowledge of the world and of the self is not as straightforward as it once seemed. It can only be attempted indirectly through the study of symbols—artistic or linguistic—or of bodily expression (Habermas, 2001). Getting to know oneself or one's world is less a matter of finding out what is "in the head" or what is "out there" as it is a gathering of expressions and practices, essentially of symbols— hence the motivation for my resolve to undertake the examination of my written work. Although in a hermeneutic universe where knowledge is always interpreted, the traditional "know thyself" has lost some of its shine, yet it has also gained potential. It may have become a window to the world: self and world as both intertwined and mutually revealing. It will remain an ongoing task of this chapter to elucidate the potential of the "know-thyself-by-examining-your-writing" enterprise, to point a finger at methodological considerations, and to render these concrete through narrative portrayals of my analytical effort.

Initial Considerations for Textual Self-Study

Where to begin? Why not with this very moment, with some of the vague, ill-defined, and seemingly unrelated mix of present tensions, unresolved pasts, and beckoning futures that are part of my current inquiry dynamic and are likely to drive upcoming research efforts? How to present these to the reader? Metaphorically and symbolically, I see them as a few notes struck at irregular intervals:

> To write I often sit by the patio door in my study, listening to Streichmusik[1] from Alpstein[2], a small town in Switzerland. I know some of the musicians. I am beginning to know the place. I will return to it, because I want to know more about its music, its landscape, and its people. They each speak to me in a special way.
>
> Ethos of place: a proposal of research as yet unfunded.
>
> The questions: Do places have moral dimensions? Can we find a language to talk about this?
>
> Why do I insist on searching for funding in such an "irrelevant" area, on such an "impossible" topic?
>
> I know I have to do it.
>
> Places—my places; people—my people; music—my music.
>
> How far is it from these emotions and thoughts to
>
> countries—my country; culture—my culture;
>
> how far to the grand "us against them" dichotomies that have haunted us as individuals and groups, seemingly forever?
>
> Language—my language;

things to write about in education—things I want to write about in education. My writing often strikes unexpected notes; seems irrelevant to those in the educational spotlight; is often not understood. What kind of quest am I on?

At this point I am not quite sure what to make of these snippets. But past experience with narrative inquiry has taught me not to ignore haphazard feelings and musings. I need to look for the stories they bring to mind, however fragile the connection initially may seem (Conle, 2000b). This then is how I shall proceed. Stories will be told about the past, themes will be struck in them. In the end—because they are my stories and driven by my inquiry dynamics—they will surely connect with the poorly defined preoccupations mentioned earlier. I know I am only in part the author of what I have written. An invisible hand seems to do some of the writing for me, pushing a certain agenda. Personal and social histories are likely involved. Perhaps looking at what I have written for a decade or so might now tell me something about that rather powerful coauthor?

What were the tensions, subtexts, and implied agendas in my texts? How do I face them now? How do I want to deal with them? It would be disingenuous to pretend that I have no notion about the results of such an undertaking. Having already explored my personal history through narrative inquiry (Conle, 1993), having reflected on this exploration (Conle, 2000b) and its academic contexts (Conle, 1999b), having in part conceptualized what such explorations are about (Conle, 2000a, 2000b; Conle, Louden, & Mildon, 1998), I more than suspect that any results will have something to do with a lived quest for cultural pluralism. But the stages of that quest, its motivation and contents, so to speak, remain vague. Is it a quest for understanding? For living? For teaching? MacIntyre (1981) suggests that the lack of definition is just the way it should be if the enterprise is inquiry. For MacIntyre, it is

> clear that the medieval conception of a quest is not at all that of a search for something already adequately characterized, as miners search for gold or geologists for oil. It is in the course of the quest and only through encountering and coping with the various particular harms, dangers, temptations and distractions which provide any quest with its episodes and incidents that the goal of the quest is finally to be understood. (p. 219)

But just as in any quest, in a quest for the mainsprings of an implicit research agenda, there are times to look back, to inspect the territory covered. Why not inspect some of the texts, name some of the tensions, and wonder about themes and subtexts? If these point to issues in cultural pluralism, a timely topic will be explored.

Alongside these personal/theoretical considerations, there are contextual and social ones as well. In the world in which we live, cultural pluralism seems inevitable and at the same time wrought with tension in current contexts: globalization in the mainstream facing protest by the marginalized; transnational formations riddled with ethnic warfare; multiculturalism struggling with national pride; the global village interfacing with pride of place. It seems urgent that an agenda of education for cultural pluralism be put on the public table of public education at this time, in Canada and elsewhere. My own journey might illuminate some of the potential components for such an education, and my guide during the quest might be to keep a look out for educational, even curricular, significance.

My effort, of course, will not be a guide for policy making and implementation. It will be a single case. Even though it will question and highlight contentious issues, success will be measured by the extent to which my effort, working one-on-one with its audience, facilitates each member's own response to similar issues. It will be judged by the extent to which the conclusions I come to become significant in the personal and educational agendas of others. Richardson (2000) reports that "many academics who read [one of her stories] recognize it as congruent with their experiences, their untold stories" (p. 932).

Where am I to look for the nonobvious, the hidden curricula of my career? Excepting a collaborative project with students (Conle et al., 2000), I seldom pronounced on the topic of pluralism itself. I will scan what I have written, looking for items that might expose subtexts and implicit agendas in four different landscapes, each corresponding to conventional ways of viewing the educational worlds we inhabit and create: (1) the systemic/sociocultural/institutional, (2) the imaginative/narrative, (3) the experiential/personal, and (4) the philosophical. In my case, since I proceed through narrative inquiry, all four landscapes fold into one another. Even though my focus may be, for example, on institutional stories, the experiential/personal and the philosophical landscapes stay on the horizon. I will examine my inquiry texts and inquiry practices to look for the impetus that seems to motivate them. My review will, I hope, allow me to construct a set of issues and themes that could help constitute agendas for educating ourselves and others to live well together in a pluralist society.

Looking for Themes

To mind comes the image of a young teenager standing by a row of windows in a classroom which had become more spacious by open folding doors which usually separate it from the adjoining room. It was gym period in a small Ontario high school in the mid 50s and two grade 10 classes were enjoying a break in routine, a snowball dance. It started with one couple, who then each asked another partner, and so on. The girl by the window was waiting. No one asked her yet. The crowd around her got smaller and smaller. Finally she was the only one left. She stayed until the bell rang and everyone filed out. "Perhaps no one noticed," she thought, but a friend remarked, "Oh, you didn't dance!" (Conle, 1993, p. 1; 1996, p. 303)

This little story, remembered in 1989 during my search for a thesis topic, became the metaphorical representation for the entire inquiry process. As a fourteen-year-old immigrant from a small German town now living in a small, predominantly Anglo-Saxon Canadian town, I felt an uncomfortable distance between me and all those others—different through language, customs, clothing, place, and educational history. I did not react openly; I did not try to bridge that gap. Instead, I pretended not to notice, tried not to remember. But as narrative inquirer many years later, I kept being drawn to similar situations: being relegated to the sidelines, peeking across fences, having to understand across difference.

Now, after ten years of research and university teaching, I sense that this inquiry is still being carried on by various means. Essential questions, transposed into many different areas, show themselves again and again: in self-study, conceptual analysis, theorizing, narrative documentation of teaching and institutional practices, collaborative efforts, fieldwork and interviewing, creating courses of study, far-flung readings—ranging from teacher education to German philosophy, from Holocaust studies and moral modeling to the ethos of place, from curriculum analysis to evaluation to literary theory.

I propose to look at my ten years of research and teaching from the vantage point of the issues of the fourteen-year-old immigrant. Those issues involve my experience of cultural difference, cross-cultural encounters, and identity formation. Reporting on what I find will, I believe, illuminate assets of cultural pluralism with regard to education and include important facets of culturally pluralistic practices that make them assets in the education of students and teachers.

Methodological Note

There are, of course, many entry points to any work. My first steps are already behind me at this point of writing. Like Richardson (1997, 2000), I first put my papers in the chronological order in which they were conceptualized. I followed this with straightforward listings of some issues and themes in all of my papers. I do not claim that any such list was, or should be, carefully analyzed and summarized. Instead, I sorted through those lists looking for the major interests that seemed to motivate each paper and picked out the contexts in which these interests were embedded, as well as the interpretations selected and conclusions reached. In what follows, the results of these efforts will be captured in narrative form. I offer institutional stories and research stories, interspersed with reflective interludes in which I try to keep track of emerging themes and issues, in other words, of a view of the world in which my work has been embedded.

What also remains is the task to search out hidden inquiries, half-starts, and points of interest that were not fully pursued in my papers, but seemed to linger in the background, watching or beckoning, so to speak. Narrative formats easily accommodate these half-starts and half-hidden issues that can be elaborated in reflective interludes. Gradually various strands come together. When clearer patterns are beginning to emerge, I report on these, adding bits of additional narrative and interpreting them with a view to the themes of cultural difference, cross-cultural encounters, and identity issues. I expect the outcome will throw light on assets of cultural pluralism in education and elsewhere, as well as on enabling conditions for productive encounters across cultural difference.

Why should the reader lend any kind of credence to what I report or reflect on? After all, there is such a phenomenon as self-deception (Crites, 1979), and I do place myself on the threshold of what Gergen and Gergen (2000) call an "infinite regress of reflections on reflections" (p. 1031). These authors point out that there are no foundational rationalities from which any warrants, claims, or challenges could be generated. Here I beg to differ. Within a hermeneutic universe and the all-pervasive presence of interpretation, a rationality can indeed be found, if the aim of communication is mutual understanding (Conle, 2001; Habermas, 1984, 1987). In other words, if I do not aim to win arguments or prove points, but instead I consistently assume that I am telling truthfully—and in as clear and competent a manner I can muster—what I understand to be the case in a particular situation, and if I assume that there are moral and ethical expectations and a communally created world to which I can refer, then I am engaged in a rational enterprise. Perhaps I deceive myself; perhaps the moral dimensions I assume need revision; perhaps the world to which I refer, and that others recognize, will eventually be seen quite differently. But I do not intentionally misrepresent, cause moral havoc, or create arbitrary universes. I am not intentionally fictionalizing. I am consistently in an inquiry mode. This kind of communicative rationality allows me the courage to move ahead. Even though my knowledge is narratively situated knowledge and even though I have to be mindful of the constructed nature of what I present, I hope that the form of rhetoric I chose is functional, perhaps even curricular, for certain audiences. On that note, I begin with two institutional stories.

Institutional Story #1

ORGANIZATIONS, SYMBOLS, AND RECOGNITION:
LIVING AUTHENTICALLY IN NEWLY CHOSEN COMMUNITIES

In 1993, I went to the University of Waikato in New Zealand. There I read Ashton-Warner's accounts of her teaching and saw the small counties and Maori communities that were probably much like the ones where she taught. I noted how she worked alone, often opposed by the administrators who came to inspect what she was doing, who criticized the method she had invented to teach the children how to read and write—a method for which she later became famous. I sensed the history of the places where she taught, and I began to read accounts of Maori history. I contacted two professors at the university who were in charge of Maori studies and spoke with them about the biculturalism that was being promoted through governmental policy.

I also visited my daughter, who was studying at Waikato to become an accountant. We traveled and rented small cottages by lakes in native forests. I helped her with her homework, which involved management studies and theories of administration. This literature was new to me, but I soon saw connections to the field of education. I began to write a paper dealing with public spaces in schools that permitted what I called social self-reflection within certain administrative conditions that allowed beginning teachers to live authentically in their new institutional environment, helping them to make the transition from "I" to "we" (Carr, 1986).

I remember reviewers of that paper mentioning that I needed to tie my themes together more effectively, and I have not often cited this paper (Conle, 1997a), written near the beginning of my career. However, writing it was very important to me. I insisted that each of the three areas it dealt with were important: community, reflection, and the shared governance of schools. What was important was the idea that institutions, organizations, and administrative arrangements are not value-neutral, but facilitate or obstruct certain moves, always keeping certain options out of view, and also that organizational arrangements are not separate from life, love, growth, self, accomplishments, or decay (Greenfield & Ribbins, 1993).

I pointed out that organizational structures shape communities, as do symbols, through what has been called the symbolic construction of community. Symbols, such as, for example, flags, songs, rituals, words, dress, or ways of relating to others, can ignore geographical and national boundaries. A particular community is therefore not bound to a certain locale but can be maintained through the manner by which diverse members orient themselves to its symbols. This orientation may become particularly important in global, multicultural communities. Ethnic minorities through the ages have relied on this fact (Assmann, 1999). Moreover, symbols may be held in different ways: perhaps not strongly enough to prevent the disintegration of a community, or else, in the other extreme, they may give rise to fanatical adherence and exclusivity. Ideally, a certain flexibility should allow for difference in the interpretation of the meaning of a shared symbol. In pluralistic societies, this certainly needs to be the case. Symbols have to do with values and identity. In pluralistic societies, symbols have to do with different values and with changing identities that may appear to one another, as they did in my teenager story, as a seemingly unreachable "otherness."

Connecting school governance and community to the stories of one of my participants in a research project, I described in the 1997 paper how Leah joined a very large primary school that allowed her, as a second-generation Canadian of Greek descent, to maintain her values and personal integrity as she joined a well-established school. Interacting at her own pace with colleagues in charge of school projects, she took full responsibility for some of these projects as soon as she felt ready to do so. By the second year, she had become a valued member of a group of teachers responsible for buying computers for the school and setting up training programs.

Leah had strong personal values she did not want to compromise. During her preservice year, Leah and I had come to recognize—through much joint, reflective work—some of these values that asserted themselves in her journals and in our conversations. We called them "not intruding," "listening," "being heard," "receiving and giving respect," and "being recognized." These values were evident in the way she came to conduct her classes in her first year of teaching, but luckily they also seemed to underpin the administration of the school and the resulting school culture. The principal used parent councils and teachers to help him govern the school in a nonimposing way. Leah could therefore become a recognized member of her new community without having to compromise her integrity as an individual; she was able to continue the narrative of her life and live authentically in the institution in which she chose to work.

I realize now that, in a sense, Leah's example illuminates issues in culturally pluralistic institutions. What can hold my three themes together in that 1997 paper is the vision of a pluralistically oriented institution that recognizes that its organizational arrangements and symbols are not neutral, but affect the lives of members directly and with great impact. Such an organization ideally would also create public spaces for groups of people to engage in what I called social self-reflection. This term evolved out of the work Leah and I did together: thinking about what is important in our lives, observing how our actions embody our values, and identifying which symbols express them. Is it such a far-fetched idea that groups of teachers engage with one another in such a way?

REFLECTIVE INTERLUDE

As I look to this institutional story in my effort to assemble strands for my theme of cultural pluralism, three of these strands begin to show, and I want to hold onto them for use in my final discussion. One strand is the idea that places, including institutional places, are not neutral, but have a moral quality, an ethos, that is felt by those who frequent them. (Readers will remember my reference to ethos of place in one of my introductory snippets.) Second, there is the idea that communities are constructed through orientations toward shared symbols and that institutions should allow flexible interpretations of the shared symbols that constitute them. Third, we must acknowledge the need for recognition in the formation of identity, including professional identity. Because recognition was granted to her, Leah did not have to go through an identity crisis but, as I phrased it, was able to live authentically in her new institutional environment. I shall come back to these ideas.

Institutional Story # 2

RECOGNITION, INTERPRETATION, AND THE ENCOUNTER OF DIFFERENCE

As I began to publish papers and put together courses in our preservice teacher education program, my own institutional story was developing. The attempt to live authentically in my chosen institutional environment and continue the narratives of my life as researcher, woman, and teacher, was not entirely successful. Partly to spite institutional realities, I suspect, I wrote a paper titled "Moments of Interpretation in the Perception and Evaluation of Teaching" (Conle, 1999a). This is another paper I do not cite often, in spite of having written it with considerable personal motivation. I wanted to challenge some of what I saw as prevalent misconceptions; I wanted to knock at some institutional blinders, protest marginalization, and draw attention to what I felt lay in the way of fairness. I'm reminded of how Richardson (2000) described how her "writing stories" made her remember "being patronized, marginalized and punished" (p. 932) by her department head and dean. Looking at her past writing concretized and clarified aspects of her institutional context for her.

I presented the paper at a national conference before I had tenure at my institution. Some people commented that it "took guts." I thought it was worth the risk. After publication, I sent a copy to an associate dean who I thought had already been a key player years before my arrival at the institution. I also used the paper in important committee work that was to establish divisional teaching assessment policy. The time of my writing (1995) was early in my career, when the feedback from my three-year-review committee was that I should write more papers that were likely to be published. Apparently, the committee (and dean) took a dim view of narrative inquiry. Luckily for me, my first published article was accepted a month or so later, in a renowned journal, and a year later still, I received an award for the way it was written. But this recognition did not change the way I felt in my institutional environment. The issues here, as in the previous institutional story, are recognition, institutional climate, and the ability of a newcomer to live authentically in her chosen institutional environment.

The evaluation of my teaching also got me into trouble. The advantages of a narrative, experiential approach to preservice education were new. Not having a clear conception of the preservice culture of which I had become a part, I was only gradually realizing the challenges inherent in a one-year preservice program and the key problems perceived by students. I was on my own in my struggle for acculturation that I only vaguely recognized as such. Only years later was I able to see my position and my tasks vis-à-vis the students more clearly and produced a paper (Conle & Sakamoto, 2002) that I use now at the beginning of my preservice courses to get my students "on board." The point they have to understand to begin to enjoy our sessions is that there is no package of information to be absorbed; but prior life experiences are to be reconstructed, interpreted, and reinterpreted. An interpretive view of truth and knowledge is the background for the experiential curriculum I have insisted on devising. This interpretive view is absent in much of the remainder of the program.

In 1995, I picked the evaluation of teaching as a focus for the previously mentioned paper in which I tried to draw attention to the all-pervasive presence of interpretation in any such evaluation—a presence that reaches right into the way phenomena we attempt to observe are perceived. The short list of teacher traits and student perceptions that, at the time, was quantitatively compiled and served as the key ingredient in merit pay considerations and promotion was worlds away from the hermeneutic view that realities are mediated by interpretation. I also made the argument about the all-pervasive presence of interpretation in the evaluation of teaching as strongly as I could in the committee that was to devise institutional policy for the evaluation of faculty for the purpose of tenure and promotion. Almost to my surprise, I found support, and a policy was written that took interpretation seriously.

The issues of recognition, interpretation, and group climate also pursued me in my classroom. In my cross-cultural education course that year, students presented experiential material, and being a culturally diverse student body, they produced very powerful autobiographical work: stories of abuse, stories of criminal behavior (youth gangs), women's stories, stories of discrimination and of religious conviction, and so forth. In a private interview, after the end of the course, one student conveyed to me that some of his male colleagues reacted negatively to what they considered "just another sob story." The content and organization of the course was questioned, and difference was received badly by some of these students. I was surprised. The gaps experienced between their own perceptual horizons and their classmates' presentations of highly diverse life experiences, it seemed, were often not bridged well.

Deciding that I had to create a teaching situation where this was less likely to happen, I designed an action research project that was to become the body of the paper mentioned earlier (Conle, 1996). The experiential work was framed by issues about interpretation and evaluation. Recognition and encounters of difference—in my classroom among the students, in my faculty among colleagues—became the themes. I described what happened when I and four graduate students observed a First Nations Elder present her issues and activities to my preservice cross-cultural education class. We five researchers compared our reactions to her in subsequent conversations. Each of us had a different background: ethnically, we were of German, Chinese, Metis, Italian, and Anglo-Canadian heritage; professionally, we brought a range of different experiences. When we compared our reactions and evaluations of the guest speaker, it was evident that we had seen very different things and had come to very different conclusions. It seemed that each of us looked from within a particular range of vision that limited and shaped everything we could see. A particular past constructed for each of us a different horizon within which certain perspectives were available and others were not. We looked and judged, each from a particular vantage point that was mediated by the languages we speak and by the cultural lenses provided by our society. A methodological point is important: the sharing was done narratively, not argumentatively. We told each other how we had experienced the speaker, listened as carefully as we could to each other, and tried to understand what each of us had perceived.

Sharing our diverse perceptions of events that had taken place in class that day was an enriching experience for me. I realized that in my cross-cultural education class that year I had not scheduled sufficient time to engage in such exchanges of perception. Nor were there in my institution public spaces for this purpose. In a rather inept way, I once attempted to create such a space by inviting faculty to a meeting in which they were asked to speak of their experiences of teaching at our institution. Many came, almost all left greatly puzzled about what this meeting had been about. Only three of us kept meeting. I had not realized how much of a gap there was between the institutional reality of the majority and my own. What seemed obvious to me was invisible to the others. My own reality had been conditioned by a graduate program of narrative inquiry and the reflection created by F. Michael Connelly at the Ontario Institute for Studies in Education since the early 1980s. Now, as a beginning teacher of future teachers, I had not been able to bridge the gap between two very different educational climates; I had not clearly conveyed the advantages of narrative reflection to my colleagues.

REFLECTIVE INTERLUDE

I believe the reader can find remnants of my dance story metaphor in this second institutional story: being relegated to the sidelines, apparently creating self-imposed borders, grappling with "I-them" dichotomies, and trying to understand across difference. However, there was progress. My transposition of the issues into a hermeneutic (interpretive) paradigm in the project I designed points to potential resolutions of the tensions described in my dance story. In the project, we did communicate across the gaps created by our prior life history. We reached out to understand one another. We did not try to argue. We did not try to win each other over to a favorite point of view. Instead, our aim was mutual understanding. As I said earlier, we told each other how we had experienced the speaker. We listened as carefully as we could to each other and tried to understand what each of us had perceived.

Even though I had created those parameters for our project meetings, the five of us communicated in this way almost automatically, because the graduate studies culture we shared was a narrative one—whereas my student teachers came to me for only a short period of time, and for some of them the narrative habit had not yet taken root. It certainly was not institutionalized the way it was at the graduate level at that time, at least in areas of some departments.

The reflective exercise we created in my project, I now believe, illustrates important ways of talking together in culturally pluralistic settings. It illustrates another facet of the social self-reflection I began to conceptualize with Leah in the earlier paper. Leah's values of listening, of being heard, fit very well into a hermeneutic world, as do narrative encounters of difference. In fact, I believe that philosophical hermeneutics (Gadamer, 1960) could easily deliver some guiding principles for living in pluralistic societies.

Since 1995, I have read much of Habermas's work, especially what he wrote in the last twenty years. I see Habermas, in spite of differences he articulated in relation to Gadamer's (1960) ideas, as firmly established in a hermeneutic world where the aim of mutual understanding is paramount. Looking back now at the little experiment I had set up for the "Moments of Interpretation" paper in 1995, I see our sharing of diverse interpretations of the same event fitting well into Habermas's description of communicative action (1984), where the aim is mutual understanding, rather than finding fault in one's opponent's position. Mutual understanding in our case, however, was attempted through the telling of experiential stories rather than through argumentation, as Habermas (1984, 1987) proposes for both theoretical and practical discourse. Again, I take this to be one of the important strands to hold on to for my discussion of potential assets of cultural pluralism.

Applying the dance metaphor to my institutional stories, I see Leah doing what I did not do: I see her crossing that line between "them" and me. I also see our experiment at mutual understanding across differences in the project just described as another way of crossing that metaphorical line. In my collegial and institutional contexts, by writing my paper, I began to walk across the line I felt existed between "them" and me, but in a sense, like the teenager in the original metaphor, I did not think I could cross over completely—perhaps because I did not want to. Perhaps I felt that "they" were too different, and I, still the immigrant, kept my distance. I remember purposely ignoring opportunities to join what I perceived to be the in-group. There were, in my view, major philosophical differences. I protested through my writing, but there were no pitched battles, and with the exception of the committee work where I faced strong opposition, there were no attempts to conquer. I wanted to be understood. In a sense, I thought I already understood "them"—perhaps a common misconception of immigrants? There was no public institutional space available that was intended to deal with these issues.

But why not attempt to join? What was the perceived danger? Why not join that other world? Looking at the 1997 "Shared Governance" paper, I notice on the first page of the introduction a passage that I now find illuminates these questions, even though it was not written for that purpose:

> When our lived histories are disrupted, when we do not find spaces to enact them, we feel alienated and cut off from our world and from who we are. Immigrants understand this well, because they find themselves having to act in worlds that are not of their own making. Unless we . . . understand our new settings and are able to negotiate a happy marriage between them and our own personal and professional histories, *we may become part of outcomes we did not intend and be made accountable for conditions we helped perpetuate inadvertently. We may be placed in the untenable position of having to shoulder onus, responsibility and blame for decisions and outcomes that are destined from the start to go askew* because the administrative environments and philosophical climate preclude certain moves or keep certain options out of view. (Conle, 1997a, p. 137; italics added)

What was I implying here? Perhaps I sensed a legitimate ambivalence toward getting involved in situations and arrangements that would make me contribute to something I would not want to contribute to, once I really understood it? Was it a fear of being held accountable for structures, the implications of which were not clear at the start and which were somehow suspect?

When do people begin to feel this way? When do they get into such situations and in what circumstances? Is it when individuals live in administratively structured environments, where their well-intentioned moves, habits, and decisions may lead to fatal consequences? Is it when people understand their actions in certain ways, but others interpret them quite differently? Newcomers in a society may find themselves in such predicaments, or people whose governments and administrators do not inform them of what is actually going on. This somehow rings true to me with regard to my own early history.

Personal Story #1

SYMBOLS, PLACES, AND WORLDS
NOT OF OUR OWN MAKING

In 1991, when I had written the second chapter of my thesis—an emotional, intense experience—I worried that I may be describing situations, showing likes and preferences, that were fundamentally flawed. I could not deny these preferences. Even now I resent that they may be flawed, and I blame I-don't-know-whom. In my doctoral work (Conle, 1993), I wrote about growing up in the aftermath of World War II in Germany, in an environment that had not yet shed the attitudes, ideas, and habits formed by an authoritarian regime. Granted, this regime was now disgraced, and the devastation it caused was obvious, but those whose patterns of desire (Booth, 1988) had been developed within the culture fostered by the regime had only gradually come to realize, specifically, what within themselves needed to change.

From 1946, when my father returned from Russia, to 1955, when I came to Canada, I had learned to love German folk songs—not unlike that Streichmusik from Alpstein to which I listen now. One of the first things my father's friends did when they returned from prisoners of war camps in 1946 was to come together again to reconstitute the hiking club they had before the war. My father took me along. I loved the singing and the listening to guitars and mandolins that accompanied every outing. This was the part of my childhood social life I treasured most. Years later, in Canada, life was harsh in the beginning, but my jobless father's Swiss friends came to our basement apartment to sing their traditional songs and play the accordion.

Thirteen years after our emigration to Canada, when I returned to Germany and talked to students of my own age at the University of Munich in 1968 (an amazing year at European universities), one remarked, "How can people today still sing those songs? How dare they!" I was dumbfounded. Years later still, I realized that even though many of those songs originated hundreds of years ago, they asserted a love of country that now seemed inappropriate. The Nazis, with their "blood and soil" slogans and their fanatic adoration of everything German—language, landscape, dress, customs—had appropriated these poems, songs, and activities; all were now tainted with a terrible past. Even my love of nature, of the landscape I hiked through, was suspect.

I had learned to love things that were now perceived as "bad." I had unwittingly contributed to the perpetuation of something that needed to be abandoned. One might say "administrative conditions" had been such that trees, mandolins, certain clothing, hiking, and songs had become symbols that, once tainted by the absolute, uniform interpretation of them demanded by the state, could subsequently no longer be recognized in a less tainted form. Nor could they be interpreted and loved in more acceptable ways. People older than I suffered much greater shock and loss. Born in 1941, I never belonged to any of those now-infamous youth clubs, where close comradeship pervaded the hiking, the sitting by evening campfires, the singing—all the while simultaneously being infiltrated by Nazi doctrines. Still, postwar youths like me and those older children were now responsible for outcomes we had never recognized. We had to learn to unlove what we treasured. Having had to act in worlds not of our own making, we were accountable for conditions we helped unwittingly to perpetuate.

This story helps me understand the wariness expressed in the paragraph I cited earlier from the "Community, Reflection and Shared Governance" paper written between 1993 and 1996. My personal story helps me understand certain subtexts in that writing.

REFLECTIVE INTERLUDE

Returning to my current environments, I recognize a particular sensitivity: I now sense certain dangers in contemporary institutional settings, because the perceptual horizon within which I operate as a result of my personal cultural history included such possibilities. The recommendation made in my "Community, Reflection and Shared Governance" article was the need for public spaces to reflectively explore how our own histories and priorities coexist with implicit demands that emerge from the contexts in which we find ourselves. If I link this to the German problems just described, I can assume that the dilemma those problems had created for me formed a tacit impetus in the inquiry involved in my article and that its recommendation of public spaces for social self-reflection can be seen as a tacit telos, a tacit end-in-view, personally for me in my life and professionally for the kind of quest that prompted inquiry in my work (Conle, 2000b).

I now believe that this is another strand to hold on to when cultural pluralism is discussed in the context of education and otherwise. Newcomers should not simply be co-opted into majority structures formed out of different cultural, political, and philosophical persuasions, without the opportunity of public spaces that encourage social self-reflection. I have not given much detail describing the kind of discursive activities I am implying here and that, I believe, would serve well in social self-reflection. To do this, I move to an analysis of another area of my research and teaching, one centered on the practice and enabling conditions for narrative inquiry.

Personal Story #2

NARRATIVE ENCOUNTERS

The discursive practices in social self-reflection I described so far are practices of narrative inquiry. The main strand in my research over the last ten years has had to do with conceptualizing facets of narrative inquiry.[3] I step back for a moment and consider this conceptualization, for it will, I believe, draw attention to some of the "enabling conditions" for social self-reflection, the reflective talk needed in culturally heterogeneous settings. I try the impossible and summarize the conceptual contents of my research in a simple list of the facets of narrative inquiry:

1. I described a rationale for narrative research, pointing out some difficulties as well as implications for the life of the researcher (Conle 1999a).

2. I worked out a particular theory of narrative inquiry, pointing to three essential facets: tensions with a history (i) that, while creating a particular inquiry dynamic (ii), moved the inquirer and her inquiry toward tacit ends-in-view (iii). Eventually, through processes of surrender to phenomena that are about to become data and through subsequent reflection on sets of such data, open-ended formulations of previously tacit ends-in-view became possible (Conle, 2000b).

3. I saw this inquiry dynamic at work in collaborative research arrangements (Conle et al., 1998), as well as in autobiographical teacher inquiry (Conle et al, 2000; Conle, Li, & Tan 2002; Conle & Sakamoto, 2002).

4. I worked out images of change to elucidate change processes that occur in and through narrative inquiry, but cannot be assimilated to technical/administrative views of change (Conle, 1997b).

5. Through the idea of "resonance" (Conle, 1996), I conceptualized interactions within narrative inquiry—when inquirer meets story, when story meets story—and how these interactions become curricular events for the people involved (Conle, 2003).

6. I delineated limits of narrative inquiry, that is to say, essential characteristics that keep it a rational enterprise and within the realms of the social sciences rather than move it into the realm of fictional narrative (Conle, 2001).

7. I pointed out claims that narrative inquirers must make and challenges they can expect (Conle, 2001).

8. I explained how narrative inquiry can be viewed as a curricular activity (as well as a research method) at universities and in schools and how it differs from other narrative curricular practices (Conle, 2003).

9. My emphasis on rationality (2001) is important in all narrative inquiry settings.

With regard to this list, what has become most widely known is what I call "resonance," the process of how experiential story meets experiential story. Resonance involves encounters of difference within commonality or perceptions of commonality through encounters of difference. Less well known is the "tensions-with-a-history-moving-toward-a-tacit-telos" inquiry dynamic

I described (2000b). It informs the inquiry of this chapter as well and will, I believe, prove useful when I discuss inquiry in culturally pluralistic settings.

I will attempt to name the story or stories implicit in this research effort. I also believe I should begin to link the various narrative activities and processes involved in this effort to formulate optimal arrangements for what I called social self-reflection and to find its enabling conditions, so to speak. However, I'm not quite ready to do this until I look at the stories in which what I conceptualized was embedded.

In various writings, I did tell my many stories: about the German child hiking through the Spessart, a now protected area of forests, streams, and villages once visited by the Brothers Grimm as they collected material for their fairy tales. Then there was the child speaking Franconian dialect in a world that valued Hochdeutsch, a German that is no one's dialect; the child living abstractions at school while making her way there along ruined houses, staircases eerily suspended in midair. There were stories about the fourteen-year-old immigrant teen learning French and English simultaneously with the aid of Latin and Greek, the only languages she had studied earlier. She was capable of great feats of abstraction—getting top marks in English grammar exercises, often failed by her English-speaking classmates. There were stories about the woman in her thirties and forties living near the ocean and stories about the teacher/researcher.

These stories were almost all stories of acculturation, where old meets new; old places, old patterns of behavior and learning, old attachments were being challenged. The old was looked at and named because it became more visible when challenged by the new. Old and new informed each other as they met, so to speak. My stories are therefore mostly stories of encounter. The old meets the new, the familiar meets difference, the teacher faces a new institution, the immigrant a new culture.

In the way I now describe them, these stories embody the quintessential hermeneutic situation, where the tension between familiarity and foreignness creates a need for interpretation. Without a break in tradition, without the jolt of the unfamiliar as it meets the taken-for-granted, there is not even the perception of a need for a hermeneutical task (Gadamer, 1986, p. 443). If there is no gap—whether spatial, temporal, or cultural—there is no perceived need for interpretation, no perceived need for inquiry. My research seems to have been motivated at a fairly deep level by the need to think about such encounters of difference and, in my writing and my teaching, to make others think about them.

The quintessential hermeneutic problem in my case is increasingly dealt with narratively. Story meets story, not only in research efforts but also in the curriculum my students and I experience. Unlike other narrative curricula, a narrative inquiry curriculum is primarily experiential. The hermeneutical gap involves someone's experience rather than a textual puzzle. Furthermore, a narrative inquiry curriculum, also unlike some other curricula that are guided by transmission of information, always involves inquiry (Conle, 2003). Inquiry here is prompted through experiential encounters of difference.

My stories then are about experiential encounters between the old and the new. One might say all learning is just that, especially in the Deweyan tradition. But it is not always portrayed that way in contemporary curriculum literature. Since my early graduate work with F. Michael Connelly at the Ontario Institute for Studies in Education, I have insisted on the portrayal of experiential encounters—quite unprompted, I even did the literature review of my dissertation that way.

REFLECTIVE INTERLUDE

The conceptual preoccupation of my research agenda as evidenced in my published papers seems perfectly compatible with the narrative content of my stories. Both deal with the urge to study experience and to conceptualize experiential encounters. In my case, my research agenda seems to be an inquiry derived from personal and cultural "tensions with a history."

The personal dilemma that acted as an invisible author in my research program seemed to push me toward certain ends-in-view that I can now begin to name: When people are involved in social situations they do not sufficiently understand, a process should be available for ongoing mutual interpretation. Newcomers and mainstream need to create conditions where interpretive talk that aims at mutual understanding is facilitated. Such interpretive talk most usefully involves the exchange of experiential narratives rather than argumentation. The aim is mutual understanding. The exchanges take place in a rational mode, involving certain claims and expectations and allowing certain kinds of challenges. The curriculum potential in these exchanges, that is to say, the potential for change in attitude and action, is realized in part through resonance and the vicarious experience (Conle et al., 2002) that is always available in storytelling. "Resonance" (Conle, 1996) names a curricular and research phenomenon in narrative inquiry that occurs when a specific set of images in someone's story suddenly and automatically call up the memory of a set of images in the listener. The two sets correspond metaphorically to one another. In other words, during the experience of an experiential story that is part of the teller's inquiry, the listener unpredictably meets up with elements of his or her own life, elements that are of particular interest or perhaps connected to some tension. If those interests are pursued narratively, the listener's own inquiry is stirred as he or she listens to stories of others. The process is very Deweyan (Dewey, 1938): it is open ended and ongoing; it is only partly available to consciousness and can never be entirely named. All of this seems perfectly compatible with the settings for social self-reflection I have in mind.

Students' Stories

CREATING PUBLIC SPACES FOR SOCIAL SELF-REFLECTION

I must give attention to the conditions conducive to inquiry in culturally pluralistic situations. In part they have been worked out in some of the educational settings I created in my teacher education classes. In the cross-cultural education course on which one of my papers (Conle et al., 2000) is based, for example, students were simply told to write experiential stories about their lives or about events in class.

It was a preservice teacher education course, not a graduate research seminar. An inquiry orientation could not be assumed. Initially, I responded to journals and copied many for the whole class to read. In small groups, each week, students shared parts of their journals. I drew their attention to the fact that they were responding differently to different kinds of texts: asserting facts drew arguments; telling about an experience prompted stories of experience among the audience.

The telling of stories of experience needed to be legitimated among students whose academic success in previous years had often hinged on argumentative discussion. I explained the rationale for my approach: that over the years I had found that students were able to explore more sensitive issues at greater depth and with greater personal significance through experiential interchange than they were able to "discuss" in the usual academic fashion. Once that sank in, some students really "took off," while others were more content to listen. Arguments disappeared. But this did not mean that all suddenly agreed. They worked out very particular issues specific to their particular lives, their lived past, and their current contexts. There were lifelong tensions, feelings of ambivalence, hidden agendas, problems of all kinds. As they talked together and kept writing their weekly reflections—more and more often in response to one another, those contentious areas in their lives that often had not even been consciously recognized began to get named and were worked on.

The 2000 paper I wrote with the help of six students gives detailed illustrations of this process. I wrote, "Each student undertakes his or her self-study from a very different position on the Canadian immigrant-mainstream spectrum" (Conle et al., 2000, p. 373). A first-generation Canadian from Guyana, second-generation Canadians from Jamaica and the Philippines, an American of Jewish-Anglo-Saxon and African American heritage, a third-generation Canadian of Irish-Scottish descent, and someone of French Canadian and Mennonite background were the students who worked with me after the course had ended to continue talking about important aspects in our cultural makeup.

Our issues were different: cultural identity, racial prejudice, living in a multicultural environment and issues of class, family culture, and the so-called normality of the mainstream. Students were very interested in each others' experiences and dilemmas. Dan remembers that after he had already handed in his final paper, he still came to class "fascinated by everyone else's presentation" (Conle et al., 2000, p. 376). Dan did not have to deal with particular tensions resulting from his ethnic background, as did some of his classmates. But even so, "the diversity among us, the combination of familiarity and socio-cultural distance, it seemed, produced a hermeneutic tension of its own" (p. 375) that helped more mainstream candidates who at first thought they had "no culture" to speak about recognize that what was considered normal was just as much the product of a particular history as the more striking differences that newcomers brought to our attention.

What each person gained was as particular as each life history: cultural self-discovery, overcoming ambivalence toward one's cultural group, accepting one's roots, recognizing important differences, crossing cultural boundaries without acting out an interloper script, and finding common ground. All of these were very significant personal gains experienced during the course and during the ensuing project. Leola gives an example of "finding common ground":

> For me, what I discovered was how similar we all are, as opposed to different. When I first came to Canada, I immediately saw the difference between me and the other students because I was in a minority in the school. I was probably the only Guyanese person in the school, except for my family members. I really saw the difference. During the process of doing my first assignment (in our cross-cultural class), that difference stayed with me: that we label ourselves as Guyanese, we label ourselves as Jamaicans, we label ourselves as Trinidadians and we've all formed our own little groups. But, while doing this work and listening to people present their journals and their different cultures, I started to pick up on how similar we are in terms of structure and of education. That was very, very wonderful to see. I remember [a classmate from Vietnam] started talking about the things that he went through with his family. Then [a woman from India] started talking about the different things that she went through in terms of her own culture. My reaction was: I went through that! I went through that! I can connect to that! So what happened for me was that I made many connections; and that was very, very surprising for me. It was great because I realized we are more alike than we are different. (Conle et al., 2000, p. 380)

I realized that what we were doing in this course was indeed significant with regard to life in a pluralistic society. We were beginning to define enabling conditions for social self-reflection. The public space created among those students might bring into educational horizons an awareness of some crucial aspect to consider in the setting up of cross-cultural, social self-reflection in pluralistic societies. People brought their complex issues, found a mode of communication to speak of these issues, and, through the ensuing conversations and the experiential responses offered by their partners in inquiry, came to a different stance vis-à-vis those issues.

At times the result was not just a new recognition, but a more valued line of action. Various students spoke of such changes. Jennifer, born in the Philippines of Chinese parents, had written journals about how she tried to come to terms with certain tensions: feeling "White on the inside," having to cope with racial slurs on the one hand and pressures to be more Chinese on the other.

> Just recently I started taking Mandarin classes all over again. That was something that was quite significant, because I had rebelled against it so much during my past. So I think the course opened up a whole can of worms for me. Eventually I was free to express and to explore a culture that had felt so alien to me. Especially our guest speaker (Xin Li[4]) from China who had lived through the Cultural Revolution, really opened up a whole can of worms. She was talking about something my grandparents went through and something I had completely forgotten about. . . .
>
> So I got to find out more about my culture than I thought I would. I was forced into it in a way. I subsequently started a lot of discussions with my parents about questions for which I had assumed to have answers. . . . I have always felt alienated as a Chinese growing up in a Filipino culture. I didn't think there were very many out there like me! [Xin Li's stories] brought that Chinese part of my grandmother, the pure Chinese part, a little closer. . . . I was able to relate to those parts of my heritage and became less ashamed, less detached, or less lukewarm towards them. I saw a relationship between the two traditions. (Conle et al., 2000, p. 381)

Another student, Arlene, had earlier in the course come to recognize her ambivalence toward her Jamaican heritage. The problem came up when she began to worry about her initial enthusiasm for teaching Jamaican-Canadian students.

> The problem, one might say, was that I questioned how was I really supposed to interact with these students in the manner I had desired, if I was not comfortable with my own feelings about where I fit in to this country, culturally speaking. The more that I thought about this dilemma, the more I realized that I was "different" from many of these students with whom I so desperately wanted to work closely. In light of various life events, I accepted the fact that something in my personality just didn't connect with the cultural confidence these students were exuding, or with their lifestyles. I asked myself where that distinction arose and why it had occurred in the first place. I needed to explore these issues in an attempt to make sense of my "crisis." (Conle et al., 2000, pp. 373–374)

By the end of the project, Arlene told us,

> Leola mentioned that in my narrative I said I was over the ambivalent stage. She wasn't quite sure why that was, or what made me get to that stage. I am thinking about it in relation to Carola [the instructor's] question, "What did you learn about the community that you now identify with?" Part of me coming to terms with this whole issue is not choosing which [community] I want to be part of.

I don't consider myself Jamaican and I don't consider myself Canadian. I consider myself half, a little bit of both in one person. And that's okay. I think that's the biggest thing that came out of what we have done together: the fact that it is okay to feel that way.

But in terms of the actual Jamaican heritage, or Jamaican culture, I did learn about a lot of things. Or rather, I allowed myself to open my eyes to things that I was overlooking before. As I mentioned during the beginning of our course, there were some behaviours or attitudes that I perceived Jamaicans exhibiting—be they my friends or be they older people—things that I wasn't entirely impressed with. I now think that I was focusing on those things and I wasn't seeing some of the other things that I should have been seeing. In our course, some people said to me: "You need to go back to Jamaica." As it turned out, I did. It wasn't until I went back to Jamaica—and I mention it in the second part of the narrative—that I saw how industrious and how innovative the people really were. I mean, everything wasn't at their fingertips, and they found a way to make what they had to make in order to survive. I was very impressed with that. I was impressed with the work ethic I could see in some people. That's not to say it was there in everybody, but I was better able to see it. . . .

I mentioned at the end of my paper here, that I feel a heightened sense of self-confidence. I'm not constantly asking myself questions that really, really bothered me. I feel like I've worked through those questions, and because of that, now I can hold my head up high and say, "Look, I am who I am. Don't ask me to be this and don't ask me to be that." I think I'm bringing that sense of confidence into the classroom with me. (Conle et al., 2000, pp. 381, 383–384)

The impetus for inquiry grew as people found themselves in a congenial space where their experiences were listened to and valued. The differences among them intensified the inquiry dynamic, and definite gains could eventually be registered. I am strongly convinced that this was not just a fluke, but that, given the right climate, cultural heterogeneity is indeed an ideal setting for inquiry. The encounter of difference in congenial settings can create the kind of inquiry dynamic particular to narrative inquiry and that I have described as tensions with a history pushing for yet unnamed ends-in-view (Conle, 2000b; Conle et al., 1998). Pluralistic societies should be environments where inquiry flourishes.

Reflective Interlude—Working Toward a Summary of Sorts

What emerges is a view of culturally pluralistic situations as being highly conducive to inquiry. Of course, one might say, what else does one do when differences face one another across a gap? Ah, but often all kinds of things happen that have nothing to do with inquiry. One of the parties involved may slip away quietly, distressed, trying to repress the whole situation in her memory. Or arguments may ensue, gang fights, wars. Yet, in any of these alternatives to inquiry, some kind of willingness to inquire lurks at the edges. The lonely youngster develops a research project in later life; some post–September 11 Americans try to understand "why they hate us so much."

Looking over the review of my texts, I see certain underlying issues that are important in cultural pluralism. They have to do with recognition, with reflection within encounters of difference, with public spaces for social self-reflection, and with discursive practices conducive to inquiry. They involve identity formation and the kind of conditions within which human beings can safeguard their identity. Some of these issues tend to be addressed in philosophical and sociological literatures, but they are not generally put on educational agendas.

I take a small detour to current European sociological/philosophical literature. Echoing American pragmatism, writers such as Habermas (1999) and Honneth (1995) concur that identities are socially formed. In a recent book, Habermas (1999, pp. 57–58) makes several important points relating to conditions of identity formation in nonheterogeneous societies. He draws our attention to unavoidable consequences of the fact that people become individuals only on the path of socialization. Recognition and respect are indispensable in this process. Reciprocal and equal respect is due as much to the members of our own group as to those outside it. The "other" needs to be included in his or her difference, without demanding that he or she should become like us. If these conditions are not obtained in a society, serious harm can come to its members. Lack of recognition and disrespect can be encountered in the physical form of bodily harm or else in social ostracism and the denial of rights, as well as in indignities that deny the social value of one's abilities (Honneth, 1995, p. 250). In their extreme forms, these losses of recognition can contribute to what may be called forms of social, psychological, and physical death.

Love, protected rights, and social solidarity are necessities. They are key in social recognition and identity formation. They are important constituents for the moral fiber of a society. In fact, morality in the view of the previously mentioned authors "inherently contains an interest in the cultivation of those principles which provide a structural basis for the various forms of recognition" (Honneth, 1995, p. 256). In my experience, narrative inquiry in culturally heterogeneous classes provided degrees of mutual recognition.

But ensuring such conditions and social interactions in our current contexts surely is too great a task for single members of our society and at the very least need institutional support, preferably being anchored in systems of law. Recognition and social solidarity need practical, everyday venues as well, where people are recognized and where they can "appear to each other in their plurality" (Bernstein, 1987, p. 518). In such encounters, as I wrote in our paper (Conle et al., 2000, p. 385), there should be the opening of a space that is "deeper and more significant than merely practical and worldly interests" (Greene, 1988,

p. 17). It must be a space where people, as newcomers, as minorities as well as established members of the mainstream, can all negotiate—through what I have been calling social self-reflection—what they perceive as problems and tensions concerning their life together. Individual identities should be able to develop authentically, without aims of expected assimilation, but having their individual and social histories taken into account.

In my vision of narrative inquiry in pluralist settings, we may create such a space by availing ourselves of modes of communication other than the ones developed in the wake of Descartes' methodological doubt, married to an academic and political culture of argumentative confrontation. It would not mean "getting into one another's heads" or reproducing one another's meanings, but we should take for granted the hope that we will come up with something new, something that arises out of narrative interaction and that, because of that interaction, can help each partner in the conversation to tell her or his story differently. The new story an individual might then tell would be better informed about the otherness of the partners, parts of whose world having been experienced vicariously (Conle et al., 2002). We know precious little about such processes, about how experiential stories are encountered and how specifically they change our own makeup during the encounter. My current research is focused in that direction.

There is a particular urgency to this research, because current social conditions make opportunities for narrative forms of socialization very difficult. Globalized administration; depersonalized, technologized environments lacking any sense of the history of their components; and the loss of cultural cohesion make communicative agreement between people often nearly possible. I notice my larger institutional environment functioning more and more according to models of organization and interaction that were originally created in the world of business. But there the bottom line is financial gain. Our bottom line should be different. Struggles for recognition pervade our current settings (Honneth, 1995). They draw attention to problems and might point out where remedies are needed. Young people in schools could be a starting point for remedial action.

The Ethos of Place

There is still another aspect to the issues of recognition and identity formation through processes of socialization. The socialization of individuals always occurs in some locality, in a particular place. Places, like organizations, are not neutral backdrops in this process. They have structural characteristics, even if these are not physically, but symbolically, evident. They have a particular ethos. Because there seems to be no theoretical language available as yet to describe and discuss ethos of place, I look to such long-term future research with a sense of personal urgency, the circumstances of which have been sounded in parts of this article. My attachment to the places where I have grown up and my resentment of their defilement and of the events that led to disrepute and shame of the cultural practices that constituted them as places has nothing to do with sentimental romanticizing, nor is it something that should be ignored or overcome.

Coda

Reworking the history of my academic writing by attending to its subtexts has been a clarification, because it lets me see connections I had previously not made and lets me name some contemporary issues more clearly. Rather than bringing solutions into view, writing this chapter has bolstered the reasons for engaging in the kind of inquiry I intend to do in the future. On the practical level of everyday life, the tensions I described at the beginning are still operative. They still motivate inquiry and shape action in a newly funded project on the interrelationship of imagination, culture, and the media. Outside my professional responsibilities and without institutional funding, I have accumulated a huge literature to find a way to describe ethos of place.[5] I have begun writing field notes in Europe that closely connect to World War II, the Holocaust, and the places left behind by the Nazis. In Germany, it is not at all clear what should be done with the sites of Nazi power (Braun, 2002; Habermas, 2001; Lutz, 2001; Reichel, 1995). On a recent trip to Nuremberg, for example, I did not inspect the huge installations that once served as backdrop for Nazi Party celebrations, because a rock festival was taking place there. Nazi sites are symbols of something we do not want as part of any community. They are reminders of something that should never be repeated. As such, they are very much part of an otherness. Should such otherness be allowed to enter into the socialization processes of young people? An important question I and others need to ask is whether there are limits to the kinds of otherness that should be drawn into reflective interaction. Should some things and some people be denied any kind of recognition and respect? If the latter, where and how can we draw the line? Pluralistic societies need to find answers for such questions.

Recommended Readings

For a different, but also similar, approach to looking at one's own written work for the purpose of fresh meaning making, I suggest *Writing: A Method of Inquiry* (Richardson, 2000). *The Asset of Cultural Pluralism: An Account of*

Cross-Cultural Learning in Pre-Service Teacher Education (Conle, Blanchard, Burton, Higgins, Kelly, Sullivan, & Tan, 2000) will give insight into the encounter of autobiographical stories by beginning teachers with diverse backgrounds, while the nature of narrative inquiry in autobiographical work is explored in *Thesis as Narrative: What Is the Inquiry in Narrative Inquiry?* (Conle, 2000b). The importance of recognition in a situation where marginalization is an issue is philosophically explored by Axel Honneth (1995) in *The Fragmented World of the Social.*

Reflective Questions

1. How do any of the issues in this chapter relate to your own life?

2. Which criteria are offered in this chapter for a productive coexistence in culturally pluralistic environments? To what extent do these apply to situations with which you are familiar?

3. Working with two colleagues, exchange your own "institutional stories."

4. Devise an exercise involving an interchange of experiential narratives among groups of four or five people. Add two observers to monitor the interchange and report to the group any likely instances of "resonance-type" responses. Discuss these responses.

Notes

1. Streichmusik (music by string instruments) from Alpstein (pseudonym) started in the late nineteenth century when groups of local musicians began to play their traditional melodies. Each group usually consists of five musicians, playing violin, cello, contrabass, and Hackbrett (a locally built dulcimer). Sometimes there is a piano or accordion as well. Musicians do not use notes, but play as a miniorchestra. Some groups play their own compositions and those of their friends; or else the originality lies in a particular interpretation of traditional tunes.

2. Pseudonym

3. At least this is what I had been telling myself and others at important moments such as tenure review or making an application for funded research. Surprisingly, as I looked over my notes on key papers in order to write this chapter, I realized I could just as well tell the story differently: I have been working on problems of cultural change and on ways to cope with them. On second thought, because of the intimate connection between culture and narrative, this is not as surprising as it first sounds.

4. My students or I sometimes invited guest speakers to tell their stories. Xin Li was one of them. Xin, who was born in China, came to one of our sessions to tell her narrative. She was a graduate student at the time, working on an autobiographical thesis. Among many things, she spoke of her experiences in the Cultural Revolution, as well as her son's present situation. He had stayed behind in China originally and had just

come to join her in Canada. A principal in a school in which she was thinking of enrolling him had suggested that she speak only English to her son.

5. I have tried but received no funding for this project and will therefore pursue it outside an educational research framework.

References

Assmann, J. (1999). *Das kulturelle Gedächtnis: Schrift, erinnerung und politische identität in frühen hochkulturen.* Munich, Germany: Verlag C. H. Beck.

Bernstein, R. (1987). The varieties of pluralism. *American Journal of Education, 95*(4), 509–525.

Booth, W. (1988). *The company we keep: An ethics of fiction.* Berkeley: University of California Press.

Braun, M. S. (Ed.). (2002). *Traces of terror. Sites of Nazi tyranny in Berlin.* Berlin, Germany: Verlaghaus Braun.

Carr, D. (1986). *Time, narrative, and history.* Bloomington: Indiana University Press.

Conle, C. (1993). *Learning culture and embracing contraries: Narrative inquiry through stories of acculturation.* Unpublished doctoral dissertation, Ontario Institute for Studies in Education/University of Toronto, Canada.

Conle, C. (1996). Resonance in preservice teacher inquiry. *American Educational Research Journal, 33*(2), 297–325.

Conle, C. (1997a). Community, reflection and the shared governance of schools. *Teaching and Teacher Education, 3*(2), 137–152.

Conle, C. (1997b). Images of change in narrative inquiry. *Teachers and Teaching, 3*(2), 205–219.

Conle, C. (1999a). Moments of interpretation in the perception and evaluation of teaching. *Teaching and Teacher Education, 15*(8), 801–814.

Conle, C. (1999b). Why narrative? Which narrative? Struggles with time and place. *Curriculum Inquiry, 29*(1), 7–32.

Conle, C. (2000a). Narrative inquiry: Research tool and medium for professional development. *European Journal of Teacher Education, 23*(1), 49–63.

Conle, C. (2000b). Thesis as narrative: What is the inquiry in narrative inquiry? *Curriculum Inquiry, 30*(2), 189–213.

Conle, C. (2001). The rationality of narrative inquiry in research and professional development. *European Journal of Teacher Education, 24*(1), 21–33.

Conle, C. (2003). Anatomy of narrative curricula. *Educational Researcher, 32*(3), 3–15.

Conle, C., Blanchard, D., Burton, K., Higgins, A., Kelly, M., Sullivan, L., & Tan, J. (2000). The asset of cultural pluralism: An account of cross-cultural learning in preservice teacher education. *Teaching and Teacher Education, 16*(3), 365–387.

Conle, C., Li, X., & Tan, J. (2002). Connecting vicarious experience to practice. *Curriculum Inquiry, 32*(4), 429–452.

Conle, C., Louden, W., & Mildon, D. (1998). Tensions and intentions in group inquiry: A joint self-study. In M. L. Hamilton (Ed.), *Self study in re-conceptualizing teacher practice: Self-study in teacher education* (pp. 178–194). London: Falmer Press.

Conle, C., & Sakamoto, M. (2002). "Is-when stories": Practical repertoires and theories about the practical. *Journal of Curriculum Studies, 34*(4), 427–449.

Crites, S. (1979). The aesthetics of self-deception. *Soundings, 62,* 107–129.

Dewey, J. (1938). *Experience and education.* New York: Collier Books.

Gadamer, H. G. (1960). *Wahrheit und methode: Grundzuge einer philosophischen hermeneutik.* Tübingen, Germany: Mohr.

Gadamer, H. G. (1986). *The idea of the good in Platonic-Aristotelian philosophy.* New Haven, CT: Yale University Press.

Gergen, M., & Gergen, K. J. (2000). Qualitative inquiry: Tensions and transformations. In N. Denzin & Y. Lincoln (Eds.), *Handbook of qualitative research* (2nd ed., pp. 1025–1046). Thousand Oaks, CA: Sage.

Greene, M. (1988). *The dialectic of freedom.* New York and London: Teachers College Press.

Greenfield, T., & Ribbins, P. (1993). *Greenfield on educational administration: Towards a humane craft.* New York: Routledge.

Habermas, J. (1984). *The theory of communicative action: Vol. 1. Reason and the rationalization of society.* Boston: Beacon Press.

Habermas, J. (1987). *The theory of communicative action: Vol. 2. Lifeworld and system: A critique of functional reason.* Boston: Beacon Press.

Habermas, J. (1999). *Die Einbeziehung des Anderen.* Frankfurt, Germany: Suhrkamp.

Habermas, J. (2001). *Zeit der Übergänge: Kleine politische Schriften IX.* Frankfurt, Germany: Suhrkamp.

Honneth, A. (1995). *The fragmented world of the social.* Albany: SUNY Press.

Lutz, T. (Ed.). (2001). *Gedenkstätten Rundbrief* (Vol. 100). Berlin, Germany: Stiftung Topography des Terrors.

MacIntyre, A. (1981). *After virtue: A study in moral theory.* Notre Dame, IN: University of Notre Dame Press.

Reichel, P. (1995). *Politik mit der Erinnerung: Gedächtnisorte im Streit um die nationalsozialistische Vergangenheit.* Frankfurt, Germany: Fischer.

Richardson, L. (1997). *Fields of play: Constructing an academic life.* New Brunswick, NJ: Rutgers University Press.

Richardson. L. (2000). Writing: A method of inquiry. In N. Denzin & Y. Lincoln (Eds.), *Handbook of qualitative research* (2nd ed., pp. 923–948). Thousand Oaks, CA: Sage.

12

The Art of Narrative Inquiry

Embracing Emotion and Seeing Transformation

Chris Liska Carger

Autobiographical Introduction

I am an Associate Professor in the Department of Literacy Education at Northern Illinois University and have worked with diverse children my entire career. I taught in a dual-language elementary school program and a migrant educational project in New York and bilingual and English as a second language (ESL) programs in Illinois before teaching at the college level. My research has centered on multicultural and multilingual education, particularly with Latino students in the area of literacy learning. My book *Of Borders and Dreams: A Mexican-American Experience of Urban Education* (1996) presents the story of an adolescent of Mexican origin and his family's struggle to find a meaningful education for a student with learning disabilities and English language development problems. I have continued tracing the Juarez family's educational sojourn for the past eight years, and this chapter shares one part of the experiences I have documented since their son dropped out of high school. In it, I challenge stereotypic notions of the characteristics of immigrant parents of an inner city Latino dropout. My chosen approaches to research are qualitative methodologies, particularly narrative inquiry. I am a former doctoral student of Bill Ayers and Bill Schubert at the University of Illinois at Chicago, and I attribute my belief in and affinity for qualitative methodologies to these two mentors, my teachers in the fullest sense of the word.

Having shared that information, I find myself wanting to say that, quite simply, "I am a teacher." I don't remember ever having envisioned myself in any other profession than that of teaching. Though I am technically an Associate

Professor, I feel that this is a pretentious title that carries with it the baggage of "the academy" and an air of superiority that I disdain. "Teacher," however, is a title I embrace fully and do not take lightly. In my qualitative research with the Juarez family, I have been both teacher and student, more often the latter. My journey of a dozen or so years with them has taught me volumes about what it means to be a member of a loving, hardworking Mexican family transplanted into the heart of Chicago and what it means to struggle for a meaningful education in an unresponsive urban educational system in America. In addition, it has helped me to understand the concept of "*bien educado*," the aspiration of many Mexican-origin families for their children: It signifies a sense of being educated that goes beyond academics to include respect, faith, moral development, and familial and community responsibility. It is a goal I have adopted for my own children.

Looking Backward

I believe that recounting and reflecting upon narratives of transformative experiences, particularly in the lives of multicultural students and their families, is a meaningful and engaging way to help teachers understand their diverse students' backgrounds. I also feel that narrative inquiry is a multidimensional research method that can include the emotion inherent in a caring relationship, such as education beckons between teacher and student, without removing it from the realm of respectable research. Furthermore, I believe that qualitative research such as mine in the area of the dropout crisis in our nation's cities can provide a longitudinal perspective on what is often a complex, cumulative process of disengagement for minority students.

These are the things I attempted to do as I told the story of Alejandro Juarez's educational experiences, the process he went through to leave formal schooling, and the repercussions of that decision upon his family and his future. In this chapter, I share a sample of narrative inquiry I wrote describing one dropout's parents' response to the loss of their son's formal education. I also reflect upon the use of qualitative research to foster understandings of "others," particularly of students and their families who are typically and tragically marginalized in a nation whose teachers often do not share their ethnicity or their backgrounds of experience. My reflections propel me to a hope for responsive educational research that is linked to responsible social action.

About a dozen years ago, I directed a center attached to a university reading and learning disabilities program in Chicago. The staff and I quickly realized that many of the children referred to the center for reading and learning problems were actually contending with difficulties developing their second (or third) language, English. So we began an outreach ESL program, in more current terminology English language learning, and sent tutors to schools to work with small groups of mainly Latino children learning to read in English. I could not find a tutor for one school, which was on my way home, so I decided to do the tutoring there myself. That was where I met Alejandro, then a struggling English language learner (ELL) in fourth grade, who also had significant learning disabilities. Eventually, I wrote Alejandro's story, focusing on his eighth-grade year in the contexts of his school, his home, and his community.

Alejandro's family was very close-knit and faced the world as a unit, and I came to know his parents very well. His mother, in particular, storied her life and came to paint vignettes and describe experiential episodes for me with candor and enthusiasm. Sadly, her firstborn son, Alejandro, dropped out of high school early in his second year there. This event caused his mother, Alma, untold disappointment and much preoccupation with the example he set for his younger siblings by failing with his schooling. I came to hear her frequent *consejos,* the giving of nurturing advice, to her younger children about not following in their oldest brother's footsteps. Her concern for Alejandro's "bad example," in her estimation, caused her to go further than *consejos* as she and her husband became stricter than they had been in limiting their children's out-of-school activities. Eventually, Alma took another step and enrolled with her husband in evening classes to prepare to undertake the test for U.S. citizenship. This action, she felt, would prove to her children the importance she and her husband attributed to schooling. She would try to counteract the bad example set by Alejandro with her own good one.

Alma's active direction of her life after an event she felt she could not control, her son's school failure, reinforced for me, once again, the appropriateness of using narrative to report the ongoing research I was doing with the Juarez family. Narratives, according to Lawler (2002), are accounts that contain transformation, action, and characters in an overall plot with setting: "They are part of the fabric of the social world" (p. 243). The episode that Alma crafted of her and her husband's bid for citizenship epitomized for me the strength of narrative inquiry as I wove her vignettes of that process into a story I titled "My Country 'Tis of Thee." The quest for citizenship is a critical experience in the Juarez's social world, a world of Latino immigrants relegated to low-paying jobs and the constant fear of loss of employment. Citizenship is an attainable, albeit challenging, goal, with clear benefits for the members of the Juarez neighborhood. Alma's own awareness of the story of this process as being one ripe for the retelling, enticed me to write it. Only her compelling border-crossing stories equaled the strong sense of narrative set in a social world that the citizenship story afforded. For it, too, is a critical story within a broader social narrative. It also tangibly captures transformation, a movement from the potential to the actual, as it affords the chance to "read time backwards" (Ricoeur, 1980, p. 183). The whole time that the citizenship story unfolds, we are on an almost inevitable march to its end, on a path easier to discern (and accept) than was Alma's son's road to becoming a dropout. Making a bid for citizenship was a big step for the Juarez parents, a class movement from disenfranchised residents to voting citizens. So, too, was their son's transformation, in their eyes, from an educated youth to a school dropout.

Looking Outward: A Dropout's Environment

Alma particularly enjoyed recounting her and her husband's struggles to study for the citizenship test. "We went to classes from 6 to 9, four evenings a week," she explained. "We'd stop home after work, wash up, and I'd cook for the kids, eat quickly, and then go right to class. We had to pay $80 for the classes, $40 each, to get the questions to study and the book. 'Do you think we can ever remember all of this book?' I'd say to Alejandro [her husband], then laugh. Which saint will pull us through this, I wondered.

"I don't know why but *me da tanta risa,* I just grinned so much as soon as we got into class. The teacher was a nice man, Puerto Rican. He seemed stern at first, but he paid a lot of attention to us; I think he liked us. At first he thought we were brother and sister, 'No, *maridos,* I told him, a married couple.' I told him I have learning problems, *problemas de aprendizaje,*" she chuckled. "I don't think I ever used that phrase so much! You know, I remembered it from when you explained it to me with Alejandro. The teacher called on us a lot. He'd ask one question of most people, but three or four of us. He'd have me go up to the board to write the sentences we had to learn over and over. And every time I'd even look at my husband I'd start to giggle. He put us on opposite ends of the classroom," she chuckled again and shook her head. "'Mr. and Mrs. Juarez cannot sit together,' he'd say. We just could not stop laughing; I think it was out of nervousness! The teacher didn't get mad at us. I felt bad for him. I think he was just a volunteer. I told him we were his two *burros* (donkeys)," she sighed.

Alicia and Ricardo or one of their other children would periodically drop into the conversation. "Yeah, Chris, they were so bad," grinned Alicia one evening around the basement table. "I tried to help them study, and they'd make each other laugh."

"Finally, Chris," Alma confessed, "one of us had to study upstairs and the other downstairs or we just couldn't concentrate. Alejandro would laugh at my English pronunciation and I'd laugh at his answers."

"Oh, remember the notebooks!" said Alicia. "I even had to show them how to use the notebooks!" Alma and Alejandro blushed. "Oh, Chris, my father, he wrote from the wrong side of the paper inwards, and her," said Alicia pointing to her mother, "she was using it upside down!"

"It's true, Chris," laughed Alma. "We didn't even know, we had so little schooling so long ago."

"You write so nicely," commented Alejandro Sr. "So quick and so nice," he said wistfully as he glanced down at my notebook.

"Look, I held it like this," said Alma, turning my field notes upside down. "I never noticed there was a top or bottom."

How did they manage to do this, I wondered, take a test in a language that was foreign to them, about random historical facts, with so little experience with literacy that they had to learn how to hold their notebooks in order to write?

"I worked with her a lot, Chris," added Alicia. "She studied a lot and so did my father. They used to have little contests on their sentences. Every time I looked at them, they were studying."

"It's the truth," said Alma. "A nice Polish man at my work, one of the mechanics, helped me study too. He kept drilling me with the questions to the beat of our machines," said Alma. "But he studied more than I did," she glanced affectionately toward her husband. "He really worked hard at it." "It'd be eleven o'clock at night, Christy," added Alicia, "and he'd still be reading. I had to tell him to go to bed."

Mr. Juarez blushed. "Well, I had to," he sighed, touching his forehead to indicate that he needed to study a lot in order to remember.

"I had to help them understand about where they needed upper and lower case letters," continued Alicia. "Yeah," attested Alma. "And I confuse b and v, to me they sound the same, and we both had trouble with i in English because in Spanish it's like an e, and we don't always hear the s at the ends of words." Recalling more and more of the specifics of their ordeal helped their story grow in stature with each retelling.

I could imagine these two people conscientiously trying to memorize these facts, one in the upstairs kitchen and one in the basement, relying on their children to help them not just with civics content, but also with basic written language skills and classroom routines. I could picture them studying in their respective factories, with kind coworkers who noticed their plight. How many people ever stop to think about the challenge of citizenship for the millions of unschooled immigrants who have managed to achieve it with pure grit and determination? It was the first time I really ever appreciated this commonplace achievement.

"I had to show them how they could check their answers in the back of their book," Alicia continued, shaking her head. "They never knew the answers were there."

"No, I never knew that," Alma confirmed. "Once she showed me them, I looked there but it was a long time before I knew anything like that."

When Mr. and Mrs. Juarez found out that they did not pass the first test comprising ten randomly selected civics/history questions and several on general information, they paid another $80 fee for eight more weeks of classes. They were very discouraged, but decided immediately to try again.

"My husband was so nervous during the test, Chris, that when they asked him if he was divorced, he said 'yes'!" Alma laughed. "I was nervous too. I heard from one of my *comadres* that they asked her what color her lipstick was," she continued. "I was so worried, I didn't wear any lipstick, and I dressed all in black. I looked like a *gangera* [female gang member], but I figured I just had to answer 'black' for any question they had about what I wore! But I knew I answered some questions wrong about the constitution, I was so scared I couldn't even think straight. I knew the minute I looked into the woman's eyes that I wasn't going to pass. I looked right at her like this," Alma fixed her gaze on my eyes. "She looked so stern," said Alma, "I knew I wasn't going to be able to handle it."

After Mr. and Mrs. Juarez took the citizenship test a second time and passed, I asked, "What made you decide to go through all of this?"

"Well," said Alma, looking off into the distance as if capturing a fleeting glimpse of her personal vision, "I wanted to show our children that their parents could succeed at something educational, especially after what happened with Alejandro," Alma told me. "We are always giving our children a little push, about school or their classes, you know, and so I thought we should push ourselves too." Once again, I saw how Alma created a curriculum for her family and how heavily her son's failed school experience blanketed her mind and influenced her actions.

It is as if the Juarezes have grasped democracy in their bare hands, holding on to their American dream and refusing to let go and settle for complete disenfranchisement. It took them more than twenty years to muster the courage to cross the latest border, but as before, they succeeded together, drawing strength from their family. Now we can exchange political opinions along with our families' stories. I find Alma and Alejandro to be thoughtful citizens who take their right to vote seriously. They are the new immigrants of the new millennium, and I feel thankful that I live in a country where this process of citizenship, albeit flawed, manages to function, sputtering and churning like a huge, old machine unaware of technological and pedagogical advances.

Looking Inward: Why I Chose Narrative inquiry

As I reflect on the story of Mr. and Mrs. Juarez's citizenship, I find myself thinking of my own father who went through a "night school" process to obtain his GED, high school equivalency diploma. Perhaps that is in some part why I find this story so touching. I remember how hard it was for my father to return to a school setting in his fifties with classmates the ages of his daughters.

I remember him studying for the test and working out math problems at our small kitchen table well into the evening after working on an aeronautical factory's assembly line all day. I remember him laughing at himself when he smelled a terrible odor in class one night. He thought to himself that the young "punks" he went to class with didn't know how to use deodorant, only to discover that he had stepped in "some dog's business." "It was me who stunk," he laughed. "Those kids were probably thinking, boy that old guy needs to shower," he chuckled. What he was really talking about was the social boundaries he had crossed in attending urban GED classes with minority young adults. Of catching up on some documentation he had missed out on, as the Juarezes had always longed for their citizenship documents. Of a transformation he quietly but doggedly decided to undertake. My father was also a dropout, of necessity in the ninth grade, to support his family when his father died in a tragic train accident during the Depression—more similarities with the narrative I have told. But my father never struggled with English as the Juarezes have. Though he could speak Polish, he was also fluent in English. Though he missed out on high school, he was literate and read throughout his adulthood. These stories and memories swirl through my mind as I write of the Juarezes' challenges, and I am connected, intimately, to my inquiry. I realize that stories help us to invent who we are and fit ourselves into the world. "If narrative makes the world intelligible, it also makes ourselves intelligible," said Henrietta Moore (1994, p. 119).

Story is the most time-honored way in which cultures preserve the past and shape the future. Embedded in the characters are the values shaped by each unique culture. In the factual information needed to survive or the inspirational example of overcoming hardship and accepting transformation or in sharing responses to daily concerns, recounting the experiences of people is a way to see the world through a particular lens in a specific context. Recounting the stories of people represents the most fundamental way in which knowledge reveals itself.

Bruner (1990), a psychologist-researcher who early in my studies made good sense to me, agreed that narrative was a natural format through which human beings make sense of life. Van Mannen (1990) nurtured my bent to look at daily lived experiences of my students and to reflect upon them deeply. Polkinghorne (1997) was another researcher whose writing encouraged me to experiment with a narrative mode of reporting or displaying my inquiries. And before I read any of these works, Schubert and Ayers, whom I affectionately refer to as the two Bills, were profound influences on me when I became not only a reader of their teacher lore research (1992) but a pupil in their classrooms a dozen years ago. They helped me to realize that research could be much more than the manipulation of events and numbers, that research could also be a venue to give attention to often silenced voices.

I have come to embrace narrative as far more than a research methodology. It is, for me, a way of thinking. I have also come to conceive research as far more than an academic exercise, something intimately tied to social action. Tierney and Lincoln's (1997) statement "The desire to create change, to lessen oppression, or to assist in the development of a more equitable world sets up a different research dynamic from that of the disengaged academic whose main purpose is to add to the stock of theoretical knowledge" (p. viii) moves me to want to sing in a Professor-Pickering sort of way, "You've got it, by God, you've got it!" I believe that the purpose of social science research is not to endorse one mandated reporting format to gain publication prowess, but rather to produce useful knowledge and understanding to improve human experiences or, specifically in my case, to improve education for Hispanic students. A narrative account, as Polkinghorne declared (1997, p. 3) "is the appropriate form of expression to display research as a practice."

Patti Lather referred to "the crisis of representation" (Lather & Smithies, 1997, p. 233) as she wrote of the search for a discourse in the human sciences. Like Lather, I reject the scientism that is pervading educational research in American universities, that is being more than endorsed by our government as pronouncements are issued that only quantitative, scientifically formatted educational studies are of value and will be funded. For example, Valeria Reyna, the deputy of the U.S. Office of Educational Research and Improvement, recently described scientifically based research during an interview. She touted a medical model of repeated clinical trials with experimental and control groups as "the only design that allows you to . . . make a causal inference." She continued to say that "the bottom line here is these same rules about what works and how to make inferences about what works, they are exactly the same for educational practice as they would be for medical practice" (Reyna, 2002).

The positivist, medical approach to educational research misses several fundamental considerations in my opinion. First and foremost, we are dealing with human beings, their behaviors, their successes, and their failures. We are not studying mice in mazes, or microbes on slides. Second, there is a temporal dimension to educational research. Very often, we are looking at human actions over time in contexts that cannot be controlled and replicated with exactness (although scientific researchers would contend that large samples will control for those variables as if referring to inanimate objects). In my own narrative inquiry, there is a definite ethnographic strain as I observe a student and his family, frequently participating in what I am observing, at first over months and now over years. Gergen and Gergen (1986) talk of the importance of narrative's "capability to structure events in such as way that they demonstrate . . . a sense of movement of direction through time" (p. 30). Through real time in real settings, I would add. Schools are not laboratories gathering information in same-time slices.

Finally, shouldn't all "scientific research," which seeks to quantify and replicate findings, be predicated upon observation? Isn't a march toward "scientific research" a march to spurious quantification and statistical analysis if it does not begin with qualitative descriptions of observable phenomena? Haven't case studies and reflective observation been cornerstones of research for centuries in the medical realm? Why must one certain model, clinical trials, be held up as the only "truth"? As Yvonna Lincoln remarked (1997), "We may need to break the science habit, and go cold turkey into a new life" (p. 51).

Bourdieu (1990), a French anthropologist, went into that "new life" and wrote about his theory of social practice. He cited three features of it that mesh with my own narrative approach to inquiry like the warp and weft of a well-woven fabric. He noted the importance of the dimensions of time and space and went further to describe the existence of an experiential type of flow that cannot be precisely planned and organized, but is not random and without thought, and an overall purposefulness with goals. In the past, I have referred to narrative as an art, and I believe that Bourdieu has captured that sense of the artistic in his description of action theory. Clandinin and Connelly (2000) also identify qualities of narrative inquiry—its temporal, contextual, and experiential nature—that convey the dynamic approach of this type of research. They continue this line of thought as they describe the three-dimensional narrative inquiry space—"with temporality along one dimension, the personal and social along a second dimension, and place along a third" (p. 50).

Another layer I add to my narrative inquiry is the cross-cultural nature of what I observe. He (2002), in describing the lives of three Chinese women teachers (of which she is one) refers to cross-cultural narrative inquiry as an approach well suited to the study of cross-cultural lives with "a close-to-life, reflective and fluid, contextualized and historicized quality that enables us to explore and portray the shifting, often paradoxical, nature of our cross-cultural lives" (p. 5). I too find that narrative inquiry offers a comprehensible unfolding and humanizing of cross-cultural situations that elude the fixed, scientifically based terminology that may frustrate practitioners who want to understand with some urgency, for example, why students' immigrant parents might not come to parent-teacher conferences, why fractions seem absolutely foreign to a bilingual pupil, why a Mexican youngster may look down at the floor when spoken to pointedly. Stories that look closely at ordinary life in a specific cross-cultural context can help to lessen home-school mismatches and answer real questions.

There remains one more feature essential to my work, and that is a concern for emotion. Like the photographer in Behar's allegory that introduces *The Vulnerable Observer: Anthropology That Breaks Your Heart* (1996), I am wont to toss aside my camera and throw my arms around a child. The true life plots that unfold before my eyes are interwoven with emotional moments.

Though I do not set out to uncover instances of injustice and racism or to discover poignant vignettes that become etched in my memory, the natural flow of the experiences I witness and share often lays those things at my feet. And I refuse to toss them aside for the sake of an imposed objectivity in research. The acclaimed author Chinua Achebe's words come to mind as I consider the debacle of objectivity and emotion in studies: "Passion is our hope and strength, a very present help in trouble," not a mere "marshalling of facts" (1987, p. 385).

Clearly, for me, research is far more than an academic exercise. I look not only outward at the inquiry landscape I study but also inward as I look at my place as the researcher in inquiry. Inevitably, when doing narrative research, my own autobiography, like a persistent song playing in my mind, surfaces repeatedly. This is a dimension that narrative research beckons, the revealing of self, the sharing of self against which most researchers are taught to combat with the mighty arm of objectivity. I have learned not to evade emotion in my inquiry, but to embrace it, to describe it richly. It is part and parcel of the art of narrative inquiry. Just as a singer can perform a song mechanically or sing it with emotion that grows from experience, the researcher has the same choice. Research crosses from an academic exercise to an art when the researcher becomes fully the author, revealing self and other in a voice that is "readable, evocative, engaging and personally meaningful" (Ellis & Bochner, 2000, p. 761).

Looking Forward

The face of America is changing, and so are its stories. Hispanics are now the largest minority group in the United States (U.S. Census Bureau, 2003). They make up the largest percentage of the "new wave" of immigrants (Lowery, 2000). They are also the group with the highest dropout rate, approximately 40 percent nationally and as high as 70 percent in large urban areas such as Chicago (Perez-Miller, 1991). In contrast, the most recent statistics on the racial makeup of elementary and secondary public school teachers in the United States show that of almost 4 million American teachers, less than 5 percent are Hispanic (King, 2003).

These numbers should send a clear message to U.S. teacher educators of the pressing need to develop cultural awareness in the nation's teachers now responsible for the education of large numbers of Hispanic students who are frequently ELL, not to mention the myriad of other ELL students from other varied backgrounds. Largely cultural assimilationist philosophies have resulted in the widespread failure of U.S. schools to successfully serve this heterogeneous Spanish-speaking population, which includes Caribbean, Central, and South American Hispanic cultures. An understanding of the values inherent in these varied cultures of origin that impact families' educational goals and behaviors seems to be a basic need often unaddressed in colleges of education. In order to teach in a meaningful and engaging manner, an understanding of, and sensitivity to, the home culture is a necessary foundation before curricula and methodology is considered.

How can colleges of education provide such a knowledge base, one that would clearly benefit from meaningful, innovative approaches? Cultural sensitivity is not something learned by rote from lists and formulas. In my opinion, it is affective knowledge learned best heart to heart and side by side. Service learning courses offer promise as college students can gain actual experiences interacting with diverse people in diverse settings. Stories that focus on cultural contexts and reveal cultural values also offer pathways to cultural sensitivity that may sidestep barriers to comprehending the unknown. The narrative form of qualitative research can promote the understanding of the experience of self and others (Diamond & Mullen, 1999). My goal as a writer of narrative research is to cultivate rich, multifaceted representations of human experiences that might begin to serve as a basis for teachers to understand diverse students. Most frequently, the experiences I till are that of an educated middle-aged White woman from a blue-collar family background of assorted Eastern and Western European ethnicities engaging with and observing the experiences of a Latino family of blue-collar workers of Mexican origin with little formal education on the part of the parents. More simply, I am a teacher, who, like many other educators in my country, comes from a White middle-class background, looking closely at the life experiences of a student I taught whose ethnicity and background experiences do not completely match my own. I say "completely," because there are some similarities I share with the family I have followed. But, like many American teachers, I found myself struggling to facilitate a meaningful curriculum for my Hispanic students, who in turn struggled in their schooling. It was as simple as that. My research arose from my general, long-standing interest in varied cultures and my more specific desire to foster smoother home-school connections for students I saw who often came from large, loving, intact families, yet found formal education to be a sometimes insurmountable challenge.

If you were to look at actuarial and statistical research on Latino dropouts, you would find that Alejandro Juarez's Mexican-origin family fits many characteristics of dropouts' families. The best predictors of Chicano school failure—low parental schooling levels and exclusive use of Spanish as the home language—are clearly present in the Juarez household. Both parents completed a second-grade level of formal education and are Spanish-dominant in language use. The characteristics of dropouts' families proceed to include a low income level, more precisely, low socioeconomic status, and a clearly at-risk home environment process profile that includes little academic guidance, no "intellectuality" in the home, and no permission for participation in clubs and organizations (Laosa & Henderson,

1991). Yet despite the formal indicators, my participant observation unveiled some very explicit encouragement of schooling and literacy-related activities and some "intellectuality" of a pragmatic sort, a transformation that entailed upgrading social status, which I relate in the excerpt of the narrative I called "My Country 'Tis of Thee" earlier in this chapter.

Alejandro's parents emerged from the margins, from a preconceived stereotypical image to a flesh-and-blood, complex, multidimensional central part of a family wrestling within a particular context. My voice emerges too as the researcher moves out of the background and an autobiographical voice wraps itself around the narrative at hand. Denzin and Lincoln (2000) envision the future of qualitative research in the twenty-first century as developing many stories and many voices "to inform our sense of lifeways, to extend our understanding of the Other" (p. 1060). I too envision a community of qualitative researchers whose work collectively informs a community of educators, educators willing to look beyond formulas and questionnaires, able to appreciate varied ways of knowing and hearing the diverse voices in their classrooms. I envision educators willing to share the stories of lives and moments of transformation through narratives, ethnographies, representation, and performance that help new and deeper pedagogical understandings to emerge.

Recommended Readings

Of Borders and Dreams: A Mexican-American Experience of Urban Education (Carger, 1996) will give a fuller picture of the student and his family described in the excerpt from "My Country 'Tis of Thee." *Researching Livid Experience: Human Science for an Action Sensitive Pedagogy* (Van Mannen, 1990) was one of the foundations upon which *Of Borders and Dreams* was built and introduced me to phenomenology and looking closely at daily life experiences. *There Are No Children Here* (Kotlowitz, 1992), a journalist's heartfelt account of his relationship with two African American boys in Chicago, was another major influence on my work. Similar in genre to my book, Greg Michie's *Holler If You Hear Me: The Education of a Teacher and His Students* (1999) is a qualitative inquiry that offers meaningful insights to teachers of diverse students. For information and insight into the struggles of Latino students, Lourdes Diaz Soto's edited book *Making a Difference in the Lives of Bilingual/Bicultural Children* (2002) is useful. Two autobiographical books for young adults also impart touching vignettes of the livid experiences of Mexican immigrants who are migrant workers. *The Circuit: Stories From the Life of a Migrant Child* (1997) and *Breaking Through* (2001), both by Francisco Jimenez, not only provide rare glimpses of the challenges faced by migrant workers in America but also include wonderful, positive images of teachers who work selflessly with ELL to help them face their academic challenges. Pat Mora, a Mexican American poet, writes eloquently of her experiences as a Latina moving between Mexico and the United States in her collection of poetry titled *My Own True Name* (2002). Appropriate for young adults and an adult audience, she uses the metaphor of a cactus—its blooms, thorns, and roots—to convey her cross-cultural experiences with sensitivity and insight. The film *My Family/Mi Familia*, directed by Gregory Nava (1995), is a wonderful portrayal of a large, loving Mexican-origin family as well as the process of immigration and cross-cultural issues for them over three generations. These materials not only offer the potential for a deeper understanding of diverse students, particularly Latinos, but also demonstrate the ability of narrative and other art forms such as poetry and cinema to provide additional avenues for cross-cultural education.

Reflective Questions

1. Did the narrative describing Alejandro's parents' quest for U.S. citizenship inform your "sense of lifeways" and extend your "understanding of the Other" as Denzin and Lincoln (2000) envisioned that qualitative research could do in the twenty-first century?

2. Do you support the idea of extending the concept of the "funds of knowledge" to include families of dropouts? Why or why not?

3. How might a program aimed at incorporating dropouts' families' funds of knowledge look in practice? How might such a program have looked for Alejandro Juarez?

References

Achebe, C. (1987). *Anthills of the savannah.* London: Heinemann.

Behar, R. (1996). *The vulnerable observer: Anthropology that breaks your heart.* Boston: Beacon Press.

Bourdieu, P. (1990). *In other words: Essays towards a reflexive sociology* (M. Adamson, Trans.). Cambridge, UK: Polity.

Bruner, J. (1990). *Acts of meaning.* Cambridge, MA: Harvard University Press.

Carger, C. (1996). *Of borders and dreams: A Mexican-American experience of urban education.* New York: Teachers College Press.

Clandinin, D. J., & Connelly, F. M. (2000). *Narrative inquiry: Experience and story in qualitative research.* San Francisco: Jossey-Bass.

Denzin, N. K., & Lincoln, Y. S. (2000). *Handbook of qualitative research* (2nd ed.). Thousand Oaks, CA: Sage.

Diamond, C. T. P., & Mullen, C. A. (1999). Art is a part of us: From romance to artful story. In C. T. P. Diamond & C. Mullen (Eds.), *The postmodern educator: Arts-based inquiries and teacher development* (pp. 13–36). New York: Peter Lang.

Ellis, C., & Bochner, A. P. (2000). Autoethnography, personal narrative, reflexivity: Researcher as subject. In N. K. Denzin & Y. S. Lincoln (Eds.), *Handbook of qualitative research* (2nd ed., pp. 733–768). Thousand Oaks, CA: Sage.

Gergen, K. J., & Gergen, M. M. (1986). Narrative form and the construction of psychological science. In T. R. Sarbin (Ed.), *Narrative psychology: The storied nature of human conduct* (pp. 29–40). New York: Praeger.

He, M. F. (2002). A narrative inquiry of cross-cultural lives: Lives in the North American academy. *Journal of Curriculum Studies, 34*(3), 323–343.

Jimenez, F. (1997). *The circuit: Stories from the life of a migrant child.* Albuquerque: University of New Mexico Press.

Jimenez, F. (2001). *Breaking through.* Boston: Houghton Mifflin.

King, G. W. (2003). *Statistical abstract for the U.S., 2002: The national data book.* Washington, DC: Diane Publishing.

Kotlowitz, A. (1992). *There are no children here: The story of two boys growing up in the other America.* New York: Doubleday.

Laosa, L., & Henderson, R. W. (1991). Cognitive socialization and competence: The academic development of Chicanos. In R. R. Valencia (Ed.), *Chicano school failure and success: Research and policy agendas for the 1990s* (pp. 164–199). London: Falmer.

Lather, P., & Smithies, C. (1997). *Troubling angels: Women living with HIV/AIDS.* Boulder, CO: Westview.

Lawler, S. (2002). Narrative in social context. In T. May (Ed.), *Qualitative research in action* (pp. 242–258). Thousand Oaks, CA: Sage.

Lincoln, Y. S. (1997). Self, subject, audience, text: Living at the edge, writing in the margins. In W. G. Tierney and Y. S. Lincoln (Eds.), *Representation and the text: Re-framing the narrative voice* (pp. 37–56). Albany: SUNY Press.

Lowery, R. M. (2000). *Immigrants in children's literature.* New York: Peter Lang.

Michie, G. (1999). *Holler if you hear me: The education of a teacher and his students.* New York: Teachers College Press.

Moore, H. (1994). *A passion for difference: Essays in anthropology and gender.* Cambridge, MA: Polity.

Mora, P. (2002). *My own true name: New and selected poems for young adults, 1984–1999.* Houston, TX: Arte Publico Press.

Nava, G. (Director). (1995). *Mi familia/My family* [Motion picture]. United States: New Line Video.

Perez-Miller, A. (1991). *An analysis of the persistence/dropout behavior of Hispanic students in a Chicago public school.* Unpublished doctoral dissertation, University of Illinois at Chicago.

Polkinghorne, D. E. (1997). Reporting qualitative research as practice. In W. G. Tierney & Y. S. Lincoln (Eds.), *Representation of text: Re-framing the narrative voice* (pp. 3–21). Albany: SUNY Press.

Reyna, V. (2002, April 2). What is scientifically based evidence? What is its logic?— Valerie Reyna: Scientifically based research. Retrieved July 11, 2003, from http://www.ed.gov/offices/OESE/esea/research/reyna.html

Ricoeur, P. (1980). Narrative and time. *Critical Inquiry, 7*(1), 169–190.

Savage, M. C. (1988). Can ethnographic narrative be a neighborly act? *Anthropology and Education Quarterly, 19*(19), 3–19.

Schubert, W., & Ayers, W. (1992). *Teacher lore: Learning from your own experience.* New York: Longman.

Soto, L. D. (2002). *Making a difference in the lives of bilingual/bicultural children.* New York: Peter Lang.

Tierney, W. G., & Lincoln, Y. S. (1997). *Representation and the text: Re-framing the narrative voice.* Albany: SUNY Press.

U.S. Census Bureau, Public Information Office. (2003, July 2). Race and Hispanic origin. Retrieved July 14, 2003, from www.census.gov/pubinfo/wwwmultimedia/LULAC.html

Van Mannen, M. (1990). Researching lived experience: Human science for an action sensitive pedagogy. Albany: SUNY Press.

Unit Six

Democracy, School Life, and Community in Multicultural Societies

13

Narrative Inquiry Into Multicultural Life in an Inner-City Community School

F. Michael Connelly, JoAnn Phillion,
and Ming Fang He

Autobiographical Introduction

In this chapter three people with different interests come together on a research landscape in an inner city Canadian school. F. Michael Connelly came to this work from science education, teacher education, and narrative studies. Beginning in 1980, in Bay Street Community School, F. Michael Connelly worked with D. Jean Clandinin for twenty-four years on teacher knowledge, classroom practice, and narrative inquiry. It was through the multicultural quality of Bay Street Community School life and through the influence of JoAnn Phillion, Ming Fang He, and others whose interests were deliberately multicultural that Michael's interests connected to multicultural education.

JoAnn's interest in Bay Street Community School grew out of her experience of teaching English as a second language in Japan and Canada and working with immigrant students and teachers. JoAnn knew about Bay Street Community School through Michael and Jean's writing. She went into Bay Street Community School and Pam's classroom (her participant) to see multicultural education up close. She worked in the school for twenty months; she observed and participated in Pam's class two or three days each week, attended staff meetings and school events, and spent weekends and after-school time in the community. Bay Street Community School continues to be a context for JoAnn's research and writing.

Ming Fang's participation in Bay Street Community School came from her experience of teaching English as a foreign language in China and as a second language in Canada. She is interested in cross-cultural approaches to multiculturalism. Her research focus at Bay Street Community School is on the impact of Chinese immigrant parents' cross-cultural experiences of school-community relations and the bearing of that experience on immigrant children's school success.

Michael, JoAnn, and Ming Fang continue to work together even though they are now in three different North American universities. The individual perspectives they brought to their collaboration challenged their notions of the purposes and outcomes of inquiry. This challenge marked the beginning of their exploration of the narrative, experiential approaches to multiculturalism in education featured in the book.

Introduction

In this chapter we explore the connection between narrative inquiry and multicultural education.[1,2] We trace the history of multiculturalism as a public discourse in Canadian social life. With this as background, we consider life in an inner-city Canadian school, Bay Street Community School, as a microcosm of Canadian social life in general. Following the ebb and flow of more than twenty years of narrative inquiry in this Canadian inner-city school, we realize that this inquiry, though defined in various terms, is ultimately a study of multicultural life. We argue that an understanding of multicultural life as democratic life process is central to an understanding of the social purposes of multiculturalism. We believe that multicultural education and narrative inquiry have the potential for profoundly productive links in the pursuit of democratic life. We conclude by puzzling over the meaning of multicultural inquiry and of the significance of cross-cultural studies for understanding multicultural life.

History and Context

Multiculturalism as a field of inquiry is comparatively new (for an overview of the history of the field, see Banks, 1995, 2004). Thirty years ago students of education would have been hard-pressed to find multicultural courses in calendars of study; there were neither multicultural journals nor multicultural conferences. Likewise, narrative inquiry, the form of experiential inquiry discussed in this chapter, was unheard of as such thirty years ago. Now, there are courses, conferences, journals, and books on narrative.

Our task in this chapter is to bring multicultural education and narrative inquiry together in the context of research in Bay Street Community School. Though there are no concrete facts or necessary logical links, we argue, using the flow of documented research life in Bay Street Community School, that there is a compatibility, a harmony, a way of thinking that underpins narrative inquiry and that is central to the social purposes of multiculturalism (Phillion, 2002a, 2002c). We also argue that multicultural education and narrative inquiry have the potential for profoundly productive links in the pursuit of democratic life. Our argument is grounded in experience in one school in downtown Toronto and in the idea that a narrative, multicultural understanding of this school and its multicultural community depends on an understanding of the political and social context: Canadian federal law and policy and the nature of public discourse within Canada. Though we believe that the general form of our argument is broadly applicable, our case is made in the Canadian context.

Furthermore, our argument recognizes that while multicultural education and narrative inquiry are relatively new, both fields have deep and long historical roots (Phillion & He, 2005). It is not that they arrived de novo on the educational inquiry landscape but, rather, that various historical threads came together and were given force by public and scholarly concerns via a naming process: multicultural education, narrative inquiry. In North America, multicultural education was first expressed in intercultural education initiatives and directly grew out of the civil rights movement, with a concern for social justice primarily as applied to African Americans (Banks, 1996). This, of course, oversimplifies an earlier history of European immigrants and later Asian immigrants as well as Latino/as and First Nations (Native Canadian) people, concern for whom takes us back to the first settlers. In Canada, multiculturalism was driven by the French-English settlement history along with concerns for First Nations people, and later European and Asian immigrants (Moodley, 1995). Similarly, narrative inquiry arrived trailing various inquiry traditions from philosophy, history, and the study of cases. Cases have played an important role in teacher education, which seems always to have relied on exemplary role models (Goodlad, 1990), and case work preceded qualitative educational research traditions. These threads are connected to current notions of narrative inquiry (Clandinin & Connelly 2000; Connelly & Clandinin, 1990; Phillion & He, 2005).

Though we have argued that multicultural education and narrative inquiry have potential for coming together in productive ways (Phillion, 2002a, 2002c), much work in multiculturalism is not compatible with narrative inquiry. Multicultural education has focused on equity for groups: African Americans, Native Americans, French Canadians, Native Canadians, and particular immigrant groups. Thus in the English as a Second Language (ESL) literature reviewed by Phillion and He (2005), research tended to revolve around programs for language teaching and learning for particular groups. Specific instances, even individuals, show up in aspects of the literature but, almost inevitably, as typifiers of a class or group. An individual is not treated as an individual as such but, rather, wears the qualities and characteristics of the group. These features of the ESL literature are found in much of the multicultural education literature.

There is a drive in multicultural research to understand, and to better educate and to make society more equitable for, classes and groups of citizens (Gutiérrez, 1995; King, 1995; Liu & Yu, 1995; Rodriguez, 1995; Snipp, 1995). In this regard, race, class, and gender—broad group categories—came to the fore. There is much potential in these studies. One potential that remains beneath the surface in the study of groups is the study of individual experience and its potential to contribute to understanding multiculturalism in education. We call this study of individual experience "narrative inquiry" (Clandinin & Connelly, 2000), a specific focus on multicultural experience "narrative multiculturalism" (Phillion, 2002d), and cross-cultural experience "cross-cultural narrative inquiry" (He, 2003). We recognize that there is little research using these methods in the multicultural education literature.

In this chapter, we trace the historical development of a more than twenty year program of narrative inquiry research in one inner-city Canadian community school by focusing on several key studies completed during this time (other studies have also been done in the context of this school). This history provides the background for a series of studies that focused on individual experience (Chan, 2004; Clandinin, 1986; Ross, 2002, 2003; Xu, in progress) and also studies that focused on a narrative understanding of Bay Street Community School itself (Phillion, 2002a, 2002b). Every study proceeds in a multicultural life context, and it is this context that gives meaning to the work. Tracing this history allows us to explore the potential of narrative inquiry in multicultural education for fostering democratic social life.

Links Between Multicultural Education, Narrative Inquiry, and Democratic Life

Why has multiculturalism become a preoccupation of educators (Kalantzis & Cope, 1992)? What gives it more holding power on the inquiring mind than the fads that pepper our intellectual academic landscape? Dewey (1938a) argued that inquiry rose out of social conditions. He said that when matters are no longer amenable to existing theoretical frames and social discourse, inquiry takes place in which both sides of the inquiry equation are a puzzle—the circumstances in question and the ideas and discourse to account for them (Dewey, 1938b).

Multiculturalism, in Canada, grew out of an increasingly puzzling and intractable social life. It is interesting that in Canadian policy and public discourse bilingualism and biculturalism preceded multilingualism and multiculturalism (Canada: Canadian Heritage-Multiculturalism, 2003). The preeminent puzzle was how to accommodate minority French Canada in majority English Canada.[3] The force of ongoing immigration to Canada, however, made the two-cultures puzzle an inadequate frame for thinking about democratic social life.

Multiculturalism is not only an academic study but also a set of ideas (or perhaps an idea and a language) for thinking about social life. Furthermore, it is not just any kind of life that is at issue but an equitable social life. There is, perhaps, no term other than "democracy" that most adequately names public discourse in Canada about how its various peoples should live together as a nation. In Canada, multiculturalism is about democratic social life. It is political in the sense of government and legislation, and it is practical and concrete in schools such as Bay Street Community School. We believe that thinking of multiculturalism as a name for democratic life and its associated policies and practices leads us to a somewhat different, complementary path to understanding multicultural education. This is where narrative inquiry, a life-based form of inquiry, is most in tune with multiculturalism. We want to show that by starting with life in narrative inquiry, rather than with social groups and classes, something new and important may be said.

Trudeau, Canadian Democracy, Bilingualism, Biculturalism, and Multiculturalism

Isajiw (1999) writes, "Virtually all nation-states in the world are, in terms of the make-up of their population, multi-ethnic" (p. 11). Using 1993 Statistics Canada data, Isajiw notes that Canada has 113 ethnicities making it, he says, "rather unique even among modern multi-ethnic nations" (p. 11). Isajiw writes that an understanding of this diversity needs to take place "in light of historical processes that have their roots in the events of the past" (p. 14). This historical dimension is central to narrative inquiry and to our understanding of multiculturalism in Canada generally and Bay Street Community School specifically.

There were a series of important steps in the development of Canada's stance toward multiculturalism: 1963–69, Royal Commission on Bilingualism and Biculturalism [French-English]; 1969, Official Languages Act [Bilingual]; 1971–72, Multicultural Policy; 1989, Multiculturalism Act; and 1997, Canadian Heritage Report. Pierre Elliott Trudeau was Canadian Prime Minister for the first four of these events. For many, he symbolizes the struggle for equitable social relations in Canada. Briefly, Canadian public discussion moved from bilingualism and biculturalism to multiculturalism and to recognition of Canada's various cultural heritages. The notion of unity in diversity where Canadian unity is seen to grow out of valuing and maintaining the identity of specific cultural groups, though not an undisputed policy, has tended to dominate multicultural thinking in Canada.[4]

Trudeau's introduction to the Multicultural Policy sets out the basic notions of multiculturalism that still play out in one form or another in Canadian public life. He wrote,

> A policy of multiculturalism within a bilingual framework (is a) . . . means of assuring the cultural freedom of Canadians. Such a policy should help to break down discriminatory attitudes and cultural jealousies. Normal unity if it is to mean anything in the deeply personal sense must be founded on confidence in one's own individual identity; . . . It can form the base of a society which is based on fair play for all. (Minister of State, Multiculturalism, 1978, pp. 45–46, as cited by Isajiw, 1999, p. 245)

Narrative Inquiry Into Life

Clandinin and Connelly (2000) argue that narrative inquiry is the study of experience. Narrative, they say, is the closest one can come to experience. For them, experience, not narrative, is the key term. They argue, using Dewey's (1938a) theory of experience, that life, experience, and education are intertwined. Building on this notion, Phillion and He (2005) argue that narrative inquiry in its most profound and elemental form is a study of life. They write, "When studying life, as in narrative inquiry, the researcher needs to attend to whatever happens in life" (p. 7). Using the notion of foreground and background, they comment on the ESL literature by showing that when one adopts life as a starting point in research, or in reading research texts, that English language learning per se fades in and out of focus depending on the life circumstances of the situation being studied. They point out that a narrative study of language learning reveals a great deal about immigrant life. They also show that much can be learned about language learning when the research emphasis is on broader life matters.

In this chapter, we build on this life-based argument. Multiculturalism names a puzzle or disquiet in social life, and it names a democratic attitude toward thinking about social life. Narrative, because it is focused on experience and on life, is a means to explore the democratic spirit that envelops the notion of multiculturalism. Multiculturalism names a way of living, and narrative inquiry is a way to think about living. The two concepts are in such harmony that Phillion (2002d) fuses them in a composite concept, "narrative multiculturalism."

Bay Street Community School, Multicultural Education, and Narrative Inquiry

Bay Street Community School is an inner-city school in Toronto, Canada. Since its construction in the 1870s, it has been located in an ever-changing immigrant community, one which reflects Canadian immigration and settlement patterns. Connelly and Clandinin entered the school in 1980, and Connelly has been involved with the school off and on ever since in a series of studies with Clandinin and various graduate students. Though Connelly and Clandinin have recently obtained research grants to study multiculturalism, multiculturalism was not the focus of their original work. There has been an ebb and flow, a rhythm, to the study of multiculturalism in this school. From the point of view of narrative and multiculturalism, multiculturalism permeates the life that runs through Bay Street Community School and its community. Dewey (1934), using the metaphor of a bird's flight, said that rhythm and harmony were neither in the bird's moments of flying nor in moments of rest but in the harmonious, rhythmic balance between them. We believe multicultural life, and our narrative study of it in Bay Street Community School, is rhythmic in this Deweyan sense.

BAY STREET COMMUNITY SCHOOL BEGINS IN THE MIDST

Narrative inquiry is a process of temporarily joining the flow of life for the sake of inquiry—to understand, make meaning, and enhance the quality of life (Phillion & He, 2005). Perhaps because of the successes of the experimental method, it tends to be taken for granted that researchers can stop life and time, impose controls, and draw new insights. Narrative inquiry is more complex in its relationship to life and less ambitious about its possible uses. Its complexity grows out of the demand that inquirers take life as it comes to them. It is less ambitious because of the recognition that life is mostly indifferent to the formalistic understandings of inquiry and that life continues when inquiry is formally completed. Furthermore, as Isajiw (1999) notes for the study of diversity in Canada, research is led by, rather than leads, social conditions. There is, of course, an interaction between research and social progress. Still, acknowledging the ongoing quality of multicultural life imposes a humble attitude toward the social implications of research.

As there is overall continuity to the flow of multicultural life in Bay Street Community School, there is overall continuity to research life in Bay Street Community School. Researchers begin in the midst of something ongoing (Geertz, 1995). Connelly and Clandinin's 1980 program of research neither stopped nor redirected the flow of life in the school. Furthermore, particular studies that started out in the university as partially clean slates in proposal pages are conducted by entering in the midst of the overall project, which is already in the midst of ongoing school life. Ming Fang He's ongoing study into the relations of school and community and Elaine Chan's (2004) study of Chinese identity began not only in the midst of Bay Street Community School's ongoing life but in the midst of JoAnn Phillion's study of multiculturalism (2002a, 2002b, 2002c, 2002d) and Vicki Ross's (2002, 2003) mathematics education study in that school. Phillion's and Ross's work, in turn, began some years earlier and was, in turn, part of Connelly and Clandinin's ongoing work. Their work, in turn, began in the midst of ongoing school life. The school did have a beginning in 1877, and it did have a first principal, Robert Maclean.[5] But, of course, the school grew out of historical conditions. The school was created as part of an educational system that began in 1850 with the formation of a school board (Tomkins, 1986). The school board grew out of various educational initiatives; wherever and whenever we start, we are in the midst.

Important to our topic of multiculturalism in education is the fact that the school was built in response to an expanding immigrant population (Phillion, 2002c). Then, as now, Toronto was one of the main settlement sites for the European immigrants that were the first immigrants to influence Canada's development. Central European immigrants were predominant in Bay Street Community School's early years, and now the Chinese are by far the largest majority group. When Connelly and Clandinin entered Bay Street Community School in 1980, Portuguese was a significant language within the school. In 2002, there were no registered Portuguese students. From its very beginnings, Bay Street Community School and its community have been home to shifting patterns of immigrant cultural groups.

Multiculturalism as a concept, idea, or label is comparatively recent (Glazer, 1997). From the point of view of "multiculturalism," the early immigration periods were a time of rest. Life was filled with what we now call multiculturalism in education but was articulated with a different language. This sense of movement is what we try to capture with Dewey's (1934) metaphor of a bird's flight and rest and the notion of rhythm.

CONNELLY AND CLANDININ BEGIN IN
THE MIDST (1980)—FROM RESTING TO FLIGHT

Initially, Connelly and Clandinin did not identify multiculturalism as a component of their work. The 1980 research was a study of policy implementation; the board of education race relations policy was one of three high profile board of education policies that they studied (Connelly & Clandinin, 1984), a process that led them into the literature and language of race relations. Thus, with no intention of doing so, the researchers were involved with

Canadian multiculturalism. Ten years earlier, the Trudeau federal government had introduced the Multicultural Policy and roughly ten years later introduced the Multiculturalism Act. However, at this time, antiracism was the language used to think about multicultural life in Toronto schools. Multiculturalism was still in the background, antiracism in the foreground. A sharp debate took place at the Race Relations Committee over anti-Semitism and whether it ought to be considered as falling within the committee's mandate. The matter was taken to the Human Rights Commission, an arms-length provincial government body, which ruled that antiracism referred to visible minorities. Though antiracism was an expression of underlying multicultural life, the language and policy of antiracism was associated with tensions in public life. We noted earlier that narrative inquirers take life as it comes to them. They tend to de-emphasize the defining of terms, putting boundaries on the inquiry and controlling conditions. Connelly and Clandinin found a race relations policy while working on other issues and while Clandinin was engaged in her study of an individual classroom and teacher (1986).

JOANN PHILLION—MS. MULTICULTURAL IN PAM'S CLASSROOM

As there is an ebb and flow to school life there is an ebb and flow to inquiry life. For a period of time, Connelly and Clandinin pursued their studies of teacher knowledge outside of the school, yet the school was in the background of their thinking and writing. Their studies of teacher knowledge, narrative, and landscape took place in other settings, and the multicultural matters that came to the foreground in Clandinin's study of a classroom and in the antiracism policy were not in the foreground of their thinking.

Multicultural life in Bay Street Community School, of course, continued to unfold. Changes took place. The studies of it stopped—there was a resting. In 1996, JoAnn Phillion entered Bay Street Community School with the purpose of studying multicultural school life. By joining Connelly's research team, Phillion brought a research emphasis on multiculturalism into the foreground. From a position of rest, the notion of multiculturalism took flight.

As Phillion entered the school, multiculturalism was, as it had always been, in the foreground of Bay Street Community School life. Robert Maclean's 1877 diaries (Cochrane, 1950) indicate the first principal's concern for the teaching of immigrant students who he thought of educating as "young scholars." Phil Bingham, principal in 1980, was also concerned with immigrant issues as he wrestled with the race relations policy.

In Phillion and Connelly's meeting to negotiate school entry, principal Steve Brown gave an account of his work. Without using the word *multicultural*, the meeting was a practical tour of one school's efforts to realize Canada's multiculturalism policy. Brown talked about school projects aimed at bridging cultural groups within the school and within the community, and he described his philosophy and specific programs for bringing the community into the school and into its decision-making apparatus. He discussed the school's motto, "*Bay Street Community School—Where You Belong*," designed to create a sense of home and community for the school's thirty-five language groups. He also discussed a list of school priorities: preservation of existing heritage language programs, the idea that the school would become the center of community life and offer a full range of immigrant social services, the possibility of offering a full day of services beginning with early morning nutrition programs to late evening homework and sports programs, and even a plan to extend the JK–8 offerings to include a full range of high school classes.

In Brown's array of actual and hoped for activities, the school's multicultural life and its community, though not named as such, were close to the surface. Phillion sensed compatibility between her ideas about democratic social life and life as she now imagined it to be in Bay Street Community School. Phillion's entry into the school not only brought multiculturalism in education to the foreground but made evident the extent to which multicultural issues, always the lifeblood of the school but often beneath the visible surface, had come into the open and were part of public discourse. The negotiation of entry meeting was a meeting on democracy in action, cultural freedom, and opportunity for students in Bay Street Community School.

Though we did not think it at the time, this meeting was fascinating for what it revealed about the rhythms of life and of inquiry and of the relationship between them. Our readings of the historical documents and of our own experience in Bay Street Community School give a sense that multiculturalism is the bedrock on which this school and its community are built but also that multicultural matters impressed themselves in varying degrees on the day-to-day working of the school. Cultural matters boil to the surface with race relations issues, but because of the public discourse around antiracism and, in Ontario, because of the formal definition of antiracism as applying only to color, what one might think of as multiculturalism as a base for a broad democratic life still remained buried beneath the surface. Phil Bingham, however, thought of race relations as human relations, trying thereby, it would appear, to defuse the dichotomies implicit in antiracism. In this way, a life-based notion of multiculturalism came closer to the surface. With Steve Brown, the multicultural life base of the school was, without use of the word *multiculturalism*, brought forward for public discussion.

In the negotiation of entry meeting with Brown, Connelly stepped back into the flow of multicultural life in Bay Street Community School, unaware that multiculturalism would soon be in the foreground of his thinking. Phillion stepped into the flow of her dissertation research and Bay Street

Community School cultural life when Brown said, "I have just the participant for you—Pam." When Phillion met Pam she was equally convinced. Pam's classroom seemed to be the ideal place for a study of multiculturalism in education. The class was composed of children from a mix of countries: Vietnam, Somalia, China, Taiwan, Pakistan, Bangladesh, and Canada. The children spoke many languages; some children, though Canadian born, spoke English as a second language and were part of the ESL program. Pam, originally from the Caribbean, had taught in the school for fifteen years.

But Phillion was in for surprises (Phillion, 2002a). The story we have told so far in this chapter is one of multiculturalism bubbling ever closer to the surface in the life of Bay Street Community School and of multiculturalism influencing the direction of studies defined in other terms. For Phillion, this formula was turned upside down. She began with multiculturalism and found that it eluded her grasp as she worked with Pam. Phillion referred to herself as "Ms. Multicultural," a person devoted to multicultural thought and someone expecting the principles of multicultural education to be at the forefront in classroom life (Phillion, 2002b). But she found herself recording what at first seemed to her to be a much more traditional classroom life—concerns for punctuality, completing assignments, discipline and order, and the standard curriculum. Life in its broadest sense was now in the foreground, with multiculturalism in the background.

Pam did certain things that Phillion felt were counter to multicultural theory, yet Pam, as a long-term member of the community, knew much about the families (Phillion, 2002a). She had a multicultural understanding of the children's lives, yet acted on it in ways that were not obviously "multicultural." There was a harmony between the Trudeau multicultural policy and the vision it entailed and multicultural life as explained by the principal and as seen throughout the school's culturally oriented programs. This harmony was not initially apparent in Pam's classroom.

Phillion turned to her understanding of narrative inquiry as a way of entering and accepting life as she found it. She adjusted her Ms. Multicultural stance to one of participation and learning from being part of classroom life. She taught herself to think narratively, which meant living in the midst with Pam rather than observing and judging Pam from the perspective of Ms. Multicultural. Ultimately, Phillion came to see that Pam lived out a version of multicultural education as equally powerful in its consequences as was the vision the principal held for the school as a whole.

Pam dealt with each child by making herself as aware as possible of the child's particular cultural/home environment that might make a difference to her or his school behavior. She did not treat or respond to a student by referring to an imagined set of cultural markers. Instead she treated such a child as an individual, with a certain background and ways of thinking. Trudeau wrote,

"Normal unity, if it is to mean anything in the deeply personal sense must be founded in confidence in one's own individual identity; out of this can grow respect for that of others and a willingness to share ideas" (Minister of State, Multiculturalism, 1978, pp. 45–46, as cited by Isajiw, 1999, p. 245). It is this aspect that came to the fore in Pam's classroom. Was multiculturalism front and center in Pam's classroom? At the obvious level it was not. Pam felt that the concern for groups was wrongheaded, but she paid much attention to her classroom's multicultural character as expressed in the individual lives of her children. This, as seen in the Trudeau quote, is close to the heart of what is meant by multiculturalism in Canadian policy.

EBB AND FLOW AT THE SAME TIME: LIFE FORCES AT WORK

Vicki Ross entered Bay Street Community School to study elementary mathematics education (Ross, 2002) as Phillion negotiated her exit from Pam's classroom. Similarly, Elaine Chan entered the school (Chan, 2003, 2004) for her study of second-generation Canadian Chinese identity development as Ross completed her work. These two studies in juxtaposition with Phillion are telling of the forces at work in school life and of our effort to understand school life and the place of multiculturalism in it. Whereas Phillion entered the school embracing ideas of multiculturalism and found her preconceived notions elusive, Ross made no reference to multiculturalism in her proposed study, yet found herself confronted on a daily basis with cultural issues.

Ross's study shows that the notion of ebb and flow that we wish to unpack is not a simple multiculturalism and life balance. Ross found her field notes filled with anything but mathematics. She found that Janine, her participating teacher, rarely divided class activities and events neatly into mathematics activities and others. She found that she needed to look for mathematics teaching and learning in the language arts program and in the links between Janine's efforts to connect the world at large with the children's curriculum. Furthermore, Janine was a dedicated social activist. A bystander to Bay Street Community School life might well have assigned Phillion to Janine because of her explicit life of social justice, and Ross to Pam because of Pam's focus on learning the subject curricula. Just as Phillion needed to teach herself to understand the flow of multicultural life in Pam's classroom, Ross needed to teach herself to see mathematics teaching and learning in Janine's broader curricular context (Ross, 2003). Thus, though it was not multiculturalism per se that flowed in Janine's class as the mathematics curriculum ebbed, it was something broader still—life itself. Living a multicultural life aimed at a broad-based social democracy was implicit in everything Janine did. Multicultural, it might be said, was the best name to call Janine's classroom curriculum.

Elaine Chan's experience supports the view that academic interests inevitably ebb and become elusive in the flow of research. Bay Street

Community School is heavily Asian as the century begins (Chan & Ross, 2002). The Chinese are the majority group and are the largest single group in William's classroom, where Chan works. Her focus is not multiculturalism per se, though this is a critical intellectual and social matrix for her work. She is explicitly interested in the development of Chinese Canadian identity and wishes to trace school influences on identity. As with Phillion before her, this explicit topic is elusive. Being Chinese does not rank high in the curricular/social life of William's classroom and, as with Ross in her focus on mathematics, the class as a whole, and children other than Chinese, come to occupy Chan's field notes. Chan found ways, as Ross did with the mathematics curriculum in Janine's class, to bring to the research foreground Chinese students and their identity issues. Chan might have found it easier to shift her topic to multiculturalism more broadly than to continue to write on Chinese identity. The reason is a version of the consequences of the ebb and flow of life that showed up so strongly in Phillion's and Ross's classrooms. Cultural issues, events, and observations are found everywhere in Chan's field notes. Just as Ross could have written a thesis or book on multiculturalism in education based on her work in Janine's classroom so too could Chan write such a document on her work in William's classroom.

EBB AND FLOW, OR ARE THEY RIPPLES?

Dewey's (1934) idea of rhythm in a bird's flight and resting, combined with the notion of ebb and flow, helped us think about the broad span of life in Bay Street Community School since 1877. But the closer we inspect the unfolding time span, the less it appears that the smooth notion of ebb and flow helps explain our life of participation. Phillion wishes to study multicultural-ism, finds her field notes filled with observations on the standard curriculum, and emerges with a new sense of multiculturalism in education that she calls narrative multiculturalism (Phillion, 2002d). Ross begins with mathematics education, finds a comprehensive life-based curriculum in Janine's classroom, understands that she could have written a multicultural thesis, and deliberately writes a mathematics education thesis by selectively attending to her field notes (Ross, 2002). Chan focuses on second-generation Chinese Canadian identity development in William's classroom but finds her field notes filled with multi-cultural and general curriculum observations. She realizes that she too could write a thesis on multiculturalism and/or general curriculum. In order to stay with her identity topic, Chan, as Ross did before her, selectively focused on relevant experiences and field notes.

As we examine these instances up close, it is clear that multiculturalism ebbs and flows in classroom life. It is as if there is a narrative researcher's law at work: "one's research interest will inevitably ebb as life flows in, over and around that interest." School life is indifferent to the academic interests of those who come to it. We believe that notions of multiculturalism also ebb and flow in society at large. In Canada, this pulsing notion is best understood against the backdrop of Canada's Multicultural Policy and Multiculturalism Act. There are important social forces, such as the concern for antiracism that drove the board of education's race relations policy during the 1980s. Overriding these forces is the ongoing life—whatever that life happens to be—that one enters into in classroom research. That too is a kind of curriculum: a particular principal, Steve Brown, with a particular teacher, Pam, with particular children, with a particular researcher, Phillion, all set in a particular board of education, a particular set of provincial government policies, within the Canadian milieu.

Each inquiry, and what may appear to be an ebb and flow, tends to dissipate into something more resembling a rippled surface. The curriculum of the inquiry, when it is a narrative inquiry with life as its driving force, tends, it would seem, inevitably to put the research interest at ebb, to force it below the surface of ongoing life. That ongoing life is a multicultural life.

UNANTICIPATED MULTICULTURALISM IN EDUCATION FLOW

When Connelly returned to Bay Street Community School in 1996, it was not to study the multiculturalism in education matters that Phillion brought with her but rather to continue studies in teacher knowledge. Connelly and Clandinin's (1995) focus had moved from the personal to the social, and they were writing on notions of landscape. Partly because of this focus, combined with Phillion's research, Connelly and Clandinin's next, and subsequent, research studies were on multiculturalism in education. Steve Brown, like Phil Bingham at the time Connelly and Clandinin first entered the school, was a community-minded principal. Brown, more deliberately activist than prior principals, found himself, in the late 1990s, in a period of budget cuts. Programs to serve the multicultural community were in jeopardy. Bay Street Community School was one of the few remaining schools with an extended-day program for purposes of offering heritage language instruction. The number of heritage languages offered was cut back, ESL support services were reduced, and two school community workers who had been nurtured within the school's budget were released. In the spring of 2002 the board of education reviewed a proposal to cut all parent centers throughout the system and to sharply reduce the services noted earlier.

Connelly and Clandinin's multicultural project was designed to study the dynamics of negotiations that take place among teachers and students over cultural matters. Though Brown supported this work, his preoccupation was with the life of the school, primarily budget matters affecting multicultural programs. Brown asked the project team to work with the school's ESL workgroup, composed of parents, teachers, and community workers, to design an every-student survey to document the multicultural status of the school (Chan & Ross, 2002). The research team met with the workgroup, listened to their discussions about ESL and associated matters, and, by recording conversations, analyzing them, and turning the discussion into measurable items, created a survey instrument and conducted a survey. This work took the better part of two years. During this time, Ross completed her work. Phillion continued to work with the team following the completion of her own study, and Chan began her research while working on this project. Ming Fang He, who had joined Connelly's research team prior to Phillion's involvement, also joined the survey work in the context of her research into the Chinese community. We draw attention to He's involvement not only because of what it illustrates about the ebb and flow of long-term intensive narrative work but also because she brought yet another dimension to the study (discussed later in the chapter).

This account of Connelly and Clandinin's project work and that of Connelly's students are important to the point of this chapter because they demonstrate how forcefully school life inserts itself into narrative multicultural work. Relations with Brown were such that it would have been possible to turn down the request for the survey. But this would have minimized access to the school and would have shut off a rich window into how multiculturalism in education was at work in the larger political and cultural context of the school. Discussions with the workgroup ranged freely from specific stories about particular refugee children to the impact of the federal government immigration policy on Bay Street Community School. Precision that one might find in carefully done narrative analysis was sacrificed for the rich multi-tentacled discourse engendered by democratic life. It was democratic life in its full sense that was at work in these discussions and in the motivations that brought people to the table and led Brown to request project team assistance.

Once again, it was not the word *multicultural* that drove discussion but, rather, particular aspects of it, especially ESL. But this was not the ESL an ESL specialist would recognize. The reason is that, for the school, ESL was embedded in life, and that life was political, communal, cultural, and relational with respect to a wide array of matters affecting ESL, such as settlement programs, out of school support, the regular curriculum, indeed, the full range of matters that one might have found at work in Pam's class, Janine's class, and in William's class. As we reflect on this overall ebb and flow of multicultural life in the school, and the ebb and flow of our study of it, we are led to the view that multiculturalism, as a language, is a language about life rather than a language of life. We do not mean to suggest that it is not important. The language of multiculturalism embedded in the Canadian Multicultural Policy and Multiculturalism Act has been a critical reference point for public discourse and for those whose research is labeled multicultural. But multiculturalism is more akin to the underlying massive tidewater that gives rise to ebb and flow than it is to the actual items that are brought forward and backward, into the foreground and into the background: "young scholars" in 1887, antiracism in 1980, ESL programming in 2002.

LEARNING TO FLY IN MULTICULTURAL CROSS-CURRENTS

Powerful as the Dewey (1934) metaphor of the rhythm of a bird's flight and rest is, this metaphor implies a constant, stable medium for flight. But even a casual observer of birds in motion will notice how air currents are inevitably used: hawks soaring high on thermal updrafts, gulls playing with the wind, swallows tacking like a sailboat to make headway upwind. He's entry to Bay Street Community School and her contribution is something like a bird's flight in an environment of moving air currents. There are elements of this, as we shall see, in Chan's work as well. Phillion's work in multiculturalism is from an insider's vantage point: someone living out the democratic multicultural life and wondering how others enter, adapt, and behave in that life. He is both outsider and insider: she came to North America (He, 2002b) after she experienced multiple cultural events in China. She puzzled about Chinese culture, Canadian culture, and the movements back and forth between them (He, 2002c, 2003). She has written that she can never truly be an insider, and she is not truly an outsider; rather, she refers to herself as being in-between (He & Phillion, 2001; He, in press).

This in-between, cross-cultural vantage point puts, we believe, a different perspective on the study of multiculturalism in education. For purposes of this chapter we used the notion of ebb and flow to help account for multicultural life in Bay Street Community School as well as our study of it. He's work is not as easily placed in this ebb and flow. In her work with Chinese women immigrants (He, 2003) and in her work with Chinese immigrants in Bay Street Community School, she is compelled by her participants and the identity issues in the inquiry to move back and forth between life in China and life in Canada. It is as if her work is a metaphorical cross-current to the rhythms of ebb and flow as recounted earlier for the study of multiculturalism in Canada. The metaphor is not altogether adequate because cross-currents tend to lead to turbulence. It is the mobile spirit of the bird's flight that best captures our sense of this cross-cultural work.

Chan's work, discussed earlier, though not as deliberately cross-cultural as He's, has some of the same qualities due to its cross-cultural narrative nature. Though Chan herself is not an immigrant, she imagines herself on a narrative thread, like He's, where, only a generation earlier, her parents too emigrated from China. This dimension, and the continual question of Chinese identity, gives Chan's work a cross-cultural quality. Tending to this sort of puzzle narratively links Chan's work in multiculturalism to the cross-cultural approach to the study of multiculturalism in He's work.

As we revise this chapter in the summer of 2004, Chan has completed her research in the school and is focused on the writing of research texts, Ross has a faculty position in the United States, and Phillion and He, also working in the United States, try to maintain connections with Bay Street Community School. In the midst of these changes, Shijing Xu, from Mainland China, has begun her doctoral research with Chinese immigrants in the school to explore how they, as well as she, negotiate their identities and a sense of home (Xu, in progress). In the ebb and flow of studies on multiculturalism, Xu's work, like He's work and Chan's work, is cross-cultural in nature. As we have seen in the studies brought forward in this chapter, however, every study proceeds in a multicultural life context, and it is this context that gives meaning to their work.

As we come to the end of this chapter, we are only at the beginning of inquiring into this puzzle of thinking narratively about multiculturalism in education. We have begun to think through, for our purposes in a Canadian setting, what the narrative study of multiculturalism in education might look like and might contribute to an understanding of democratic social life. We have begun to puzzle over the significance of cross-cultural narrative work and how this work harmonizes with and strengthens ongoing work in narrative multiculturalism. Following the tenets of narrative inquiry, we believe that we will make progress in working our way through these puzzles by continuing to work in multicultural life situations like Bay Street Community School. We expect that Bay Street Community School life will continue to flow and that multiculturalism will continue to ebb and flow, bringing us unanticipated but real and meaningful situations where, working with these different flows and working with cross-currents, we will also make progress in understanding democratic social life in Canada.

Recommended Readings

Work in five different disciplines has influenced our thinking about narrative, experiential approaches to multicultural life issues in schools and societies: education, anthropology, philosophy, ethnography, and literature. Our work is grounded in Dewey's experiential theory of education, in particular his *Education and Experience* (1938a), and Schwab's theory of the practical (Westbury & Wilkof, 1978). Anthropologists have influenced our thinking on how to engage in fieldwork, how to relate to participants—particularly those from different cultural backgrounds—how to narrate our experience in Bay

Street Community School, and how to perceive the fluidity of culture. Readers will find these influences in Bateson's (1994) *Peripheral Visions: Learning Along the Way* and Geertz's (1995) *After the Fact*. Philosophers have also influenced our work. Greene's (1995) notion of cultural imagination in *Releasing the Imagination* and Nussbaum's (1997) notion of narrative imagination in *Cultivating Humanity* allow us to see that narrative, experiential approaches demand passionate involvement, commitment, and advocacy from the researchers and have the potential to cultivate hope for better lives in multicultural societies. These ideas are also demonstrated in ethnography, particularly in Valdés's (1996) *Con Respeto*. The work of Valdés and other ethnographers (such as that of Soto, Hermes, and Deyhle in this book) helped locate our inquiry at Bay Street Community School in a more complex social context. The language, culture, and identity issues explored in literature, particularly in life-based literary narratives such as Chamoiseau's (1997) *School Days* and Hoffman's (1963) *Lost in Translation* developed our in-depth understandings of lived experience from the perspective of the participants. These life-based literary narratives affirmed that narrative, experiential approaches humanize research by situating research in life contexts and lived experience.

Reflective Questions

1. Compare and contrast what you have learned about multicultural policies in Canada and the United States and/or your home country. What do the differences in these policies tell you about the differences in societies? How do the differences impact multicultural education in these societies?

2. How has a reading of this chapter expanded your notion of what counts as educational research? How can we make research more relevant to communities, parents, teachers, and students?

3. In what cases and in what ways do you think narrative inquiry would be useful in multicultural education research? What do you think would be some of the challenges and concerns in using narrative inquiry?

Notes

1. This chapter is adapted from Connelly, Phillion, and He (2003). The work was originally presented at Experiential Approaches to Multiculturalism in Education, a conference sponsored by Curriculum Inquiry/Blackwell Publishers, Toronto, Canada, May 16, 2002.

2. The research on which this chapter is based is funded by research grants from the Social Sciences and Humanities Research Council of Canada.

3. Of course, from a French Canadian perspective the puzzle was framed somewhat differently and placed more emphasis on the autonomy and independence of the province of Québec.

4. For an introduction to multiculturalism in Canadian public policy, see the federal government Web site on multiculturalism (Canada: Canadian Heritage-Multiculturalism, 2003).

5. Other than the researchers, all names, including the name of the school, are pseudonyms.

References

Banks, J. A. (1995). Multicultural education: Historical development, dimensions, and practice. In J. A. Banks & C. A. M. Banks (Eds.), *Handbook of research on multicultural education* (pp. 3–24). New York: Macmillan.

Banks, J. A. (Ed.). (1996). *Multicultural education, transformative knowledge and action: Historical and contemporary perspectives.* New York: Teachers College Press.

Banks, J. A. (2004). Multicultural education: Historical development, dimensions, and practice. In J. A. Banks & C. A. M. Banks (Eds.), *Handbook of research on multicultural education* (2nd ed.; pp. 3–29). New York: Macmillan.

Bateson, M. C. (1994). *Peripheral visions: Learning along the way.* New York: Harper Collins.

Canada: Canadian Heritage-Multiculturalism. (2003, April 3). Retrieved October 20, 2004, from www.pch.gc.ca/mult/index.html

Chamoiseau, P. (1997). *School days.* Lincoln: University of Nebraska Press.

Chan, E. (2003). OP-ED. Ethnic identity in transition: Chinese New Year through the years. *Journal of Curriculum Studies, 35,* 409–423.

Chan, E. (2004). *Narratives of ethnic identity: Experiences of first generation Chinese Canadians.* Unpublished doctoral dissertation, Toronto, Canada: University of Toronto.

Chan, E., & Ross, V. (2002). Report on the ESL survey. Sponsored by the ESL Workgroup in collaboration with the OISE/UT Narrative and Diversity Research Team. Toronto, Canada: Centre for Teacher Development, Ontario Institute for Studies in Education of the University of Toronto.

Clandinin, D. J. (1986). *Classroom practice: Teacher images in action.* London: Falmer.

Clandinin, D. J., & Connelly, F. M. (2000). *Narrative inquiry: Experience and story in qualitative research.* San Francisco: Jossey-Bass.

Cochrane, M. (Ed.). (1950). *Centennial story: Board of Education for the City of Toronto: 1850–1950.* Toronto, Canada: Thomas Nelson & Sons.

Connelly, F. M., & Clandinin, D. J. (1984). *The role of teachers' personal practical knowledge in effecting board policy (Volumes 1–4). Vol. 2: Development and implementation of a race relations policy by Toronto Board of Education.* Toronto, Canada: Ontario Institute for Studies in Education.

Connelly, F. M., & Clandinin, D. J. (1990). The cyclic temporal structure of schooling. In M. Ben-Peretz & R. Bromme (Eds.), *The nature of time in schools: Theoretical concepts, practitioner perceptions* (pp. 36–63). New York: Teachers College Press.

Connelly, F. M., & Clandinin, D. J. (1995). *Teachers' professional knowledge landscapes.* New York: Teachers College Press.

Connelly, F. M., Phillion, J., & He, M. F. (2003, Winter). An exploration of narrative inquiry into multiculturalism in education: Reflecting on two decades of research in an inner city Canadian community school [Special series on Multiculturalism in Curriculum Inquiry]. *Curriculum Inquiry 33,* 363–384.

Dewey, J. (1934). *Art as experience.* New York: Capricorn Books.

Dewey, J. (1938a). *Experience and education.* New York: Collier Books.

Dewey, J. (1938b). *Logic: The theory of inquiry.* New York: Henry Holt and Company.

Geertz, C. (1995). *After the fact: Two countries, four decades, one anthropologist.* Cambridge, MA: Harvard University Press.

Glazer, N. (1997). *We are all multicultural now.* Cambridge, MA: Harvard University Press.

Goodlad, J. I. (1990). *Teachers for our nation's schools.* San Francisco: Jossey-Bass.

Greene, M. (1995). *Releasing the imagination: Essays on education, the arts, and social change.* San Francisco: Jossey-Bass.

Gutiérrez, R. A. (1995). Historical and social science research on Mexican Americans. In J. A. Banks & C. A. M. Banks (Eds.), *Handbook of research on multicultural education* (pp. 203–222). New York: Macmillan.

He, M. F. (2002a). A narrative inquiry of cross-cultural lives: Lives in China. *Journal of Curriculum Studies, 34*(3), 301–321.

He, M. F. (2002b). A narrative inquiry of cross-cultural lives: Lives in Canada. *Journal of Curriculum Studies, 34*(3), 323–342.

He, M. F. (2002c). A narrative inquiry of cross-cultural lives: Lives in North American Academe. *Journal of Curriculum Studies, 34*(5), 513–533.

He, M. F. (2003). *A river forever flowing: Cross-cultural lives and identities in the multicultural landscape.* Greenwich, CT: Information Age Publishing.

He, M. F. (in press). In-between China and North America. In T. R. Berry & N. D. Mizelle (Eds.), *From oppression to grace: Women of color and their dilemmas within the academy.* Sterling, VA: Stylus Publishing.

He, M. F., & Phillion, J. (2001). Trapped in-between: A narrative exploration of race, gender and class. *Race, Gender, Class in Education, 7*(4), 47–56.

Hoffman, E. (1963). *Lost in translation: A life in a new language.* New York: Penguin Books.

Isajiw, W. W. (1999). *Understanding diversity: Ethnicity and race in the Canadian context.* Toronto, Canada: Thompson Educational Publishing.

Kalantzis, M., & Cope, W. (1992, November 4). Multiculturalism may prove to be the key issue of our epoch. *The Chronicle of Higher Education,* pp. B3, B5.

King, J. E. (1995). Culture-centered knowledge: Black studies, curriculum transformation, and social action. In J. A. Banks & C. A. M. Banks (Eds.), *Handbook of research on multicultural education* (pp. 265–290). New York: Macmillan.

Liu, W. T., & Yu, E. S. H. (1995). Asian American studies. In J. A. Banks & C. A. M. Banks (Eds.), *Handbook of research on multicultural education* (pp. 259–264). New York: Macmillan.

Minister of State, Multiculturalism. (1978). Statement by the Prime Minister, House of Commons, October 8, 1971. In *Multiculturalism and the government of Canada* (pp. 45–46). Ottawa: Minister of Supply and Services Canada.

Moodley, K. A. (1995). Multicultural education in Canada: Historical development and current status. In J.A. Banks & C. A. M. Banks (Eds.), *Handbook of research on multicultural education* (pp. 801–820). New York: Macmillan.

Nussbaum, M. (1997). *Cultivating humanity.* Cambridge, MA: Harvard University Press.

Phillion, J. (2002a). Becoming a narrative inquirer in a multicultural landscape. *Journal of Curriculum Studies, 34*(5), 535–556.

Phillion, J. (2002b). Classroom stories of multicultural teaching and learning. *Journal of Curriculum Studies, 34*(3), 281–300.

Phillion, J. (2002c). Narrative inquiry in a multicultural landscape: Multicultural teaching and learning. Westport, CT: Ablex.

Phillion, J. (2002d). Narrative multiculturalism. *Journal of Curriculum Studies, 34*(3), 265–279.

Phillion, J., & He, M. F. (2005). Narrative inquiry in English language teaching: Contributions and future directions. In J. Cummins & C. Davison (Eds.), *The international handbook of English language teaching* (Vol. 2). Norwell, MA: Springer (formerly Kluwer Academic Publishers).

Rodriguez, C. E. (1995). Puerto Ricans in historical and social science research. In J. A. Banks & C. A. M. Banks (Eds.), *Handbook of research on multicultural education* (pp. 223–244). New York: Macmillan.

Ross, V. (2002). *Living an elementary school curriculum: Rethinking reform through a narrative classroom inquiry with a teacher and her students into the learning of mathematics/life lessons from Bay Street Community School.* Unpublished doctoral dissertation, University of Toronto, Canada.

Ross, V. (2003). Walking around the curriculum tree: An analysis of a third/fourth-grade mathematics lesson. *Journal of Curriculum Studies, 35*(5), 567–584.

Snipp, C. M. (1995). American Indian studies. In J. A. Banks & C. A. M. Banks (Eds.), *Handbook of research on multicultural education* (pp. 245–258). New York: Macmillan.

Tomkins, G. F. (1986). *A common countenance: Stability and change in the Canadian curriculum.* Scarborough, Ontario: Prentice-Hall.

Valdés, G. (1996). Con respeto: Bridging the distances between culturally diverse families and schools: An ethnographic portrait. New York: Teachers College Press.

Westbury, I., & Wilkof, N. J. (Eds.). (1978). *Science, curriculum, and liberal education: Selected essays of Joseph Schwab.* Chicago: University of Chicago Press.

Xu, S. (in progress). *In search of home: Chinese families on cross-cultural landscapes of schools in transition.* Unpublished doctoral dissertation, University of Toronto, Canada.

14

Creating Communities of Cultural Imagination

Negotiating a Curriculum of Diversity

Janice Huber, M. Shaun Murphy,
and D. Jean Clandinin

Autobiographical Introduction

In the fall of 1990, Jean joined the faculty of education at the University of Alberta. As both a faculty member and Director of the Centre for Research for Teacher Education and Development, Jean continued a program of research with F. Michael Connelly and graduate students and teachers in schools and classrooms in which her interests in experiential and narrative understandings of teacher knowledge and professional contexts shaped her work alongside teacher education and graduate students in curriculum, teacher education, and narrative inquiry courses. It was in the context of a graduate course in curriculum studies, Life in the Elementary Classroom, that Janice and Shaun first met Jean. Within this course, Janice, in 1990, and Shaun, in 1996, found spaces where their experiences as teachers mattered, spaces where, as they began to tell stories of their experiences as teachers, they were, at the same time, inquiring into who they were and who they were becoming as teachers. Not only did this kind of

AUTHORS' NOTE: The authors wish to acknowledge the support of a research grant from the Social Sciences and Humanities Research Council of Canada to F. Michael Connelly and D. Jean Clandinin.

personal, experiential, and narrative inquiry shape Janice's and Shaun's teaching in elementary classrooms among diverse children, youth, and families, but it also shaped sustained relationships among Jean, Janice, and Shaun.

Over the years, questions of knowledge, contexts, identity, and diversity became threads of inquiry linking Jean's, Janice's, and Shaun's lives in research funded by the Social Sciences and Humanities Research Council (SSHRC) grants held by Jean and Michael. In the fall of 2000, we, alongside other teacher researchers and researcher teachers, had an opportunity to work and engage in inquiry together with children, youth, and families in a city centre school in Edmonton. In part, we came to our work there with questions of who we were and who we were becoming as White teachers teaching among the First Nations children and families in the school. We also came to our work thinking hard about possibilities for shaping narrative inquiry spaces with children, youth, and families. Peace candle gathering spaces, spaces where we and children shared stories of our lives as we negotiated an experiential curriculum in our classrooms, became an interconnecting inquiry thread among us. In time, as we found ourselves no longer working on this shared school landscape, yet, still involved in negotiating peace candle spaces, we were drawn toward more fully understanding these negotiated, tension-filled, story-filled spaces. Our chapter shows some of our unfolding experiences in relation to the negotiation of peace candle gathering spaces in two elementary school contexts. We continue to puzzle over questions of how these spaces, shaped by the bumping up of the stories of the children's and our experiences and stories of school, might help to shape more intentional possibilities for staying at the work of negotiating a relational, temporal, experiential, narrative curriculum of diverse lives.

Beginning With a Peace Candle Moment

Thirty bodies, including Janice's and Jean's adult-sized bodies, were crowded into the small carpeted corner where the children gathered after morning recess. It was a hectic morning, and the classroom seemed too close, too small for so many bodies. It was late January, and the day in this northern Canadian city was filled with a wintry pale light. Janice leaned over and lit the candle in the globe-shaped container. It was time for a peace candle gathering. Maybe, Janice and Jean thought, bringing the children around the peace candle was a way to move forward, to talk about how the children were making sense of their experiences, a space for children to speak their stories, to listen to others' stories.

The children were still high, and Janice tried to get the children to talk about what happened in the gym that morning. The storied emotion around what happened shaped the classroom rhythm.

The triggering event happened early in the morning during the regular physical education time. After a game of skittles, Ryley,[1] Damien, and Kotef were running around with some of the balls, trying to shoot baskets. As Rachel and Lia attempted to collect the balls, Lia ran over to Damien to get his ball, couldn't stop, and ran into him, pushing the ball into his stomach. He doubled over in pain and began to cry. Ryley, seeing his friend in pain, knelt beside him, and Damien told him Lia punched him in the stomach. Ryley's reaction was immediate as he ran out of the gym saying he was going to get even with Lia. Damien ran after him.

Moments later, in the coatroom, Ryley, Damien, and other children gathered around Lia as Ryley and Damien shouted accusations at her. Lia, feeling unheard and unjustly accused, ran into the hallway. Ryley followed, calling out to older children gathered there that Lia was crazy and that they should look out for her. When some older children in the hallway laughed, Lia stormed back into the room. Janice asked her to go into the cozy corner as we waited for the other children to put on coats, boots, hats, and mittens. Jean and Janice talked with her quietly while the others were outside. Lia explained she had not meant to hurt Damien but had run into him and had pushed the ball into his stomach. We said we understood. Perhaps a peace candle would help.

And so the moment of the peace candle was with us. The children would not focus, would not talk about what happened. Finally, Janice sensing that dialogue would not come, asked if Lia would make a wish out loud, part of the peace candle rhythm, and blow out the peace candle. Lia said she would make a quiet wish rather than an out-loud wish and she would blow out the peace candle. Ryley, engaged with Damien, missed the negotiation between Janice and Lia and asked if he could make an out-loud wish and blow out the candle. Without waiting for Janice's assent, he moved closer to the candle. In that instant, he saw Lia also moving into the candle. He put his hands up and began to move back and then . . . he changed course and moved in to the candle again. They sat there, facing each other with the peace candle between them. Lia made a quiet wish and Ryley wished for a better afternoon, an afternoon where people would listen to each other. He said, "On my count" and they both blew out the peace candle. (Reconstructed notes to file, January 28)

The Research Sites

We began with this moment of a peace candle gathering to explore ways we see children making sense of talking across what they see as differences to understanding. We chose this moment because Ryley and Lia were two children who called us to explore their lives, lives that at this moment and at other moments bumped against each other as they lived in this Year 3–4[2] city centre classroom. This moment was one of many we experienced as we, Jean and Janice, joined Karen, a full-time school board teacher, at City Heights School[3] for a full school year. Janice and Jean worked as teacher researchers in the classroom. We participated in and, at times, helped plan activities. We also wrote field notes of our participation in the classroom. Janice was in the classroom two and a half days per week, and Jean was in the classroom one half-day per week. As Jean's and Janice's relationship with the children and families developed, Jean, Karen, and Janice also engaged in tape recorded and transcribed research conversations with eight children and four mothers.

Some months after this school year ended, reconstructing this January field note of a peace candle gathering called us to consider how children used the peace candle space to explore the tensions they felt as they lived in the classroom. Janice and Jean wondered what we might learn about the meeting of diverse lives in schools and about curriculum making by attending to peace candle moments. We also began to wonder what children might say of these peace candle gatherings. We invited Shaun, a primary-division teacher also inquiring into peace candle gatherings in his Year 1 classroom, to join us in this research. Shaun is a full-time teacher researcher. Shaun, still engaged with the children in his classroom, asked the children what they thought of the place of the peace candle gatherings in their classroom. In this chapter, we draw together field texts of peace candle moments in the Year 3–4 classroom at City Heights School and in Shaun's Year 1 classroom at Strawberry School.[4]

We have been exploring the making of peace candle gatherings since 1994 when Janice and a teaching colleague began playing with the possibility of such spaces. We see them as a space and time to foreground the tensions that emerge among children's stories, teachers' stories, and stories of school. Rather than paper over the tensions in an attempt to smooth away, to make invisible the tensions of lives lived in relation, we work to create curricular spaces where children's stories are attended to in relation with each other. Our intention is to explore the making of a curriculum of diversity. Janice, in trying to describe peace candle gatherings, wrote, "Our conversation moved deeper into the underground; uncovering self-truths that were shaping the surface of our classroom landscape. Listening to the stories we told shifted our understanding of the possibilities for living community on the in-classroom place" (Huber, 1999, p. 19). In another chapter (Huber, Huber, & Clandinin, 2004) we wrote of peace candle gatherings as spaces for narrative coherence, spaces where children could tell the stories of who they were and who they were becoming as they lived alongside other's stories and as they tried to live within the storied landscape of schools (Clandinin & Connelly, 1996). In this earlier work, we had not attended to the possibilities of using the peace candle space as a place for negotiating a curriculum of diversity.

When Shaun began to shape peace candle gatherings, he wondered, as had Janice (Huber, 1999), if they might be a place to help shape the classroom community. However, while the peace candle process came with no instructions, Shaun realized that they evolved out of the experiences the children and he brought to the space. He had a sense that, if the students had a space where they could talk about their lives at school, it would influence the classroom as a whole. Shaun had the everyday concerns of a teacher embarking on a new process with a group of young children. As a teacher, a certain part of him wanted to know how to run a peace candle gathering. What were the right ways to manage the space? What kinds of directions did he need to give first-year students in order for them to participate in the peace candle gathering? As the year evolved, the students began to call more regularly for peace candle gatherings. They typically came in from recess and asked for a peace candle gathering. In the gathering, the children began to talk about what was happening to them at recess. They often told stories of conflicts and incidents that happened when playing outside. Occasionally, a student asked for a gathering first thing in the morning. Usually they asked after they had been at school for some part of the day. Shaun's more recent inquiries into peace candle gatherings as a curricular space drew on our earlier research and practice.

Peace candle gatherings have been research spaces in both the Year 3–4 classroom at City Heights and the Year 1 classroom at Strawberry School, spaces that allow us to see, to become awake to, to attend to the tensions that, too often, are buried beneath the taken-for-granted living out of the dominant story of school, which silences stories of diversity. As researchers and teachers, these spaces helped us attend more closely to children's and families' stories as they bump against the stories of school that teachers and administrators live and tell. Although Janice and Jean had only field notes in the City Heights site, Shaun kept audio recordings of some of the gatherings in his Year 1 classroom.

Narrative Concepts of Diversity in Curriculum Making

Our wonderings about the making and remaking of curriculum relating to diverse children and families comes out of the ongoing narrative research of Connelly and Clandinin (1988) and Clandinin and Connelly (1992, 2000), who suggest that curriculum "might be viewed as an account of teachers' and students' lives together in schools and classrooms. . . . [In this view of curriculum,] the teacher is seen as an integral part of the curricular process . . . in which teacher, learners, subject matter, and milieu are in dynamic interaction" (Clandinin & Connelly, 1992, p. 392). In this chapter, as we explore peace candle gathering spaces in the making of a curriculum of diversity, we share their "vision of curriculum as a course of life" (p. 393). For us, a classroom curriculum is shaped by the expression of the diverse narratives of experience in a classroom. However, because classrooms are nested in a broader epistemological, social, cultural, and political context, teachers' stories, stories of teachers, school stories, and stories of school (Clandinin & Connelly, 1996) also shape the making of curriculum. Attending to this nested set of stories and their relationship in the making of a curriculum of diversity between and among ourselves and diverse children and families helped us to see moments of bumping up among the dominant stories of school and the diverse stories we and children were living, telling, retelling, and reliving in our curriculum making in two elementary classrooms.

Attending to this temporal storying and restorying of lives in relation as curriculum making helped Connelly and Clandinin (1999) shape a narrative understanding of teacher and principal identity as "stories to live by." Stories to live by attend to the historical, the temporal, the contextual, and the relational. Stories to live by interconnect teachers' personal, practical knowledge with their professional knowledge contexts. Connelly and Clandinin wrote that "personal practical knowledge is a moral, affective, and aesthetic way of knowing life's educational situations" (1988, p. 59). Stories to live by are fluid, evolving, and profoundly experiential. We imagine something similar for children, that is, stories to live by connect their school contexts with their embodied narratives of experience. Thinking through curriculum and identity in narrative ways means that stories to live by are at the heart of the making and remaking of a curriculum of diversity.[5]

Working together as children, teachers, and researchers to make a curriculum of diversity, we were increasingly drawn to focus "on the ways in which the curriculum is being lived as each learner constructs new meaning and learns to live a new but connected story" (Clandinin & Connelly, 1992, p. 393). The negotiation of a curriculum of diversity is, then, a curriculum that unfolds moment by moment in a particular place with people in relation. How we understand and negotiate a curriculum of diversity is intimately connected with the life stories of each person and the intermingling of storied lives in the life space of the classroom. In this way, we see the negotiation of a curriculum of diversity as inextricably linked with what Florio-Ruane calls cultural imagination, which she describes as "people making culture together, reshaping, in their moment-to-moment encounters, their . . . histories and futures" (2001, p. 148).

Intentions in the Making of a Curriculum of Diversity

In early September, months before the January morning described at the beginning of the chapter, Janice wrote about the meaning that peace candle gatherings have for her in a letter to Karen.

> I loved being part of the peace candle conversation this morning and I want to think more about this space . . . its value . . . its possibilities. As both a participant in and an observer of the conversation, I couldn't help but think about what a different beginning to a school year many children and teachers experience when they don't know one another. I felt a strong sense of "knowing one another" and of "connection" as our conversation unfolded. . . . Even for those children who were

just coming to the conversation this morning, many shared stories of themselves. I imagine that Azim might have already felt more connected to you and the other children because of the stories he knows of last year from Norman, Darwin and Joseph (and probably even their mothers). I wonder what Azim experienced when you responded to his stories by letting him know that you knew of his Kokum [Cree word for *Grandmother*] and of the significance of the place he and his larger family continue to return to. I was struck by the openness of his story and of the vulnerable place he positioned himself in when he talked about not having running water at his Kokum's house.

I am so intrigued by the conversation that opened up around learning a different language this morning and of my and Caleb's telling of the fear . . . [and] anxiety we have sometimes experienced in speaking a new language. Sometimes I've wondered if I would have felt as apprehensive about speaking Dutch and now Spanish if I had been learning at a younger age and yet, hearing Caleb say that he too, at times, also feels like I do, was really important. . . .

Karen, did you see Tommy when you shared your story about getting engaged! He seemed excited about your news but at the same time, he also seemed as though you had just told them a secret . . . like something highly confidential!

There is something profoundly amazing that happens in peace candle spaces, and in thinking further about this tonight, I think it's a different kind of knowing that emerges and is shaped in these spaces than the knowledge our mandated curriculum documents are built around. (Letter to file, September 2)

At this early time in the school year, Janice wrote of the peace candle gathering space as a curriculum space, a space of coming together to make visible who we each are in the stories we tell of ourselves. Family stories, language stories, relationship stories were ways of connecting as the class members met at the gathering. Janice attended to how children might have connected to stories of the classroom they knew from other children and their mothers who were at the school the year before. She noted the impact of hearing Karen's personal plans on Tommy, a child. She wondered about how such spaces redefine what curriculum means.

Unpacking the January Peace Candle Moment

As we interpreted the ways the peace candle gathering space shaped a place for the day-to-day negotiation of a curriculum of diversity, we slid backward in time from the moment of the January peace candle gathering described earlier to tell something of the two children whose lives created the urgency in the classroom that January morning.

To understand the moment that brought Lia to the peace candle, we needed to know something of the many narratives of experience that lived within Lia. Lia, child of Somalia, child of war, child of Islam, a daughter and sister, girl child within a cultural narrative that stories girls as less than boys, storyteller, friend to children in school. A child who knows herself as capable and visible, seeking relationships, telling stories, helping others, a child who also knows she is "less-than" in her family cultural narratives.

To understand the moment that brought Ryley to the peace candle, we needed to know something of the many narratives of experience that lived within Ryley. Ryley, child of Aboriginal heritage, child of a mother who was present in the school, boy child within a cultural narrative, child of a mother who told her story as one who cared for all children—a fierce protector of her son. A child who knows himself as someone who is listened to in the class-room, as a friend to others, as a good athlete, as someone strong and able to exert physical force.

Knowing the multiplicity of stories that Ryley and Lia were living helped us see something of why these two embodied narratives of experience might have collided on that morning, and on other mornings in the classroom. Lia, trying to be helper, to live her storyline as girl child, as capable, was helping to collect the balls. When she ran into Damien, Ryley's friend, she at first tried to live a story that fit her plotline of helper, as female in relation to male, but she was unable to sustain it. Instead, she burst out of the plotlines with anger at being accused and unheard. We imagine the cultured, gendered plotlines became too restrictive, and Lia burst from them and, in this stepping outside the familiar plotlines she lived within, shaped space to attempt a new story to live by in which she could be angry.

Ryley, living his story of physical, powerful friend, was playing, resisting the bounds of the story of physical education cleanup when the accident hap-pened. He immediately began to live the story as friend and protector as he sought to punish Lia for her transgression. The collision of these two narratives of experience was the moment when Lia broke free of her familiar story. We imagined that had Lia not broken free, there would not have been tension. We also imagined that the moment would have gone unnoticed by us. Ryley could then have stayed with his familiar plotline as protector of his friends.

As we gathered around the peace candle, we were unable to negotiate a space in which the children told their stories in words. Unlike other gatherings, when words were possible, on this January morning neither Ryley nor Lia could move outside the story lines swirling around the event. Nor were Janice and Jean able to help them pick a story thread with which to begin the conver-sation. In the absence of negotiating meaning through telling stories, it was the embodied knowing of this space, knowing at the end of the peace candle time that a child makes a wish and blows out the candle, that finally created the opening for Ryley and Lia to restory their difference in that moment. Our embodied knowing of this space was a knowing of intimacy, knowing that wishes were made out loud, and a public display of blowing out the candle signaled the end of this time and the return to other less intimate curriculum undertakings. Our embodied knowing of what happens in this space moved with us as we moved away to other spaces such as math centers, inquiry spaces, and the gym.

Even as the children gathered in the peace candle space on that January morning, they came living the knowing of all the other peace candle gatherings: gatherings where they told stories of themselves as children new to Canada, children speaking many languages, children who moved between family members and extended families. In the moment when Janice realized that words would not come, she drew on this shared knowing of the rhythm of the peace candle as she invited Lia to make an out-loud wish and to blow out the candle. Lia accepted partially and agreed to make a quiet wish, but not to risk further visibility. We imagined that by now, Lia, her anger dissipated, resumed a more comfortable story of girl child in her cultural narrative. But Ryley appeared to be in the midst of another story. He was not attentive in the peace candle space. He continued to talk with Damien and, drawing on his knowing of the peace candle rhythm, demanded that he make the wish and blow out the candle. It is only in that moment when he faced Lia across the space created by the candle that he seemed to face himself, realizing he could restory his relationship with Lia, at least in that moment. We do not know what his wish might have been at his first demand. We do sense that, after facing Lia, he moved from being in the midst of this peace candle space inward to face himself. What emerged is his restorying made visible in his wish for "an afternoon where people would listen to each other."

As we laid Janice's reflections on the first peace candle gathering alongside our unpacking of the January peace candle gathering, we noticed that, at least on that January day, the children were still learning to listen, learning to tell their stories in words in a place of angry tension. We noticed that, in January, they imagined reaching across the space between, a space created by anger, trusting that they would be respected for who they are, in all their multiplicity. Ryley and Lia used their multiple story lines as they reached across that space of anger, a space between them, to "meet" each other, allowing possibility for them to imagine how they might come to restory one another and their living in relation in the Year 3–4 classroom space. Ryley, by engaging in this restorying, stepped outside the plotlines of stories he was familiar living. By so doing, we imagined that they both temporarily lived and told new stories with one another. In this shifting of their stories to live by, they came to know something different of each other, of themselves, and of their living in relation. Ryley and Lia continued to know the peace candle space as a space where the tensions of their diversity were recognized and respected, a space where cultural connections were imagined. In this space, we lived a curriculum in the making, a curriculum that requires liminal space to become a curriculum of diversity.

A Curriculum of Diversity as a Liminal Space

In our research around peace candle gatherings, we attended closely to the tensions created when diverse lives met in classroom contexts. Rather than creating a curriculum where tensions were erased, we tried to create a curriculum where we, the children and ourselves, stepped outside comfortable plotlines of who we were in school and entered a place we understood as a place of liminality, "a state of necessary in-betweenness" (Heilbrun, 1999, p. 98). Heilbrun wrote about a place of liminality as "never designed for permanent occupation" but as a place "between destinies . . . the place where we write our own lines and eventually our own plays" (pp. 101–102). In Kennedy's (2001) narrative inquiry with teachers, she explored a space of liminality that called "forth new scripts, improvisations that reflect a different way of being in the classroom. As a process-oriented activity it calls upon all members of the classroom to participate in the creation of new ways of being in the classroom" (p. 137). Kennedy wrote that

> liminal space is the in-between space, the space between what was and what might be, where one engages with future possibilities. Its apparent lack of structure is both its strength and its weakness, a strength because of what it offers to those who engage with it and its weakness because in the structured society in which we live, there is a fear of the chaotic. (p. 130)

As we interconnected the January peace candle moment with the earlier incident in the gym and the multiplicity of narratives of experience embodied by Ryley and Lia, we were drawn into puzzling further over the place of liminality in the negotiation of a curriculum of diversity. In the peace candle moment, there was an instant when Ryley almost did not come to the space of negotiating across difference. However, he did choose that moment to reach across to Lia, to step into liminality to try to create a new plotline where they would blow out the candle together and try to compose a new story for the afternoon. As Florio-Ruane wrote, "To reach a place of 'affirmation, solidarity, and critique,' learners must probe more deeply their own formations and their relationship with others. To accomplish this kind of cultural understanding can be risky" (2001, p. 9). In their own, although different, ways, Lia and Ryley each took risks. Lia risked living an imagined new story just after the event in the gym. Ryley risked imagining a new story, a story of "people listening to each other," as the peace candle gathering came to a close. The peace candle gathering space, being a liminal space, is a temporal space we come to for the purpose of understanding our stories to live by in school. It is a move away from a more scripted way of being in classrooms. We know from our work with the children that the creation of this liminal space is important to them as a making-sense space for moments in their lives in school.

Only as we began to consider peace candle gatherings as places of liminality did our naming of them as "peace" candle spaces become problematic. Why were we naming these *peace* candle spaces? What was the significance of peace in their negotiation? We knew that our understanding and negotiation of peace candle gathering spaces with diverse children was not linked with national movements such as Safe and Caring Schools and character education, movements that do involve visions of peace. As we experienced these movements, we did not see their vision of peace in liminal terms but rather as smoothing over tensions, as silencing, as remaking diverse stories to live by to fit within a dominant story of school. These were not the kinds of experiences we were trying to negotiate with children.

The Meanings of Peace in the Peace Candle Gatherings

We were intrigued as we explored the meanings of peace as "the state existing during the absence of war"; "a state of harmony between people or groups"; "a state of stillness, silence or serenity" (*Collins English Dictionary and Thesaurus*, 1993, p. 837). For us, as teachers, peace candle gathering spaces were liminal spaces in which children, teachers, and researchers could tell stories, and in hearing others' stories, could imagine other possibilities, restorying our own and our relational stories. In so doing, we were attempting to negotiate a curriculum of diversity. We knew that negotiating such a curriculum involved tension, something that is sometimes seen as in contradiction to peace. As we talked about the peace candle, we wondered about the children's understandings of peace. At City Heights, peace candle conversations were not generally tape-recorded, but Shaun was tape-recording his classroom's peace candle conversations. We had a research opportunity to ask one group of children about what sense they made of peace. In a conversation, Shaun asked his Year 1 children to talk about what peace meant.

The definitions of peace in this conversation demonstrated a range of understandings. Melissa equated peace with the idea of peace and quiet. She talked about how the peace of the library was interrupted by the arrival of louder students. Throughout the conversation the children referred to peace by looking for opposites. Wally introduced the idea of swear words, which made us wonder whether, for him, the absence of peace was illustrated by the use of swearing. The conversation about "swears" continued when, to illustrate an understanding of what happens when peace breaks down, Mark said, "It's almost like it takes over peace. . . . It's so bad that it makes peace disintegrate." They spoke of tension and war in order to discuss the idea of peace.

They know there is peace when they "get to have fun and play . . . people play with you and are nice to you." Jamie said, "And it's a wonderful time out there . . . b-because you get to play and do stuff outside." In this discussion on peace, the children made an initial reference to defining the gathering when Cory explained that we call it the peace circle "because it has to be quiet and we have to make a circle." Melissa responded with, "Because it makes you feel better." In these two responses we saw how they explained the peace candle gathering. In their comments, there were elements of definitions of peace suggested by the *Collins* dictionary in their references to war and swearing, to playing together, and to quiet. Their responses demonstrated an understanding of the requirements of quiet in order to hear other people's stories.

The children's understandings affirmed for us that peace candle gatherings require stillness, not only in the physical sense but also in the sense of quieting our own stories to hear another's. In that hearing there was the possibility of imagining other ways of being. Peace, as stillness, allowed the possibility for lives, with all their ambiguity, uncertainty, tension, and complexity, to be expressed. Peace, as stillness, allowed the possibility of moving away from the certainty and arrogance of knowing to the uncertainty and humbleness of not knowing (Baylor, 1997). As Kennedy wrote, "Reconceptualizing my understanding of a classroom as a liminal space would provide opportunities to stay with the story of our experience and to explore its ambiguities, contradictions and tensions" (2001, p. 138). Peace candle gatherings as a living experience allowed us to stay with the diverse narratives of our experience and to explore their ambiguities, contradictions, and tensions. Peace candle gatherings, as liminal spaces, allowed us to imagine new ways, new stories to live by in schools.

The Challenge of Staying With Liminality in Making a Curriculum of Diversity

The living out of new stories to live by was not an easy undertaking. As we studied the field texts from the peace candle gatherings in both research sites, we searched for moments when we felt we were moving toward living in liminal space and for moments when we were not. In the January peace candle gathering we felt the experience as a liminal space.

During the peace candle gatherings in Shaun's classroom, he and the children talked about the issues they felt relevant. Problems at recess, an issue on the school bus, and the experience of being in Year 1 at school with so many other children were all topics. Children tried to make sense of managing their bodies and space in the shared place of school. Sometimes an individual shared a positive moment on the playground, a time when they had fun, and friends were easy to be around. Other times, Shaun asked a question such as when he asked about peace. He asked how they would tell another class or teacher about the peace candle gathering, what they liked or disliked about it. At other times,

Shaun wondered out loud about how they participated in the peace candle gathering, why some children were often silent, while others were very vocal.

For the children, the peace candle time was a favorite time of day. Shaun often thought that, given the chance, they would hold the peace candle gathering all afternoon. He had a sense that, for them, it was a space and time when they were in control of what was talked about, a time alive with their lives at school. During peace candle gatherings, children became passionate about the conversation, they could barely wait for their turn, they interrupted each other, and they got mad when the time was over. Emotions ran high.

Just as in the January story of the tensions existing in the peace candle gathering between Ryley and Lia, tensions were part of the peace candle gatherings in Shaun's classroom. Students called out, trying to be heard over each other, and sometimes Shaun intervened. Often, he found himself bringing their attention back to their purposes, refocusing them on listening and taking turns. Some students lost focus, started to have conversations with each other, played. Shaun tried a variety of means to redirect them, catching their attention, putting his finger to his lips, and when that failed, he paused the tape in order to refocus them and to talk about appropriate behavior. During a research interview, Shaun said that he "paused the tape in order to talk to the children" (Transcript, March 10). Later he wrote,

> In discussing the interview the other day I shared the fact that at times I pause the tape in order to ask different children to pay better attention, to stop fooling around, or to stop talking so that others can be heard. When I thought about the pause button I realized that I was trying to have a smooth story of the peace candle gathering where everyone was attentive all the time and there was no need for a teacher to tell them how to behave. But that isn't true and I often make eye contact or gesture for a student to stop talking or stop playing. I am essentially editing out the real life of the peace candle gathering, part of its complexity. (Notes to file, March 10)

As Shaun related the story of hitting the pause button, we realized this was a moment when he stepped away from liminality to bring the story of school to the peace candle time. He enacted a common teacher story of good classroom management, a story of imposing order. That he puts the tape recorder on pause when he fell into this story showed he was aware he was stepping outside the liminality of the peace candle gathering. Shaun also showed us he was not comfortable with this shift in his story. The field note indicated he wanted to present a smooth story of the peace candle gathering, avoiding the tensions when diverse stories to live by are negotiated in a classroom. As Shaun reflected on pushing the pause button, he was in part struggling with letting others know that staying with liminality in peace candle gathering spaces was not easy. His inner tension was shaped by knowing that in peace candle gatherings, people need to hear one another. His felt tension called forth, from his embodied knowing, a teaching story of imposing his authority on the gathering. Aware that this was movement away from liminality, he paused the tape recorder in order to hide the complexity of negotiating meaning in peace candle gatherings. Shaun's pushing of the pause button raised questions about the challenge of staying with liminality as he attempted to negotiate a curriculum of diversity.

Unpacking an April Peace Candle Moment

We found another moment of tension in an April peace candle gathering at City Heights when we again slipped away from liminality. In our exploration of the January peace candle gathering we were drawn toward narrative understandings of the bumping up of Lia's and Ryley's diverse stories to live by. We saw the peace candle gathering space as shaping an opening for Ryley and Lia to negotiate across difference, a space where they might, momentarily, come to know one another differently. We saw the space as a liminal space for them. Three months later, in April, another peace candle gathering was also a time of attending to the diverse experiences of children. This time, however, the peace candle gathering was interrupted and became a different kind of space. Again the events that led to this peace candle gathering began in the morning in the gymnasium.

> First thing in the morning Janice and the children headed down to the gym. It was a bit ragged when we first got there, lots of running around the gym. The basketball game was passionate from start to finish. Janice knew Ryley was getting higher and higher as the game went on. . . . We were in the last few minutes of the game when the ball went out alongside the benches and Van picked it up and threw it in. Janice stopped the game and asked him not to do this, as he wasn't on the court at the time. Lia was beside him so Janice gave her the ball, and Lia threw it in. The game resumed. Janice saw Lia and Ryley arguing along where the benches were. Janice stopped the game and asked the children to line up. Lia and Ryley continued to argue, and Lia said that Ryley called her a bitch because she had also told Van not to throw the ball in.
>
> We were beginning to line up and Ryley and Lia's voices were becoming angrier. Janice asked Lia to go to the front of the line and Ryley to the end. Ryley shoved his way through the line of children, following Lia. She was just by the door when he reached her. He lunged to push her and, in the act, Nina's head hit the door frame and she scratched her face. Janice called out to Ryley that he needed to leave, he needed to go to the office. He turned and looked at Janice and said, "That's where I want to go." Nina was crying and her face was bleeding. Lia took her to the bathroom, and the rest of us went to the classroom.
>
> Karen and Janice decided to have a peace candle gathering after recess. As the children came in they gathered them. We were just about to begin when the

principal came in. She talked for about fifteen minutes, telling the children that they needed to learn what to do when they became angry, that she wanted everyone to think about how they'd contributed to the situation. It was silent. At one point Karen said she was concerned because it seemed like blaming was happening, and she didn't think this helped the situation. The principal agreed that talking about people didn't help them. When the principal left, Janice realized that Ryley had come in with the principal and was also seated in the cozy corner. Karen asked if he wanted to go to the bathroom or to get a drink as he had missed recess. He got up then and he had the hood on his top pulled down over his head and eyes. (Notes to file, April 28)

In our attempts to further understand the place of peace candle gatherings as a space helping to shape a curriculum of diversity, our rereading of this April peace candle gathering stopped us. Initially, we were halted by considerations of how the space of this peace candle gathering was unlike others we experienced and described in our unfolding field notes of life in this Year 3–4 classroom. As we continued to try to make narrative sense of this April peace candle gathering, we were drawn toward questions of how we might give an account of the children's and our lives during this moment, of how we might understand the spaces among the children, among the children and ourselves, and among the children, ourselves, and stories of school.

Exploring these questions drew us backward from the peace candle moment to the earlier tensions shaping it. A number of diverse stories to live by bumped up in the last few moments of the passion-filled basketball game. As the physical education class unfolded, Lia appeared to be living out her familiar story lines of being capable and a helper. When Van, a boy new to Canada, threw the ball from the sidelines onto the court, Lia told him not to. We do not know what Lia said to Van. What we do know is that her involvement in that moment with Van shaped tension between Ryley and her. The bumping up of their diverse stories to live by became visible as they argued at the edge of the game. Tension built between them as Ryley, appearing to live his familiar story lines of being a good athlete and as strong and able to exert physical force, called Lia a bitch. Tensions built until Nina was eventually injured when Ryley, attempting to reach Lia, lunged forward through a group of classmates and, in the act, pushed Nina's face into the door frame.

It was at this point in the unfolding moment that the multiplicity of Janice's stories to live by becomes visible. At first Janice seemed to be living a story of negotiation. She negotiated with Van to help him understand more about the rules of basketball, and she negotiated with the children to get the game going when Lia, a player on the court, threw the ball back in. However, seeing Ryley and Lia arguing seemed to shift Janice's story of negotiation. Instead of negotiating with Lia and Ryley to help them move forward from their tension, Janice abruptly halted the game and tried to separate Ryley and Lia from one another.

Janice's shift toward living a story we could name as a familiar teacher plotline, a plotline of being responsible for what happened in the classroom, did not appear to bump against Lia's stories to live by. However, Janice's living of this common teacher plotline bumped against Ryley's stories to live by. Not only did he not move away from Lia as Janice requested, but he stayed within his familiar stories by attempting to follow Lia. When Nina was injured, Janice's and Ryley's stories to live by continued bumping up, and Janice, slipping even further from living a story of negotiation, told Ryley to "go to the office."

By falling into this scripted story of school, a storyline common on many school landscapes and a story Ryley seemed to know well, we could say that Janice enacted a story of exclusion with a plotline smoothing over moments of conflict. We might also say that, in this passion-filled moment of tension and complexity, Janice's response of falling into these two familiar plotlines, a teacher plotline of being responsible and a plotline of school of sending children to the office in moments of tension, significantly limited future possibility for individual and communal negotiation and living of new stories in relation to the tension. Ryley, appearing to stay within his familiar story line of being strong, headed for the office. Lia, appearing to stay within her familiar story line of helper to others, took Nina to the bathroom. In this multiplicity of the bumping up of diverse stories to live by, the tensions between Ryley and Lia, between Ryley and Nina, and between Ryley and Janice were suspended. No movement across difference happened.

As we moved forward from the events in the gym to the peace candle moment, Janice's and Karen's stories to live by were visible through their decision to call a peace candle gathering. This forward movement also took us to an in-classroom place, which the gym and hallways are not.

The peace candle gathering after recess, intended as a space to make meaning of the events of the morning, began as usual. Markers we knew the peace candle rhythms by were all there: everyone was gathered together on the carpet, the candle was lit and sitting somewhere in the middle of our gathering space, the window blinds were likely drawn, a quiet stillness enveloped the space. Not unlike the January peace candle gathering space, silence, shaped in the earlier moments of tension in the gym, influenced the beginning of the April peace candle space. However, unlike the January peace candle gathering where Lia and Ryley eventually reached across the space between them to imagine how they might restory one another and their living in the classroom, there was no reaching across the spaces between Lia and Ryley, the spaces between Ryley and Janice, the spaces among us as a classroom community and stories of school. The imagined conversation and negotiation of understanding, the rhythms we knew the peace candle gathering space by, never did happen, and it was attention to these silences that helped us to see another layer of the bumping up of diverse stories to live by against stories of school.

As already described, the April peace candle was, in part, shaped by Janice's response of sending Ryley to the office. However, the April peace candle gathering space was also shaped by the lived and told stories of the principal, who, appearing to enter into the space in a spirit of helping also seemed caught in familiar stories of school. Not unlike Janice's response on the out-of-classroom place of the gym, the principal's response to the tension shaped by the bumping up of diverse stories to live by seemed to come as a story of certainty, of determining right from wrong, of fixing up problems. Neither quieting her own story to hear another's nor imagining other ways of being, she appeared to lecture the children, telling them "that they need to learn what to do when they become angry." A story of blame wove into the space when she said that she "want[ed] everyone to think about how they contributed to the situation." We could say that the principal did not seem to come to the peace candle space embodying the rhythms of peace candle gathering spaces, of narrative listening, of narrative response, of ambiguity, of liminality. At least in this moment, negotiating meaning across difference appeared outside the range of stories of school she felt able to live by. Possibilities for imagination, risk taking, and restorying were not nurtured in the face of these dominant stories of school. We did not hear Ryley's, Lia's, Van's, Nina's or Janice's stories. Even Karen, the teacher in this in-classroom space, was unable to shift the stories of school with plotlines of certainty and blaming, of the principal as holding the authority, and of the need for solutions and answers, shaping the peace candle gathering space. In this April peace candle gathering, our negotiation of a curriculum of diversity was halted.

Working with this field note in our present contexts, now many months since our year alongside Karen and the Year 3–4 children and families at City Heights, it was the silence, the lack of negotiation, the lack of making meaning across difference that drew us in. Reading the moment of this April peace candle gathering as more attentive to our movement across in- and out-of-classroom places and story lines raised new questions for us about the very tenuous negotiation of a curriculum of diversity on school landscapes. Both the January and the April peace candle moments were shaped by events in the gym, an out-of-classroom place. On both days, a peace candle gathering was called to talk about the tensions, to learn by listening to diverse stories. What seemed to separate these two peace candle moments was that the April peace candle gathering was shaped not only by the bumping up of diverse children's stories to live by but also by the bumping up of the diverse stories to live by of children and teachers and the bumping up of teachers' diverse stories to live by and stories of school. We wonder if certainty wove into our April peace candle gathering space, in part because the tensions shaping our gathering happened on an out-of-classroom place, a place that seemed to shape who Janice became, especially as blood appeared on Nina's face. Janice's response of sending Ryley to the office and Ryley's action of going told us something of tensions around diversity on out-of-classroom places. We also wondered about how the bumping up, not only of children's diverse stories to live by but of Ryley's and Janice's stories to live by, shaped the peace candle gathering. In spaces, such as peace candle gathering spaces, where intentions for shaping a curriculum of diversity were negotiated, knowing was shaped in relation, moment by moment as stories are lived and told, intermingling one with another. This intermingling often shaped moments of discomfort, feelings experienced as we hover on the threshold between certainty and uncertainty, knowing and unknowing as we step out of familiar and into unfamiliar story lines. The peace candle gathering, often a liminal space of uncertainty, unknowing, and unfamiliarity, vanished as a certain story of school was imposed. On this April morning in the out- and then in the in-classroom place of City Heights, both Ryley and Janice seemed unable to move beyond familiar stories for children and teachers to live by. That they were unable to move into unfamiliar story lines raised additional questions for us about the negotiation of a curriculum of diversity on school landscapes.

Summary

Our experience across these moments in two research sites showed us the complexity of attempting to negotiate a curriculum of diversity. As we returned to Florio-Ruane's (2001) call for cultural imagination, we realized that to engage children's and our cultural imagination in negotiating a curriculum of diversity required liminal spaces. As Kennedy wrote, "Incorporating liminality in the educational practices or rituals that are set out to suppress liminality creates an onerous burden for teachers" (2001, p. 129).

For us, peace candle gathering spaces offer possibilities for attending to the diverse narratives of experience of children and teachers. In the research moments described in this chapter, we attempted to create liminal spaces where we could step away from the scripted stories of school in order to negotiate a curriculum of diversity, a curriculum that fit the moment and the lives being lived there. The peace candle gathering allowed us to begin to do the work of attending to each other without an imposed script of school. What became evident to us were the tensions that were present in the peace candle gatherings. These tensions could not be smoothed over if we were to attend to the lives gathered in that space. The peace candle gathering created a space where the multiplicity of the lives of children and teachers could be attended to in a negotiated manner that tried to respect the diverse stories to live by of children and teachers. As Kennedy points out, this curriculum work is difficult work given the stories of school that shape teachers' and children's lives in school. Attending narratively to lives in relation in schools highlights the complexity of curriculum making in classrooms of diversity. Our exploration of the peace candle gathering space as a place for shaping a curriculum of diversity shows that we did, at times, like Kennedy, find liminality an "onerous burden" (2001, p. 129). However, our exploration also shows us that liminality is an urgent burden if our intentions are to continue the making of a curriculum of diversity.

Recommended Readings

Teachers as Curriculum Planners: Narratives of Experience (Connelly & Clandinin, 1988) has had an important place in each of our lives as teachers and researchers. As Shaun and Janice engaged in the curriculum course, Life in the Elementary Classroom, this book was a central reading and, as they remember it, shaped important spaces where they began a process that continues today of inquiring into who they, children, and families are and who they, children, and families are becoming as their lives meet in curriculum situations. Jean continues to draw from this book in her current teaching of the Life in the Elementary Classroom course with Pam Steeves. In this way, too, *Teachers as Curriculum Planners: Narratives of Experience* has held a central place in her teaching and research. In puzzling through possibilities of peace candle spaces in helping to shape a curriculum of diversity, our ideas were significantly shaped by understanding curriculum as experience and as shaped, reshaped, and negotiated in the meeting of children's and teachers' lives in classrooms.

Paley's books *White Teacher* (1979), *The Boy Who Would Be a Helicopter: The Uses of Storytelling in the Classroom* (1990), and *Kwanzaa and Me: A Teacher's Story* (1995) are, in so many rich ways, showings of the moment-to-moment curriculum negotiated and experienced in situations that Connelly and Clandinin explore in *Teachers as Curriculum Planners: Narratives of Experience* (1988). Important to the idea of negotiating a curriculum of diversity is that Paley does not work to smooth out the complexities and tensions she experiences as a teacher alongside diverse children and families. Instead, she pulls these threads forward as central to her gradual awakenings of herself as a teacher in relation with the stories lived, told, relived, and retold by diverse children and families.

In *School Days* (1997), Chamoiseau, through sharing stories of his memories as a child, helps readers to understand something more about the meeting of his life with structures and practices in a particular school and classrooms. Chamoiseau's memories of this time and place in his life are deeply remembered and, when read with attention to questions of the meeting of diverse children's and teachers' lives in the negotiation of a curriculum of diversity, helps to shape new imaginings of how his experiences might have been otherwise.

Reflective Questions

1. What are some of your life experiences with tensions, uncertainty, and liminality, and how might these experiences shape the curriculum you negotiate with children and families?

2. How do you, as a teacher, work with children to inquire into the tensions they experience in schools and classrooms?

3. How might you understand your inquiries with children into their experiences with tensions as curriculum making?

Notes

1. All children's names and the names of the schools are pseudonyms. Some of the children selected their own pseudonyms.

2. Because of the multiage organization of the school, we refer to the children's year in school rather than grade. Year 3–4 refers to the group of diverse eight- and nine-year-old children in the classroom. Over the yearlong inquiry, the number of children in the room fluctuated from twenty-one to twenty-eight children. Children and families new to the classroom came from diverse contexts including neighboring schools, other schools in the city and province, and schools in other locations in Canada and the world. This mix of familiarity and unfamiliarity with the school and classroom was also present in the children's out-of-school lives. Some children did see one another outside of school hours; other children did not see classmates outside of school.

3. City Heights is the name we gave to the city centre school where this narrative inquiry unfolded. Located in a western Canadian city, the community surrounding City Heights was developed in the early 1900s, with some ongoing redevelopment since that time. The most recent neighborhood profile indicates that single-parent, transient, low-income, and unemployed families are a high proportion of the neighborhood. Property is described as dilapidated and poorly maintained. There is little green space, a high crime rate, and high traffic noise and congestion. Statistics Canada (1996) reported that the ethnicity of the community is diverse with high numbers of people of Chinese and Aboriginal backgrounds. Nearly one-fourth of the community's adults are described as having less than a Year 9 education.

4. Strawberry School is the name we gave to a rural school where part of this narrative inquiry unfolded. Located outside of a western Canadian city, the school was built in the 1980s in response to the acreages in the area. It is a kindergarten through Grade 9 school, and the students come from acreages and farms in the surrounding area. The school population, predominately middle class and White, totals approximately 600 students, and the majority of these are bussed into the school.

5. We situate our study within other narrative classroom studies of diversity. For example, Paley's (1979, 1990, 1995) inquiries into life in the kindergarten classrooms she shares with children attend to who she is and who she is becoming as a White teacher in relation with African American children and to ways, such as story playing, in which children's lives shape the curriculum made in the classroom. Oyler (1996) also

sees children's diverse lives and experiences as part of curriculum making as she explores ways children and a teacher share authority in a classroom context. We also draw on memoirs of children's experiences in school such as Chamoiseau (1997), hooks (1996), and Littlechild (1993).

References

Baylor, B. (1997). *The other way to listen.* New York: Aladdin Paperbacks.

Chamoiseau, P. (1997). *School days.* Lincoln: University of Nebraska Press.

Clandinin, D. J., & Connelly, F. M. (1992). Teacher as curriculum maker. In P. Jackson (Ed.), *Handbook of research on curriculum* (pp. 363–401). Toronto, Canada: Macmillan.

Clandinin, D. J., & Connelly, F. M. (1996). Teachers' professional knowledge landscapes: Teacher stories/stories of teachers/school stories/stories of school. *Educational Researcher, 25*(3), 24–30.

Clandinin, D. J., & Connelly, F. M. (2000). *Narrative inquiry: Experience and story in qualitative research.* San Francisco: Jossey-Bass.

Collins English Dictionary and Thesaurus. (1993). Italy: HarperCollins.

Connelly, F. M., & Clandinin, D. J. (1988). *Teachers as curriculum planners: Narratives of experience.* New York: Teachers College Press.

Connelly, F. M., & Clandinin, D. J. (1999). *Shaping a professional identity: Stories of educational practice.* New York: Teachers College Press.

Florio-Ruane, S. (2001). *Teacher education and the cultural imagination.* London: Lawrence Erlbaum.

Heilbrun, C. (1999). *Women's lives: A view from the threshold.* Toronto, Canada: University of Toronto Press.

hooks, b. (1996). *Bone black: Memories of girlhood.* New York: Henry Holt and Company.

Huber, J. (1999). Listening to children on the landscape. In F. M. Connelly & D. J. Clandinin (Eds.), *Shaping a professional identity: Stories of educational practice* (pp. 9–19). New York: Teachers College Press.

Huber, M., Huber, J., & Clandinin, D. J. (2004). Moments of tension: Resistance as expressions of narrative coherence in stories to live by. *Reflective Practice, 5*(2), 181–198.

Kennedy, M. (2001). *Race matters in the life/work of four, white female teachers.* Unpublished doctoral dissertation, University of Alberta, Edmonton, Canada.

Littlechild, G. (1993). *This land is my land.* San Francisco: Children's Book Press.

Oyler, C. (1996). *Making room for students: Sharing teacher authority in room 104.* New York: Teachers College Press.

Paley, V. (1979). *White teacher.* Cambridge, MA: Harvard University Press.

Paley, V. (1990). *The boy who would be a helicopter: The uses of storytelling in the class-room.* Cambridge, MA: Harvard University Press.

Paley, V. (1995). *Kwanzaa and me: A teacher's story.* Cambridge, MA: Harvard University Press.

Statistics Canada. (1996). Profiles: Total immigrant population—An analysis of selected demographic and socio-economic characteristics. *Immigration Research Series.* Toronto: Statistics Canada.

15

Narrative and Experiential Approaches to Multiculturalism in Education

Democracy and Education

Ming Fang He, JoAnn Phillion, and F. Michael Connelly

Reflection on Chapters

Multiculturalism, for us, is not only the key issue across disciplines including education but also the way people live their lives in an increasingly diversified world. People of different cultural beliefs and values are in continual interaction, and, as in North America, multiculturalism is a concept increasingly found around the world for addressing equality and justice in living among people of different cultures. In *Narrative and Experience in Multicultural Education*, we focused on multiple cultural and ethnic groups and on experience and the meaning of experience from the perspective of individuals in these groups. Both conceptually and methodologically, this book contributes to new ways of thinking about multiculturalism by emphasizing the experiential and narrative quality of multicultural life.

This book reflects nuanced ways in which educational researchers foster equality and justice by studying the details of multicultural life. In North America, partly because of its history, partly because of unresolved injustice, tensions between Black and White have foregrounded the discussion of multiculturalism. The issue of American neighbors and its indigenous people has also gripped North American multicultural thought. While these issues have been represented in the structure of this book and in the choice of particular chapters, we must remember that North America is broader and more culturally complex than defined by the groups represented in this book; Asian American, Muslim American, and many other groups need to take their place in our thoughts on multicultural life. Internationally, the broad concerns for multicultural life seen in North America are the same; however, the details hinted at in chapters in this book are vastly different. There are also many other important issues in multicultural education that we were unable to discuss in this book. We touched on this matter in Chapter 1.

The scholarship featured in this book is work that looks beyond—or perhaps a better metaphor is peers beneath—the blanket of rhetoric of multiculturalism to come in touch with life as it is lived out in schools, classrooms and communities. The purpose of featuring the scholarship in this book is to better understand multicultural life and, by virtue of our understanding and acting upon our understanding, make life more equitable and just. This is why we believe that the narrative, experiential work brought forward in these chapters has so much potential. As readers reflect on the chapters of this book, we hope that they will feel, and imagine, the potential and power that we feel and imagine for experiential and narrative approaches to multiculturalism to create more equitable, democratic lives in North America and in the world.

In putting together this book, we drew upon a group of scholars who have developed inquiries that focus on multicultural issues and who carry on these inquiries in daily life and practice. The authors in this book develop their research questions, perspectives, and inquiry methods by drawing on what they care about passionately. Through detailed exploration of specific topics and inquiry into life situations, each author raises our awareness of important multicultural educational issues. The inherent potential of these inquiries lies in possibilities to effect social change, beginning with the individual and expanding into the greater community. Researchers engaged in these inquiries focus on experience, make meaning of experience in context, and transform understanding of experience into action for educational and social change.

We began this book with an overview of multiculturalism across disciplines and multiculturalism as a force in educational thought. We pointed out that the idea of multiculturalism has woven its way into the literature of academic disciplines. Many see multiculturalism as a central, perhaps *the* central, issue confronting many countries as immigration changes the country's cultural composition. Multiculturalism is a global issue as the world becomes more integrated through technologies, transportation, and commerce (UNESCO, 2003). These global and national concerns are urgently expressed in education. Perhaps no other field devotes as much attention and inquiry to multiculturalism as does education.

We argued, in the opening chapter of the book, that the study of multiculturalism, particularly in education, needs among other things a focus on how people live, and are educated in, multicultural lives. We said that multicultural research tended to focus on cultural groups and to explore the demographics and social treatment of groups. Much, if not all, of this research is driven by a democratic ideal of equality. There are, however, limits to the study of groups. It is in response to these limitations that this book takes its place. We also said in the opening chapter that there was a turn to narrative and experience in the field of educational research. This is a turn from characteristics of groups to qualities of individual experience. The experiential question in its most general sense is "How do people, individual people, experience their multicultural lives?"

This book sets the stage for understanding this inquiry turn in multiculturalism by bringing forward a series of experientially oriented studies. Though the turn is a turn inward from the group to its individual members, the authors in this book show how an understanding of individual experience sheds light on the group and strengthens our insights, passion, and commitment to the democratic ideals driving multicultural research.

The book brought forward thirteen studies organized into six units, three dealing with specific groups—African Americans, Latinos/Latinas, Native Americans, one on teacher education in the international context, one on experiential inquiry, and one on the democratic drive. This division into units is more arbitrary and convenient than it is hard and clear cut. For instance, Chris Liska Carger's "The Art of Narrative Inquiry" in Unit 5 on experiential inquiry could as easily be placed in Unit 2, which focuses on the study of Latino families. There is also a strong sense of the social inequities in the family's life that would permit its placement in Unit 6 on democracy, school life, and community. In addition, an imaginative reader could develop consequences for teacher education in North America and elsewhere, and the chapter could thereby be placed in Unit 4 on multicultural teacher education. Donna Deyhle's "Journey Toward Social Justice," placed in Unit 3, which focuses on Native American educational issues, is also a study filled with discussion of teachers and what their education might be, a topic featured in Unit 4. The study brings forward twenty years of work aimed at bettering the lives of Navajo children and their communities to ensure equal educational opportunity with others in the school board, a topic explored in Unit 6. The duration, intensity, and wide range of Deyhle's field texts also have much to say about how to carry out experiential inquiry, featured in Unit 5 and discussed in all chapters.

Similar readings of the other chapters are possible. We invite readers to return to one or more of their favorite studies and do a similar reading, ignoring the artificial boundaries set up by the units. These are rich studies: rich in the sense of a spotlight shining on a specific setting and nuances of that setting brought forward, and rich in the sense of illumination of individual experience. There is a saying that "the world can be seen in a grain of sand." It might be a stretch to apply that saying to each of these chapters. Still, each chapter, examined closely in the spirit that the authors have explored their topics, reveals much about our multicultural world.

Reading With an Experiential Eye, Reading With an Imaginative Eye

We began Chapter 1 by inviting readers to read with an experiential eye. By reading with an experiential eye, we intended to draw attention to the details of experience brought forward in each of the studies. We wanted readers to vicariously travel with each author into her or his research setting, situate themselves in that setting, and experience, in some small, vicarious way the lives of her or his participants. Narrative, experiential inquiry has potential to foster a lifelike relationship between reader and text. We hope that readers will have treated these texts as life-based literary narratives (Phillion & He, 2005) discussed in Recommended Readings for Chapter 1. By reading these texts with such an experiential eye, readers will, in some small way, carry on the inquiries alongside the authors and will see, hear, and feel the multicultural lives of those under study.

We also asked readers to read with an imaginative eye. It is often said that it is possible to lose sight of the forest for the trees. Experience is like the trees. There is an endless amount of experience. If one reads only with an experiential eye, one might become lost in the experience of each of the studies and wonder what the inquiry is all about. The imaginative eye permits readers to see an author and the author's participants in context. The imaginative eye also enables readers to recognize broad multicultural educational issues. If one reads only with an imaginative eye, one sees only forms and categories—the outlines of the forest. Reading with both an experiential eye and an imaginative eye brings the worlds of idea and experience together in mutually illuminative ways. The experiential detail grounds the ideas and issues, and the ideas and issues explain the experience.

Democracy and Education

With both an experiential eye and an imaginative eye, we invite readers to join us as we further explore the meaning of the chapters in the book. We borrow John Dewey's (1916) key concepts in *Democracy and Education* to conclude our book for several reasons. First and foremost, the concept of multiculturalism, and therefore the study of it, is a democratic concept, and because this book is by and for educators, *Democracy and Education* aptly names what this book is about. This idea, as we said in Chapter 13, is formally embedded in Canadian statutes. The idea is also evident in every chapter in this book. In order to grasp the full significance and meaning of each of the studies, it is necessary to hold in mind this idea of democracy and education as the particular lives of teachers, students, parents, and community members are played out on the pages of each study.

Saundra Murray Nettles's (Chapter 2) account of her work in Stanton Elementary School is best read with a sense of the democratic vision infused in her work. Stanton was a low-achievement inner-city school of poor and working-class children. The text is not presented as an argument or illustration of democracy. The word *democracy* is not used nor is the standard language of antiracism, equity, and social justice found in the text. But this is a work that tells us much about those matters as the chapter describes the school-community effort to strengthen the academic performance of students. Part of the power of this text arises from the fact that Nettles grew up in a community similar to Stanton's. She spent the better part of her academic career in socially active research attempting to improve the lives and opportunities of children like those in Stanton Elementary School. Moreover, Nettles, as she began the Stanton study, was far removed from the impassioned rhetoric of opportunity so often written by those at a distance. Instead, she was at a point of despair, feeling that situations like those in Stanton Elementary School were indifferent to the words and deeds of academic activists like her. A reader of this text cannot help but feel the force of the democratic ideal as it struggles to reemerge in Nettles's spirit and as Ms. Robinson, the school's principal, forcefully carries the school, and Nettles, along a path of educational improvement. Ostensibly, this is a study of one school's efforts to raise achievement scores. But achievement is advanced as a worthwhile aim because of its potential relationship to opportunity and the democratic vision. The relationship with Ms. Robinson points to a democratic vision subtheme in her work, namely, the collaborative spirit that pervaded Nettles's relationship with Ms. Robinson and with members of the community. For those who have become jaundiced by the passionate critical rhetoric of multiculturalism, this is a chapter that will, as Nettles's work in Stanton Elementary School did for her, renew a democratic vision.

This notion of democratic vision is expanded into international contexts in Lourdes Diaz Soto's chapter (Chapter 8). In her study, teachers and students struggle to come to grips with the tragic events of September 11, 2001. As they rise above their horror and anger, they ask democratic questions on a global scale. Grace Feuerverger's study (Chapter 10) of her university classroom can be viewed as one, like Soto's, in which students and teachers engage in a critical dialogue about their place in the world and the potential of this understanding for realization of a democratic vision. Readers may wish to explore the notion of democratic vision as it is expressed in other chapters.

These Deweyan readings of the texts in this book are important also for the reason that Dewey's experiential philosophy led him to view democracy as "more than a form of government; . . . as . . . primarily a mode of associated living, of conjoint communicated experience" (Dewey, 1916, p. 80). For Dewey, for experiential inquirers, and for the authors of this book, it is not enough to have statutes and laws at the governance level nor is it enough to have broad and impassioned rhetoric of democracy and education, equality, and equal opportunity. It is necessary to see, and experience, these matters in life as lived, not merely in government statutes and in the ideas of academics and reformers. Freema Elbaz-Luwisch (Chapter 9), as with other authors in the book, links her reflective, narrative text to the concreteness of life experience. She begins the experiential part of her chapter by describing how she twisted her ankle on the way to class and how her bodily response to this told her how much she dreaded going to class. The dread, it appears, was because life in and out of the classroom was not going well. It was the time of the "intifada uprisings" and the recipro-cally retaliatory Palestinian suicide bombings and Israeli military attacks. Not only is she puzzled about how to think about life in such a situation, but it is her job to teach a class of teachers in training in this environment. These teachers face the same issues when they enter their classrooms as does Elbaz-Luwisch in her daily life, and, in addition, the classroom reflects, in words, the societal sit-uation. The class consists of Arab/Palestinian Israelis and Jewish Israelis who in turn are of mixed cultural origins, Sefardic and Ashkenazi. Elbaz-Luwisch adopts the question "Is education possible?" as the driving puzzle of her inquiry, but she might as well, in a Deweyan spirit, have asked "Is multicultural life pos-sible?" and by this she would have meant at home and on the streets outside the university classroom, as well as inside the walls of her classroom. The experien-tial life quality of Elbaz-Luwisch's inquiry is strengthened by references to her narrative history—that she is the daughter of Jewish immigrants to Canada who lost family members in the Holocaust and that she was committed to a life in Israel. Because Elbaz-Luwisch's inquiry is so deeply connected to her class-room life as a teacher and to her public life as an Israeli citizen, it is perhaps no surprise that her inquiry ends on a note of uncertainty, not unlike nearly any place one might stop telling or living a life story.

Still another reason for using Dewey's (1916) concepts in *Democracy and Education* as a touchstone is the connection Dewey makes between democracy and equality. For Dewey, equality in life is implied by the notion of democracy. He wrote, "Belief in . . . the democratic creed . . . means faith in the potential-ities of human nature . . . irrespective of race, color, sex, birth, and family, of material or cultural wealth" (Winn, 1959, p. 25). Mary Hermes' (Chapter 6) study of Native American education in Ojibwe Tribal Schools is driven by a democratic vision and a search for equality for Native American children. As it was with Nettles, Hermes does not use the language of democracy and equality. Hermes lets her White teacher participants choose their own language. Their language, of course, is shaped by the research selection process, that is, by the fact that Hermes set certain criteria for the selection of teachers and by the fact that hers are tribal schools with a culture-based curriculum aimed at fostering Ojibwe students' culture. The inspiring strength of her chapter arises out of the balance between her drive to foster equality for Ojibwe children and her ability and readiness to listen as the situation speaks to her. This is not a study where the ideology of the inquirer and his or her research proposal shapes the data and the interpretation. Hermes tells a reader that she is a Native American and that she is rearing two children for whom she wishes equality and cultural understanding. Perhaps because her thinking is governed by the democratic ideal and the urge for equality, not by ideology and the rhetoric of equity and social justice, Hermes is able to listen rather than to shape. She is convinced by her participants that it is poverty more than cultural difference that accounts for the Ojibwe children's school difficulties. She allows this, for her, contrary thought, while maintaining her belief in systemic injustice. A telling point in the chapter occurs when she accepts her participants' interpretation of student difficulties as being a question of poverty and interprets poverty in terms of a "history of oppression." Hermes' is a chapter in which equality means more than empty words. It means concerns for the education and community life of the Ojibwe children in her study.

This idea of equality is also seen in Carola Conle's (Chapter 11) "quest for pluralism" as she explores the democratic urge in the autobiographical record of her inquiries. Reflecting on a decade of her writing, Conle makes the case for the creation of a space to engage dialogue as part of democratic life. The consequence of an education conducted in the *absence of multiculturalism* and, accordingly, in the absence of equality is also seen in Alma Rubal-Lopez's and Angela Anselmo's study (Chapter 4) of their experiences growing up as Puerto Rican girls in New York. By examining their lives, they realized that there is a lack of inclusion of the experience of immigrant children in mainstream schooling. Alma Rubal-Lopez and Angela Anselmo call for a multicultural curriculum that respects the experience of immigrant children and creates a democratic space to provide equitable education for all.

We could as easily have chosen any other chapter to make these points. For instance, we might have read Meta Y. Harris's chapter (Chapter 3) as illustrative of the idea of equality that is central to the democratic ideal. Harris discusses autobiography as a means to place power into the hands of Black women writers to critique stereotypical and distorted images of Black women and to enable them to define who they are in their own terms. Black women writing their own lives, when historically their identity has been constructed by others, is therefore in itself a democratic process. In her chapter, Harris extended the democratic act of Black women writing their own lives into the use of autobiography in multicultural education.

Still another reason for the use of Dewey's title *Democracy and Education* (1916) is that this is a book about education. Every chapter addresses education either directly in the title or via the content of the inquiry. For Dewey, education and life are two sides of a coin in which the capacity to live effectively in everyday life marked what he called educative experience. Following this line of thought, it would be possible to explore the idea of democracy and education in out-of-school settings by paying attention to other areas and aspects of life apart from the formal educational system. For instance, we could read Sofia A. Villenas's chapter (Chapter 5) as illustrative of what we need to ask ourselves about democracy, who we include and exclude, and how we can embrace the voices of those who are marginalized. In engaging in her research, in listening attentively to the women's voices, Villenas created a democratic space for Latina immigrant mothers to raise concerns about the challenges they face in schooling their bicultural children as they forge new communities in the borderlands. Hearing the women's conversations about their personal struggles and their dilemmas in educating their children, delving into the spaces between the "telling and the told" created by Villenas, forces us to recognize that to be democratic means to value and respect the voices of all immigrants and the experiences of all those who are marginalized. Readers might wish to undertake a similar exploration of democratic notions in other chapters in the book.

Everyone is involved in the educational system in some way, at some time, and in some place. For parents, their involvement was as children and now as parents of children. Life for children in educational institutions is a microcosm, an educational training ground, for life as a whole. The school could be a place of democracy, in the sense we have described it in this chapter, in the making. If people cannot live democratically in schools, how can we expect our society to function democratically? Janice Huber, M. Shaun Murphy, and D. Jean Clandinin (Chapter 14) address democratic school living directly as they explore life in a peace candle school ceremony. The peace candle ceremony is an activity, carved out of the daily schedule, in which students, teachers, and researchers gather together to share issues, concerns, troubles, and difficulties. It is a space that provides the moments of democratic living for people with disparate life positions. As the chapter unfolds, discussions have ups and down, triumphs and failures. As such, the peace candle ceremony and the democratic space it provides do not represent an idealized version of democracy; rather, it is democracy in action. This chapter, as with the other chapters in the book, needs to be read as a study of a democratic classroom society.

As we summarized ideas of democracy and education found in the book, we drew on specific chapters to make our points. We used Nettles's to illustrate democratic vision, Elbaz-Luwisch's to illustrate a democratic mode of living, Hermes' to illustrate democracy and equality, and Huber, Murphy, and Clandinin's to illustrate democratic educational life. We could as easily have chosen any other chapter to make any of these points. For instance, we might have read Meta Y. Harris's (Chapter 3) African American study as illustrative of the idea of democracy, as a study of African American life, as an exploration of equity, or as a study of democratic education as lived. Similarly, we might have read Sofia A. Villenas's (Chapter 6) on Latina mothers' narratives and children's schooling in these four ways. These possible readings apply to all chapters, and we invite readers to think through the idea of democracy and education for each inquiry of special interest to them.

Narrative and Experiential Inquiry

A final reason for using Dewey's (1916) *Democracy and Education* for this section is that the experiential forms of inquiry brought forward in this book share the spirit of democracy in education. Dewey wrote on a wide array of topics as he developed his theory of experience. Just as it is important to see his ideas on democracy as an expression of his theory of experience, it is important to understand his notions of inquiry as expressions of the same theory. Inquiry, education, democracy, and experience are linked by the same theoretical frame. A key element in Dewey's theory of experience is the continual interplay between fact and idea (Dewey, 1938). For Dewey, facts that fit, and facts that do not fit, require new theoretical explanations that, in turn, generate new views of the factual, experiential world with new facts that fit and facts that do not fit. Growth in inquiry, as in education, develops through this continuous interplay of fact and idea. It is in this spirit that we ask readers to read this book with an experiential eye and an imaginative eye. We believe that reading of the text in this way is consistent with Dewey's notions of the development of inquiry and of educational growth.

More than this, however, we believe that narrative, experiential inquiry as seen in this book exhibits certain qualities that one might call democratic. In *Democracy and Education* (1916) Dewey wrote, "A democratic society repudiates the principle of external authority" (p. 90). This notion of authority applies to the role of inquirers in narrative, experiential inquiry. The inquirers in this book neither control the research setting nor determine in detail what steps shall be followed in pursuit of the inquiry. Rather, they act as participants not as authorities.

With this democratic, nonauthoritarian orientation, acting not only as researchers but also as concerned, involved participants, the authors in the book take action and work toward a more democratic environment in their research settings. These actions are taken within context and are themselves democratic acts as each researcher, as participant, not as authority, recognizes injustices and gives voice to actions that he or she believe would bring about improvement. His or her democratic action is not taken by virtue of imposed authority but by virtue of participation in, and commitment to, the life under study.

Associated with the participatory, nonauthoritarian role, researchers in narrative, experiential inquiry tend to join the lives of the people and situations studied. Joining the flow of life becomes a way of defining participation in narrative, experiential studies. This means that researchers neither stand outside the flow of life under inquiry nor control it for purposes of the inquiry. Rather, they enter that life and, to a greater or lesser extent depending on circumstances, become part of that life.

One of the dilemmas for narrative, experiential researchers adopting a democratic, nonauthoritarian stance in which they join the lives of their participants is that the tables may seem to be turned and the researcher may seem to be powerless and voiceless in the research situation. There are moments in Elbaz-Luwisch's study (Chapter 9), for instance, when she despairs of making progress. In our chapter (Chapter 13), we discussed how we were caught up with the flow of life in Bay Street Community School; partially set aside our research agenda; and worked with teachers, administrators, and community workers to create, develop, and implement a survey to assist the school in assessing second language learners' needs. We put aside our academic authority, acted as participants, and joined the flow of life in the school. It is when researchers and participants develop a level of equality that productive, democratic, experiential inquiry is underway. At that point, researchers and participants experience a democratic, collaborative environment. In this way, narrative, experiential inquiry of the sort brought forward in this book mimics and models the democratic life and democratic ideals of the larger society.

Another dilemma for narrative, experiential researchers adopting a democratic, nonauthoritarian stance in which they live in the midst of their participants' lives is that the intimacy, closeness, and caring that may develop can create vulnerability. The more intimately the inquirers become involved in their inquiries, the more they may come to care for their participants and their inquiries. With increased involvement of the inquirers, participants begin to develop trust. As the level of trust accelerates, participants may reveal "sacred and secret stories" (Crites, 1971), which may make inquirers and participants vulnerable. Deyhle (Chapter 7) exposes the fundamental inequalities existing in a Navajo community not only at the present time but also in the past. This revelation of inequality makes her and her participants vulnerable to backlash from the larger community.

Narrative and experiential inquirers are also vulnerable within the academic community. From the Western scientific perspective, discussed in Chapter 1, any one of the studies in this book might be shown, if one wished, to be inadequate. For instance, Nettles's and Hermes' chapters could be criticized by using the Western scientific perspective. But their work is convincing and credible. Three key points make them credible. First, data are presented in a lifelike way; readers vicariously experience people and situations. Second, Hermes and Nettles link their auto/biographies to their studies. This conveys an aura of trustworthiness, a sense that they know what they are talking about and that the data presented are merely surface signs of an ocean of underlying experience. Third, the "signature" of both authors is convincing; neither are strident and both have a quiet commitment and a sympathetic, understanding tone toward the plight of the participants under study. Credibility is demonstrated by the other authors in the book in similar and other ways.

In conclusion, as we reflect on the chapters in the book and examine them in the light of Dewey's *Democracy and Education,* we believe that a democratic vision, one of justice and equality for all, permeates the book. The authors bring forward the conviction they have of the importance of their topic and their commitment to creating democratic spaces in their environments. These convictions are apparent in every detail of the chapters, from the micro interactions in a Canadian inner-city school around a peace candle gathering to a university classroom filled with tension in Israel. These convictions are also apparent as we learn of the time commitment of the authors, from working with a Latino family over a span of years in Chicago to struggling alongside the Navajo for decades. These convictions are affirmed as the authors trace their autobiographical connections to their inquiries. Leading us through their inquiries, providing us with details of life as it is lived in the inquiries, the authors' commitments have become our commitments. Their vision of a democratic society, with equality and justice as not only catch words but as genuine possibilities, is a vision of a multicultural democratic life.

References

Crites, S. (1971). The narrative quality of experience. *Journal of the American Academy of Religion, 39*(3), 291–311.

Dewey, J. (1916). *Democracy and education: An introduction to the philosophy of education.* New York: Free Press.

Dewey, J. (1938). *Logic: The theory of inquiry.* New York: Henry Holt and Company.

Phillion, J., & He, M. F. (2005). Narrative inquiry in English language teaching: Contributions and future directions. In J. Cummins & C. Davison (Eds.), *The international handbook of English language teaching* (Vol. 2). Norwell, MA: Springer (formerly Kluwer Academic Publishers).

UNESCO. (2003). *Education in a multilingual world.* Paris: Author.

Winn, R. B. (Ed.). (1959). *John Dewey: Dictionary of education.* New York: Philosophical Library.

Index

About the Editors

F. Michael Connelly is Professor Emeritus and former Director of the Centre for Teacher Development and Chair of the Department of Curriculum, Ontario Institute for Studies in Education/University of Toronto (OISE/UT). He is Director of the Hong Kong Institute of Education/OISE/UT doctoral program and a Founder and Editor of *Curriculum Inquiry*. Professor Connelly was the recipient of the 1987 Outstanding Canadian Curriculum Scholar Award of the Canadian Society for the Study of Education, the 1991 Canadian Education Association Whitworth Award for Educational Research, the 1995 Ontario Confederation of University Faculty Associations Outstanding Teaching Award, and the 1999 Lifetime Achievement Award in Curriculum Studies from the American Educational Research Association (AERA). He has written widely, with his collaborator D. Jean Clandinin, in science education, teaching and teacher knowledge, curriculum, and narrative inquiry.

Ming Fang He is Associate Professor of Curriculum Studies at Georgia Southern University. She received her Ph.D. from the Ontario Institute for Studies in Education of the University of Toronto at the Centre for Teacher Development with F. Michael Connelly. She taught English as a Foreign Language in the People's Republic of China and English as a Second Language to immigrant adults and children in Toronto, Canada. She currently advises doctoral students, directs doctoral dissertations, and teaches graduate courses in curriculum studies, multicultural education, and qualitative research methods. Her preservice teacher education courses are in foundations of education. She has also taught doctoral level courses in Hong Kong and currently advises doctoral students and serves on dissertation committees for the Ontario Institute for Studies in Education's cohort-based doctoral program for Hong Kong Institute of Education faculty members. Her work is on cross-cultural narrative inquiry of language, culture, and identity in multicultural contexts; cross-cultural teacher education; and curriculum studies. She has also written the book *A River Forever Flowing: Cross-Cultural Lives and Identities in the Multicultural Landscape*. She is Professor of Curriculum, an Editor of *Curriculum Inquiry*, and an Associate Editor of *Multicultural Perspectives*.

JoAnn Phillion is Associate Professor in the Department of Curriculum and Instruction at Purdue University. She received her Ph.D. from the Ontario Institute for Studies in Education of the University of Toronto at the Centre for Teacher Development with F. Michael Connelly. She was awarded the AERA Division B Outstanding Dissertation Award in 2000. She was past Chair of Division B Equity Committee and member of AERA Affirmative Action Council. She is an Editor of *Curriculum Inquiry*. Her research interests are in narrative approaches to multiculturalism, teacher knowledge, and teacher education. She teaches graduate courses in curriculum theory and multicultural education, and an undergraduate course in preservice teacher development. She is involved in international teacher development in Hong Kong and Honduras. She published *Narrative Inquiry in a Multicultural Landscape: Multicultural Teaching and Learning* in 2002.

About the Contributors

Angela Anselmo was born of Puerto Rican/Dominican parents in New York City. She was raised in the south Bronx as well as in Puerto Rico. She graduated Summa Cum Laude, Phi Beta Kappa from the City College of New York in 1972, where she majored in psychology. A year later, she received her first master's degree in the area of guidance and counseling from the Consortium for Bilingual Counselor Education (a consortium of colleges involving CUNY and the University of Puerto Rico). Angela received two other degrees from Yeshiva University—a master's of art in psychology in 1988 and a combined doctorate in psychology and linguistics in 1991. While writing her doctoral dissertation, Angela attended The New Seminary in New York City and was ordained as an interfaith minister in 1990. She has worked for 29 years at Baruch College as a counselor, Director of Counseling, and Director of the SEEK Program. Angela enjoys lecturing in the areas of spirituality, bilingualism, and cultural diversity.

Chris Liska Carger is Associate Professor in the Department of Literacy Education at Northern Illinois University. She received her Ph.D. in curriculum and instruction from the University of Illinois at Chicago. Her area of concentration was reading and English language learners. Her research interests are literacy development for bilingual children, integrating multicultural children's literature and the arts, ethnographic research, and narrative inquiry related to teacher education.

D. Jean Clandinin is Professor and Director of the Centre for Research for Teacher Education and Development at the University of Alberta. She is a former teacher, counselor, and psychologist. She is the coauthor with F. Michael Connelly of four books and many chapters and articles. Their most recent book, *Narrative Inquiry: Experience and Story in Qualitative Research*, was published in 2000. She is part of an ongoing inquiry into teacher knowledge and teachers' professional knowledge landscapes. She is past Vice President of Division B of the American Educational Research Association (AERA) and is the 1993 winner of the AERA's Early Career Award. She is the 1999 winner of the Canadian Education Association Whitworth Award for educational research. She has worked closely with Janice Huber and M. Shaun Murphy on research projects on teacher knowledge.

Carola Conle teaches courses in cross-cultural education, foundations of curriculum, and narrative inquiry at the Ontario Institute for Studies in Education of the University of Toronto. Her work has been published in *American Educational Research Journal, Teaching and Teacher Education, Educational Theory,* and other journals. She received an Outstanding Writing Award from the American Association of Colleges for Teacher Education in 1997 and is currently engaged in funded research on ethics and the imagination.

Donna Deyhle is an educational anthropologist at the University of Utah, where she holds joint appointments in the Department of Education, Culture, and Society and the Ethnic Studies Program, as well as an adjunct appointment in the Department of Anthropology. Deyhle has worked with such diverse groups as the Karaja in the Brazilian Amazon, street youth in New York City, and among preservice teachers at Acoma and Laguna Pueblos and the Navajo Nation. Deyhle has worked with one Utah Navajo community—San Juan County and the Navajo Nation—and its schools for almost twenty years. Deyhle's early research was framed by a "cultural difference" perspective, which argued that much of the conflict and failure experienced by these youth was due to cultural differences between the home and the school. Deyhle has published articles on testing in *Curriculum Inquiry,* the *Journal of Educational Equity and Leadership,* and the *Peabody Journal of Education,* on culture and child development in *Theory into Practice,* on parent involvement in the *International Journal of Qualitative Research in Education,* break-dancers in the *Anthropology & Education Quarterly,* and dropouts in the *Journal of Navajo Education.* Deyhle's current research examines how power and racial relations contribute to the academic struggles of Navajo youth. She has published articles focused on cultural integrity and racism in the *Harvard Educational Review,* on Navajo mothers and daughters in the *Anthropology & Education Quarterly,* on break dancing and heavy metal in *Youth & Society,* cultural identity and dropouts in the *Journal of American Indian Education,* and in a review of the field of American Indian Education in the (AERA) *Review of Research in Education.*

In 2002, Deyhle received the George and Louise Spindler Award for Distinguished Career in Educational Anthropology from the American Anthropological Association. In addition, she received the Distinguished Achievement Award from the Educational Press Association of American for her article "Cultural Differences in Child Development: Navajo Adolescents in Middle Schools." She has also been the recipient of three faculty research awards from the University of Utah and two Spencer Foundation research grants as well as a Spencer Fellowship from the National Academy of Education at Harvard

University. At the University of Utah, Professor Deyhle teaches undergraduate courses in multicultural education and American Indians in the American experience and graduate courses in qualitative research, ethnographic research, cross-cultural education, and anthropology and education.

Freema Elbaz-Luwisch is Associate Professor in the Department of Education, Haifa University, in Haifa, Israel. She teaches teachers and postgraduate students in narrative methods and multiculturalism. She is especially concerned with the mixed Jewish Palestinian student body at Haifa, which has an open policy on admission and encourages a mix of students.

Grace Feuerverger is Associate Professor in the Centre for Teacher Development, Department of Curriculum, Teaching and Learning at OISE/University of Toronto. As the daughter of immigrants and refugees, Feuerverger grew up in a multicultural and multilingual home in Montreal and brings her personal and professional experiences to bear on her teaching and research work. Feuerverger was educated at a variety of institutions—McGill University; the Università per Stranieri in Perugia, Italy; the University of California, Berkeley; the University of Alberta; the Hebrew University in Jerusalem; and the University of Toronto. She was a French immersion teacher in Alberta and Ontario before she began her university career, and her heart is never far from the classroom. Her research interests focus on theoretical and practical issues of cultural and linguistic diversity, ethnic identity maintenance, and minority language learning within multicultural educational contexts, as well as on conflict resolution and peacemaking in international settings. Her courses at OISE/University of Toronto and her research projects explore the personal and professional texts of those who live within and between various cultural worlds, struggling to find voice, meaning, and balance in their lives and their implications for teacher development. She continues to direct a multicultural literacy project in various schools in Toronto where she has developed an inservice teacher's guide and video programs. Feuerverger is also principal investigator of an individual large-scale Social Sciences and Humanities Research Council research study, which focuses on the school experiences of immigrant and refugee students in Toronto and Montreal. Her recent book *Oasis of Dreams: Teaching and Learning Peace in a Jewish-Palestinian Village in Israel* (Routledge/Falmer) is a reflexive ethnography about an extraordinary bilingual-bicultural educational endeavor.

Meta Y. Harris is currently an Assistant Professor at Georgia Southern University. She holds an Ed.D. degree from The University of Alabama in administration of higher education and a Ph.D. in women's studies from The University of Manchester, England. She is currently involved in research on mothering of daughters in the southeastern United States. Other research interests include gender roles in Europe and Africa, and she is beginning a new research on women's participation in politics in the African countries of Nigeria and Botswana. She is a mother of two children.

Mary Hermes is a member of the Ojibwe tribe. She is an Assistant Professor at the University of Minnesota, Duluth, where she works in teacher development and teacher education. Her research is the area of language, culture, and identity, particularly as related to Native Americans. She also serves as Director of a bilingual school on a nearby reservation.

Janice Huber is an Assistant Professor at St. Francis Xavier University in Nova Scotia. She is a former elementary teacher. She completed her Ph.D. at the University of Alberta in 2000 and has worked with D. Jean Clandinin and F. Michael Connelly on various research projects since 1991. She is the author of several chapters and articles. Her most recent article, coauthored with Karen Keats Whelan and D. Jean Clandinin, is published in the *Journal of Curriculum Studies*.

M. Shaun Murphy is currently a doctoral student at the Centre for Research for Teacher Education and Development at the University of Alberta. He has been an elementary teacher for seventeen years. His research interests focus on students' knowledge of school contexts and teachers' professional knowledge.

Saundra Murray Nettles is Professor and Chair of the Department of Curriculum, Foundations, and Reading at Georgia Southern University. Her scholarship includes theoretical reviews to explore emerging fields (e.g., psychology of Black women, gender equity in schools, and community involvement in youth development), case studies of school improvement, program evaluation, and empirical studies in the psychology of Black women. Her work has appeared in *American Educational Research Journal, Review of Education Research, Education and Urban Society, Feminist Studies, Social Psychology of Education, Psychology of Women Quarterly, Journal of Adolescent Research*, and *Peabody Journal of Education*. In her book *Crazy Visitation: A Chronicle of Illness and Recovery*, she developed a narrative self-inquiry into the experience of risk and recovery from a brain tumor. She was Associate Professor of Human Development at the University of Maryland, Principal Research Scientist at Johns Hopkins Center for Social Organization of Schools, and Director of Field Services for a large antipoverty agency in Washington, D.C.

Alma Rubal-Lopez is currently a faculty member at Brooklyn College, where she is the Program Head for a bilingual teacher education program as well as the Deputy Chair. Her research interests are in the fields of sociology of language, where she has written extensively on the global spread of English as well as on the sociolinguistic situation of the Puerto Rican in New York City. Her most recent research is in the area of multicultural education, where she has written various articles on bilingual education and multicultural teaching as well as her latest book on becoming Nuyoricans, a recollection of her and her sister's childhood experiences in the South Bronx.

Lourdes Diaz Soto is a graduate of Hunter College and The Pennsylvania State University. Her publications include *Language, Culture, and Power: Bilingual Families Struggle for Quality Education* (SUNY Press) and two edited volumes titled *Making a Difference in the Lives of Bilingual/Bicultural Learners* and *The Politics of Early Childhood Education* (Peter Lang). Scholarship and collegial opportunities have taken her to Puerto Rico, Costa Rica, Greece, Spain, and Uruguay. In addition, she has published numerous articles and book chapters examining issues of social justice and equity. She is currently involved in collaborative community action projects with her students in order to benefit linguistically and culturally diverse populations.

Sofia A. Villenas is Associate Professor of Cultural Studies in Education in the Department of Curriculum and Instruction at the University of Texas at Austin. She is a mother of four children and a former bilingual school teacher, and she currently teaches and researches in the areas of multicultural education and Latino family education. She is coeditor with Laurence Parker and Donna Deyhle of *Race Is . . . Race Isn't: Critical Race Theory and Qualitative Studies in Education*. She is also coeditor of *Chicana/Latina Education in Everyday Life: Feminista Perspectives on Pedagogy and Epistemology* in production with SUNY Press. Her work has appeared in *Harvard Educational Review,* the *International Journal of Qualitative Studies in Education,* and *Anthropology & Education Quarterly,* among other journals. She is currently finishing a book on her research with Latina mothers and race relations in North Carolina.